Psychology and the Bible

PSYCHOLOGY AND THE BIBLE

A New Way to Read the Scriptures

VOLUME 3
From Gospel to Gnostics

Edited by
J. Harold Ellens and Wayne G. Rollins

Foreword by Donald Capps

PRAEGER PERSPECTIVES

Psychology, Religion, and Spirituality

PRAEGER

Westport, Connecticut
London

Library of Congress Cataloging-in-Publication Data

Psychology and the Bible: a new way to read the Scriptures / edited by J. Harold Ellens
and Wayne G. Rollins; foreword by Donald Capps.
    p. cm.—(Psychology, religion, and spirituality, ISSN 1546–8070)
    Includes bibliographical references and index.
    Contents: v. 1. From Freud to Kohut—v. 2. From Genesis to apocalyptic vision—v. 3.
From Gospel to Gnostics—v. 4. From Christ to Jesus.
    ISBN 0-275-98347-1 (set : alk paper)—ISBN 0-275-98348-X (v. 1 : alk paper)—
ISBN 0-275-98349-8 (v. 2 : alk paper)—ISBN 0-275-98350-1 (v. 3 : alk paper)—
ISBN 0-275-98462-1 (v. 4 : alk paper)
    1. Bible—Psychology. 2. Psychoanalysis and religion. I. Ellens, J. Harold, 1932–
II. Rollins, Wayne G. III. Series.
BS645.P89 2004
220.6′01′9—dc22   2004050863

British Library Cataloguing in Publication Data is available.

Library of Congress Catalog Card Number: 2004050863

ISBN: 0–275–98347–1 (set)
       0–275–98348–X (vol. I)
       0–275–98349–8 (vol. II)
       0–275–98350–1 (vol. III)
       0–275–98462–1 (vol. IV)
ISSN: 1546-8070

First published in 2004

Praeger Publishers, 88 Post Road West, Westport, CT 06881
An imprint of Greenwood Publishing Group, Inc.
www.praeger.com

Printed in the United States of America

The paper used in this book complies with the
Permanent Paper Standard issued by the
National Information Standards Organization (Z39.48–1984).

10 9 8 7 6 5 4 3 2 1

CONTENTS

FOREWORD

Donald Capps

I learned about the psychological study of the Bible as a PhD student, when, in a psychology of religion course taught by David Bakan, I was introduced to an essentially psychoanalytic approach to the Bible. Before that, despite two years of intensive graduate study, not one of my professors had ever breathed a word about the psychological study of the Bible. Even in Bakan's course, the idea that the Bible could be approached psychologically seemed idiosyncratic and odd, yet strangely compelling. At the time, Bakan was mostly interested in what he called the "infanticidal impulse," the desire of adults to kill children, and he viewed the story of Abraham and Isaac in Genesis 22 as illustrative not only of the infanticidal impulse itself but also of its displacement through animal sacrifice (see Bakan, 1968).

I might not have gotten hooked by this field of study had my introduction to it involved merely abstract theorizing, or had I not been introduced to it when young men were being sent by their political fathers to fight in a controversial war in Vietnam. In any case, I did get hooked, and the psychological study of the Bible has been the primary, perhaps the sole, means by which I have remained faithful to the religious legacy that was imparted to me as a child. I am sure that many others whose work is presented in these four volumes could make similar testimonies to the personal value and importance of the psychological study of the Bible and would subscribe to the view that the way to renewed faith and trust is not around but through psychology.

The field of the psychological study of the Bible has come a very long way since my introduction to it in the mid-1960s. As Wayne G. Rollins documents in *Soul and Psyche: The Bible in Psychological Perspective*, a "sheaf of articles and books in the late 1960s and early 1970s appeared from within the orbit of biblical scholarship," calling "for a fresh look at the contributions psychological and psychoanalytic research might bring to the task of biblical interpretation" (1999, 68). Many scholars both within biblical studies and in fields such as the psychology of religion, which had manifested considerable but erratic interest in the Bible in previous decades, responded to this call. Over the next two decades, so much interest had been generated that in 1991 the Society of Biblical Literature approved a proposal to establish a program unit on Psychology and Biblical Studies. This program unit would assess the significance of the approaches employed to date and would provide a forum for developing the future agenda of psychological criticism as a subdiscipline within biblical studies. The faithfulness with which these responsibilities have been carried out accounts to a large extent for the fact that, some thirteen years later, J. Harold Ellens and Wayne G. Rollins had little difficulty finding willing contributors to this four-volume collection titled *Psychology and the Bible*.

Both editors of these volumes have offered their own characterizations of the field. In a special issue on psychology and the Bible in *Pastoral Psychology*, a journal whose editor, Lewis R. Rambo, has been unusually receptive to psychological studies of biblical texts, J. Harold Ellens, who guest edited the issue, assessed the state of the field and clarified its focus. In his guest editorial, "Psychology and the Bible: The Interface of Corollary Disciplines" (1997a), he pointed out that, beginning in the early 1960s, a consciously crafted critique of the positivist assumptions of the Enlightenment had given rise to interest in interdisciplinary studies, and that one of the most significant of these was the application of interdisciplinary approaches using scientific models and methods for investigation of religious traditions, practices, and experiences. As one such scientific discipline, psychology has played an increasingly important role in these interdisciplinary approaches. As Ellens notes, "we found ourselves teaching courses and doing research in the sociology of religion, the psychology of religion, the Bible in Western literary traditions, psychotheology, psychospirituality, transcendental psychology, and the like. This undertaking was influenced, as well, by the birth of sturdy concerns to investigate the interface of many of the great religions of the world, particularly the encounter between Eastern and Western psychology and spirituality" (1997a, 159–160).

In his essay "The Bible and Psychology: An Interdisciplinary Pilgrimage" in the same issue of *Pastoral Psychology*, Ellens noted that one of the fruitful products of this new interest in interdisciplinary studies was the publication of many significant books and articles on the interface between the disciplines of psychology, theology, and biblical studies, and suggested that the focus of interdisciplinary work in psychology and biblical studies is that of bringing "the insights and models of psychology to bear upon a biblical text, assessing the nature and function of the author, of the implied or stated intended audience, of the real audiences in the church's history which interpreted the text, together with their interpretations, and thus assess the reasons, healthy or pathological, for the constructs that were expressed in the text and in subsequent uses of it" (1997b, 206). Note, here, the assumption that biblical texts have not only been used—misused—to legitimate pathological ideas and behaviors, but that the original texts themselves may also reflect pathological as well as healthy ways of thinking and behaving.

A very tangible reflection of this understanding of what psychology may contribute to biblical studies is the recent publication of four volumes titled *The Destructive Power of Religion: Violence in Judaism, Christianity, and Islam* (2004), edited by Ellens. One of the four volumes is devoted exclusively to sacred scriptures. In his own essay "Toxic Texts," Ellens notes that "sacred scriptures motivate ordinary people to amazing achievements in spirituality, religion, and cultural creativity." By the same token, "the inspiration of sacred scriptures can also be devastatingly destructive, spiritually, psychologically, and culturally" (2004, 3:1–2). To illustrate their destructive side, he explores the story in John 9 about Jesus' healing of a man who was born blind, noting that this text "is generally prized by Bible scholars and religious devotees," yet it "has a dangerous subtext or underside that has been ignored," a subtext that "can have a destructive effect on persons, communities, and cultures by the negative archetypes that it may generate at the unconscious psychological level" (2).

In "Rationale and Agenda for a Psychological-Critical Approach to the Bible and Its Interpretation, Biblical and Humane" (1996), published at nearly the same time as Ellens's two *Pastoral Psychology* articles, Wayne G. Rollins identified what he termed "a psychological-critical approach" to the Bible. The goal of this approach "is to examine texts (including their origination, authorship, and modes of expression,

their construction, transmission, translation, reading, and interpretation, their transposition into kindred and alien art forms, and the history of their personal and cultural effect) as expressions of the structure, processes, and habits of the human psyche, both in individual and
collective manifestations, past and present" (1996, 160). Key here is
the understanding that the original texts, their transmission, and
their transposition into other forms are all expressions of the human
psyche, its cognitive and emotional structures and processes, its habits
of mind and heart.

Three years later, in *Soul and Psyche*, which comprehensively reviews
both past and present work in this burgeoning interdisciplinary field,
Rollins cited a third effort to characterize the field and commended it
for its accuracy and succinctness. This is Antoine Vergote's proposal
that the purpose of psychological biblical criticism is "to understand
the mental universe of the biblical tradition" (1999, 78). Building on the
idea that the "mental universe" of the biblical tradition is its appropriate focus, Rollins went on to suggest that the fundamental premise that
informs research in the field of psychological biblical criticism and that
constitutes the insight that gave birth to the discipline can be stated as
follows: "From a biblical-critical perspective, the Bible is to be seen as
part and product, not only of a historical, literary, and socioanthropological process, but also of a psychological process. In this process, conscious and unconscious factors are at work in the biblical authors and
their communities, in the texts they have produced, in readers and
interpreters of these texts and in their communities, and in the individual, communal, and cultural effects of these interpretations" (1999, 92).

This premise not only includes the view that the Bible is part and
product of "a psychological process" but also introduces the idea,
emphasized by psychodynamic theorists such as Freud, Jung, and their
followers, that both conscious and unconscious factors are at work in
this process. Thus, one of the primary purposes of the "psychological-
critical approach" is to make that which is unconscious conscious.
Rollins goes on, however, to emphasize that what is especially under
examination in a psychological-critical approach "is the *psychological
context* and *psychological content* of the Bible and its interpretation"
(1999, 93). Together, these two prongs of critical examination have
the larger objective of enhancing the repertory of critical perspectives
on the Bible (historical, literary, socioanthropological) "by adding to it
a vision of the text as itself a psychic product, reality, symptom, and
event, and as a source of commentary on the nature, life, habits,
pathology, health, and purpose of the psyche/soul" (1999, 94). Thus,

endorsing Ellens's view that a central focus of interdisciplinary work in psychology and biblical studies is to "assess the reasons, healthy or pathological, for the constructs that were expressed in the text and in subsequent uses of it," Rollins suggests that in addition to being "a source of commentary" on matters of pathology and health, the Bible, as itself a psychic product, may reveal both healthy and pathological mental and emotional structures and processes.

Because one of my own special interests is the pathogenic characteristic of some biblical texts, I am both impressed and encouraged by the fact that whether explicitly or implicitly, the essays included in these four volumes are concerned with the pathology and health of the psychological process at work in the biblical authors and their communities and in their subsequent interpreters. For Rollins, as for Ellens, this concern is part of the second of two agendas in the psychological study of the Bible, the exegetical and the hermeneutical. In a section of his chapter "The Hermeneutical Agenda" in *Soul and Psyche*, bearing the heading "The History of Biblical Effects in Psychological Perspective: Pathogenic and Therapeutic Effects," Rollins notes: "It is no longer a secret in scholarly and even ecclesiastical literature that the Bible and its interpretation can have pathogenic effects on individuals and cultures—an acknowledgment that has been both liberating and dismaying for those who treasure the text" (1999, 175).

By the same token, the very recognition of the pathogenic effects of the Bible and its interpretation has reawakened interest in its therapeutic effects:

> Scholarly interest in the pathogenic aspects of the Bible has been matched at the end of the twentieth century with renewed interest in its therapeutic dimension. As much as the Bible provides evidence of pathogenic potential, even more does it provide evidence that it can transform consciousness, change behavior patterns, and open up a new cognition of reality in ways that have affected individuals and shaped entire cultures for generations. (Rollins, 1999, 177)

Rollins concludes that a major undertaking for psychological biblical criticism in the future

> will be to develop a critical method for identifying, measuring, and assessing the degree to which the text presents itself as the mediator of a therapeutic agenda, to come to an understanding of the strategies it recommends for achieving this agenda, to compare it with contemporary therapeutic models, and to consider what insight it can add to collective scholarship and thought on the *cura animarum* in our own time. (1999, 179)

Although the psychological-critical approach to the Bible has much in common with other critical approaches, these other approaches are not as likely to give sustained or systematic attention to the fact that the Bible has both pathogenic and therapeutic aspects. The psychological-critical method bears a special responsibility for recognizing and pointing out the difference. Attempts throughout history to make the case that certain biblical texts have priority over other biblical texts because they are more central to the Bible's own intentionality—the so-called canon within the canon—have been exposed as misleading and self-serving. However, those who endorse (as I myself do) the view of the editors of these four volumes that the psychological study of the Bible entails the assessment of the pathogenic and therapeutic aspects of biblical texts may well accord the healing stories in the New Testament Gospels a special status as a "source of commentary" on matters of health and pathology, and thus as valuable in their own right for assessing the healthy and pathological constructs in other biblical texts and interpretations thereof. This means that it is not merely a matter of bringing twenty-first-century understandings of health and pathology to bear on biblical texts—after all, these understandings are implicated in the very constructs that they intend to assess—but also of using the biblical tradition's own understandings of what makes for health and pathology to assess its own psychological processes. Perhaps this is why Erik H. Erikson could both endorse the spirit of Thomas Jefferson's attempt to provide Native Americans an abridged version of "the philosophy of Jesus of Nazareth" extracted from the four Gospels and critique his decision to eliminate "all references to Jesus' healing mission" (Erikson, 1974, 40–50).

Finally, the very fact that the Bible continues to have an emotional as well as intellectual attraction even for those of us who acknowledge its pathogenic features is itself a question that invites and warrants psychological examination and assessment. Three or four years before I was introduced to the psychological study of the Bible, I read Erik H. Erikson's *Young Man Luther: A Study in Psychoanalysis and History* (1958). This book—which, with its advocacy of a psychohistorical method attuned to religious themes, was itself an indirect contributor to the development of the psychological study of the Bible field—advances a psychological theory of the attraction that the Bible held for Luther. I suggest that this theory may have wide application and that it may be one of several emotional links creating a bond between all of the essays (and essayists) in these four volumes. The theory occurs in the midst of a discussion of Luther's "passivity," which

Erikson emphasizes is not mere indifference but the activation of perceptions and their emotional counterparts that existed before Luther's—and other children's—development of will and willfulness. Thus, it is the "passivity" of active reception, the kind of reception that occurs when readers allow a biblical text to "speak" to them. Erikson asks:

> Is it coincidence that Luther, now that he was explicitly teaching passivity, should come to the conclusion that a lecturer should feed his audience as a mother suckles her child? Intrinsic to the kind of passivity we speak of is not only the memory of having been given, but also the identification with the maternal giver: "the glory of a good thing is that it flows out to others." *I think that in the Bible Luther at last found a mother whom he could acknowledge: he could attribute to the Bible a generosity to which he could open himself, and which he could pass on to others, at last a mother's son.* (1958, 208, my emphasis)

Noting that Luther spoke of being reborn "out of the matrix of the scriptures," Erikson adds, "matrix is as close as such a man's man will come to saying 'mater'" (208).

As we have seen, for editors Ellens and Rollins, the psychological process to which the psychological-critical approach attends occurs in the biblical authors and their communities, in the texts they have produced, in the readers and interpreters of these texts and in their communities, and in the individual, communal, and cultural effects of these interpretations. This psychological process *is* the very matrix of the Scriptures. Thus, the essays included in these four volumes attest to the generosity of the Bible, to the fact that it is, indeed, the "good book" (although by no means perfect book) that richly rewards those who come to examine it, assess it, and take its measure. Undoubtedly, its greatest rewards are reserved for those who are unabashedly— perhaps hopelessly—in love with it. In the course of reading these essays, the reader will find, however, that examination, assessment, and love—all three together—are integral to the psychological process to which the Bible itself gives testimony.

Decades from now, our successors will surely wonder how such a monumental undertaking as these four volumes on psychology and the Bible could ever have come about. This undertaking is a reflection of the organizational and administrative acumen that the two editors have also displayed in their work on behalf of the Psychology and Biblical Studies program unit of the Society of Biblical Literature. It is also a tribute to the respect in which they are held by their colleagues. But these four volumes also testify to the editors' exquisite sense of timing. As Jesus' own illustration of the children in the marketplace attests (Matt. 11:16–17), one can pipe a tune, but if no one is either willing or able to dance, nothing much happens. According to my count, aside from the editors themselves, thirty-two responded to their invitation to write essays, and some more than once. Had Abraham done even half as well, the city of Sodom would have been spared. Ellens and Rollins clearly discerned that there are scholars out there who, if asked, are not only willing but able to set aside their inhibitions and fear of self-embarrassment and to venture out on the dance floor, secure in the knowledge that there is safety in numbers. May this monumental undertaking inspire others to make a similar venture.

References

Bakan, D. (1966). *The Duality of Human Existence: An Essay on Psychology and Religion.* Chicago: Rand McNally.

Bakan, D. (1968). *Disease, Pain, and Sacrifice: Toward a Psychology of Suffering.* Chicago: University of Chicago Press.

Ellens, J. H. (1997a). Psychology and the Bible: The Interface of Corollary Disciplines. *Pastoral Psychology, 45,* 159–162.

Ellens, J. H. (1997b). The Bible and Psychology: An Interdisciplinary Pilgrimage. *Pastoral Psychology, 45,* 193–209.

Ellens, J. H., ed. (2004). *The Destructive Power of Religion: Violence in Judaism, Christianity, and Islam* (4 vols.). Westport: Praeger Publishers.

Erikson, E. H. (1958). *Young Man Luther: A Study in Psychoanalysis and History.* New York: Norton.

Erikson, E. H. (1974). *Dimensions of a New Identity.* New York: Norton.

Rollins, W. G. (1996). *Rationale and Agenda for a Psychological-Critical Approach to the Bible and Its Interpretation, Biblical and Humane,* D. Barr, L. B. Elder, & E. S. Malbon, eds. Atlanta: Scholars Press, 153–172.

Rollins, W. G. (1999). *Soul and Psyche: The Bible in Psychological Perspective.* Minneapolis: Fortress.

Series Foreword

J. Harold Ellens, PhD

The interface between psychology, religion, and spirituality has been of great interest to scholars for a century. In the last three decades a broad popular appetite has developed for books that make practical sense out of the sophisticated research on these three subjects. Freud expressed an essentially deconstructive perspective on this matter and indicated that he saw the relationship between human psychology and religion to be a destructive interaction. Jung, on the other hand, was quite sure that these three aspects of the human spirit—psychology, religion, and spirituality—were constructively and inextricably linked. Anton Boisen and Seward Hiltner derived much insight from both Freud and Jung, as well as from Adler and Reik, while pressing the matter forward with gratifying skill and illumination. Boisen and Hiltner fashioned a framework within which the quest for a sound and sensible definition of the interface between psychology, religion, and spirituality might best be described or expressed (Aden & Ellens, 1990). We are in their debt.

This set of general interest books, so wisely urged by Greenwood Press, and particularly by its editor Debbie Carvalko, defines the terms and explores the interface of psychology, religion, and spirituality at the operational level of daily human experience. Each volume in the set identifies, analyzes, describes, and evaluates the full range of issues, of both popular and professional interest, that deal with the psychological factors at play in the way religion takes shape and is expressed, in the way spirituality functions within human persons and shapes both religious formation and expression, and in the ways that spirituality is shaped and expressed by religion. The primary interest is psychological. In terms of the rubrics of the discipline and the science of psychology, this set of superb volumes investigates the operational dynamics of religion and spirituality.

The verbs *shape* and *express* in the previous paragraph refer to the forces that prompt and form religion in persons and communities, as well as to the manifestations of religious behavior in personal forms of spirituality, in acts of spiritually motivated care for society, and in ritual behaviors such as liturgies of worship. In these various aspects of human function, the psychological drivers are identified, isolated, and described in terms of the way they unconsciously and consciously operate in religion and spirituality.

The books in this set are written for the general reader, the local library, and the undergraduate university student. They are also of significant interest to the informed professional, particularly in corollary fields. The volumes in this set have great value for clinical settings and treatment models as well.

This series editor has spent an entire professional lifetime focused specifically on research into the interface of psychology, religion, and spirituality. These matters are of the highest urgency in human affairs today, when religious motivation seems to be playing an increasing role, constructively and destructively, in the arena of social ethics, national politics, and world affairs. It is imperative that we find out immediately what the psychopathological factors are that shape a religion that can launch deadly assaults on the World Trade Center in New York and murder 3,500 people, or a religion that motivates suicide bombers to kill themselves and murder dozens of their neighbors weekly, or a religion that prompts such unjust national policies as preemptive defense—all of which are wreaking havoc on the social fabric, the democratic processes, the domestic tranquility, the economic stability and productivity, and the legitimate right to freedom from fear in every nation in the world today.

Of course not all of the influences of religion now or throughout history have been negative. Indeed, most of the impact of the great religions upon human life and culture has been profoundly redemptive and generative of great good. It is just as urgent, therefore, that we discover and understand better what the psychological forces are that empower people of faith and genuine spirituality to give themselves to all the creative and constructive enterprises that, throughout the centuries, have made of human life the humane, ordered, prosperous, and aesthetic experience it can be at its best. Surely the forces for good in both psychology and spirituality far exceed the powers and proclivities toward the evil that we see so prominently in our world today.

This set of Greenwood Press volumes is dedicated to the greater understanding of psychology, religion, and spirituality, and thus to the profound understanding and empowerment of those psycho-spiritual drivers that can help us transcend the malignancy of our pilgrimage and enormously enhance the humaneness and majesty of the human spirit, indeed, the potential for magnificence in human life.

Reference

Aden, L., & Ellens, J. H. (1990). *Turning Points in Pastoral Care: The Legacy of Anton Boisen and Seward Hiltner.* Grand Rapids: Baker.

CHAPTER 1

INTRODUCTION

J. Harold Ellens and Wayne G. Rollins

> People will read the gospel again and again and I myself read it again and again. But they will read it with much more profit if they have some insight into their own psyches. Blind are the eyes of anyone who does not know his own heart, and I always recommend the application of a little psychology so that he can understand things like the gospel still better.
>
> —Jung, 1973, 463

On December 24, 1995, the *New York Times Magazine* carried an article that is symptomatic of an important movement afoot in biblical studies and in the field of psychology. It is a scholarly quest that brings psychological and psychoanalytic insight to bear on the history, interpretation, and significance of the Bible. In that Christmas reflection, entitled "Jesus Before IIe Could Talk," Pulitzer Prize essayist Jack Miles, formerly a Jesuit and currently an Episcopal layman, proposes that "for most of the hundreds of millions who . . . will hear the story again on Christmas Eve, what counts in it is neither theological nor historical but psychological." With a Harvard doctorate in Old Testament Studies, Miles attributes the enduring effect of biblical stories not only to their theological sublimity and narrative elegance but above all to their ability to activate archetypal truths anchored deep in the soul.

Miles voices an opinion that has been increasingly affirmed by biblical scholars since the 1970s. It is the conviction that the critical repertory of biblical scholarship needs to be expanded beyond the

historical-critical and literary-critical methods to include "psychological criticism." What does a psychological perspective add to the mix?
It helps us see Scripture as the product not only of historical, social,
economic, and literary processes but also of a psychic process in which
unconscious and conscious factors are at work in the original writers,
in their communities and traditions, as well as in biblical interpreters
and the communities they address. From a psychological perspective,
the Bible is a book that tells us not only about the past but even more
about the present and perennial experiences of the human soul, its
trials, troubles, successes, and victories. The Bible is a text that *informs*,
but it is also a text that from time to time *transforms* its readers. Psychological biblical criticism contends that as important as the historical, social, political, economic, and cultural factors are in determining
how the text came into being, it is the psychic factors that are pre-
eminently important in determining what was recorded in the text,
why it is remembered, how it is said, to whom and for what purpose it
is said, how it is read, how it is interpreted, and how that interpretation is received, shaped, and translated into life.

What sorts of questions does psychological criticism ask and what
new areas or types of research does it propose? Jack Miles identifies
one of seven key areas of research that occupy psychological criticism
today: research into *the nature and power of symbols, myths, and archetypal
images*, resting on the judgment shared by Freud and Jung that the
"symbolic process" is a natural and spontaneous function of the psyche
(Bregman, 1990). This symbolic process has generated figures such as
the divine child, the tree of life, the satanic trickster, the virginal
mother of the demigods, the sacred mountain, and the golden age, all
of which recur in myths, fantasies, fairy tales, and dreams across time
and cultures. Walter Wink observes that such classical images
"appear so frequently in widely scattered mythic traditions that we are
justified in regarding [them] . . . as a standard component in spiritual
development" (1978, 142).

A second area of research, in collaboration with literary critics, is
inquiry into the *psychodynamics in biblical stories and narratives* to
observe how biblical characters and story structures illustrate the common traits of the human psyche. For example, one finds instances of
the psychological mechanism of denial (Adam and Eve in the garden),
intellectualization (the Johannine Pilate in conversation with Jesus),
projection (Peter's acclamation of Jesus as a victorious Messiah), and
rationalization (Adam's passing the buck to Eve and Eve's to the serpent), along with patterns of obsessive compulsion (Paul's persecution

of the Way in his earlier career) and the mitigation of cognitive dissonance (the creation of apocalyptic scenarios to resolve the problem of evil).

A third area of inquiry is *the psychology of biblical personalities.* This research can take one of three routes: character analysis of the literary construct of biblical figures, such as Saul, Jonah, Jacob, King Herod, and Paul; second, the analysis of the roles that biblical personalities can come to play as models or exemplars for readers, as Moses did for Freud and the Christ figure for Jung. A third approach is psychoanalytic. Although in the strictest sense psychoanalysis of biblical figures is ruled out by the absence of the analysand, a number of recent studies have suggested that psychoanalytic observations in the hands of seasoned analysts can provide compelling insight into biblical authors and their characters, just on the basis of the data we do have available in the texts.

A fourth area of inquiry is psychological commentary on *biblical religious phenomena*, a kind of redux of William James's (1902/1985) classic, *The Varieties of Religious Experience*, focusing on three phenomena: religious experience (for example, prophetic visions, martyrdom, speaking in tongues, and dreams), religious practice (for example, sacrifice, baptism, eucharist, purification rites, the experiences of forgiveness, and salvation and rebirth), and paranormal experience (for example, faith healing, exorcism, clairvoyance).

A fifth area is the broad field of *biblical psychology*, which involves the study of the biblical concept(s) of the psyche/soul/self, explored in conversation with contemporary psychological models of the self, comparing concepts of human illness and human wholeness and the routes to both.

A sixth area is in the field of hermeneutics, the "world between reader and text," examining *how texts affect readers and how readers affect texts*, an inquiry that will be done in collaboration with contemporary ideological, reader-response, feminist, and rhetorical critics.

A seventh and final area is the *psychology of biblical effects*, to examine how reading and living with Scripture has affected people, individuals and whole cultures, pathogenically or therapeutically. We are all aware of the pathogenic effects of certain biblical positions on slavery, women's rights, children's rights, violence, war, and internecine tribal warfare. Moreover, we can find directly opposite examples of biblical opinion on each of these issues, reinforcing the judgment of Carl Jung that the Bible and religions at their best "are psychotherapeutic systems in the truest sense of the word. . . . They express the whole range

of the psychic problem in mighty images; they are the avowal and recognition of the soul, and at the same time the revelation of the soul's
nature" (Jung, 1953–1978, 367).

The present volume, third in this set on *Psychology and the Bible: A
New Way to Read the Scriptures*, focuses on a psychological approach to
the literature of the "New Testament Era," from the earliest writings
to the emerging Gnostic tradition. The essays touch on a range of literary genres: the four Gospels, Matthew, Mark, Luke, and John; the
parables of Jesus; the passion and resurrection narratives; Paul's second letter to the Corinthians; the book of Revelation; the biblical words
for soul, psyche, and self; and Gnostic literature. The psychological
approaches employed in this volume include learning theory, cognitive psychology, depth psychology, the psychology of grief, object
relations theory, and archetypal psychology.

Sixteen scholars have joined us to develop this volume. What they
have in common is their desire to bring into focus the view of the
meaning and message of the Bible that can be seen through the lens of
psychology. As a way of introducing them and their ideas, we offer
snapshots of their articles.

The Foreword, introducing all four volumes in this set, is written by
Donald Capps, the William Hart Felmeth Professor of Pastoral Theology at Princeton Theological Seminary. His own prodigious writing
has covered a wide range of topics bridging the fields of psychology,
religion, Scripture, and counseling. He has long been associated with
the work of the Psychology and Biblical Studies group of the Society
of Biblical Literature. His Foreword expresses in detail the development of his interest in reading the Bible through the lens of psychology, citing the introductory work to the field found in Wayne Rollins's *Soul and Psyche: The Bible in Psychological Perspective* (1999), Erik
Erikson's *Young Man Luther: A Study in Psychoanalysis and History*
(1958), and J. Harold Ellens's *God's Grace and Human Health* (1982) as
well as other related works.

It is appropriate that immediately following this incisive and articulate Foreword we should turn first to Walter Wink's (1975) essay,
"Snagged by the Seat of My Pants While Reading the Bible." It was
one of the earliest popular articles published in the United States to
report on the use of psychological models in biblical interpretation.
Wink starts off with an autobiographical yarn about an existential/
professional "snag" he discovered in 1962 while serving as a parish
pastor in southeast Texas, trying at the same time to complete a doctoral dissertation. When a member of the church learned of Wink's

work on the dissertation, he asked him why he was not sharing some of this in his preaching. Wink was nonplussed to discover that he had no idea how this type of scholarship would ever apply to the real people in the pew. He simply attributed to his own escapism this grand canyon between his biblical scholarship and his biblical preaching.

But in 1967, when he was on the faculty of Union Theological Seminary, the question of the Bible's relevance to war resistance, curriculum reform, and black economic development flared up. His sense of "snag" sharpened. What resulted was his landmark book, *The Bible in Human Transformation: Toward a New Paradigm for Biblical Study* (1973), which announced his judgment that historical-critical approaches to biblical study had become "bankrupt," not dead, but "no longer able to accomplish their avowed purpose," caught up as they seemed to be in a "trained incapacity to permit these texts to evoke personal and social change"—that is, to bite into one's own life and ministry.

The snag in all of this was the web of intellectual objectivism, the pretense of detachment, and the "disembodied observation and uninvolvement" of the scholar. But it was not enough to criticize. What was needed was a new paradigm for the field of biblical scholarship. Wink found the new paradigm, quite by accident, in the Guild for Psychological Studies in San Francisco, which had developed a learning setting in which Jungian depth psychology was used as an aid to opening up the Scriptures. This development in Wink's young career shaped the decades to follow.

Wink hit a second and related snag that led to another advance in his thinking about the Bible and life. The snag this time was the discovery that he and most readers of the Bible were preoccupied with the personal meaning of Scripture, with little or no interest in its social and political implications. No matter how much he tried to turn discussion in the direction of the problems built into social structures and systems, he hit the invisible wall of privatized interpretation. What got him off the snag this time was a book recommended to him by a colleague. The book, *The Hidden Injuries of Class* by Richard Sennett and Jonathan Cobb (1973), described a broad swath of society in which, no matter how hard individuals work, they find it impossible to get up and over the invisible glass ceilings of class-oppressing systems. This snag was to set Wink on a decade-long project of unmasking the principalities and powers of systems of social, political, and economic domination. Wink's snags, as uncomfortable as they were, had a point, and we are feeling the effects in his scholarship.

In his essay on "Object Relations Theory and Mark 15:33–39: Interpreting Ourselves Interpreting the Bible," Ralph L. Underwood applies to the phenomenon of textual interpretation the object relations theory of Freud and the post-Freudians Melanie Klein, W. R. D. Fairbairn, and Don Winnicott. This essay focuses on the relationship that comes to life between a biblical text and a reader, a process in which the text becomes a living object for the reader, internalized by the reader, and installed as part of the reader's psychic makeup.

As a case study of the dynamic interchange between text and reader, Underwood introduces the crucifixion account in Mark 15 as "text" and one of his own Lenten sermons as a response to the text. In his analysis of the transaction, Underwood likens the exchange between text and reader to Winnicott's "squiggle" therapy, in which he invites a child "to make something of" a "squiggle" the therapist has drawn on a piece of paper. Underwood emphasizes that a sermonic response to a text illustrates the object relations theory that creative responses to squiggles are demonstrations of the universal penchant of the human psyche to make meaning of the suffering, ambiguity, or paradox with which we are confronted in a story such as Mark 15, with its troubling images of the sundering of the veil of the sacred sanctuary and of a "suffering God."

In Chapter 4, "The Parable and the Centered Self: Erickson's Confusion Technique as Hermeneutic for the Stories of Jesus," Kamila Blessing introduces a new way of approaching the therapeutic and transformative effects of parables, namely, through the hermeneutic use of psychologist Milton Erickson's "confusion technique" and the "therapeutic story." Blessing tells us that "the specific elements of Erickson's therapeutic story are exactly the same as the specific, defining elements of parables." Erickson's approach helps us understand how and why a story works and how it induces change in the hearer.

Providing a brief biographical sketch describing how Erickson came to his theory, Blessing goes on to describe confusion technique as a story-telling strategy. It constructs a story that progressively introduces elements of confusion—for example, unfamiliar changes of setting, discontinuities, cryptic word plays, paradoxes and the "double bind"—toward the end of inducing an initial state of cognitive dissonance in the hearer. Ultimately, however, it goads the reader psychologically and spiritually into making sense of the story and rearranging the confusing elements into a meaningful whole. Blessing demonstrates the principle with a series of Gospel parables: the story of the Prodigal Son, for example, in which the reader surprisingly finds himself or herself identifying with the offending prodigal rather than with the "good" elder son; or the story of the hidden treasure in Matthew 13:44, in which Jesus puts the reader into a double bind by comparing the finding of the kingdom of God to a man who unscrupulously buys a field without informing the owner that he has found buried treasure there. Blessing finds similar "confusing" and paradoxical qualities in the story of the rich man and Lazarus (Luke 16:19–31), the parable of the talents (Matt. 25:14–30), the parable of the two sons (Matt. 21:28–31), and the parable of the wedding feast (Matt. 22:1–14). The culminating example is the parable of the unjust steward in Luke 16:1–8, which ends incredibly with the master commending a steward who, when he discovered he was going to be fired, cooked the books for his master's debtors to incur an indebtedness that would be of help when he was on the outs. The final moral is that with parables as "therapeutic stories," paradox and confusion can be the parent of *metanoia*, the biblical term for a change of mind, heart, and perspective; a conversion of spirit, attitude, and behavior.

Because the four Gospels deal extensively with the death of Jesus, Kari Syreeni finds it reasonable to suppose that the psychology of the grief process might cast light on the content and orientation of the Gospels. In his article on "Coping with the Death of Jesus: The Gospels and the Theory of Grief Work," Syreeni describes his approach as a "psychoanalytically oriented hermeneutical theory" that aims to take notice of phenomena in the Gospels otherwise easily overlooked and to help us carry on the personal quest for a better understanding and integrating of the Gospels, ourselves, and the universal experience of grief.

Syreeni begins with an engrossing review of contemporary grief process theory, from Sigmund Freud to Elisabeth Kübler Ross and on to the more recent cognitive and humanistic psychological approach of Kenneth Pargament. He offers keen observations on the strategies we employ to adapt and reorient ourselves after experiences of death or extreme loss, taking note of those strategies that are adaptive or maladaptive, regressive or progressive. Syreeni concludes that "successful grief work results in recollecting and incorporating what is left of the deceased person and in welcoming new replacements that maintain and develop the symbolic universe of the individual or the group."

In the second section of the essay Syreeni turns to the Gospels themselves, with the surprising initial observation that "what the Gospels tell us about the events immediately after Jesus' death conforms to the initial phases of grief work," namely, signs of shock, search for the absent one, experiences of his presence, refusal to believe that the death has occurred, and even euphoria in the conviction that the loss is greatly to the advantage of the bereaved. Syreeni also observes that not all early Christian groups centered their faith on the death-resurrection motif, noting that one of the earliest compilations of the life of Jesus, the Q source, had no account of the death of Jesus and no clear allusions to his resurrection or appearances. In the letters of Paul, however, we find a recreative interpretation of Jesus' death on the basis of resurrection belief, cultically symbolized in the language of being "in Christ," being baptized with Christ, and being part of the Body of Christ. Syreeni concludes that all of these means of coping "symbolically sustained the sense of Jesus' postdeath presence while in practice substituting for the absent Jesus," and he adds, "the Gospels do the same."

In his closing section on "the Gospels as grief work," Syreeni observes that a primary function of the Gospels is to create a symbolic universe for the Christian community that acknowledges and integrates the loss and absence of Jesus. Syreeni further reports that Mark, Matthew, Luke, and John reflect a progressive hermeneutical change in the historical situation and symbolic universe of the early church. The achievement of the Gospels as grief work is to teach "us to interpret our losses through the original loss inscribed in the Gospels." All the variety of grief work is already there, from desperate attachment to the past, through self-reproach and accusations, to recollection and reorientation toward the future. Even though we find ourselves in a new interpretive situation with respect to the facts in the Gospels, "our options are the same."

"Reading Mark for the Pleasure of Fantasy," by Petri Merenlahti, Chapter 6 in this volume, offers psychoanalytic reflection on texts and readers from three perspectives: Umberto Eco, Jacques Lacan, and Merenlahti's own interest in "how a psychoanalytic reading of Mark relates to ancient Greco-Roman conceptions of masculinity and femininity." Eco's semiotic theory proposes that every text has a *model reader*. This means that encoded in the composition of a literary text is an ideal audience and an ideal reading strategy that the text anticipates and tries to create. Every text, in Eco's view, is written with a strategy to evoke in readers the questions, interests, and even fantasies that the text is written to address.

Jacques Lacan, in Freudian tradition, would argue that there is more to the model reader than meets the eye. Lacan locates this "more" in the reader's unconscious, and its name is "desire." Lacan takes us back to infancy and the infant's desire for the mother. As the child grows, he or she develops language that can put a name on that real flesh-and-blood "mother." But when he begins to use the word "mother," something happens. He realizes that the term "mother" is no real substitute for the "mother herself" and in fact is prima facie evidence that the *real* mother is lacking. Therefore, reading any text, filled with such symbols and substitutes for reality, occasions desire for what is lacking in the words themselves. It is with such desire for what is lacking in the words themselves that we come to the Gospels. As Merenlahti observes, "The living, immediate presence of Jesus in the (oral) kerygma is substituted by the distant, objectifiable Jesus of the text, so that the latter effectively marks the lack of the former. On the other hand, it is only through this lack that the lost living Jesus first becomes desirable." Desire for what? The answer is "identity," and the text leads us to the image of Christ as the lure for our "fantasy" about that identity.

The fantasy is twofold. On the one hand, it is the fantasy image of the healer, teacher, mystic, subverter of conventional religious practice, and social integrator. On the other hand, it is the fantasy of a submissive obedience to death and renunciation of oneself. From a Freudian perspective, this can be seen pathologically as "voluntary castration." From another perspective, it can be seen as an inverted Oedipus complex, in which the boy child, instead of hoping to defeat the father, wishes to replace the mother as the object of the father's desire and so becomes the "bride" of Christ. A third perspective is the model of one who serves as a loyal subject or as one who, in transcending death, enters a state of mystic, ineffable joy. Merenlahti concludes with the observation that in some canonical texts, and certainly among the Gnostics, the Greco-Roman homogenization of the "male" image to include both males and females in one single mode of "manhood" may be operative in the Gospel. This invites the identity-fixing fantasy of both male and female readers as they read the text in their "desire" for what is lacking.

As background to the study of "The Psychology of Johannine Symbolism," Michael Willett Newheart provides, in Chapter 7, a history of earlier approaches to the rich symbolism of the fourth Gospel, from the existentialist approach of Rudolf Bultmann to more recent social-scientific and literary-critical approaches. Because of the need to probe the unconscious factors at work in symbols, Newheart insists that a psychological approach is essential. Opening with a virtual primer on Jungian analytical psychology, Newheart unpacks the archetypal value of the symbols of water, light, and bread and the picture of Jesus

as an archetypal image of the self. Newheart demonstrates how analytical psychology can be used as a window to gain insight into the
psychic tensions within and between first-century Jewish and Christian communities, adding a helpful excursus on the antisemitism inadvertently triggered in the fourth Gospel as a demonstration of psychological projection.

In Chapter 8, Paul N. Anderson offers us "The Cognitive Origins of
John's Unitive and Disunitive Christology." He employs two cognitive-
oriented psychological models to solve the vexing problem of the
apparent contradictions, polarities, and discontinuities in the portrait
of Jesus in John's Gospel. On the one hand, the Christology is high
(Jesus as the eternal logos), on the other hand, it is low (Jesus as human
"flesh"); on the one hand, Jesus is portrayed as omniscient, on the
other hand, he is portrayed as anxious and perplexed; on the one hand,
Jesus is seen as the Son equal to the Father, on the other, he is seen as
a son subordinate to the father.

In the first section of the chapter, on "diachronic solutions to John's
theological tensions," Anderson reviews the attempt of Rudolf Bultmann, one of the leading New Testament scholars of the twentieth
century, to solve the problem of the unitive and disunitive Christology
in John and its *aporias* (discontinuities), using a multiple-source theory, suggesting that the Gospel is a compilation of three disparate
sources with disparate points of view from different time periods in
the history of the formation of the Gospel. In the second and third sections, Anderson turns to "two research-based models of cognitive
analysis" for a more satisfying solution to the problem.

In his second section, on "the evangelist's ambivalence toward Jesus'
signs," Anderson introduces the developmental theory of James Fowler
on "stages of faith development" to account for the polarized attitude
toward the miracles (signs) of Jesus. On the one hand, the popular
interest in miracles is extolled; on the other hand, it is repudiated as an
inferior and less authentic basis for faith. Fowler's schema of the six
stages of faith puts this difference of opinion in historical perspective
as expressions of different levels of faith: intuitive-projective faith;
mythic-literal faith; synthetic-conventional faith; individual-reflective
faith; conjunctive faith (both/and); and universal faith.

Section three, on "the flesh and glory of Jesus," employs John
Loder's cognitive work on the process of "convictional thinking."
Loder's works suggests that the bioptic tension between the Gospel's
portrait of Jesus as both human flesh and glorified savior is to be seen
as an expression of different stages in a cognitive process, reflecting

the historical and personal experience within the Johannine community as it severs its relationships with the synagogue past and breaks
out on its own. Anderson concludes with the observation that these
same *aporias* and discrepancies are characteristic of developmental and
cognitive processes at work in the evolution of all faith communities,
typifying "the religious question across time and culture."

Anthony Bash opens Chapter 9, "A Psychodynamic Approach to 2
Corinthians 10–13," with a rationale for the application of psychological critical insight to the interpretation of Paul's writing. Bash contends that it is critically necessary to ask "whether a particular form of
behavior by a person in the Bible might at least be affected by psychological processes." In fact, as he demonstrates, biblical scholars have
long asked such questions, inquiring for example whether Paul's
behavior in 2 Corinthians 5:13 might not be an "example of megalomania." Bash's special aim is to engage in "psychodynamic criticism"
in an attempt to provide insight into how and why Paul said and did
what he did in the blustering passage in 2 Corinthians 10–13.

The specific issue at work in 2 Corinthians 10–13 is Paul's tirade
and ad hominem reproof of his Corinthian audience. Paul is clearly
under attack and angry. But angry with whom? Bash unpacks the
dynamics of the passage by identifying three factors: Paul as author,
the Corinthians as recipients of the letter, and an unnamed third group,
a shadow group, who have been roiling the waters against Paul. Bash
uses the psychology of defense mechanisms, particularly "displacement," "denial," and "splitting," to provide insight into what is happening. The odd twist in these four chapters is that Paul's behavior
and language can be seen as an instance of displacing his anger from
the "shadow group of dissidents," the real enemy, and turning it
against those who had been his loyal friends in Corinth. In his careful
exegetical explication of these psychological dynamics, Bash demonstrates how psychological criticism, as one arm of historical research
and literary interpretation, adds to our arsenal of insights into biblical
texts. It helps us to see the texts "as expressions of structure, processes, and habits of the human psyche," processes and habits that
may provide the key to understanding crucial aspects of certain biblical narratives.

"Differentiation in the Family of Faith: The Prodigal Son and Galatians 1–2" is the title of Chapter 10. Kamila Blessing applies the family
systems theory of psychiatrist Murray Bowen to the analysis of two
New Testament texts, a parable and a hortatory text in Paul. Bowen
is "the first to create a self-consistent theory of the relationship within

the family" and within society in general as a system. When one person moves, others are pulled along. The system exercises prodigious influence on the lifestyle, health, and identity of its members. Religions are family systems, and relationships within biblical stories are embedded in such family systems, which provide a psychodynamic backdrop for virtually all biblical texts.

Blessing selects three concepts of Bowen as hermeneutical tools for understanding what is happening in the systemic worlds reflected in the story of the Prodigal Son and in Galatians 1–2. One is differentiation, which denotes the degree to which an individual within the confines of the family system can enter the emotional arena without losing rational control. Anxiety is the major factor in determining the health or illness of the family system. Differentiation of self is the major determinant of our response to anxiety. A second concept is the "triangle" (many of them) into which family relations tend to coalesce. A third is the "fugue," or flight from the triangle(s), that an individual makes when anxiety runs high. Bowen's therapeutic ideal is to develop a heightened level of differentiation in the individual and to convert what begins as fugue into healthy independence and interdependence. Analyzing the various triangular relationships that develop in the story of the Prodigal Son between God, the prodigal, the pigs and starvation, the elder brother, the father, Jesus, and the reader, Blessing focuses on the parable's hope for a systemic community in which the worthy and unworthy are welcomed, including the implied reader.

Kamila Blessing's treatment of Galatians 1–2 appropriates an additional set of Bowen concepts, that of the "pseudoself" and "solid self." The pseudoself is a person whose feeling system dominates the intellectual and who lives by the principle of conformity; the solid self marches to his own drumbeat. Galatians 1–2 provides a compelling example of both in the person of Paul as a "solid person" and Peter, whom Paul denounces as a "hypocrite," as the "pseudoperson." Both are caught within the constraints of Gentile custom and Judaic law and ethos. Peter is the "conforming disciple," beholden to the social pressure of the Judaizers, especially in their insistence on the necessity of circumcision for Gentile members of the Christian community. Paul dares to operate out of his "faith" orientation "system," in which "spirit" rather than law is sovereign. Bowen's theory finds in these two pieces of Scripture an implicit invitation to form a system of differentiated selves who respond to systemic anxieties out of the strength of the solid self rather than that of the conforming disciple, whether in the form of the elder brother or Peter.

In his essay in Chapter 11 on "Paul's Letter to the Galatians in Social-Psychological Perspective," Dieter Mitternacht explores what is conventionally thought to be the conflict simmering under the surface of Galatians. The tension is evident at the very beginning of the letter, where Paul appears to be denouncing a group of "Judaizing" Christians who are exercising influence on the community, imposing circumcision on Gentile Christians. Mitternacht helps us to view this crisis through the lens of epistolary-rhetorical and socio-psychological analyses, which see the crisis in Galatia in a different light.

The epistolary-rhetorical approach opens our eyes to literary formulae at work in ancient letter writing that Paul adopts in Galatians, for example, the "rebuke formula" at the beginning of the letter and the "request formula" midway through the letter.

The bulk of the essay, however, is devoted to a socio-psychological analysis of the dynamics at work in the situation in Galatia, with special emphasis on role adoption theory. The traditional view of Galatians is that Paul's mission was under attack from intolerant and exclusivist opponents, demanding that Gentile converts be circumcised or suffer the possibility of being "lost."

Instead, this theory asserts that the circumcision activities in Galatia were the result of societal pressures. No agitators were demanding that Gentiles be circumcised. Nor was it a movement directed against Paul. It was a social acclimatization movement, Gentiles seeking social acceptance within a predominantly Jewish-Christian social milieu. The issue for the "opponents" was not legalism, law versus gospel, works versus faith, but rather a matter of social role adoption in which they, as Gentiles who had been ostracized for their faith in Christ, wished to be accepted as full social members in a Jewish-Christian ethos. It was not so much a matter of circumcision being demanded as circumcision being desired. Paul's objection is that these Gentiles adopted a role model other than that of Christ.

Mitternacht's thesis rests on the mythical role adoption theory of Hjalmar Sundén, which holds that in all cultures certain archetypal roles become encoded in a people. These have the potential of shaping role patterns over successive generations. Although the individual may lapse from the role from time to time, the mythical role remains in the mind as a latent structure of experience that can be activated as soon as a relevant stimulus occurs.

Paul's issue with the Gentiles in Galatia is that they have adopted a role far beneath the role that Paul would have them emulate. This is the role of Christ, as one who dwells in them (Galatians 2:20), as a role for which they have been set apart from their mother's womb (Galatians 1:15), as a role that is seeking to be formed within them (Galatians 4:19), as a role that Paul has adopted and that he invites them to adopt (Galatians 4:12). Paul calls them to a life focused not on social conformity but on the relentless imitation of the crucified Christ that integrates the possibility of suffering, even persecution, into their lives.

In the following chapter, the psychological root of apocalyptic thinking is explored by Charles T. Davis in his wide-ranging essay, "Revelation 17: The Apocalypse as Psychic Drama." Using Jungian archetypal theory, Davis identifies the lurid language of Apocalypse, populated by heroes and dragons, Christs and Antichrists, as expressive of a battle that originates within the human psyche and is projected on anyone within reach who might be perceived as the enemy. Davis takes us on a guided tour of such "enemies" over the last 2,000 years, beginning with Rome and Nero during the early Christian persecutions, continuing with the Muslim infidels during the Crusades, the Franciscans during the reign of Boniface VIII, the Pope or Luther during the Reformation, and David Koresh in Waco, Texas. Davis sees the same projection at work in the literary scenario of Sherlock Holmes versus Moriarty and Batman versus Shreck, suggesting the need for psychological insight into the toxic effects of apocalyptic projection today.

J. Harold Ellens opens Chapter 13 on "Psychological Aspects of Biblical Apocalypticism" with the thesis that there are two "master stories" within the Judeo-Christian tradition. All master stories, he would add, are constructed of three resources: the spiritual imagination of the community, the historical experience of the community, and the metaphors, myths, and scenarios with which the human psyche habitually formulates such experience. One of these master stories is expressed in the Pharisaic and Talmudic traditions, with their celebration of the presence of the transcendent in the Torah. The second, which occupies center stage in this essay, is Jewish apocalypticism, rooted in the world view of Daniel 7–9 and I Enoch 37–71, manifested in the cloistered Essenism that produced the Dead Sea Scrolls, and transmuted into the Jesus movement, the Son of Man image, and early Christian apocalyptic tradition. The historical experience out of which Jewish apocalypticism emerged is the memory of suffering, disempowerment, and meaninglessness associated with their forced exile from Judea to Babylon in the sixth century B.C.E. Accordingly, apocalyptic metaphors, visions, and mythic ideations emerged out of the psychological need to rethink and reconceptualize the role of the transcendent in human history. The inspiration for this reformulation is found in the exodus. Ellens writes, "Exodus tradition is essentially a psychological perspective . . . that . . . seeded the eschatological and apocalyptic formulations of postexilic Judaism, including that form of it that became Christianity." Living in the experience of exile, the community rerationalized the role of transcendental forces, finding in the memory and metaphors of the exodus a ready-made storehouse of images for speaking of divine intervention in history, which will now be portrayed in eschatological, metahistorical terms.

Within the earliest levels of the Christian movement, the apocalyptic trajectory is extended in the adoption, first by Jesus and later by the community, of the Son of Man image. The image was envisioned in three forms: the Son of Man as earthly teacher and healer; the Son of Man as a suffering servant who dies and is exalted; and the Son of Man as a future eschatological figure returning in judgment at the end of history. Ellens argues that all three images were implicit in the teaching and life of Jesus but that the latter became the psychological lodestone for the emerging Christian community as it began to process its own experience of "exile" in its encounter with Rome.

In her essay on "The Bible and the Psychology of Shame," Jill McNish explores one of the last "four-letter" words in the English language, "shame." She offers a riveting range of examples of this phenomenon that everyone knows firsthand but no one wants to talk about. Surveying the sources of shame as an aspect of our "embodied" existence from infancy to old age, McNish provides insightful analysis of shame's liabilities but also its assets, appropriating the psychological resources of Helen Lynch, Carl Jung, and D. W. Winnicott. At the heart of McNish's work is the psychological judgment that shame has a formative and revelatory potential in life, a point adumbrated in the biblical accounts of shame, beginning with the "original shame" of Adam and Eve and concluding with the shame of the fatherless and crucified historical Jesus.

David L. Miller opens Chapter 15, "Biblical Imagery and Psychological Likeness," with a 1958 *Cosmopolitan* magazine survey of prominent preachers, theologians, and psychologists on the question, "What would happen if Jesus were to return to earth?" Carl Jung, one of the respondents, replied that Jesus "would see himself banalized beyond all endurance." Miller proceeds to consider the way in which classical biblical interpretation may have banalized the Bible since the eighteenth century by approaching the Bible either as a book of theology or as a book of history, relegating the meaning of the Bible either to the future (salvation and heaven) or to the past (the history of God's acts in past time). Miller suggests a third way in which the meaning

of the Bible addresses the here and now, addressing not just the theologian's or historian's intellectual ego but also the reader's soul. This
third route is the "imaginal realm," in which the meaning of the Bible
is plumbed not by theological doctrine or historical facts but by
examples or likenesses rendered in metaphors, stories, and images
that provide a "feel," an experience, a spiritual contextualizing of what
the text is saying about us. In fact, as Miller points out, "the Biblical
text [itself] is a treasure-house of images . . . in a variety of genres
(myth, history, parable, poetry, letter, prophecy, and apocalypse)" that
provide "profound psychological life-likenesses" of those realities in
life that need naming: the experience of lost paradise, of deluge and
flood, of bondage, of walking on dry land through a tempest, of finding
something sacred in a virginal place, of being "nailed" and betrayed
by friends, and of being lifted up above death, suffering, and oblivion.

The Bible is a treasury of likenesses that illumine life and "body
forth the unconscious complexes of a rich and multifaceted psyche."
As Miller contends, the art of creating such likenesses is also the task
of the biblical interpreter, whose business it is to make plain how text
and soul relate. Miller illustrates how Origen of Alexandria understood that well, in the third century, and how the poet Wallace Stevens
understood it in our own time. Miller concludes his essay with a skill-
ful defense of a depth-psychological approach to the text as a method
that seeks to find the meeting place between text and psyche. He
addresses and counters three critiques of this approach—the Essentialist critique, the Comparativist critique, and the Reductionist
critique—with an *apologia* rich in learning and classical "likeness."

In his essay in Chapter 16 on "Psyche, Soul, and Self in Historical and
Contemporary Perspective," Wayne Rollins contends that we live in a
culture in which just about everybody uses the words *psyche*, *soul*, and
self, but virtually no one, with the exception of depth psychologists,
defines them to any satisfactory degree. The goal of Rollins' essay is to
provide a history of these three terms, unpacking their meaning today
as virtually synonymous. The history of the term *psyche* begins with
Aristotle's classic *Peri Psyches* (concerning the Psyche), the first "systematic psychology" in the West, and continues with an exploration of
Patristic treatises on the *psyche*, the introduction of the term "psychology" by a biblical scholar in the sixteenth century, the repudiation of
the term by empiricists and behaviorists, and its reclamation by Freud,
Jung, and humanistic psychology in the twentieth century. Freud and
Jung used the word *soul* (German: *Seele*), without its religious connotations, as a translation term for psyche. Theologians and psychologists

in the mid-twentieth century tended to disuse the term because of its ambiguity. The last quarter of the century witnessed its remarkable return as a cultural word of choice. Finally, the word *self* is surveyed in history: its adoption by Aristotle, Descartes, Kant, and Hume; its disuse by British Associationists; its revival in the twentieth century by William James, Erik Erikson, Karen Horney, and Heinz Kohut; and its adoption by cognitive and developmental psychologists as the best term to express the "inner" structure of the human person. In the end, Rollins will argue that all three terms, with slightly nuanced differences, constitute the best available symbols to denote the total system of conscious and unconscious life in the human personality.

In the wake of the enthusiasm surrounding the Gnostic documents from Nag Hammadi, biblical scholars are reassessing the strange, imaginal world of Gnosticism that flourished in the first few centuries C.E. Their writings were banned from orthodox Christian circles by the fourth century, but traces are evident in the New Testament. In Chapter 17, "'Begotten, Not Created': The Gnostic Use of Language in Jungian Perspective," Schuyler Brown, a seasoned New Testament scholar, examines what at one time had seemed to be a passing phenomenon within early Christianity. Brown is convinced that the exclusion of Gnostics from the Christian Church was more damaging from a psychological point of view than any subsequent church schism.

What has Gnosticism to offer? Brown's thesis is that it represents a way of thinking, a way of reading, and a way of using language that is compensatory to the rationalism, the dogmatism, and the objectivism of an orthodox approach to theology. Brown provides a catalogue of differences between orthodoxy and Gnosticism. Orthodoxy is the voice of logical, ordered, objective thinking; in Freudian terms it is secondary process thought. Gnosis is right-brained thinking, commercing in fantasy, poetry, and dream images (i.e., primary process thought). The root metaphor of orthodoxy is the Logos, the spoken "masculine," proactive, creative, shaping word, dedicated to the ego-conscious power of speech and communication. The root metaphor of Gnosis is the feminine Sophia, "begetting" new creation and new being, dedicated to the depth-psychological power of procreation and imagination beyond the conscious ego.

Brown reports that Jung developed keen interest in Gnosticism, despite his initial bafflement, because of Gnosticism's access, through its intuitive closeness to the wisdom of the unconscious, to parts of the human "being" that rational discourse could not reach. Orthodoxy seems confident of its ability to define the holy, once and for all. Gnosis, in concert with contemporary deconstructionism, realizes the ineffability of all objective reality. This does not mean that rationality is abandoned; it is transcended and deepened to include the dimension of the ineffable. How are we to read the Gnostics and the Nag Hammadi texts, the Gospels of Thomas and Philip? Brown tells us that they are to be read as poetry that seeks to arouse rather than define and that can help us reclaim the "psychic matrix" of theological language in experience.

In conclusion, it is our conviction in producing these volumes that anyone who is serious about the quest for meaning in human life will need to pay close attention to the Bible and the biblical tradition of understanding both the human and the transcendent world. Furthermore, anyone who is serious about understanding the Bible and its impact upon the human quest and human history must look carefully at the biblical text through the lenses of literary analysis, historical analysis, other relevant forms of critical analysis, and psychological analysis. These four volumes are about looking at the Bible through the lens of careful and responsible psychological perspectives in the hope that it will produce more light and truth about who we are as human beings and what we are about.

References

Bregman, L. (1990). Symbolism/Symbolizing, *Dictionary of Pastoral Care and Counseling*, R. Hunter, ed. Nashville: Abingdon, 1249.

Ellens, J. H. (1982). *God's Grace and Human Health*. Nashville: Abingdon.

Erikson, E. (1958). *Young Man Luther: A Study in Psychoanalysis and History*, New York: Norton.

James, W. (1985). *The Varieties of Religious Experience*. New York: Penguin Classics. (Original work published 1902)

Jung, C. G. (1953–1978). *The Collected Works of C. G. Jung*, R. F. C. Hull, trans. (Vol. 20). Princeton: Princeton University Press.

Jung, C. G. (1973). *C. G. Jung Letters: Vol. I, 1905–1950* (addressed to Frau Schmit-Lohner, May 20, 1947). Princeton: Princeton University Press, 463.

Miles, J. (1995, December 24). Jesus Before He Could Talk. *New York Times Magazine*, 28–33.

Rollins, W. (1999). *Soul and Psyche: The Bible in Psychological Perspective*. Minneapolis: Fortress.

Sennett, R., & Cobb, J. (1973). *The Hidden Injuries of Class*. New York: Vintage.

Wink, W. (1973). *The Bible in Human Transformation: Toward a New Paradigm for Biblical Study*. Philadelphia: Fortress.

Wink, W. (1978). On Wrestling With God: Using Psychological Insights in Biblical Study. *Religion in Life*, 47, 136–147.

CHAPTER 2

Snagged by the Seat of My Pants While Reading the Bible

Walter Wink

> Bible study must give equal time to both psychological and sociological issues lest we fail to do justice to its passion for transformation.
>
> —Author

The otherwise even flow of my life as a scholar-for-the-church has so far hit two snags. Both have irreversibly changed my course.

I was hooked by the first snag in 1962. Having completed work on my PhD except for the dissertation, I was at last established as pastor of a church in southeast Texas, trying to write my thesis with one hand and take care of pastoral duties with the other. The church was generous in allowing me time to study—and I needed that time for my psychic health, because I had walked in on a congregation in a shambles. It was no little relief to be able to retreat into the first century and thus escape the conflict and pain of the parish. The worse the storm outside, the more I fled to my study inside. Within nine months I had the writing finished.

Once during that period the chairman of the church's official board asked me why I never preached on any of the New Testament passages that I was so exhaustively exegeting. I did not know. It was odd: I could not say why, but I was very certain that I could not. It would be somehow—wrong. It would be to sully the texts, to contaminate them. It would seem almost a prostitution to take these texts, which I had analyzed with the purest objectivity of which I was capable, and apply them somehow to this bickering yet beloved parish. No. I could not explain why, but I could not preach on those texts.

Five years passed. I was preaching two different sermons every Sunday at first, then, mercifully, only one. In five years I must have preached upward of 350 sermons. Yet on only a couple of occasions could I bring myself to use those dissertation texts.

The Bankruptcy of Historical Criticism

Now it is characteristic of most of us that when we uncover such anomalies as these, we dismiss them as aberrations of our own personal experience. That was where I was inclined to leave it. After all, I could scarcely blame my teachers for the problem. No more profoundly engaged teacher has taught Bible in our time than my Old Testament professor, James Muilenburg. And in New Testament there was the existentially involved Chris Beker and the perceptively human work of John Knox. And all the rest—W. D. Davies, J. Louis Martyn, Samuel Terrien, George Landes—were deeply committed to the truth claims of the Scriptures. So I dismissed my snag as the peculiar problem of an escapist parson.

Then in 1967, Union Theological Seminary invited me back to teach New Testament. In this more exposed setting, dealing with students embroiled in war resistance, black economic development, curriculum reform, and the "Columbia Bust" of 1968, the question of the Bible's relevance for modern life was stridently and insistently posed. At the same time I was meeting more and more pastors to whom I would put the question—at first very tentatively, almost as if to make conversation: What role does historical criticism *really* play in your preaching, your personal Bible study, your leadership in congregational study? The answers varied widely, but enough were sufficiently disturbing that my sense of the anomaly grew. I was not off the snag. I was impaled on it, *and so were they*. I would never be rid of it till I plunged into the water and dug out its roots.

The fruit of that effort was published under the title *The Bible in Human Transformation: Toward a New Paradigm for Biblical Study* (1973). I had at last located what was for me at the base of the anomaly, thanks to the help of others who had pointed the way. Simply but quite precisely put, the historical-critical approach to biblical study had become bankrupt. Not dead: the critical tools have a potential usefulness, if they can only be brought under new management. But on the whole, the American scholarly scene is one of frenetic decadence, with the publication of vast numbers of articles and books that fewer and fewer people read. Most scholars no longer address the lived experience of actual people in the churches or society. Instead they address the current questions of their peers in the professional scholarly guild. The net result has been a gathering malaise, a crisis of morale, and a dawning recognition that what was once a vital contribution to the emancipation of people from the constrictions of dogmatism has become a new constriction in its own right.

I heard this report: The chairman of a university religion department, a biblical scholar by specialization, walked into the office of a colleague and flung my book on his desk. "Have you read this?"

"No."

"Then read it and tell me what you think."

The next day the colleague dropped in on the chairman. "Well, I read it."

"What do you think?"

"He's right, of course."

"Do you realize what that means for me?"

"You must have already known that, or you wouldn't have asked me what I thought."

At this point my memory, already no doubt enlarging on the tradition, breaks down. When it picks up again, the chairman is confiding that he does not know for whom he's writing books any longer, or why anyone would want to read them.

Caught in the Web of Objectivism

That dialogue tells me that my once private snag has now gathered quite a company. Hooked are hundreds of scholars whose original intention in entering biblical studies has long since been compromised, squeezed out, or suppressed. Most of us found ourselves *drawn* to the Bible. It chose us, as it were, or something in it chose us, something that comes to speech in it. We were attracted to it—not out of curiosity or mere historical interest but because we believed it could evoke human transformation. Biblical scholarship would be our ministry, our self-offering to the Kingdom of God.

Then, ineluctably, we found ourselves jettisoning the very questions and interests that led us to begin. We were caught in the web of intellectual objectivism, with its pretense to detachment, disembodied observation, and uninvolvement as the ideal stance of the researcher. Rudolf Bultmann had already so clearly exposed the false consciousness of objectivism that it seems incredible that, rather than being in decline, it is flourishing. I can only guess that one key reason is the history of denominational pluralism in America and the understandable reluctance of universities and colleges to permit the teaching of religion in a way that smacked of sectarianism. Hence, objectivism with a vengeance: the more religion could be taught as an exact science, the less offense it would cause. This at a time when the physical sciences were beginning to repudiate objectivism!

Other departments in the university felt no such pressures. In the department of philosophy, a logical positivist might be busy demonstrating the folly of all previous philosophies before the moment he himself began his doctoral studies. Over in psychology, a Skinnerian or a Freudian unabashedly propounds his own school's thought as if it were normative for the entire field. No one was objecting, because that was what these scholars were paid to do: to be profess-ors, to represent a position, to incarnate it even, if they are capable, yet with enough critical distance to be open to criticism and dialogue and even to changing one's mind.

But over in the religion department, scholars might still be churning out papers justifying the study of religion on the college campus. And any teachers of religion who are effective are so because they have courageously refused to knuckle under to this absurd demand for detached, uninvolved, disinterested study of the ultimate questions of existence.

I had finally named the anomaly for myself. It was the inability to study these texts in such a way that the intention of the texts themselves was honored. It was the trained incapacity to permit these texts to evoke personal and social change. It was not my professors who had trained this capacity out of me. I had caught the disease from the general ethos of the field, the meetings and journals of the professional societies and the endless flood of monographs.

But it was not enough to criticize the old mode of biblical scholarship. What was needed was an alternative, a new paradigm, a way beyond the anomaly. I was planning a "normal" scholarly sabbatical in Tübingen, Germany, when two of my former students persuaded me to look into a program in San Francisco with the Guild for Psychological Studies. Using Jungian depth psychology as an aid in interpretation, Dr. Elizabeth Howes and her colleagues were studying the Bible in a total context aimed at the healing of persons. I visited that summer, found it the answer to my need, and reversed directions on my sabbatical.

The approach of the Guild for Psychological Studies provided just the distance I needed to fight free of the hold that the objectivist paradigm still exercised over me. From my studies during that sabbatical and during each of seventeen summers, I not only received necessary training in the Guild's Jungian approach for use in my own work but was able to articulate an alternative to the current scholarly paradigm that, I hoped, might be at least one way to release others who were caught on the snag. From the outpouring of responses, I must say that it seems to have hit home.

The Glass Wall of Individualism

Meanwhile, in the flow, I had hit another snag, as important as the first and as intractable. But by that time I had learned to respect my snags, to believe in them as a certain kind of voice. So I honored this one.

I had, in my book, discussed the importance of "exegeting the exegete," of bringing under analysis not only the analyst's attitudes and reactions to the text but also his social situation, his vested interests, the political implications of his or her work. I had no clear idea of how to proceed, nor had any of my subsequent work helped me significantly. In fact, my preoccupation with psychological insights tended to eclipse social and political questions.

I thought to myself, "Surely it is the people involved; they are not politically aware." But then I led Bible study with the most politically aware and intellectually astute of all our students; I worked with an ecumenical and interracial group in East Harlem; I went to every conceivable class of church. Still it did not happen. No matter how much I wanted discussion to verge on the social, it generally tended to remain privatized, individual, personal. At first, the sheer excitement of what was happening to people at a personal level mesmerized me. I was willing to leave it at that. Later, they would become social activists, I hoped.

Finally, I had to concede that it was not going to happen, and for exactly the same reason that it almost never happens to Billy Graham's converts, or people in psychotherapy or the human potential movement, or devotees of Eastern religions, or simply students of theology. It would not happen because it *could not happen.* There has been erected an invisible glass wall between ourselves and the social system. Whenever we try to move against the system itself, we hit the glass wall, we are deflected, and we rise to transcend the discomfort of injustice or institutional evil by purely private means. It is the ideology of individualism, and in this country it exists to protect racism, sexism, and the class system of capitalism.

An Accursed Freedom

I did not discover this on my own. For three years I had puzzled over the anomaly: I want to address social, political, and economic realities, yet in the groups I lead we seemed to move further and further into ourselves. What is happening is good; but why can we not connect it with the social? I pressed the question with Professor Beverly Harrison. She put into my hands *The Hidden Injuries of Class*, by Richard Sennett and Jonathan Cobb (1973). Suddenly I saw what I had been looking at without really comprehending.

Sennett and Cobb's study focused on working-class males in Boston. Generally accused of being materialistic by intellectual friends and foes alike, these blue- and white-collar workers were in fact trying to amass goods, get promoted, buy two cars, and move to the suburbs because these are the things that society tells them they must do to win a sense of personal dignity and worth. But in fact, even success on society's terms does not bring the longed-for satisfaction:

> The fear of being summoned before some hidden bar of judgment and being found inadequate infects the lives of people who are coping perfectly well from day to day; it is a matter of hidden weight, a hidden anxiety, in the quality of experience, a matter of feeling inadequately in control where an observer making material calculations would conclude the working man had adequate control. (Sennett & Cobb, 1973, 33–34)

For these laborers, freedom is no longer merely the freedom to eat. Now it is a matter of how much choice one has and the development of the human potential of people in what is for them a postscarcity society. Such people do not feel that their work allows them to express enough that is unique in themselves to win others' respect as individuals. They envy "cultured" people whom society has put in a position to develop their "insides." And yet their outrage that society permits this inequity of opportunity rebounds on them as self-doubt and accusation: if only I had tried harder in school, if only I had had the breaks. It is an accursed freedom, which tells everyone in this society, rich and poor, plumber and professor, that he or she must validate the self in order to win the respect of others and of oneself. Yet the system will not and cannot deliver that respect, even when all of the players play the game by the rules.

The system says, for example, that if you strive to excel, like Horatio Alger, you will succeed; if you fail, you have no one to blame but yourself. But in a given plant there may be 3,000 workers eligible for six foreman jobs over a period of several years. Perhaps 1,500 would like to be promoted; only about 150 may be genuinely qualified. Six are selected. The others—do they lead a revolt? Organize a factory takeover by workers? No. They blame themselves. They are angry and unsure of their right to be angry.

Flawed Humanism

It is the glass wall. Just at the moment when inequities might be confronted, the ideology of individualism blocks the view. And now the plot thickens. For it was just this dynamic that I saw happening week after week in my Bible study classes. Somewhere, way back there, we were all told that if we succeeded it was by the grace of God; if we failed, we had only ourselves to blame. But more: we were told that all were created equal. That is the voice of the Enlightenment. If all were created equal, then by George,

> those who are the most intelligent or able or competent have demonstrated more character in manifesting a potential that flows through all; don't they deserve to be treated with more respect than others, or at least to be entrusted with more power? This would be only reasonable, after all; they showed themselves to be better in practice when all began the same. (Sennett & Cobb, 1973, 255)

The cause of class inequality proves in our case to be—belief in equality!

This "flawed humanism," as Sennett and Cobb call it, provides a perverse justification of the inequities of the class system and confirms those on the bottom or middle or even uppermost rungs in their anxiety about their lives. We do not in fact deserve to be respected. We must earn it. The authors cannot restrain themselves; they finally call it by its theological name: justification through works.

Given such a situation, the preaching of the Good News of God's free acceptance of each of us should come as the word of a real deliverance. And there is no better way to break the karma of this cycle of self-depreciation. The message of justification by grace was never more timely in the whole history of the church.

But—and this is a huge qualifier—*if* that message of justification by God's undeserved love is preached apart from an unmasking of the actual power relations that have aggravated these feelings to the level of a social neurosis; *if* people are released from the rat race of upward mobility only privatistically, with no critique of the economic and social ideology that stimulates such desperate cravings; *if* people are liberated from a bad sense of themselves without any sense of mission to change the conditions that waste human beings in such a way, *then* justification by faith becomes a mystification of the actual power relations, and the Christian gospel is indeed the opiate of the masses. And study of the Bible that avoids facing these issues becomes a justification of the status quo.

Still Caught on the Snag

Do not misunderstand me. I am not merely referring to the need for social involvement. Nor am I speaking of making the Bible relevant to modern society. The anomaly is far deeper; it has to do with the way the very social systems themselves are continually rendered invisible, perpetually withdrawing themselves from examination, leaving us only ourselves to blame or change.

We must not be deceived; the anomaly has not disappeared. We are still skewered on the snag. But we can now see what it is that has us hooked. It is the ideology of individualism, the flawed humanism of the Enlightenment, and an interpretation of Christianity that resolutely avoids addressing the principalities and powers. I learned from Carl Jung, Elizabeth Howes, and others something about how persons can relate to the source of their own transformation. Now I am beginning to delve for this new set of roots. I am content to stay at the task for as long as it takes. The very integrity of the Good News is at stake.

It is not, of course, a task that one can manage alone. The vicious individualism of scholarship itself must be superseded; new kinds of relationships and communities must be formed. Liberation theologians, to be sure, have seen this for some time. But the large task of changing the way we wrestle with the Bible has scarcely even been acknowledged. It must be begun, despite the enormous resistance of the biblical guild. The resistance is understandable. We cannot change our scholarship unless we change our lives.

Epilogue: September 30, 2003

This programmatic essay from 1975 set forth an agenda for the rest of my scholarly life. The first step seemed to me to be the development of a Bible study methodology that would make personal and social transformation possible. That effort occupied most of the 1970s and resulted in two books, *The Bible in Human Transformation* (1973) and *Transforming Bible Study: A Leader's Guide* (1980; 2nd ed., 1989). During that time I devoted myself to the study of Carl Jung's works to understand better the intrapsychic processes involved in human transformation. It was the consensus of most biblical scholars of that period that the Bible has no social ethic, just a personal ethic. I found that preposterous. At that juncture I came across William Stringfellow's *Free in Obedience* (1964), which introduced me to the principalities and powers as present realities. That interest eventuated in a trilogy on the Powers: *Naming the Powers: The Language of Power in the New Testament* (1984); *Unmasking the Powers: The Invisible Forces That Determine Human Existence* (1986); and *Engaging the Powers: Discernment and Resistance in a World of Domination* (1992), supplemented by other works on the Powers: *Violence and Nonviolence in South Africa* (1987); *Cracking the Gnostic Code: The Powers in Gnosticism* (1993); *The Powers That Be: Theology for a New Millennium* (1998a); *When the Powers Fall: Reconciliation in the Healing of Nations* (1998b); and *Peace Is the Way: Writings on Nonviolence from the Fellowship of Reconciliation* (2000), among others. In all of these works I have tried to maintain a balance between the personal and the social.

Note

From W. Wink (1975, September 24). Snagged by the Seat of My Pants While Reading the Bible. *The Christian Century, 92*, 816–819. Reprinted with permission of the publisher.

References

Sennett, R., & Cobb, J. (1973). *The Hidden Injuries of Class*. New York: Vintage.

Stringfellow, W. (1964). *Free in Obedience*. New York: Seabury.

Wink, W. (1973). *The Bible in Human Transformation: Toward a New Paradigm for Biblical Study*. Philadelphia: Fortress.

Wink, W. (1984). *Naming the Powers: The Language of Power in the New Testament*. Philadelphia: Fortress.

Wink, W. (1986). *Unmasking the Powers: The Invisible Forces That Determine Human Existence*. Philadelphia: Fortress.

Wink, W. (1987). *Violence and Nonviolence in South Africa*. Philadelphia: New Society Publishers.

Wink, W. (1989). *Transforming Bible Study: A Leader's Guide*. Nashville: Abingdon.

Wink, W. (1992). *Engaging the Powers: Discernment and Resistance in a World of Domination*. Minneapolis: Fortress.

Wink, W. (1993). *Cracking the Gnostic Code: The Powers in Gnosticism*. Atlanta: Scholars Press.

Wink, W. (1998a). *The Powers That Be: Theology for a New Millennium*. New York: Doubleday.

Wink, W. (1998b). *When the Powers Fall: Reconciliation in the Healing of Nations*. Minneapolis: Fortress.

Wink, W. (2000). *Peace Is the Way: Writings on Nonviolence from the Fellowship of Reconciliation*. Maryknoll: Orbis.

CHAPTER 3

Object Relations Theory and Mark 15:33–39: Interpreting Ourselves Interpreting the Bible

Ralph L. Underwood

Among a variety of different psychologies useful for biblical studies, the key contribution of object relations theory is the way in which this perspective calls on scholars and religious adherents alike to reflect on the relational qualities and dynamics of biblical study and meditation. The focus, in other words, is on the relationship between the text and the person studying and interpreting the text, a process in which the text may come to be like a living "object" in a communication event. A summary overview of object relations theory orients readers to this psychological approach. Several working principles that describe and analyze patterns of relational dynamics of biblical interpretation prepare readers for an examination of Mark 15:33–39 and the dynamics of its interpretation as embodied in a sermon. Object relations perspectives guide reflections on this interpretation of the text.

Object Relations Theory: Propositions on Textual Interpretation

First, then, a brief summary of aspects of object relations theory salient for a relational approach to the interpretation of a text. Object relations theory is a school of thought within the psychoanalytic tradition. Freud himself inaugurated the theory of object relations but only partially developed it. Freud thought that in part the ego structure of the psyche is formed through identification: an external object is taken into the ego (Freud, 1927, 35–41). The general idea in object relations theory is that very early relationships between infant and caregivers, primarily the mother, come to be represented within the psyche of the infant in tandem with the infant's development of a sense of self. Psychologically, sense of self and sense of others virtually define each other. The internal representation of another person within the psyche comes to have its own stability or becomes an object present to the infant even when the other person is not present. The term "object" refers to relationships or relationships as represented in mental images. The term derives from libido theory, according to which psychic energy or libido seeks satisfaction in an object. In Freud's thinking, the nature of the object is not as important as is the need for satisfaction. In contrast, for contemporary object relations theory, the nature of the personal object is critical. As the infant develops images of others, so the child forms images of self; these self-images are objects in which psychic energy is invested, as are the internal objects that represent others.

Freud's focus, however, was on the Oedipal complex and not on earlier stages of infant development. Others in the psychoanalytic movement were trying to account for internal conflicts that preceded the Oedipal stage and developed further the theory of object relations. Noted for her attention to the way infantile mental images are split into good and bad, Melanie Klein focused on the first three years of the life cycle. Following her were W. R. D. Fairbairn and Don Winnicott. The latter is a central figure for contemporary theory.

The most significant task of early development in object relations theory is that of acquiring and forming internal images of self and others that are realistic. Even under good conditions, no self is complete without conflicts, unconscious and primitive objects, or unrealistic elements. Studying these dynamics of development, object relations theorists came to emphasize the inherently relational nature of the human psyche.

With this admittedly cursory introduction to object relations, let me proffer several propositions about object relations and textual interpretation. The first addresses a bivalence quality in interpretation. A text, when interpreted, "speaks" on at least two levels: the primordial and the creative. The second proposition holds that the process of interpretation relocates text and reader in transitional space. In this space, reading a text becomes relating to a text. The third concept propounded is that creative interpretation entails a suspension of disbelief. Such suspension fosters exploration of primordial and creative dimensions of text-reader relationships. Critical interpretation is an essential dimension of the interpretive process. Even so, suspension of the critical-analytical frame of mind enables a kind of leap of faith with one's eyes open. Finally, primordial self-understanding and cultural self-understanding conspire to evoke creative possibilities in the text.

For purposes of presenting and illustrating these propositions, this chapter offers a scriptural text and an interpretation of it in the form of a sermon. Discussion of these proposed concepts about object relations and interpretation follow.

Mark 15:33–39, NRSV: A First Reading and an Anomaly

When it was noon, darkness came over the whole land until three in the afternoon. At three o'clock, Jesus cried out with a loud voice, "Eloi, Eloi, lama sabachthani?" which means, "My God, my God, why have you forsaken me?" When some of the bystanders heard it, they said, "Listen, he is calling for Elijah." And someone ran, filled a sponge with sour wine, put it on a stick, and gave it to him to drink, saying, "Wait, let us see whether Elijah will come to take him down." Then Jesus gave a loud cry and breathed his last. And the curtain of the temple was torn in two, from top to bottom. Now when the centurion, who stood facing him, saw that in this way he breathed his last, he said, "Truly this man was God's Son!" (Mark 15:33–39)

This text is part of a narrative on Jesus dying on the cross. Verses 33 to 37 take the reader from the darkness at noon to the moment when Jesus breathes his last (Greek: *exepneusen*). Verse 38 takes the reader to another scene, the curtain at the temple, and verse 39 returns the reader to the crucifixion scene as the centurion witnesses Jesus' last breath and declares, "Truly this man was God's Son!" From the viewpoint of the structure of the narrative, verse 38 introduces the anomaly. The story reads smoothly without verse 38. The reference to the temple curtain calls for interpretation (i.e., it places a demand on the reader). Along with references to darkness, the anomaly of the temple curtain is present in the synoptic gospels, not in John. Like Mark, Matthew's version (27:51f.) locates the torn curtain element of the story immediately after Jesus breathes his last, but Matthew adds the elements of the earth shaking, rocks splitting, tombs opened, and many bodies of saints raised before the author returns to tell of the centurion and others' testimony concerning Jesus. Luke's account (23:44–47) places the torn curtain before Jesus' moment of death, and the centurion testifies simply that Jesus was innocent. In all synoptic versions the torn curtain seems to interrupt the narrative and yet belong to it.

A background text concerning the curtain is Exodus 26:31–33. The curtain separates the holy and the holy of holies. Only the high priest on the day of atonement enters the holy of holies to make atonement for his own sins and the sins of the people. Hebrews 10 offers a theological interpretation of the meaning of the curtain.

Interpreting may begin with initial observations such as the above and proceed to become embodied in more elaborate and critical exegesis and commentary, in personal journaling, in teaching, in preaching, or in other forms of reflection and communication. This chapter comments on a sermon. The following is a sermon based on the Mark 15 passage, delivered by the author as part of a Lenten series of worship services. The reader, of course, will want to keep in mind that the following gives expression to particular Christian beliefs in the context of a worship event.

A Sermon: "When God Suffers," Mark 15:33–39, Austin, Texas, Spring 2003

It is post-9/11 and we are at war. Naturally, we are focused on human suffering. It is Lent, and we even give thought to voluntary sacrifice and suffering. As Christians we are called to complicate the question of human suffering because of a central belief. In Jesus God became human and in Jesus God suffered. The Nicene Creed uplifts him as "God of God, Light of Light, Very God of Very God." Accordingly, in Jesus God was suffering. Not only the majestic words of the Nicene Creed, but even these elusive words of a centurion testify to the divine power of this event: "Truly, this man was God's Son."

One of the most profound books of the Old Testament is Job, and Job addresses the question of good people suffering, even at the hands of God. But Job does not venture into the arena of our question—why should God suffer? Does something wondrous happen when God suffers? And what is that something?

Some religions find this concept to be nonsensical, and do we understand it ourselves? We say something like this: whatever else God may be, God is love, and on earth in this life, love must suffer. Here God suffers because God is God, God is love.

And we have a related question: cannot God do more than suffer with us? Years ago as a chaplain I was on call on Christmas Eve at a major midwest hospital complex. That night I shuttled between three children and their parents. All three children died early Christmas morning. I spent time with them and their families in their pain. Again and again I saw how a little child seemed to transcend pain, smile, and play with a doll or toy. I saw how the pain and suffering returned, and finally took the child away. And then at 8 a.m. on Christmas day I went off duty to be with my wife and two little girls to celebrate as best I could and share gifts. What was I supposed to do with my anger toward God?

Yes, God is love, we say, but why can't God be God enough to do more than suffer with us? Why doesn't God intervene? Ease up, God, and be more playful, be magical and miraculous, just a bit more. Why are love and suffering so wedded?

I bring these questions to Mark's account of Jesus' suffering and death. This text is a straightforward narrative, except for verse 38, "And the curtain of the temple was torn in two, from top to bottom." Strangely, our text juxtaposes two disparate places: the holy of holies and the dung hill where blood and gore reek in the air. In the religious place is a world so packed with meaning that only symbols hint at the fullness of truth, while outside Jerusalem a secular centurion guards a place so barren of life and justice that it dares anyone to presume to speak of truth.

The holy of holies was a twenty cubit cube (approximately thirty cubic feet). The symmetry of space indicates holiness. The inner curtain matches the draped walls and ceiling of the holy of holies. The high priest enters one time each year for the atonement of the people. Oh, we know this place. In our hearts we know that the holy of holies is real; it is there, only it is often so inaccessible. This is a place of wonder. The wonder of the sacred testimony of a final veil to divine holiness, not lifted or removed, but torn.

We have our holy places today, including here in this beautiful sanctuary. Notice the openness between pews and the table. The most holy place is fully accessible. We can see everything. That is why the choir has to show up sober on Sunday mornings! Not so for our Eastern Orthodox brothers and sisters. A large screen called an iconostasis hides from view the altar and the bishop's chair. A royal door in the middle opens and closes during worship, and there is a curtain there behind it, as in the Jewish temple.

And so I wonder, with all this openness, seated on our padded pews, what does it take for us to sense the mystery of God in this place? What speaks the unspeakable to us?

Now come with me back to the scene of the crucifixion. Not Jesus' disciples, who were far away in shock; not his mother and other women who were near in unspeakable grief; but a Roman soldier, of all people, testifies to something divine about Jesus. This outsider and stranger, carrying out his secular duty, hears Jesus cry aloud and breathe out his last breath. Then he says, "Truly this man was God's Son." Can we know the centurion's wonder? Does it have meaning for us, or are we situated too far from the cross?

I can hear a chorus of ancient Christians who might question our capacity to understand. To them we are too pleasure-minded, too committed to our own selves, to be in any position to comprehend or discern the depths of God's love. They fasted and denied themselves in many ways—some of these were ways we would not regard as very therapeutic—but they were positioning themselves to be near the cross and to begin to understand. They knew that something wondrous happens when God suffers—what is that something?

Two places: the beautiful temple and the horrific hill of Golgotha. Two places of wonder examined side by side in this gospel passage. Was God in both places? What was God doing? What was happening to God? And today we see two kinds of places. The one is beautiful, our renovated sanctuaries where we behold—or do we behold?—the divine beauty. The other kind of place is horrific, the places of war, the places of abuse, the places of agony. In my mind's eye I see Baghdad burning. Is God in both of these places? What is God doing in Baghdad? What is God doing here? What is happening to God in Iraq? What is happening to God here and now? How is it that God is putting these two places side by side in our hearts? God takes places that do not seem to belong together, and God positions these places alongside each other in our hearts. Who is this God who opens suffering to the inner reaches of holiness and opens holiness to the darkest suffering?

Reflect with me on our own experiences. Many times our own hearts, selfish as they may be, are touched by others' suffering. It may be the pain of a loved one or a friend, or it may be the grim realities of war we see on television or read of in the paper, but our hearts are touched. Battle scenes invade our middle-class peace. And near or far sometimes our hearts really go out to others, strangers though they may be, and a bond of some kind of love is formed, and they are in our hearts. When God's compassion reaches us, suffering of some kind makes its home with us. And when this happens, perhaps we are near the cross, and perhaps we can ask, "Does something wondrous happen when God suffers?"

The Book of Hebrews hints at this wonder when it tells us that for the joy that was set before him Jesus endured the cross (12:2). Or consider the way social psychologist Gordon Allport envisions the expanse of religious experience. He observes that the religious motive or sentiment "holds everything in place at once, and gives equal meaning to suffering and to joy, to death and to life" (Allport, 1978, 21). Equal meaning? How are these to be contained, how held together?

Mr. Ari had fought guerrilla warfare against the Soviet invasion of Afghanistan. He was captured and severely tortured. Later in this country, he was to tell his story to a psychotherapist, but at first he only wept. Seeing the concern on the therapist's face, he finally spoke: "In my country we have a saying: One asks the candle, 'Why do you burn?' The candle says, 'I must burn to give off my light.' For me, I must let the tears fall from my eyes, to give off my light. How else can I live?" (Griffith & Griffith, 2002, 137).

Do you see? It is not just that God is our companion in suffering, fundamental a truth as that may be. It is that the power of God's presence in suffering, the power of God's own suffering, transforms everything about suffering, and everything about us. When God suffers, everything about suffering changes. Sacred love redeems and forgives, sacred suffering transforms. Somehow the suffering gives off a kind of light. This light shines in the darkness. Mark's gospel tells us of the darkness in the sky throughout the crucifixion, and how the centurion, of all people, discerns something of the sacred in the agony of the cross. Something wondrous happens when God suffers, a something that makes itself known to us, something that transforms life.

I am reminded of a Sufi saying: "When the heart has wept for what it has lost, the spirit laughs for what it has found." If only we could know God's suffering, that we may know God's joy! This kind of wholeness, if that is what it is, is no psychiatric perfection and no self-actualizing fulfillment. It is coming to terms with God's suffering and with our suffering and with that of others, and it is being surprised by the joy of suffering transformed. It is living with agony and joy of the heart, traversing between sacred places that house a torn mystery and agonizing places of suffering. Such cargo of the heart spans immeasurable distances!

When God suffers we know that we are not alone. When God suffers we know that God loves us. When God suffers we can sense the beginnings of new life. When God suffers we can expect transformation. When God suffers we are taken beyond ourselves into the wonder of all that is holy and incomprehensible, all that is compassionate and eternal.

Who is this God? This is the God of the temple. This is the God
of the cross. And this is the God of the resurrection. The God of the
temple is the God of the cross. The God of the cross is the God of
the temple. The God of the cross is the God of the resurrection. The
God of the resurrection is the God of the cross. This is one God! Who
is this God? And who is called by this God to speak the unspeakable?
Whose heart is positioned with this agony and this joy? Who?

Analysis of the Sermon in Light of Text-Reader Propositions

With the above sermon as illustration, object relations perspectives
on text-reader relations can be examined briefly. The first perspective
addresses a particular kind of bivalence in the text and the reader. The
object relations approach looks for primordial, often hidden meanings,
yet it does not require that the meaning or meanings of a text be
reduced to a primordial level in terms of developmentally early fragments of experiencing and/or conflicts. One clue to this bivalence is
anomaly. While typically we think of an anomaly as in the text, the
very recognition of an "anomaly" may say as much about the reader's
relation to the text as about the text itself. Accordingly, the locus of an
anomaly lies in the relationship between text and reader. The anomaly
of verse 38 in Mark 15:33–39 in one sense is in the eye of the beholder
and at the same time is in the text. Unwittingly, early childhood internalizations become frameworks for interpreting new experiences. Such
frameworks may be manifested consciously as a sensitivity to anomalies, such as the one in Mark 15:38.

This relational way of thinking, so characteristic of an object relations approach, is represented well in the squiggle game Don Winnicott played with his patients. When a child came to Dr. Winnicott, he
had the child play this game. It called for a stack of blank sheets and
two pencils. The child would draw a squiggle, then the therapist would
"finish" it by trying to make something recognizable from it. Then the
roles were reversed: Dr. Winnicott would draw a squiggle and the
child would make something of it. They kept on playing in this fashion
for a good while, at the end of which Dr. Winnicott said that he had a
diagnosis: not a diagnosis of the child but a diagnosis of his relationship with the child (Winnicott, 1971).

Let us think of the squiggle game as a parabolic representation of
much of object relations thinking, its relational self-understanding and
its bivalence. The squiggle represents the primordial, the unformed,

the irrational, the unrecognizable. In texts, an anomaly is like a squiggle. The response to the squiggle, to the primordial, is an attempt to build or help construct a relationship. It is making meaning of chaos in the presence of another and in response to that other. This response in the squiggle game represents the creative. There is a suggestive power in text and reader that opens ways to make something of the squiggle.

In addition, the squiggle game image speaks to other dimensions in the dynamic of reading a text. To consider the reader without the reader's context is to be abstract. One reads for oneself and for one's community(ies). This is true for all readers, whether pastors and members of a religious community or scholars in an ongoing relation with a community of scholarship. A certain bivalence continually reproduces itself at various levels. Anomalies of texts do not submit readily to preconceptions of individuals or communal traditions. When a religious leader reads a text, he/she reads with rich images of the religious community (past, present, and future) in mind, and the process of interpretation is an attempt to advance or realign the relationship with this community. When a scholar reads a text, he/she reads with nuanced images of a particular scholarly community in mind (past, present, and potential) and intends that the process of interpretation will make a difference in the ongoing development of this community. Actually, for both religious leaders and scholars, mental images of various communities operate, at times in the background and at times in the foreground. A biblical scholar, for example, reading a text in the process of preparing a biblical commentary has in mind that the commentary will be read by scholars, pastors, teachers, and perhaps others. The biblical scholar's contributions are part of a larger creative process the consequences of which authors do not control. Preaching, lecturing, or writing, authors anticipate audience response, and this dynamic enters into the interpretive process. At the same time, authors do not possess accurate foreknowledge of audience responses and do not predetermine responses. Thus, reading ourselves reading the text calls us to reflect on our personal and professional communities, our relationships. In such processes, some persons and communities may discover that their very relation with the divine is being transformed by the reworking of their images of God.

Let me comment on the second proposition above: interpretation relocates text and reader in transitional space. In this space, reading a text becomes relating to a text. Subject and object, reader and text, are taken up into each other such that neither is distinct and the external-internal divide is bridged in a kind of third realm that blends the two. Object relations theorizes that creative involvement with a text such as a Scriptural passage has qualities not unlike those early childhood experiencing processes in which mental objects (persons as internalized in the developing psyche of the child) are not completely stable and fixed. Transitional space in the interpreting process is the "place" where everything is in transit: there is movement, change, an alive experiencing in which meaning and self-understanding evolve or are radically transformed. The assumed meaning(s) of a text somehow is conjured and opened for fresh reconsideration. The text made alive in the processes of encounter, attending, and interpreting addresses and relocates the person and/or the community (Underwood, 1997).

Questions emerge when traditional images (for example, temple and cross) are readmitted into transitional space. How is an inaccessible God made accessible through sacrifice (temple, worship) and suffering? Who is this God? And who is called by this God? Questions make demands; they also can open the way for nondemanding time, for attending. They sustain transitional "play" or experiencing/reflecting. That is, they invite hearers to take time with the wonder of a text. Wonder is a mark of transitional space.

As a transitional process, biblical interpretation induces the primordial, the analytical, and the creative into a kind of unpredictable conference with one another.

A third proposition emphasizes that creative interpretation entails a suspension of disbelief. Such suspension fosters exploration of the primordial and creative dimensions of text–reader relationships. Critical interpretation is an essential dimension of the interpretive process. The very concept of suspending assumes the existence of "disbelief" or questions of truth and its verification. Once engaged in analytical approaches to a text, suspension of the critical-analytical frame of mind enables a kind of leap of imagination. Paul Ricoeur's vision of a hermeneutical process of first naïveté, followed by a hermeneutics of suspicion, which yet is open to a second naïveté, relies on similar assumptions (1970).

Finally, a fourth proposition proffers that primordial self-understanding and cultural self-understanding conspire to evoke creative possibilities in the text. The juxtaposition of cross and holy of holies in the text is an anomaly, a squiggle. The reading of the text embodied in a sermon is a rendering, a making something of the squiggle. There are many possibilities; the sermon expresses but one. Its authenticity in retaining the primordial and its fruitfulness in terms of creativity can be envisioned in a limited manner by way of responses in the lives and thinking of speaker and listeners as a relational community.

An object relations perspective on the above sermon could claim that its interpretation of Mark 15:33–39 and the torn curtain image envisions creative possibilities at a pre-Oedipal level, that is, at a developmental stage close to where splitting of good and bad images occurs and the consequent challenge of learning to interrelate such images. At a glance, one could imagine Hebrews 10 as an interpretation of the curtain image (see verse 20) at a more Oedipal-like level (i.e., at the level of guilt and processes of its resolution). Accordingly, when a therapeutically minded culture is inclined to attend to the primordial in terms of pre-Oedipal internalizations, new possibilities for the interpretation of a text such as Mark 15:33–39 emerge. The Mark text becomes an exemplar or even a parable-like representation of soul action when persons are responding to the challenges of internalizing contrasting images or objects and interrelating diverse relational realities. For example, if one were to interpret the loud cry of verse 37 as a triumphant cry, as has been done by some interpreters, another kind of contrast with the darkness and agony depicted in the text is put into play.

When one considers that readers of such a text embody within themselves an inevitable socio-cultural hermeneutic, the task of reflecting critically on our own perspective and assumptions is an elusive challenge to our capacities. Even within a psychotherapeutic framework, for example, the question might be raised, "Does the dominance of psychological categories usually signal a countertransference as well as a subtle kind of projection onto the text?" Such dynamics may be inevitable, but awareness of them may undergird an ongoing openness of inquiry in relationship to the Scriptural text. Object relations theory provides a framework for focusing on the process of interpretation more than on the content or substance of the interpretation. This means that object relations does not provide a new language into which the contents of ancient texts or traditional theologies are to be commuted in order to become meaningful in terms of contemporary culture. Rather, an object relations approach assists readers to sustain a playful or flexible distance from their ways of construing the meaning of texts, whether these ways be more traditional or exploratory. Object relations is weak as a cryptotheology. Its strength is as a vehicle by which we attend to ourselves attending to texts: we develop an awareness of what is happening to us as we interpret texts. The principal location of an object relations approach, I am suggesting, is the dynamic process of interpreting; its primary value derives from this locus.

References

Allport, G. (1978). *Waiting for the Lord: 33 Meditations on God and Man*. New York: Macmillan.

Freud, S. (1927). *The Ego and the Id*. London: L. and Virginia Woolf at the Hogart Press and the Institute for Psycho-analysis.

Griffith, J. L., & Griffith, M. E. (2002). *Encountering the Sacred in Psychotherapy*. New York: Guilford.

Ricoeur, P. (1970). *Freud and Philosophy. An Essay on Interpretation*. New Haven: Yale University Press.

Underwood, R. (1997). Primordial Texts: An Object Relations Approach to Biblical Hermeneutics. *Pastoral Psychology, 45*(3), 181–192.

Winnicott, D. W. (1971). *Playing and Reality*. London: Tavistock.

CHAPTER 4

The Parable and the Centered Self: Erickson's Confusion Technique as Hermeneutic for the Stories of Jesus

Kamila Blessing

A different orientation to life is assumed by those who take their cues from parables rather than from dogmas or pious sayings. They realize . . . that life is risky and open ended; and that surprising things happen *in it*.

—McFague, 1975, 180

Friedrich August von Kekule was said to be neither a particularly good practical chemist nor an inspiring professor of chemistry.[1] Yet he had what has been called "the most important dream in history since Joseph's seven fat and seven lean cows" (Weisberg, 1996). In 1865, a major problem in chemistry was the structure of benzene; no one could figure out why it had the properties it had until Kekule's dream. Here is the way he described it:

> I turned my chair to the fire . . . and dozed. Again the atoms were gamboling before my eyes. . . . [The atoms were] all twining and twisting together in snakelike motion. . . . One of the snakes had seized hold of its own tail, and the form whirled mockingly before my eyes. As if by a flash of lightning I awoke . . . [and knew that benzene atoms form a ring!] Let us learn to dream, gentlemen.[2]

The entire field of organic chemistry as we know it evolved out of that dream and that previously unconsidered ring structure. It seems so unscientific, so unreasoned. Nevertheless, much of what we call genius rests on the sudden insight, the intuitive flash, the creative moment. We are all created with that capacity. The inner self, after much incubation—or in some unusual context—suddenly sees what it did not see before. It is not that it is unreasoning, but it makes use of a different aspect of our reason, a part of the soul that creates with God. We might think of this capacity as having "the ears to hear."[3]

Parables, Jesus' principal means of teaching about the kingdom of heaven, intentionally appeal to that aspect of the hearer. They invite the sudden flash of insight, the solution to a problem one would never ordinarily have reached. They connect the teller of the parable with the innermost self of the hearer and evoke a response beyond the hearer's everyday capacity. Parables are not just story, just heard; they invite the hearer to become new. It is like a recent tourism campaign by the state of Louisiana, which consists of the words: "Come as you are. *Leave different.*" To put it another way, parables have the specific purpose of producing an intrapsychic event in the hearer: in Greek, *metanoia* (literally, a turn-around).

It is for this reason that it is not sufficient to interpret the parables of Jesus as simply literary works, folktales, or moral lessons. There must be some way to reach inside the parable to understand the way in which it produces such a change. The literature on parables is voluminous and addresses, among other things, the literary techniques that are involved. However, there is another approach that will tell us why those techniques do what they do. That is the hermeneutic use of the psychology of Milton Erickson, specifically his "confusion technique." The confusion technique is a way of telling the therapeutic story. What makes this concept useful for interpretation is this: the specific elements of Erickson's therapeutic story are exactly the same as the specific, defining elements of parables. Knowing how and why a story works the way it does for Erickson will yield new insight into the way the parable works its change in the hearer.

Two cautions are in order. First, in doing this work, we are not analyzing an intrapsychic event in the text, nor are we directly analyzing such an event within the hearer. We are looking for textual and contextual elements in the parable that evoke observable change in the hearer. From such change, we can infer *metanoia* in both its psychological and its spiritual aspects.

Second, it should be apparent that while we are addressing issues that are literary on the one hand and psychological on the other, the specific type of change evoked is not just a change of mind but a turning of the innermost self toward God. Biblical cultures do not see the spiritual, psychological, and physical as separate but as aspects of the total person. Analyzing the psychological effect of the story does not deny the spiritual aspect of *metanoia* but may provide some small view into it. From a biblical standpoint, the Holy Spirit is not absent in the effect of the parable.

In what follows, we introduce Erickson and the confusion technique. We then list the basic elements of the parable and the therapeutic story and illustrate them using the parables. Finally, we provide an extended illustration using the parable of the unjust steward in Luke 16:1–8.

Erickson and the Confusion Technique

Erickson's Therapeutic Hypnosis

Psychiatrist Milton Erickson (1901–1980) developed hypnosis as a clinical tool. This kind of hypnosis bears little resemblance to that of magic tricks. Clinical hypnosis is simply an exceptionally focused state of concentration—one in which, however, the person is receptive to the best of his own inner self. Today, many people know this state of concentration as the "relaxation response" (Benson, 1997) or as the state of quiet achieved by means of centering prayer. For this reason, what Erickson found in the course of developing hypnosis as a tool should be of interest to everyone.

Erickson's particular kind of hypnosis, generally referred to as "unobtrusive hypnosis," focuses the hearer's attention upon one or more stories. One of his greatest contributions was to demonstrate the way in which these narratives can change the "inner person." In fact, he made a life work of studying people's intrapsychic responses specifically to the oral story.

Erickson's Background

Erickson's background shows something of the way he came to his discoveries. In his early childhood, he was afflicted with polio—not once, but twice. The resulting difficulty in communication and general functioning made it necessary for him to become sensitive to the subtlest of human responses. This sensitivity allowed him to develop verbal techniques that incisively addressed the client's unconscious response to words. Often, the client (and any observers) did not realize that therapy was being done. Yet, with astonishing regularity, his patients experienced major breakthroughs upon listening to Erickson's stories.

The Confusion Technique: Definition

Perhaps his most important tool in the therapeutic use of the story was the confusion technique, which is defined as follows:

The Confusion Technique [is] a play on words . . . that introduces progressively an element of confusion into the question of what is meant,
thereby leading to an inhibition of responses called for but not allowed
to be manifested. . . . Thus the whole becomes a medley of seemingly
valid and somehow related ideas that leads the subjects to try to combine
them into a single totality . . . literally compelling a response. (Erickson,
1989, 290)

The confusion is introduced by means of wordplay, abrupt changes
of context, irrelevancies, and other mechanisms that produce discontinuity or absurdity. The overriding purpose of the confusion technique
is to depotentiate the hearer's conscious-level responses—repeatedly,
with the occurrence of each new discontinuity. The "unconscious" opens
up briefly, in what Erickson calls the "creative moment": the hearer is
open to new categories of experience, and new responses are formed.[4]

Discontinuity is often created by a play on words, exemplified by
these (presumably spoken) sentences from Erickson:

a) Write right right, not wright or write.
b) A man lost his left hand in an accident and thus his right (hand) is his
left. (1989, 258)

A biblical example might be a play on Matthew 22:14 (NIV), "Many
are invited but few are chosen." The many are many of all there are,
but the few might be few of the many, or few of all there are, or perhaps the few are really many, but too few in God's view.

An entire story might contain a series of such sentences, interacting
in complex fashion. However, the discontinuities and other confusions
might also be a property of the story as a whole—as when the kingdom of heaven is said to be like something that we do not find immediately appealing, such as a treasure that has been stolen.

A particularly effective discontinuity is one called the double bind,
in which the hearer is asked to choose between two alternative explanations that are inherently contradictory (discussed below). At the
creative moment, the hearer will do one of two things. Either he will
respond in a way that is entirely new for him, or he will avoid the issue
(but not the resulting mental dissonance); in the latter case, the dissonance remains in the background until some other such choice forces
him into a new response. That response is often explosive or sudden,
as in the example of the nurse below.

The Hearer's Ownership

Although the storyteller provides the stimulus, the hearer's resolution of such ambiguities, and any resulting change, must be the client's

own. Zeig summarizes Erickson's philosophy of therapy thus: "The power to change is something that lies dormant within the patient and needs to be reawakened. Anecdotes can be used to guide" this process (1980, 11). We add that, if the patient's power to change is (or is augmented by) a gift of the Holy Spirit, this is exactly the character of biblical *metanoia*.

Erickson's Nurse: The Power of Erickson's Stories

A literal *metanoia* (turn-around of life) was demonstrated during one of Erickson's teaching seminars. One of the subjects for the demonstration was a nurse whose depression had not yielded to any therapy over a considerable time. Erickson was telling one of his stories that was not obviously related to her in any way. In the middle of it, the woman suddenly left the stage—and her old life, leaving behind all of her possessions. It was assumed that she had committed suicide, and Erickson was blamed for it. However, five years later, Erickson received a note of thanks from her. His story had made her realize that her depression stemmed from living the wrong life. She had immediately left and begun a new career in the military, and she had been a new, emotionally healthy person ever since. Such was the effect of Erickson's therapeutic stories.

In general, stories employing the confusion technique have three effects: they bypass the hearer's resistance to addressing problems, they approach the person's needs indirectly, thereby making inner change possible.

This last occurs even in extreme circumstances, such as profound depression, physical pain, or hostility toward the storyteller.

The Confusion Story Compared with the Parable

The Nature of the Parable

There are many definitions of the parable, but let us begin with the simplest. A parable is a story with a beginning, a middle, and an end— rather than being only a simile, an aphorism, or metaphorical language. Parables are also not allegories (stories that refer to something only symbolized by their elements). Parables are metaphorical, however; they describe that which human beings cannot know directly, concerning the in-breaking of the kingdom of heaven into the natural world. Parables convey a depth of knowledge that the more propositional kind of theology does not. I can assert that there is a God, for instance; but hearing the parable of the lost sheep, I experience an aspect of

God's love in a way that I can only recall, but not exhaust, with words. My heart is changed even before I can articulate the learning I have had. Unlike an allegory, the parable's content, and my experiencing of it, *is* the message.

McFague (1975, 3) says that parables are always triangular. Meaning is always constructed in relationship among the storyteller, the story, and the hearer. In this relationship, the hearer is confronted with two logics, two ways of reasoning. One is that of merit, and one is that of grace, and the hearer is always implicitly asked: which will you follow? Like Erickson's nurse, the hearer is presented with a choice. It is not the "obvious" kind of choice, between the religious and the secular. It is this choice: having experienced the import of the story, which logic will the hearer apply to everyday life?

Jesus' Reason for Parables

Jesus' stated reason for speaking in parables evokes the intentional confusion of Erickson's technique. Jesus says (Matt. 13:11–15, NIV): "This is why I speak to them in parables: though seeing, they do not see; though hearing, they do not hear or understand." Why would a healer take such an approach to potential disciples? Either Jesus' words are ironic and he does want them to understand; or, like Erickson, Jesus is bypassing the hearer's cognitive function to speak to the innermost self. This is not to say that Jesus was "doing psychology." However, Erickson merely articulated the human response to the stress-creating ambiguity of such stories; this response is simply an aspect of human nature. Jesus' listeners may well have exhibited such a response. The resulting inner change would have been available even to the many hostile listeners to whom the New Testament says Jesus preached.

Further Parallels between the
Parable and the Confusion Story

The parallels between the parable and the confusion story go further, however. To demonstrate this resemblance, the Erickson story may be compared with the parable as described by McFague (1975). McFague's work is considered common knowledge among scholars of the parable; it reflects much of the best work on parables, such as that of Crossan (1975). However, her work is completely independent of Erickson's. Her description is of further interest because, participating as it does in reader response criticism, it details the rhetorical structure of the parable in terms that address those responses. Comparison with the confusion technique adds what reader response criticism cannot: insight into the intrapsychic dimension of the response.[5]

The first parallel may seem obvious. Parables, like other parts of the Bible, were originally given orally, for a time passed down orally, and even today continue to be transmitted by oral reading. The hearer cannot go back a sentence or paragraph to analyze the story, as with a written piece. Hence the parable was and is presented in a way that, in fact, augments the confusion. Another aspect of orality remains unstated by McFague but is implicit in many Bible passages and explicit in Erickson's writings. The storyteller speaks with the utmost earnestness, as if to indicate every expectation that the listener will understand even the discontinuities. The other major parallels are shown in Table 4.1. The attributes of the story or parable are given, as much as possible, in Erickson's and McFague's own words.

Table 4.1 can be read as follows. The oral story or parable makes contact with the hearer's own experiential world (parallel 1). The hearer's immediate responses are prevented (4) by the combination of word-play, including unexpected reversals of meaning (2), disjunctions of context (3), and the consequent rapt attention to the story (5). According to Erickson, these elements predispose the construction of an entirely new response by the hearer (6) and also the intrapsychic change or "opening up" that is required for that response. Obviously, shorter parables (such as the one-verse "buried treasure" in Matt. 13:44) will not contain all of these elements. However, those that form an extended metaphor for ordinary life, newly seen against the backdrop of God's imminent (and immanent) presence, do contain these powerful elements of the confusion technique. Thus, the parable by its nature potentially bears all of the critical attributes that bring the hearer to the type of response predicted by Erickson.

Illustration: The Prodigal

To illustrate these elements, let us look briefly at the parable of the Prodigal Son in Luke 15. In Chapter 10, we present an extended analysis of the Prodigal Son, interpreted using Bowen theory. There, the triangle of storyteller, story, and listener is made explicit using the triangles of Bowen theory (and coinciding with McFague's use of the triangle to describe parables). Here, we will not recapitulate the entire parable but merely show how the interpretation is augmented when we identify the various elements of the confusion story.

First, like all parables, the story begins with common experience (Luke 15:11): "There was a man who had two sons." The younger

Table 4.1: Parallels between
the Confusion Technique Story and the Parable

The Confusion Technique Story[6]	The Parable (McFague)[7]
1. *Experiential*: "Evoke[s] responsive behavior based upon the subject's own experiential past."	1. *Experiential*: What counts here is "the details of the story" with which the hearer can identify.
2. Based upon "*wordplay*": double meanings, reversals, two "opposite" words coming to designate the same thing.	2. Many parables turn upon such *wordplay*—easily seen when the parable is read in Greek; McFague writes of words taking on unexpected meanings in unexpected contexts.
3. *Disjunctions of context* are central, including non sequiturs and irrelevancies; a word or phrase "taken out of context [of the overall narrative] appears to be . . . sensible. Taken in [the overall] context they are confusing, distracting, and inhibiting and lead . . . to the subjects' . . . need" for resolution.	3. Parables very purposefully "set the familiar in an unfamiliar *context*"; "an old word or story is suddenly seen in a new setting, [prompting] an insight with implications for one's belief and life."
4. The hearer's normal cognitive *responses are disrupted*, "leading to an inhibition of responses called for but not allowed to be manifested"; often, the hearer is shocked into nonresponse.	4. "The transcendent comes to ordinary reality and disrupts it"; "the shock, surprise, or revelatory aspect [of the parable] . . . *disrupts the ordinary dimension*" of response.
5. *Rapt attention* to the story is demanded by the "medley of seemingly valid and somehow related ideas" that, however, taken together, contain elements of confusion.	5. The parable "demands *rapt attention* on itself and its configurations, it is open-ended, expanding ordinary meanings" (see no. 6).
6. The entire configuration "leads the subjects to try to combine them into a single totality of significance . . . literally compelling a response." The response *will not be from among the hearer's usual cognitive repertoire*.	6. ". . . so that we . . . are shocked into a new awareness"; "the radical dimension . . . which disrupts the ordinary dimension . . . *allows us to see it anew as re-formed*" and thus *to act newly in response to it*.

son's wanting his part of the inheritance during his father's lifetime may be unsavory, but it is only a complication of an issue (inheritance) that is part of everyday life. In this parable, the reversals of meaning are not so much created by wordplay as by concept play: the significance of the two sons is reversed during the course of the story. The "bad" younger son takes his inheritance and leaves, spends it all, and is about to starve when he decides to beg his father to take him back as a servant. So far, he is unequivocally unacceptable. But then the crisis results in his "coming to himself"—growing up and taking responsibility for his actions before his father and God. Suddenly, he becomes a model of *metanoia*. When the "good," hard-working older son spitefully refuses to enter into the father's heartfelt celebration of the Prodigal's return, his image also reverses. He has rejected a great gift from God of the restored family and of repentance and redemption.

The parable abruptly ends there, leaving the hearer to respond to an "unfinished" story—a disjunction. The ordinary response to a story has been disrupted, invoking the possibility of an unplanned new kind of response—a *metanoia* in the hearer. This moment corresponds to the creative moment in Erickson's analysis. If the hearer, attempting to supply what is missing, resolves to be like the younger son, then the new response has occurred. It is a new *kind* of response—not just a reaction to the content of the story but a difference in the self. It is notable that between the Prodigal's redemption and the hearer's, the *context* has suddenly, yet silently, changed. What was a story about a father and two sons on a farm is now a story about the hearer and Jesus, or the hearer and the kingdom of heaven.

The element of rapt attention is present also; when the sons' significance changes, the hearer has to pay a new level of attention to see where this story is going. When the moment of resolution comes, the hearer who has been brought to a resolution of his own is thoroughly engaged in the story.

A Further Look at Disjunctions

Different parables contain the various elements of the confusion story in varying degrees. The disjunctions, reversals of meaning, abrupt endings, and changes in context can sometimes be very evident in even the smallest parables. They also vary in kind from one parable to another. Let us therefore take a more thorough look at them, including the particular mechanism called the double bind.

The Hidden Treasure

The parable of the hidden treasure (Matt. 13:44) contains a disjunction of context that is typical of Jesus' stories. It says:

The kingdom of heaven is like treasure hidden in a field. When a man found it, he hid it again, and then in his joy went and sold all he had and bought that field.

The story begins with Jesus' usual opening, "the kingdom of heaven is like . . . ," and goes on to the commonplace, a field, a man, and a purchase of property. Also, the hidden treasure was a very common theme in ancient folklore. In this story, the disjunctions quickly take over. A man finds a treasure and is very joyful. He sells all he has to get that field. But wait! The kingdom of heaven is like . . . what? A treasure that remains hidden from its owner? The kingdom of heaven is like a treasure that is the occasion of . . . fraud? What? This is a discontinuity. For the hearer, there is no rewind, and questions hang in the air. The story just ends.

The literary mechanism is augmented by a psychological disjunction, the double bind. In the double bind, recall that the hearer is forced to choose between two options. Each of the options is internally contradictory. Here, one option is: accept Jesus' description of the kingdom as a treasure that is the occasion of fraud; then Jesus is probably not a teacher we would desire to follow. The other option is: Jesus' story is incorrect about the nature of the kingdom as represented here; but then Jesus is not the teacher we thought he was. The question is, what will the hearer do with these options? The double bind effectively disables all of the usual responses simply by making each response impossible.

The double bind sets the hearer up for one of two things: a refusal to deal with the story at all, or an effort of soul to reach for some response that has heretofore been outside of the repertoire. Usually, the hearer's frustration or even anger over this strange and abrupt ending will propel him to some inner change, if only of perspective. The hearer must look at the story differently, find some context in which this parable's assertion about the kingdom makes sense. This is the creative moment.

The first thing to notice is that the object of the story is not the obtaining of treasure in the sense of having more money. It is the act of finding what was hidden. Jeremias (1972, 200–201) says that the joy of finding what was hidden propels the finder to abandon all else and totally surrender to the thing found. But notice that the man found what was hidden, hid it again, and then had joy. It is like a magician's sleight of hand; one action or shiny object demands your attention while the real action, the "magic," is happening right in front of you, but unseen. That is what happens in the parable. The real action is the finding and hiding, followed by the appropriation of it as hidden. It never says he dug it up again, by the way. At the end of the story, that is only a possibility, and it is not even quite implied. It is another discontinuity.

What, then, can this story mean? Suppose the treasure is in fact just what the parable says ("the kingdom of heaven is like a treasure"). That is, for the purpose of the story, the treasure is the kingdom. Suppose it has suddenly been revealed to you. It might not be possible to appropriate it in any way that makes it unhidden for others. They do not yet have the eyes to see, or they would have seen it. All you can do is hold your secret knowledge to yourself and devote all you have to it—with the hint that in some future time you might also enrich others from it. That is one way to hear this parable.

It is noteworthy that the realization of hidden knowledge was greatly valued by some early Christian groups, specifically the Gnostics—but not limited to them. Jesus, in telling his followers not to tell the things he has done, inherently gives them to know that they have something valuable, something that is only theirs, in the special knowledge that he has revealed to them. Some of the parables turn upon the theme of hiddenness, such as the yeast (Matt. 13:33; Luke 13:20–21) and the growing seed (Mark 4:26–29). The former of these presumes that the expansion of the dough depends on something the baker cannot see. The latter makes that hiddenness explicit: the planter waits for what he cannot see and does not understand. Both realize an increase as a result. In other literature, some pre-Gnostic documents place a high premium on this finding of hidden knowledge as the key to salvation (including, for example, the Gospel of Thomas). So the finding of the hidden is itself a treasure.

In light of this theme of hiddenness, the true context is not that of buying and selling or of truth and (implicitly) lying but of the kingdom and the finder of it. The hearer will have identified with the one who finds the treasure; it is only a short step to see himself as the finder. But at the same time he is suddenly seeing another treasure that until now was *hidden in the hearing* of this parable—the discovery that the treasure is the kingdom, or put another way, the experience-through-story of finding the kingdom. Now, not only can the hearer mentally picture himself in the story, but inwardly he has in fact become the finder. The parable has worked a change—that of actually making the hearer a treasure finder—by the way it is worded and by its discontinuities. Such is the effect of the double bind.

There is another version of the parable of the hidden treasure in the Gospel of Thomas, a collection of sayings attributed to Jesus.[8] In this version (Logion 109), the man has actually bought the field before finding the treasure. The kingdom is likened to the man who originally owns the field but does not know about the treasure. He bequeaths it to his son, who also does not know and who sells the field. The buyer then finds it. Jeremias (1972, 33) says that this version of the story focuses upon the rage of the man who loses the opportunity of finding the treasure. However, the logion does not actually address that point. The story is simply one of the good fortune of a man who has succeeded in land speculation. Any hearer will identify with him and gladly disengage from any thought of the seller. The story is concluded with no ambiguity.

In the Gospel of Thomas version, the lack of the discontinuity destroys the original point. Furthermore, the discontinuity and the consequent abrupt ending are highly typical of Jesus' stories. They in fact mark the Matthean version as more likely to be original than that in the Gospel of Thomas.[9] This type of realization gives the Ericksonian focus on discontinuity an inherent value for the interpreter.

Other Instances of Discontinuity

The discontinuities vary in intensity and in the place they hold in the story. Some examples follow. This list is not by any means exhaustive but only illustrative. In the rich man and Lazarus (Luke 16:19–31), the discontinuity is simply an irony, a departure from ordinary expectation: the beggar Lazarus is saved while the wealthy and prominent man is sent to Hades.

In the parable of the talents (Matt. 25:14–30), another irony reverses the ordinary values. The man who carefully saved his talent by the means usually considered secure in that culture, burying it, is condemned. Those who engaged in speculation are praised and given more responsibility. "For everyone who has will be given more. . . . Whoever does not have, even what he has will be taken from him" (verse 29). How unfair! But in the context of the kingdom, the reward is for spreading the one thing of real value—the knowledge of the kingdom—around as much as possible. It cannot be lost in that way, only increased.

In the two sons (Matt. 21:28–31), Jesus asks which son is obedient: the one who says yes and then does not do the work assigned him, or the one who says no but then does it anyway? This is a true Ericksonian discontinuity, with elements of the double bind. In verses 31 and 32, Jesus resolves the ambiguity by analogy, saying that the tax collectors and prostitutes are entering the kingdom of heaven ahead of the elders and priests; thus, the second son is the obedient one.

In the wedding feast (Matt. 22:1–14) and the wicked tenants (Matt. 21:33–40; Mark 12:1–11; Luke 20:9–18), the discontinuity is escalated. In the former, the outrageous treatment of the king's servants by the prospective wedding guests and the king's revenge upon them shows that there is something that cannot be explained by the social context of the surface story. In the latter, the tenants who have killed the landlord's son escalate the stakes further. Both their violent response and Jesus' "prediction" of the landlord's response to them show that the mere collecting of rent cannot be the issue. In each, the issue of course is the kingdom of heaven. Acceptance of the invitation to the kingdom is vital to salvation; receptiveness to the Son is of the essence. The discontinuity is in the context.

Finally, some of the discontinuities are very sophisticated. The parable of the unjust steward (Luke 16) contains multiple discontinuities of context, extraordinarily clever wordplay, layered disjunctions of actions that lead to the outcome, and a final "resolution" that is "anything but." We now turn to that parable for an extended example of the Ericksonian analysis of the wordplay, absurdities, and disjunctions of the parable at their fullest.

In the section below, the object is to show the way in which the parable would have affected the first-century hearer. However, the principal elements of confusion will be accessible even for readers who do not understand the Greek or the ancient customs.

Luke 16:1–8 Interpreted by the Application of the Confusion Technique

The Story

The parable of the unjust steward begins when the steward has been accused of mismanagement. The master ("rich man") asks, "What is this I hear about you?" He then commands the steward to give account of his management because he can no longer be steward. The steward, having lost his job, decides that he can neither dig nor beg for a living. He therefore calls several of the master's debtors and tells each to rewrite his bill to reduce the amount of the debt. Presumably, these people will later welcome him (and give him a new position). Then the moment of accounting arrives. Luke 16:8a, the last verse dealing with the steward, says: "The master commended the dishonest manager because he had acted shrewdly." Abruptly, the story concludes without reasonable resolution.

Analysis

The contradictions and ambiguities begin with the first verse of the parable. The confusion centers upon three terms: the Greek "steward," *oikonomos;* "accuse," *diaballein* (both in Luke 16:1); and "shrewd," *phron-imos* (Luke 16:8a).[10] These terms together form a frame of contradiction, confusion, and absurdity around the entire story. Each of them bears differing meanings, depending on context. Furthermore, these meanings represent highly familiar aspects of the Middle Eastern cultures of the first century, thus entering into the experiential world of the original hearer.

The accusation that initiates the narrative contains the first confusion. The Greek *diaballein* means either "accuse" (justly, as in a court of law) or "bear false witness." With the latter meaning, in Greek, the master here implicitly has the role of a *diabolos* ("demon"), equivalent to the Hebrew *satan* ("false accuser"), from which the name Satan is derived. The master may have heard a false accusation. He may be intentionally making a false accusation. Or he may be making a true accusation.

The Greek *oikonomos* is the equivalent of an ancient Middle Eastern social institution called (in Hebrew) the *shaliach.* As a *shaliach,* his hands are legally the master's own hands. His judgment and actions are, by the definition of his role, trusted. A biblical example is Joseph in Potiphar's house (Gen. 39), and even more so, Joseph as the ruler of all Egypt under Pharaoh (Gen. 41:40ff.). Thus, if such a steward forgives a debt, it is as if the master himself has forgiven it. A *shaliach* would not be rebuked for such action because any benefit from it actually accrues to the master.

However, in this context, there is an implicit contradiction: the foremost requirement (also assumption) of a *shaliach* is faithfulness; but this steward's faithfulness is in question. In verse 8a, he is called "the unrighteous steward," *ton oikomon tēs adikias,* presumably in summary of his just-recounted actions; but that is a contradiction in terms. On the one hand, the storyteller apparently assumes that he is stealing from his master. Also, the hearer is predisposed to think of him as dishonest because of the introduction to the story. On the other hand, let us suppose that he did not have the normal immunity of a *shaliach.* Is it likely that he would do something obviously illegal, knowing that he was required shortly to account for the master's assets?

One possible resolution is that here, *oikonomos* bears one of its other common meanings: he is merely an accountant or treasurer, and a stupid one. It must be remembered that the *oikonomos* is not absolutely linked with social status. Particularly in the Old Testament, an *oikonomos* is first of all a slave—rather than a high (free) official. Thus, there is at least a conundrum, if not an outright contradiction, on the surface in the description of the steward. He holds a high post, or is just an employee; if he holds the high post, he is, paradoxically, both unrighteous *and* a *shaliach*.

Phronimos, "shrewd," also has two meanings. It can be used in the worldly sense. In verse 8a, it more likely represents a particular kind of shrewdness, a self-knowledge that comes about when the person suddenly becomes aware of being face to face with the Judgment. This is the way in which Luke uses the term in his only other use of it in 12:42 (part of the parable in 12:42–48). However, the term also contains a contradiction that results from a characteristic of the New Testament. The writers of the New Testament imparted authority to their message very purposefully by alluding to usages in crucial parts of the Old Testament. The first and most striking use of *phronimos* in the entire Bible occurs in Genesis (Greek Septuagint, Gen. 3:2, corresponding to English 3:1): the serpent was more *phronimos* than any of the wild beasts the Lord had made. This meaning of *phronimos* resonates with the possibly evil actions of the steward and with (spiritual or material) damnation rather than salvation. Thus, there is a potential contradiction between the office of *shaliach* and his acting "shrewdly."

Finally, verse 8a seals the hearer's sense of confusion, discontinuity, and absurdity. The surprise ending of commendation is in apparent contradiction with the possibly illegal forgiving of debts in verses 1 to 7. Thus, the narrative as a whole (verses 1–8a) contains a significant element of confusion. More immediately forceful, within verse 8a, there are at least two conceptual non sequiturs, which seal the inscrutability of the narrative (see Figure 4.1).

"Unrighteous" contradicts "commended." Then, "dishonest" contradicts "shrewdly." This puts the hearer in a difficult position. When the master praises the steward, the hearer must choose between the master and (seeming) justice. How can the master be just and praise the unjust? To be on the master's side now is also to be on the side of the steward. But this is all wrong—or is it? This is the double bind.

The discontinuities of verses 1 and 2 are now fully manifest. The contradictions in verse 8a force the hearer to reevaluate the role of

---

> The master *commended* /
> the *dishonest* manager /
> because he had acted *shrewdly*
> (Greek **phronimōs**).

Figure 4.1. Discontinuities within verse 8a

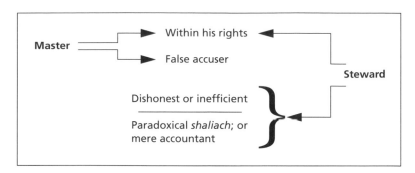

Figure 4.2. The double meaning of Steward's and
Master's positions in the parable

the steward in the story as a whole—anything to provide a resolution
to the contradictions. Thus, together, *oikonomos* and *diaballein* somehow represent two or more completely different stories. The possibilities are represented in Figure 4.2.

The "Second Story"

The confusion does not end here, however. There is actually
another story, one about God and the person under judgment, superimposed upon the simple story of a master and steward. In fact, this is
the "real" parable. There are several cues to this second story of the
story; they also are found in the key terms. In classical and late antique
secular texts in Greek, and in Rabbinic literature as a Hebrew word
(transliterated from Greek), the term *oikonomos* does tend to carry
a simple meaning such as "estate manager." However, the biblical
usage of this term is distinctive. Furthermore, the usage of the term
in the New Testament differs significantly even from that in the Old
Testament.

In Luke 16, it is likely that this steward actually reflects what is evidently a commonly held first-century conception of the believer. This
is the figure of the "*oikonomoi* of the mysteries of God" (1 Cor. 4:1, here
in apposition to "servants of Christ"). In the parts of the New Testament that were written before the Gospels, specifically Paul's letters,
the status of the steward comes from his faithfulness (1 Cor. 4:2); his
role is radical obedience to Christ in acting upon the Gospel. This
usage of *oikonomos* continues from the earliest books of the New Testament (mid first century) to the latest (possibly early second century,
for example, Titus 1:7 and 1 Pet. 4:10) and thus through the period
when the Gospels were written.

This usage opens the distinct possibility that the steward in Luke 16 is the *shaliach* of Christ. If so, it is as if he is taking literally the petition in the Lord's Prayer as it appears in Luke 11:4: "Forgive us our *sins* [*hamartias*], for we also forgive all of *those who owe debts* [*opheilonti*] to us."[11] However, allowing for *phronimos* as the shrewdness of the serpent, another contradiction appears. Is the steward a heaven-wise servant of Christ or a *diabolos* corrupting the message of salvation? In the latter case, the original accusation is fully justified, albeit in a spiritual sense.

In this context, ironically, the master may be the Judge (God) calling his servant (good or bad) to eternal account. As God, the master has the sole option of approving his servant, regardless of his past, by grace, thus removing any contradiction in the final outcome. On the other hand, he may be Satan, the original false accuser of the faithful (cf. Job 1:8–12).

Thus, a spiritual story is superimposed upon an earthly one. The hearer now suddenly is within a new and surprising context, specifically of the Judgment. One is thrust toward an awareness of the moment of accounting to God. However, the absurdity of verse 9 proclaims that only paradoxical solutions are available; no resolution is to be provided for the hearer. (The need for resolution may be the reason that further verses were added to the parable after verse 8a.[12] That they were added—a point of interest to Bible scholars—is evident from the absurdity of the advice there given.)

The response must be to place oneself at the mercy of the master. Suddenly, the hearer is living one of the petitions of the Lord's Prayer and casting about for whose debts might be forgiven—even if those (moral or physical) debts have been dearly clutched to the heart for a lifetime. It is at this point that the creative moment occurs. If the hearer goes anywhere at all with the story after this, it must be in a new direction. If open to such a change, the hearer enters into new possibilities. If, however, the hearer is not open to new categories and new paths, the confusion will not disappear. It will merely wait for the next discontinuity, the next creative moment. When it does come to fruition, the conversion will seem, like Saul's on the road to Damascus, explosive, abrupt, and out of keeping with the surface level of the person's character.

A Fundamental Change

The multiple perceptions of the story are thus not the most fundamental change effected by the confusion technique. The most fundamental effect is that the hearer acquires a new power to change, a change in ability to change. This, along with the prompting of the Holy Spirit, is the opening to *metanoia*.

Thus, the parable of Luke 16:1–8 contains all of the hallmarks of the confusion technique story. The entire scenario comes from the experiential world of the intended original hearers (Table 4.1, parallel 1). The original hearers' rapt attention (parallel 5) to this story cannot now be observed. However, that type of attention is created by the hearer's need to deal with the story's confusions, of which there are quite a few. The wordplays (parallel 2), including contradictory meanings for single terms, occur in 16:1–2 and 16:8, forming a frame for the story. A sophisticated juxtaposition of contexts (parallel 3) is implicit in the term "shrewdly" as well as in the metaphor of servant and master (the person and God) so typical of the parables. The absurdity and contradictory nature of the story create for the hearer a double bind. Is the master unjust in his judgment, in which case, do we reject him? (But what if he turns out to be God?) Or is he just, in which case we must accept a conclusion that is thoroughly absurd?

The double bind disrupts the usual responses (parallel 4) and creates in the hearer a need for some psychological resolution. If any inner change occurs, Erickson's technique predisposes it toward a whole new level of soul resolution (parallel 6).

Conclusions

Erickson's confusion technique shows that the analysis of the fractured nature of the parable has inherent value. It provides insight, in some cases, into the origin of the text by identifying elements of the parable that are genuinely like the ones that are typical of Jesus. It also provides a view into the hearer's response that is more systematic than that obtained by other methods. Most Bible scholars are already aware of the parable as a means by which the hearer is prompted to an interior change. What Erickson's clinical technique adds is that such change is now seen as a normal aspect of our response to the paradoxical.

What that systematic view into the hearer's response shows us is the very function of the parable in process. That process can be summarized by analogy with the following visual "parable." Figure 4.3, of the ambiguous woman, is an illustration frequently found in elementary psychology books. This is a picture of an old woman, but also of a young woman. Both cannot be seen at the same time because each uses the entire set of lines and shapes. But once both are seen, the

Figure 4.3. Ambiguous woman

viewer is somehow essentially different; he can now see both. Further-more, having experienced the ability to move between the two mean-ings of the drawing, he has changed in his ability to change. That, with the help of the Holy Spirit, is incipient *metanoia*. The confusion technique shows us that moment in the life of the hearer when, having come as he is, he is suddenly prepared to "leave different."

Notes

1. According to a website, www.rod.beavon.clara.net/kekule.htm, which adapted the information from Farrar (1994).

2. As recorded at the website http://members.ozemail.com.au/~caveman/ Creative/Brain/kekule.htm.

3. In describing the role of the parable, McFague addresses this inner change as fundamental. It is interesting that she does so thus: "It is the basis of scientific discovery, the intuitive flash, the overview . . . which surveys the terrain from the heights, eventually to return to earth" (1975, 56–57). Thus, she also connects the sudden insight directly with the change we call *metanoia*.

4. Via, a scholar of the New Testament, puts this concept another way: "Response [to the text] is elicited from the reader to deal with the fact that the text both reveals and conceals. . . . [To bring about understanding of the text,] the reader must bring to light a layer of his or her own personality that could not previously be made conscious. The old and the new are merged" (1967, 204).

5. As we begin to address the hearer's response, it is important not to commit the "affective fallacy" of placing the entire meaning within the hearer. We look for the response the hearer must have but always interpret it with reference to the original story.

6. Quotations taken from Erickson (1989, Chapter 10). The terms used here should be read in the context of the entire chapter to grasp fully what Erickson is saying. Likewise, the quotations from McFague.

7. Quotations taken from McFague (1975, 258, 290–291).

8. The Gospel of Thomas is not actually a Gospel in form and does not appear in the New Testament. However, some elements of it carry the possibility of bearing witness to some sayings of Jesus that were not otherwise recorded.

9. For an example of a parable of the Gospel of Thomas that appears to be original to Jesus, see Blessing (2002b); the article makes reference to the confusion technique.

10. It is not known whether Jesus told these stories in Greek, Aramaic, or Hebrew. However, the Hebrew equivalents of *oikonomos* and *phronimos* also carry both a positive and a negative meaning as well as a specialized and a day-to-day language meaning. The parable can be analyzed now, however, only in the language in which it was transmitted. For the various meanings of these two Greek terms and their history of usage, see the appropriate articles in Kittel and Friedrich (1967).

11. This usage is significant because it occurs earlier in the same work by the same author. Compare Matthew 6:12, where only "debt" and "owing" terms appear in these places. It is further interesting that the early church emphasized this aspect of owing and forgiving debts. In *The Didache, a Commentary by Kurt Niederwimmer* (Attridge, 1998, 134–135), the Lord's Prayer in both Greek and English follows the Matthean version. This translation reads: "Cancel for us our debt, as we cancel [debts] for those who are indebted to us."

12. After Jeremias (1972), who posited that the parable ends with verse 8a. Luke 16:9 says, "I tell you, use worldly wealth to gain friends for yourselves, so that when it is gone, you will be welcomed into eternal dwellings." This sentence hardly makes sense of the preceding story, even if one is willing to accept this instruction for itself.

References

Attridge, H. W., ed. (1998). *The Didache, a Commentary by Kurt Niederwimmer*, L. M. Maloney, trans. Minneapolis: Fortress Press.

Benson, H. (1997). *Timeless Healing. The Power and Biology of Belief.* New York: Simon and Schuster.

Blessing, K. (2002a). The "Confusion Technique" of Milton Erickson as Hermeneutic for Biblical Parables. *Journal of Psychology and Christianity*, *19*(1), 161–168.

Blessing, K. (2002b). Gospel of Thomas 97, *The Lost Coin: Parables of Women, Work and Wisdom*, Mary Ann Beavis, ed. Journal for the Study of the New Testament Supplement Series. London: Sheffield Academic Press.

Crossan, J. D. (1975). *The Dark Interval. Towards a Theology of Story.* Allen: Argus Communications.

Erickson, M. H. (1989). The Confusion Technique in Hypnosis, *The Nature of Hypnosis and Suggestion: Vol. 1. The Collected Works of Milton H. Erickson on Hypnosis*, Ernest L. Rossi, ed. New York: Irvington Publishers, 258–291.

Farrar, W. V. (1994). Friedrich August Kekule, *Biographical Dictionary of Scientists*, T. Williams, ed. New York: HarperCollins.

Jeremias, J. (1972). *The Parables of Jesus* (2nd rev. ed.). New York: Charles Scribner's Sons.

Kittel, G., & Friedrich, G., eds. (1967). *Theological Dictionary of the New Testament.* Grand Rapids: Eerdmans.

McFague, S. (1975). *Speaking in Parables, a Study in Metaphor and Theology.* Philadelphia: Fortress Press.

Rollins, W. G. (1999). *Soul and Psyche: The Bible in Psychological Perspective.* Minneapolis: Fortress Press.

Via, D. O. (1967). *The Parables, Their Literary and Existential Dimension.* Philadelphia: Fortress Press.

Weisberg, R. (1996). *Creativity, Beyond the Myth of Genius.* New York: W. H. Freeman.

Zeig, J. K. (1980). *Teaching Seminar with Milton H. Erickson, M.D.* New York: Brunner/Mazel.

CHAPTER 5

COPING WITH THE DEATH OF JESUS: THE GOSPELS AND THE THEORY OF GRIEF WORK

Kari Syreeni

The four canonical Gospels deal extensively with the death of Jesus. For the movement he inaugurated, this was a dramatic new situation that had to be coped with. For these reasons alone, grief work, as an instance of coping, seems a promising angle to Gospel literature. I also argue that the fact that the Gospels also narrate the life of Jesus and proclaim the vindication of his death by no means diminishes the value of a grief work approach. And surely, coping with death was just as much a practical issue for all ancient readers of the Gospels as it is for us today.

My discussion is in two main parts. I first sketch a theory of grief work as coping. The sketch is eclectic, and the reader should know that my approach represents "psychoanalytically oriented hermeneutical theory" (Rollins, 1999, 172) rather than any specific psychological tradition. I hope that this hermeneutical framework will help interpreters of the Bible to see phenomena otherwise easily overlooked (the *unveiling* function of hermeneutics), to pose useful questions for further scrutiny (hermeneutics as the *common ground* for human sciences), and to carry on the personal quest (the *primary* hermeneutical task) for the significance of the Gospels (an instance of the *ultimate* goal of hermeneutics, viz., understanding "the other").

The second main part applies the theory of grief work to the Gospels, addressing first some basic historical questions "behind" the documents. Then, the extant canonical Gospels are approached from a grief process perspective. Finally, there is a brief discussion of the modern interpretative situation "in front of" the Gospels. This threefold structuring conforms to a practical, hermeneutically oriented arrangement of exegetical methods (Tatum, 1997). However, there is much more to interpretation than this simplified diachrony (Syreeni, 1999), and my discussion of the Gospels in the middle section is not quite about grief work "in" the Gospels. The changing concrete, ideological, and artifactual reality constitutes a complex historical system. We necessarily use assimilating concepts to reduce and master the complexity. Even if we wish to focus solely on the Jesus of the Gospels, it may turn out that we are actually behind or (more often) in front of the Gospels. And strange as it is, we are inadvertently speaking of *many* deaths and losses when speaking of the death of Jesus.

Grief Work and Coping: A General Introduction

Most basic elements of the theory of grief work, such the idea of grief as *work*, the notion of *working through*, and the concepts of *mourning* and *melancholia*, derive from Sigmund Freud. A Freudian psychoanalytic legacy is evident in the concentration on death as a prime example of loss and in the tendency to view grief work from a pathologic viewpoint; the therapist's task is to distinguish between normal and abnormal, healthy and unhealthy responses. Further typical foci of attention are *denial*, that is, the mourner's inability to "face reality" and "to act reasonably," the role of the *unconscious*, and the ego's *defense* mechanisms.

The Freudian approach is perhaps best articulated in Yorick Spiegel's book *The Grief Process*[1] (1978). A professor of practical theology, Spiegel combines psychoanalytical insights with a broader sociological perspective and a keen theological interest. In an epilogue entitled "The Death of Jesus and the Grief of the Disciples," he offers a Bultmannian interpretation of John 16. Freud's impact is less evident in Elisabeth Kübler-Ross's seminal book *On Death and Dying* (2001), which provides practical guidance for therapists and counselors meeting terminally ill patients. Kübler-Ross's very readable treatise established the notion in the minds of her readers that working through the experience of loss is a process in various stages. She suggested five stages: from initial denial and isolation to anger, then bargaining, and through depression to final acceptance (Kübler-Ross, 2001, 34–121).

A number of other descriptions of the stages or phases of grief work have also been advanced. The influential model developed by Bowlby and Parkes reckons with four phases (numbing, yearning and searching, disorganization/depression, and reorganization/recovery). Originally, as explained in the third and last volume of *Attachment and Loss*, written between 1969 and 1980, the model only had three stages, with the first two stages counted as protest (Bowlby, 1998, 85–96). The interest in distinguishing between healthy and unhealthy, or adaptive and maladaptive, traits in the grief process is obvious throughout in Bowlby, as is the stress laid on defense mechanisms (1998, 44). Essential to this model is the Freudian emphasis on childhood traumas as explanations for adults' reactions to a loss. Thus, besides death, another archetypal form of loss was highlighted: the infant's or the young child's separation from the mother figure, be it final (at the parent's death), temporary (occasioned by a stay in a nursery or hospital), or partial (as with weaning). The mother figure is usually the biological mother but may also be another person to whom the child is attached. The Bowlby-Parkes "attachment model" views grief work as an object relation in which the object of attachment is absent or unavailable. This basic idea lays the foundation for a positive view of grief work as a process that leads to personal growth and reorientation, as is apparent in the case of weaning. While suggesting that the mourner, in due time, should find novel objects of attachment to substitute for the absent one, it also involves the idea that the function of grief work is not to detach the survivor from the absent person but rather to reorganize that relationship (Bowlby, 1998, 100; Attig, 1996, 163–192). As the theory of grief work has been carried further, increasing attention has been paid, by Parkes (1998) and others, to the different kinds of attachment and loss and to the various personal and situational factors that shape the process.

Although most expositions of grief work center on the individual experiencing a loss, in the context of Gospel studies it is vital to view this phenomenon from a broader anthropological or social-psychological angle. Grief work then appears to be a transition from one status and social role to another through successive adaptive procedures (Spiegel, 1978, 101–133). Using a general three-stage description instead of more nuanced clinical distinctions, we may say that the initial stage is often a shocking and perplexed experience, asserting itself in a protest in which the loss is denied as not real or permanent. The deceased person may be felt as still present or is expected to return soon, so that no adaptive long-term procedures seem needed. In some cases, the mourners may see the deceased person in visions or dreams, and they may anxiously seek for the deceased in familiar places. Sometimes the painful event is kept isolated. The middle stage is marked by the recognition that the loss is irrevocable and has to be confronted. Typical responses include retrospective reactions like anger, self-reproach, negotiating, mania, and despair, which normally will be overcome, but also more permanent adaptive mechanisms that prepare the mourner for a new social role (Spiegel, 1978, 173–342).

Most coping mechanisms fulfill both *retrospective* and *prospective* functions. Therapeutically, backward-looking strategies that only seek to adhere to the past state of affairs may be termed regressive, whereas strategies that help the bereaved adequately to cope with the new situation are progressive. Not all retrospective responses are necessarily regressive. At the end stage, the mourner has fully taken on the new status emotionally, intellectually, and in real life. Some adaptive mechanisms have become a permanent part of the individual's and the larger community's new way of constructing reality. To use a sociology-of-knowledge concept, the adaptive mechanisms are integrated into the individual's and the group's changed "symbolic universe" (for the concept, see Berger & Luckmann, 1984, 110–122; for my reasons to use it, see Syreeni, 1999, 35–40). Thus, grief work proceeds from *denial and disorganization* toward *acceptance and reorganization*, or from adherence to the *past* status to reorientation toward the *new* status. The status change includes the deceased person, whose new role is being shaped simultaneously with that of the mourners.

During the process, the mourners become more and more aware of what is *left* of the deceased. The image of the beloved one's character is shaped in the minds of those who mourn and may become a source of inspiration and guidance in their lives, as the neo-Jungian psychologist James Hillman (1999) stresses. Using Freudian-type concepts, we may speak of the *recollection* and *incorporation* of the deceased in the memory of the survivors. While they conserve elements of the past relationship, these adaptive mechanisms, by compensating for the loss, function as partial *substitutes* for the absent person. Recollection, incorporation, and substitution are intimately connected and sometimes indistinguishable, but in principle they differ in the subject-object relation. Recollection refers to the remembered image of the departed person as distinct from (although related to) the mourner, incorporation refers to the recollected image of the departed within the mourner, and substitution refers to the construction of another object of attachment and significance to replace the past one (Spiegel, 1978, 301–342, with modifications).

Recollection sometimes includes regressive elements that attach the bereaved persons to the deceased one so as to prevent them from developing coping strategies for the new situation. By contrast, substitution often involves progressive procedures that help the bereaved go on in the new social status. Successful grief work results in recollecting and incorporating what is left of the deceased person and in welcoming new replacements that maintain and develop the symbolic universe of the individual or the group.

Already Freud, in his *Mourning and Melancholia*, noted that the lost object need not be a person but may be an abstract concept such as "liberty" or "one's country." Peter Homans has developed this Freudian idea into the concept of *symbolic loss* (2000, 19–22, 225–238). In this view, the processes of mourning are not just a response to an individual's death but have validity for our understanding of history, social institutions, and cultural symbols.

Such a wide cultural approach intensifies the problem, raised already in the narrower context of clinical study, of whether the theory of grief work, advanced in a modern Western culture, applies to phenomena from distant cultures and ancient times. In recent years, some efforts have been made to widen the scope cross-culturally (Parkes, Laungani, & Young, 1997). These efforts are promising but have not remained unchallenged. This is a real problem, and much more work toward a historical understanding of psychological phenomena is certainly needed. In any case, however, I find the well-known New Testament scholar Klaus Berger's program for a "historical psychology" inconclusive. Berger rightly states that "(t)here is no such thing as *the* historical psychology of *the* Bible" (2003, 18). However, his wholesale rejection of all modern psychology, together with his emic (insider's) perspective and his focus on the otherness of the ancient texts, cannot but encourage the notion of a specific "biblical" (New Testament, Pauline, etc.) psychology. It is one thing to pay close attention to the cultural and religio-social differences between ancient and modern constructions of identity and experience. Here, Berger's exegetical and tradition-historical observations are most valuable. It is quite another thing to ban modern psychological insights in principle.

It is especially demanding to bring a modern psychological theory to bear on ancient literature. The phenomenon of textuality involves a further level of analysis in addition to the loss itself, which is an event in real life, and the process of mourning, with its impact on the mourners' symbolic universe. I will return to this problem in the exegetical discussion. However, the pervasiveness of Freud's original ideas, by now of course in substantially modified forms, and their continuing fruitfulness in various cultural and literary approaches may indicate that here is, at least, a useful instrumental metaphor (Merenlahti, 2002, 131–132) for describing and understanding phenomena that are, on the most basic level of reality, common to all human beings.

Grief work as an instance of coping entails another uneasy methodological combination. Although grief work theorists coming from Freudian traditions may speak of coping and defense mechanisms without distinction (Spiegel, 1978, 173–174), modern coping theory, as Kenneth I. Pargament (1997) presents it and applies it within the psychology of religion, is embedded in a cognitive and humanistic psychological approach. This approach differs markedly from both Freudian psychoanalysis and a constructionist view of reality, and Pargament is intent on keeping the traditions distinct. In describing his own bias, he notes that one of the appeals of coping theory is its "ennobling" vision of the human condition, in contrast to the "degrading" legacy of Marx, Darwin, and Freud (1997, 16).[2] I do not subscribe to such a pejorative understanding of the Freudian legacy, which is still providing fresh insights, not least in the study of culture and religion (DiCenso, 1999), but no doubt modern coping theory's humanistic view is a counterweight against naturalism. In addition, it is not difficult to appreciate Pargament's further appeal that coping theory rests on a commonsense view of life.

Coping theory emphasizes the intentionality of human activity (Pargament, 1997, 91). This explains why the theory does not favor speaking of defense mechanisms, which are largely unconscious or preconscious. However, while it is a commonplace that people usually do what they intend to do, it is also an everyday experience that people do not fully recognize the motives and internal forces at work when choosing between different courses of action.

Pargament's basic tenet is that human beings seek significance. Significance is a concept congenial with general hermeneutics and helps to widen the concept of attachment. Admittedly, in Bowlby the concept of attachment is unduly narrow (Roberts, 2002, 181). Significance, in contrast, quite naturally covers both personal relations (objects of attachment as significant others) and more abstract or symbolic entities (such as commitment to political and religious values). The main model in Pargament's coping theory distinguishes between ends ("destinations of significance") and means ("pathways to significance"). Coupled with the distinction between conservation and transformation, it results in a matrix with four methods of coping: *preservation* (conserving both ends and means), *reconstruction* (conserving ends but transforming means), *reevaluation* (transforming ends but conserving means), and *re-creation* (transforming both ends and means) (Pargament, 1997, 111).

Pargament examines coping with death as an instance of reevaluation and as a rite of passage. Reevaluation combines change and continuity. Old objects of significance and attachment must be relinquished and replacements must be found; yet in the midst of loss and change, a way of life must be sustained (Pargament, 1997, 235). Pargament's other example of reevaluation is the seeking of religious purpose. This is to be distinguished from conversion, which is a re-creative response and involves a radical change of faith and life. In conventional rites of passage, the duality of change and continuity is especially clear. These rituals occur at life's crucial "once and for all" transitions: at birth, coming of age, marriage, and death. The community's fixed rituals provide a secure path from the old status to the new through a period of transition (Pargament, 1997, 239–246).

There is a natural analogy between the rite of passage and the main aspects of grief work ("working through" the grief from disorganization toward reorganization), as many grief work theorists have noticed (Grainger, 1998, 123–137). However, while grief work theory focuses on the individual's or the group's grief, or *mourning as it is experienced*, Pargament's focus is on the socially available *mourning practices* that regulate the status change. In other words, grief work theory is primarily about grief or about mourning as it is experienced, whereas Pargament is mainly concerned about socially available mourning practices.[3]

Pargament's way of dealing with mourning in the context of reevaluation raises some very puzzling questions as we turn to early Christian responses to the death of Jesus. On the one hand, does not the early Christian veneration of Jesus (Hurtado, 1988) indicate such a strong attachment that it is problematic to speak of a reevaluation? Even after 2,000 years, Christians continue to pray to Jesus and wait for his coming. This would rather seem an instance of preservation, and a highly regressive coping mechanism. On the other hand, the proclamation of the raising of Jesus from the dead seems suggestive of the most radical coping method, namely, re-creation. The followers of Jesus did not simply return to normal life after a period of mourning. Rather, they, or some of them, had an altered destination of significance (a changed symbolic universe) along with transformed means (a new way of living their daily lives). The hermeneutical challenge is to understand this perplexing combination of contradictory forces.

"We Have Seen the Lord": Resurrection Faith as Coping

Historically, the coping with Jesus' death coincides with the birth of the post-Easter community by virtue of what is customarily called resurrection faith. We are then far *behind* the written Gospels, and the methodological problems we meet are substantial. Not only is resurrection faith a hotbed of theological debate. It is also clear that any historical reconstruction of the decisive events after Jesus' death will remain conjectural.

However, it is striking that much of what the Gospels tell us about the events immediately after Jesus' death conforms to the initial phases of grief work. Signs of shock, searching for the absent Jesus, and experiences of his presence appear in the two main strands of tradition that narrate Jesus' vindication of death: the visions (with auditions) and the empty tomb. Visions of the dead and a strong sense of the deceased person's presence in familiar places and typical situations are well attested in both the New Testament world (Berger, 2003, 99–100) and in modern case studies (Bowlby, 1998, 86–90). It is interesting that in many appearance stories Jesus shares a meal with his disciples, as he did during his earthly life (thus Luke and John). This may reflect early Eucharist theology but is equally understandable in the opposite direction: the experience that Jesus was present at the table furthered the development of a cultic meal. The more ecstatic vision experiences, which may have found an echo in the early Christian emphasis on the Spirit and joy ("unspeakable joy"; 1 Pet. 1:8), might be compared with modern cases of euphoria, which show at least two quite distinct forms. The euphoric response is sometimes "an emphatic refusal to believe that the death has occurred combined with a vivid sense of the dead person's continuing presence." In other cases, however, "the loss is not only acknowledged but is claimed to be greatly to the advantage of the bereaved" (Bowlby, 1998, 169). "No simple theory can cover both," Bowlby concedes (1998, 169). Oddly, resurrection faith combines both kinds of responses, the former by insisting on the living Jesus and the latter by envisaging a new joyful era of salvation and the empowerment of the believers through the Spirit.

The empty tomb tradition suggests that the women were seeking Jesus at a place where they hoped to find him. The literary motifs of misapprehension, nonrecognition, and unbelief (cf. John 20:14–15; Luke 24:15–16; Matt. 28:17) may reflect earlier traditions, in which the elusiveness of Jesus' postdeath appearances was more pronounced. Moreover, the (male) followers of Jesus had fled before or at Jesus' arrest, a fact that remained a traumatic memory (Mark 14:27, 14:50; John 16:32). The tradition of Peter's denial, recorded in all of the canonical Gospels, was not just about an individual disciple but, considering Peter's central role, evoked the failure of all the disciples. Whatever the historical Judas did, the widespread tradition that "one of the twelve" was a traitor reveals another traumatic experience. "There is, in short, much to be said for the Gospels' portrayal of the disciples as despairing and despondent, as very far from confidently expecting the resurrection of the crucified Jesus" (Wedderburn, 1999, 45).

The experiences of failure and the fact that the disciples did not witness Jesus' bodily death and were unable to perform the rite of burial may have encouraged feelings of self-reproach and anger (cf. Bowlby, 1998, 90–91). A further factor is that Jesus' crucifixion was the shameful death of a criminal. Admitting to this shame without qualification[4] would have greatly inhibited any positive recollection of Jesus' traditions and the shaping of the mourners' new status as the followers of the crucified one. Why remember and carry on the mission of a leader who died a villain's death? Some, possibly several, of Jesus' followers originally came from the circle of John the Baptist, and presumably some more after John's imprisonment and death (cf. Matt. 11:2–19; Luke 7:18–35). John the Baptist's death could easily be interpreted as the fate of a noble martyr or of a prophet. Facing the new loss, his former disciples could either cope with it in terms of preservation ("more of the same": Jesus was yet another martyred leader) or adopt a more transformative strategy ("enough is enough"; cf. the Q sayings in Luke 11:47–51 and 16:16). Resurrection belief ensured that Jesus and his followers were right after all and not in shame before God.

To be sure, not everything in the early traditions fits in neatly. The record that Jesus appeared to over 500 people at once (1 Cor. 15:6) is certainly exceptional. Paul, who by virtue of his call vision (Gal. 1:15) became a convert to the new movement, cannot be said to have mourned after Jesus' death.[5] The earliest form of the empty tomb tradition obviously did not include an appearance by Jesus (Mark 16:1–8, in contrast to Matt. 28:8–10 and John 20:10–18).

While the secure historical data are too few to allow definite psychological explanations, it is clear that resurrection belief can be seen as a coping device for those mourning after the death of Jesus. However, what we usually call resurrection faith need not render precisely that which all of the earliest believers became convinced of. According to Berger (2003, 101), the Easter visions can be reconstructed as (1) experiences of the presence of Jesus, (2) experiences of continuity

(Jesus is "with" his followers and guides the transmission of tradition), (3) legitimation of successors in authority (commissioning), and (4) experiences of revelation (of momentous speech by the Exalted One). Thus, the visions could be understood as Jesus' manifestations from his new heavenly realm without necessarily thinking of his bodily resurrection from the tomb.

Some documents indicate that not all early Christian groups centered their faith on a death-resurrection scheme. Among these are the letter of James and the *Didache*, which are taken by some scholars as very early Jewish Christian writings, and the Gospel of Thomas. Unfortunately the tradition history and date of these documents are debatable. More promising, although hypothetical, is the sayings Gospel Q, which Matthew and Luke presumably used in addition to Mark. It has no passion account, no clear allusions to Jesus' resurrection, nor any appearance stories. Modern Q research is largely unanimous that the writing reflects a strand of early Christianity in which the proclamation of Jesus' suffering, death, and resurrection was not the focal point. At the same time, the Q people believed in the vindication of Jesus' death in some way or another. They may have believed that Jesus was exalted by God to sit at his right hand and to be the heavenly Son of Man (cf. Ps. 110 with Dan. 7:13–14; Mark 14:62; Acts 7:56) or that Jesus just disappeared from this world and was removed to heaven, where he is held in reserve for a future role (cf. Luke 13:35b), in analogy with such Old Testament figures as Enoch and Elijah (Kloppenborg Verbin, 2000, 369–379). These possible alternative conceptions have their partial counterpart in the traditions entertained by the Fourth Gospel, in which it is suggested that Jesus is "going away" or "hiding himself" from the world (John 7:33–36, 12:36, 13:33, 14:22) but also that Jesus' crucifixion is the exaltation or "lifting up" of the Son of Man (John 3:14; 12:32, 12:34b).

The curious features in the Gethsemane tradition might indicate that some followers of Jesus were reluctant to accept even the fact that Jesus had been arrested and executed. Mark's account of Jesus' prayer in Gethsemane includes some bargaining (Mark 14:36; cf. Kübler-Ross, 2001, 72–74). Mark also has a young man fleeing naked at Jesus' arrest (14:51–52), obviously only to reappear in a white robe at the empty tomb (16:5). It is conceivable that this strange piece of tradition reflects an early deviant understanding of Jesus' death with heavy symbolic overtones (Myllykoski, 1994, 169–170). Matthew (26:53) adds to the arrest scene Jesus' words that he could have asked God to send more than twelve legions of angels to rescue him. John (12:27–

33) has a peculiar scene with echoes from a Gethsemane tradition mentioning an angel's voice. While this Johannine episode rejects any idea that Jesus would be "saved from this hour" (verse 27), Hebrews 5:7 oddly suggests that Jesus' prayer for rescue was heard.

Again, we cannot make too much of such scattered observations, but three general conclusions can be drawn. First, resurrection faith can of course be seen as a denial of historical reality, and obviously the unbelieving contemporaries of Jesus' followers thought so. Yet, this is not as extreme a denial as some other beliefs concerning the vindication of his death might have been. Resurrection faith admitted—and the canonical Gospels came to emphasize it heavily—that Jesus suffered a bodily death. Second, while admitting the factuality of Jesus' death, resurrection belief implies a radical protest against accepting Jesus' death as a bare fact. It is a "yes, but" answer that admits to what cannot be explained away but develops an argument to reevaluate the consequences of the fact. Jesus died *but* was raised. Hence, a positive understanding of the significance of Jesus' death was called for. Third, this bold move made a *re-creative* method of coping possible, although not necessary. While allowing for the movement to carry on the proclamation of Jesus despite his tragic death (a *preserving* strategy) or to develop new and more appropriate means to achieve what Jesus was hindered from doing (*reconstruction*), it could also fuel a re-creative strategy that involved a radical change of faith and a new way of life.

Among the New Testament writers, Paul in particular advanced the re-creative interpretation of Jesus' death on the basis of resurrection belief. In Paul, we see how this strategy pushed the nascent Christian movement toward a completely new identity. They were no longer Jews or Gentiles but those "in Christ" (Gal. 3:28). Membership in the new gathering of God's people was through baptism, a rite of initiation modeled on the death and resurrection of Jesus (Rom. 6:3–11) and signaling a religious conversion. The rapid development of Christology shows that the identity of Jesus was construed in novel ways. Interestingly, Paul's theological achievement was not the direct result of a grief process. Paul was not one of Jesus' original followers and mourners. Indirectly, by receiving the tradition and perpetuating the visionary response of the original followers, he was influenced by their memories, experiences, and ways of coping with Jesus' death. Yet, Paul's different background may help explain why any recollection of Jesus' "fleshly" life was unthinkable to him (2 Cor. 5:16–17). What the individual Christian should incorporate or participate in was the dead Jesus and the resurrected Lord, the new creation (Gal. 6:15; 2 Cor. 5:17).

Despite its transformational potential, resurrection faith is not a single coping strategy. As noted, it could be adopted without drawing all of the Pauline conclusions. Moreover, resurrection faith is a feature of the symbolic universe rather than of social life and practical behavior. A hermeneutical bifurcation takes place: the symbolic universe in part molds the practical life, in part becomes a system of beliefs without immediate effects on the flow of everyday reality. Resurrection belief became a cornerstone of the emerging Christian symbolic universe, then a dogma of the orthodox creed. However, since the brave new world was not really here, the actual coping strategies, although not unaffected by the faith, had their own ways. It is here that we see the traces of grief work. Soon, a number of substitutes for the absent Jesus appeared, and they were interpreted as carriers of the presence of the exalted Lord. From the beginning, the Spirit was involved in the visionary, ecstatic response to Jesus' death and was therefore an apt substitute for Jesus: in fact, he was often taken as his alter ego. The charismatic leaders and missionaries were the human carriers of the Spirit's workings. With them came the incipient institutionalization of community structures, which stood in some tension with the pneumatic tradition, according to which the individual believer immediately incorporates the Spirit of (the risen) Jesus. Cultic practices (especially the Eucharist) and the community itself as the "body" of Christ also mediated the presence of the Lord, as did the oral Jesus tradition. While all this could be interpreted and legitimized on the basis of Jesus' resurrection, the procedure is fully understandable as progressive grief work.

All of these means of coping, bred by resurrection faith, symbolically sustained the sense of Jesus' postdeath presence while in practice substituting for the absent Jesus. In principle, the Gospels do the same, but in recollecting the life and death of the earthly Jesus the evangelists and their communities faced the problem of Jesus' absence anew, this time on a literary level. As a result, the grief work that had seemingly ended long before seems to begin again, if only as a secondary phenomenon.

"These Are Written That You May Believe": The Gospels as Grief Work

With the written Gospels, we enter into the sphere of textuality with its own methodological problems. Especially a narrative text may have an almost seductive appeal as it creates a mimetic world for

the reader to dwell in. The drive toward a text-internal reading tri-
umphed in the narrative critical approach to the Gospels during the
past two decades and, in another way, in reader-response criticism.[6]
To focus on the text's inner world or the reader it constructs may
surely be rewarding, even for the more historically minded scholar
(Syreeni, 2000). In this case, a narrative approach allows us to observe
the various ways in which grief work as a literary theme is reflected in
the Gospels. This is not enough, however. As will be seen, there is a
remarkable development from the earliest Gospel to the later ones.
Grief work is, as it were, at an early stage in Mark, and it is more
advanced in Matthew. As far as the canonical Gospels are concerned,
it was brought to an end in Luke-Acts, with John standing near Luke
but in an ambivalent way. To understand what is going on in this
large process, we must take a broader perspective on the Gospels *as*
grief work.

Some preparatory remarks will clarify the general idea of the Gospels as grief work. To begin with, if the Gospels, written decades after
the death of Jesus, were involved in what resembles grief work, then
the process is obviously of *secondary* nature in relation to the original
loss (although already the first survivors after Jesus had experienced
previous losses). To the extent that it is grief over Jesus, we must realize that the identity of Jesus was (re)constructed differently from the
way the earliest followers had. Second, we must look for *subsequent*
losses: the death of the first generation of Jesus' disciples and apostles,
the catastrophe of the Jewish war and the destruction of the Temple,
the progressive separation from Judaism, the religious "mother figure" of early Christendom, the gradual fading of the expectation of a
near end ("the delay of the parousia"), and conflicts within the communities. For example, when in Matthew's passion narrative the crowds
shout, "Crucify him!" and "His blood be on us, and on our children!"
(27:22, 27:25, NEB), we sense behind the crowd's voice the narrator's
aggression toward those responsible for Jesus' death. Such a regressive response may seem odd at this late stage of synoptic grief work,
but obviously it reflects enmities experienced in Matthew's contemporary situation. Third, many of these events and developments imply
symbolic losses that were not necessarily experienced as traumatic
but nevertheless changed the *symbolic universe* of the communities and
called for new coping strategies. Lastly, we must observe the impact
of *textuality*, which explains, among other things, the paradox that the
Gospels provide both a sense of the living and present Jesus (the character Jesus is permanently available in the text world) and a sense of

his absence (the character is only a literary presentation). Textuality thus paves the way to ever new turns of (tertiary, as it were) grief work for readers of the life and death of Jesus.

The grief work approach to the Gospels does not presuppose distinctive and opposite "hermeneutics" for oral and written texts, as suggested by Kelber (1983). (Against Kelber, see Dunn, 2003, 199–204.) The oral Jesus tradition did not naturally and inevitably lead to the Gospels, but the relatively new interpretative situation that resulted in Q, Mark, and the later Gospels was mainly due not to textuality but to changes in the historical situation and the symbolic universe.

Nevertheless, there is a hermeneutical change from the earliest period to the time of the written Gospels and again when we approach the middle of the second century. This should not be dismissed, as happens in Dunn's discussion of the motifs of "witnessing" and "remembering Jesus" (2003, 177–180). Certainly, both phenomena (but not the literary motifs) were there from the first. Yet it is hardly accidental that the two latest canonical Gospels, Luke and John, are those that pointedly refer to eyewitness testimony. This new emphasis is precisely the sign of an experienced and recognized *loss* of eyewitnesses, as Luke makes clear in his prologue: "Many writers have undertaken to draw up an account of the events that have happened among us, following the traditions handed down to us by the original eyewitnesses . . ." (Luke 1:1–2, NEB). In John (20:25, NEB), Jesus says to Thomas: "Because you have seen me you have found faith. Happy are they who never saw me and yet have found faith." In this sense, the Gospels substitute for the eyewitnesses who no longer live, and in the last analysis, for Jesus himself.

The motif of "remembering" Jesus does surface early, but notably in the cultic context of the last supper: "Do this in remembrance of me" (1 Cor. 11:24–25; Luke 22:19). For Pauline Christians, this was a reminder of the death of Jesus that brings new life, not a command to gather up the memory of the earthly Jesus. The Gospel writers do not describe their texts as "memoirs of the apostles"—that is Justin (1 Apologies 66:3; Dialogue 100:4) well into the second century. Dunn is correct, however, in stressing the identity-shaping function of remembrance (2003, 178, referring to Schröter, 1997, 462–663). Indeed, religion can be understood, when it comes to its diachronic dimension, as "a chain of memory" (Hervieu-Léger, 2000; for my modification, see Syreeni, 2001, 550). It is only vital to realize that this memory is typically shaped in retrospect and gradually, as the events have been experienced, interpreted, objectified, and finally legitimized.

Another side of retrospection is to attribute to Jesus himself the intention of leaving the message to be remembered and witnessed. In Acts 1:8 the risen Jesus says, "You will be my witnesses," and in Matthew 28:16–20 Jesus refers to the teaching that is to be transmitted. A further variant of attributing to Jesus the intention of transmission is the notion of Jesus' "last will." The form of the literary testament emerges already in the Old Testament. The Gospels do not apply this literary pattern to structure the whole text, but some elements of it may be discerned in Jesus' end-time speech in Mark 13 and in Luke's account of the last supper (22:14–38).

The most extensive application of the testament form is in the Johannine farewell speech and scene (John 13–17). It illustrates many typical features of grief work at its various stages. Jesus begins by describing a very regressive response: he knows that the disciples will seek him, as "little children" seek their lost parent (13:33). Later, though, the disciples are granted the status of Jesus' friends (15:14–15). The most progressive view comes in the final prayer, as Jesus now sends the disciples into the world, as his own Father had sent him (17:18). The confusing variety of regressive and progressive responses indicates that the Johannine community was really struggling with the implications of Jesus' death and would not easily let Jesus go. Yet there are several signs of advanced coping, such as the notion of the Spirit (Paraclete) as the substitute for Jesus (16:7). The Paraclete will remind the disciples of what is left of Jesus, namely his words and especially his love commandment, but he will also teach them new things that they were not able to learn previously (16:12–14). In John, the theme of "remembering Jesus" has become a vital part of the grief process; but this new emphasis belongs to a relatively late stage. A late redactor even introduces a reliable eyewitness: the beloved disciple (from 13:23 on), who is eventually identified as the author of the Gospel (21:24).

The grief work approach has consequences not only regarding the literary motifs and forms used in the Gospels but also for their genre as a whole. Martin Kähler's famous dictum was that "one could call the Gospels passion narratives with extended introductions" (Kähler, 1964, 80 no. 11). A provocative overstatement, later a worn-out slogan, it makes two points that I think are still valid. First, Kähler hoped to draw attention away from the Gospels as (modern) biographies designed to show the development of Jesus' self-consciousness and growth as a person (Carroll & Green, 1995, 5). This plea was heard by the form critics, but recently the *bios* thesis has become quite popular again. True, the Gospels stand close to ancient biography, and no doubt the evangelists and their churches had some—obviously growing—biographical interest in knowing about Jesus (Dunn, 2003, 184–186).

However, a mere literary comparison (typically Burridge, 1992) does not reveal the hermeneutical nature of the Gospels. What the grief work approach contributes is a wider understanding of the Gospels as recollections of the life and death of Jesus, and not only that. As noted, this recollection also involves coping with subsequent, mainly symbolic losses. The "biographies" of Jesus in the Gospels thus became unusually multilayered, loaded with symbolism that actually deals with something other than Jesus. Or is it something else? At the same time, the overloaded hermeneutical structure of the Gospels implies a massive conceptual enrichment of Jesus (for the term, see Syreeni, 2001, 546–549). The Jesus of the Gospels becomes the merger and bearer of a whole symbolic universe, assuming more or less of the significance attached to other objects—many of them concretely or symbolically lost. In relation to Judaism, the emergent new movement's "mother religion," this multilayered Jesus assumes the role of the now lost (or worse, abandoned) parent (thus especially in John). In relation to the early beginnings of the movement, he takes on the death of the martyred witnesses and becomes an exemplary sufferer (thus, with rather different accents, in Mark and Luke). In relation to the community factions, he becomes the symbol for the unity of the church: its only teacher (Matt. 23:8), its sole source of life, love, and nourishment (John 15:1–17).

In mimetically shaping and maintaining the identity of Jesus, the Gospels simultaneously articulate and enhance the identity of the "survivors"—the Christian community. If Jesus is the parent, the community is the heir: the new Israel, the disciples of the true teacher, the branches in the vine. This double identity shaping was the natural task for the second and later generations after Jesus; they *legitimate* the new symbolic universe that already exists (Berger & Luckmann, 1984, 110–146). As such it is a strategy for preservation and maintenance, but it includes variations, degrees, and development. The incipient legitimation in Mark provides just an etiology ("beginning story"; Mark 1:1) of the Gospel that is now proclaimed. The legitimation of the new Christian order has proceeded considerably by the time we come to the latest synoptic Gospel, Luke-Acts (Esler, 1987). In different ways, however, all of the Gospels shape and make plausible the significant past of the Christian movement.

Kähler's second point highlights the centrality of the passion story.

This is especially true for Mark, whose lasting contribution was to unite the passion story, hitherto in all likelihood a separate account, and other mainly narrative material that covered the public "ministry" of Jesus. This combination brought about, if not precisely a "life of Jesus," then a recollection of the memory of the Jesus who proclaimed the Gospel (Mark 1:14–15) and is now preached *in* and *as* the Gospel (1:1). The Pauline reservation against reviving Jesus apart from his death is not completely removed. The "Gospel" (8:35, 10:29, 13:10, 14:9) has echoes of the Pauline proclamation (Marxsen, 1969, 117–150). The "ministry" of Jesus is ultimately the giving of his life "as a ransom for many" (Mark 10:45).

It is remarkable how filled with passion the Markan story is. The shadow of the cross is cast early in the narrative (3:6). The three passion predictions on the way to Jerusalem in the middle of the Gospel (8:31, 9:31, 10:31–33) allow the reader to feel anticipatory grief (cf. Parkes, 1998, 78; Spiegel, 1978, 83–86). The pain in Peter's bitter self-reproach (14:72) is unmistakable. After Jesus' death, only the burial and the strange incident at the empty tomb are narrated. The story ends with the shocked women who flee from the tomb (16:8). A reunion of the risen Jesus and his disciples in Galilee is promised but never narrated. The Gospel of Mark attaches the reader to the life and death of Jesus in a strange way. This is an ethos of following Jesus from the initial calling (1:17, 1:20) to the cross. In 8:34, this ethos of following Jesus is expressed aggressively in terms of *following to death* (cf. Spiegel, 1978, 256–277).

The Markan recollection of Jesus is less concerned with the sayings of Jesus, despite its appreciation of Jesus' teaching (1:22) and the programmatic statement that the words of Jesus will last forever (13:31). This aspect is prominent in Matthew's recollection, in which Mark's Gospel is mainly used to provide the narrative frames for Jesus' teaching. The five great discourses of Jesus, thematically arranged and clearly marked by the evangelist, recollect the ethical will of Jesus so that the risen Lord is able to refer to the totality of the teaching as "all that I have commanded you" (Matt. 28:20). Also, Matthew sets the history of Jesus in a wider context. The genealogy and the birth narrative (chapters 1 and 2) give Jesus' "ministry" a salvation-historical framework, and the story now extends beyond the empty tomb. The women hurry away from the tomb, not frightened as in Mark but "in awe and great joy" (28:8), and the risen Jesus appears to them. In the end, the reunion of Jesus and his disciples on a mountain is narrated, and the mission of the church is introduced (28:16–20). All of this makes Matthew's Gospel much less death-centered and more filled with "realized eschatology" than was Mark's. Luke shares with Matthew the salvation-historical framing of Mark, and he fills in some further gaps in the "life" of Jesus. More important, in the second volume (Acts) the story is extended beyond Jesus' resurrection and ascension to encompass the story of the Gospel's victorious route "all over Judaea and Samaria, and away to the ends of the world" (Acts 1:8 NEB). The story of Jesus is thus firmly embedded in a history of salvation; it is the theological "centre of time" (Conzelmann, 1954) between Israel's and the church's time.

Thus, the synoptic grief work proceeds from Mark's death-permeated recollection through Matthew's less painful image of the teaching of Jesus for new generations to Luke's full-fledged legitimation of the new order. While Matthew's final scene still metaphorically attaches the community to Jesus, portraying the only teacher who will be "with" his disciples "to the end of time" (28:20), Luke's second volume lets Jesus go, and the substitutes for his presence, the Spirit-filled apostles, occupy the scene. Strikingly, Luke has a 40-day period between Jesus' resurrection and ascension (Acts 1:1–11), which marks the status change of both Jesus and those after him. It is the middle stage of the rite of passage, ensuring that the disciples are able to carry on the teaching of Jesus and are fully prepared for their new role as the messengers of the kingdom. This is subsequently confirmed by the promised outpouring of the Holy Spirit. Thus, the Gospels display a progressive grief work that certainly has to do with Jesus, but particularly the end of Acts shows that it is much else as well. Luke, living in a church that is aware of its debt to the Pauline mission, will not let Paul go but pictures him alive and well preaching the gospel (Acts 28:31), much as Matthew portrays the resurrected and present Jesus.

Space does not permit a more detailed survey of how the identity of Jesus (Christology) and his followers (ecclesiology) is shaped in each Gospel. It is obvious, however, that the surviving and expanding community becomes more explicitly included in the recollection of Jesus (from Mark's disciples to Matthew's *ekklêsia* and the Johannine imagery with sheep, vine, etc.), up to the point where Luke lets Jesus go and takes the initiative to recollect the memory of the holy apostles of the church. The first circle of grief work was closed when resurrection belief became the objectified interpretation of Jesus' death. With Luke, the orthodox narrative version of the Christian symbolic universe is complete, and the second circle of grief work is being closed. However, the process does not stop there.

Letting Jesus Go: Coping with Death in Front of the Gospels

Whenever later generations experience bereavement, the loss is always new: "Do not weep for me, but weep for yourselves and for your children" (Luke 23:28). The Christian tradition has taught us to interpret our losses through the original loss inscribed in the Gospels. The cross is there, and it is ours (Mark 8:34). And all the variety of grief work is already there, from desperate attaching to the past, through self-reproach and accusations, on to recollection and orientation to the future.

In seeking words of hope, it is tempting to ask for instant satisfaction and let oneself be absorbed in the words of the Gospels. In John 11:25–26, for instance, Jesus assures that he is the resurrection and the life. Whoever lives and believes in him shall never die. The immediate consolation we may receive diminishes, however, if we recognize that the Jesus who is speaking "to us" is just as huge an assimilation as our bypassing of all the historical distance is a hermeneutical short circuit. Already the Johannine Jesus has many voices. The one we hear in these words hardly comes from the community's ripest theological reflection. Hard lessons were yet to come, some through acquaintance with the synoptic Jesus (cf. John 12:24–26 with parallels) but most through the community's own hardships, as the multilayered farewell speech shows.

The Gospels are not ready-to-use textbooks for counseling or other practical purposes, but if we read them carefully there is much to learn. It might seem natural to see the risen Jesus in Luke's Emmaus story as "an excellent bereavement counsellor" who "does not reveal himself straight away—that would be to deny their grief before they had fully had chance to accept it but gives them opportunity to talk through their feelings" (Walters, 1997, 32). This may be a plausible modern therapeutic ideal, but in fact the Lukan Jesus rebukes the two disciples for their mourning and disbelief (Luke 24:25–27). However, he does more than that. He stays with the disciples some time, long enough that they recognize him at the (Eucharistic) meal, and then disappears. The disciples learn to let Jesus go. The Johannine Jesus, a late one but perhaps not the latest in the Gospels, makes a similar point: "It is for your good that I am leaving you" (John 16:7 NEB).

Have we learned that much, or should we? Much depends on whether we assume that our interpretative situation, nearly two millennia after Jesus and the Gospels, is qualitatively new. For Luke or

John, letting Jesus go did not imply denying his resurrection and parousia. These were part and parcel of the now objective Christian symbolic universe, although coming there may have been painful for the Johannine Christians. After the Enlightenment and the rise of critical biblical scholarship, after Darwin and Freud, can we still live in that premodern universe? Surprisingly, many seem to think so, but some exegetes have raised serious doubts.

Gerd Lüdemann concludes that "(w)ith the revolution in the scientific view of the world, the statements about the resurrection of Jesus have irrevocably lost their literal meaning" (1995, 135). Obviously, we need not wait for his coming, either. Somewhat unexpectedly, Lüdemann yet believes that "this Jesus was not given over to annihilation through death" and that "the unity with God experienced in faith continues beyond death" (1995, 137). A. J. M. Wedderburn (1999) is slightly less explicit about what "really" happened to Jesus. He does show, however, very ostensibly how even critical exegetes tend to become obscure when it comes to the resurrection accounts in the Gospels. He recommends agnosticism (which he almost sees in Mark), a "vulnerable" faith, and the need to go "beyond" resurrection.

Certainly the great majority of biblical interpreters articulate a more conventional standpoint, sometimes with philosophical sophistication (Frei, 1997, 174–183) or recasting it as a postmodern stance (Gunter, 1999). However, especially the last-mentioned example is indicative of a new interpretative situation in which the traditional Christian symbolic universe has lost or is losing its plausibility. If this is the situation in which we find ourselves, then interpreting the Gospels involves a new and crucial symbolic loss. If we no longer feel at home in the world of bodily resurrection, ecstatic visions, and endtime expectations, what comfort can the Gospel story, or rather the several stories of the Gospels, give us?

No doubt the Christian community at large may find such a loss painful to acknowledge and work through. However, I would not concur with Lüdemann that "the Christian faith seems reduced almost to a minimum," leaving the Christians "to live by the little they really believe" (1995, 137). In fact, all of the canonical Gospels are left for us, and by all means the Gospel of Thomas and the other recently found documents from Christianity's childhood. The cross remains, for we still have to die. The variety of responses we see in the Gospels is available, and our options are the same. Even resurrection faith is an option: not as a belief or a dogma concerning the body of Jesus but as the possibility of transformation.

Such a letting go would not mean forgetting the Jesus of the Gospels. Rather, it means, as in any grief work, a process of "relearning the world" (Attig, 1996, 99–127), "relearning our selves" (128–162), and "relearning our relationships with the deceased" (163–192). "Let go we must but not entirely" (174) because "we continue to love and cherish the stories of lives now ended" (178). By calling us to follow the way of Jesus (Mark), to remember his lasting wisdom (Matthew), to grow toward a mature discipleship (John), and to go on fulfilling our mission in the world (Luke-Acts), the Gospels from a bygone world may give us a significant past and a path to the future.

Notes

1. The 1977 Abingdon Press publication renders the original 1973 German subtitle, *Analysis and Counselling*.

2. Here, Pargament quotes approvingly a writer who ridicules the assumptions of Marx, Darwin, and Freud, who would "make monkeys of us all" (1997, 16). Pargament continues: "How, I wonder, with our own feet mired in the muddy soil of this assumptive world, can we help our clients who are stuck in theirs? Coping theory, I feel, rests on a broader set of assumptions, one that recognizes the potency of internal and external forces, but one that also recognizes the potential to transcend our personal and social circumstances."

3. I follow Bowlby (1998, 17–18), who retains the term "mourning" to refer to all the psychological processes, conscious and unconscious, that are set in motion by loss, whereas "mourning customs" are public expressions of mourning. Homans would like to reserve the term "mourning" to denote "a ritual" or "the culturally constructed social response to the loss of an individual" (2000, 2).

4. There is a sense in which the grief work after Jesus' death *did* result in admitting to the shame, although not in an unqualified manner but by reverting it to a paradoxical honor. This phenomenon of self-stigmatization—I would define it as the voluntary acceptance and symbolic reversal of a denigratory identity trait attributed to one by outsiders—is seen by many as a prominent feature in the early Jesus movement and in Paul. It is instructive that resurrection belief and self-stigmatization share the same "yes, but" pattern: Jesus died *but* was raised, he suffered a shame *but* turned it into an honor.

5. Lüdemann (1995) explains the appearance to more than 500 brethren as "mass psychosis" (99) and Paul's conversion as resulting from a "Christ complex" (126). This is rather speculative, of course. It seems a more plausible suggestion that Peter's denial of Jesus was a psychological factor that contributed to his appearance vision; Lüdemann interprets Peter's Easter experience as a "process of mourning" (93).

6. See the entries on narrative criticism and reader-response criticism in

Aune (2003, 315–317, 397). I agree with much of Aune's heavy criticism of the (older) narrative-critical approach, but at places the attack is unfair. There have been efforts to widen the scope of narrative analysis. It is also pointless to regard focusing on particular narrative aspects of the Gospels, such as characterization, as "atomistic."

References

Attig, T. (1996). *How We Grieve: Relearning the World*. New York and Oxford: Oxford University Press.

Aune, D. E. (2003). *The Westminster Dictionary of New Testament and Early Christian Literature and Rhetoric*. Louisville and London: Westminster John Knox.

Berger, K. (2003). *Identity and Experience in the New Testament*, C. Muenchow, trans., Minneapolis: Fortress. (German original 1991)

Berger, P. L., & Luckmann, T. (1984). *The Social Construction of Reality: A Treatise in the Sociology of Knowledge*. Harmondsworth, Great Britain: Penguin (Pelican). (First published in the United States 1966; in Great Britain 1967)

Bowlby, J. (1998). *Attachment and Loss: Vol. 3. Loss: Sadness and Depression*. London: Pimlico.

Burridge, R. A. (1992). *What Are the Gospels? A Comparison with Graeco-Roman Biography*. Society for New Testament Studies, Monograph Series 70. Cambridge: Cambridge University Press.

Carroll, J. T., & Green, J. B. (1995). *The Death of Jesus in Early Christianity*. Peabody: Hendrickson.

Conzelmann, H. (1954). *Die Mitte der Zeit: Studien zur Theologie des Lukas*, G. Bruswell, trans., Beiträge zur Historischen Theologie 17. Tübingen, Germany: Mohr. (Translated as *The Theology of St. Luke*, 1960, New York: Harper and Row)

DiCenso, J. J. (1999). *The Other Freud: Religion, Culture and Psychoanalysis*. London and New York: Routledge.

Dunn, J. D. G. (2003). Jesus Remembered, vol. 1. *Christianity in the Making*. Grand Rapids: Eerdmans.

Esler, P. F. (1987). *Community and Gospel (Luke-Acts): The Social and Political Motivations of Lucan Theology*. Society for New Testament Studies, Monograph Series 57. Cambridge: Cambridge University Press.

Frei, H. W. (1997). *The Identity of Jesus Christ*. Eugene: Wipf and Stock.

Grainger, R. (1998). *The Social Symbolism of Grief and Mourning*. London and Philadelphia: Jessica Kingsley Publishers.

Gunter, W. S. (1999). *Resurrection Knowledge: Recovering the Gospel for a Postmodern Church*. Nashville: Abingdon.

Hervieu-Léger, D. (2000). *Religion as a Chain of Memory*. New Brunswick: Rutgers University.

Hillman, J. (1999). *The Force of Character and the Lasting Life.* New York: Random House.

Homans, P., ed. (2000). *Symbolic Loss: The Ambiguity of Mourning and Memory at Century's End.* Charlottesville and London: University Press of Virginia.

Hurtado, L. W. (1988). *One God, One Lord: Early Christian Devotion and Ancient Jewish Monotheism.* Philadelphia: Fortress.

Kähler, M. (1964). *The So-Called Historical Jesus and the Historic Biblical Christ.* Philadelphia: Fortress.

Kelber, W. H. (1983). *The Oral and the Written Gospel.* Philadelphia: Fortress.

Kloppenborg Verbin, J. S. (2000). *Excavating Q: The History and Setting of the Sayings Gospel.* Minneapolis: Fortress.

Kübler-Ross, E. (2001). *On Death and Dying.* London: Routledge.

Lüdemann, G. (in collaboration with Alf Özen). (1995). *What Really Happened to Jesus: A Historical Approach to the Resurrection.* Louisville: Westminster John Knox.

Marxsen, W. (1969). *Mark the Evangelist: Studies on the Redaction History of a Gospel.* Nashville: Abingdon.

Merenlahti, P. (2002). *Poetics for the Gospels? Rethinking Narrative Criticism.* Edinburgh and New York: T&T Clark.

Myllykoski, M. (1994). *Die letzten Tage Jesu: Markus, Johannes, ihre Traditionen und die historische Frage, Band II.* Annales Academiae Scientiarum Fennicae B 272. Helsinki: Suomalainen Tiedeakatemia.

Pargament, K. I. (1997). *The Psychology of Religion and Coping: Theory, Research, Practice.* New York and London: Guilford Press.

Parkes, C. M. (1998). *Bereavement: Studies of Grief in Adult Life* (Reprint of the 3rd rev. ed.). Harmondsworth: Penguin.

Parkes, C. M., Laungani, P., & Young, B., eds. (1997). *Death and Bereavement Across Cultures.* London: Routledge.

Roberts, R. C. (2002). Attachment: Bowlby and the Bible, *On Being a Person: A Multidisciplinary Approach to Personality Theories,* Todd H. Speidell, ed. Eugene: Wipf and Stock, 174–199.

Rollins, W. G. (1999). *Soul and Psyche: The Bible in Psychological Perspective.* Minneapolis: Fortress.

Schröter, J. (1997). *Erinnerung an Jesu Worte: Studien zur Rezeption der Logienüberlieferung in Markus, Q, und Thomas.* Wissenschaftliche Monographien zum Alten und Neuen Testament 76. Neukirchen-Vluyn, Germany: Neukirchener.

Spiegel, Y. (1978). *The Grief Process.* London: SCM. (German original 1973)

Syreeni, K. (1999). Wonderlands: A Beginner's Guide to Three Worlds. *Svensk Exegetisk Årsbok, 64,* 33–46.

Syreeni, K. (2000). Characterization, Ideology and History in the Gospels: Narrative Criticism as a Historical and Hermeneutical Approach, *A Bouquet of Wisdom: Essays in Honour of Karl-Gustav Sandelin,* Karl-Johan Illman,

Tore Ahlbäck, Sven-Olav Back, & Risto Nurmela, eds. Åbo, Finland: Åbo Akademi, 171–196.

Syreeni, K. (2001). Identity, Remembrance and Transformation as Key Concepts in Biblical Hermeneutics. *In die Skriflig, 35*(4), 537–556.

Tatum, W. R. (1997). *Biblical Interpretation: An Integrated Approach* (Rev. ed.). Peabody: Hendrickson.

Walters, G. (1997). *Why Do Christians Find It Hard to Grieve?* Carlisle, UK: Paternoster.

Wedderburn, A. J. M. (1999). *Beyond Resurrection.* London: SCM.

CHAPTER 6

READING MARK FOR THE
PLEASURE OF FANTASY

Petri Merenlahti

In this chapter I present a reading of Mark's Gospel that draws on three sources. First, I employ Umberto Eco's theory of semiotics, especially his idea of the *model reader*. In Eco's vocabulary, this term refers to an ideal reading strategy presupposed by and encoded in the formal composition of the literary text. Second, I supplement the model reader concept with insights taken from psychoanalytic criticism, especially as inspired by Jacques Lacan's reading of Sigmund Freud's writings. Using Freud's and Lacan's thoughts as intertexts for interpretation, I look for traces of the model reader's unconscious, pleasure-driven side. Third, recognizing that sexuality (which, according to Freud's original thesis, is the key to the constitution of the unconscious) may mean different things to different cultures at different times, I ask how a psychoanalytic reading of Mark relates to ancient Greco-Roman conceptions of masculinity and femininity.

The Model Reader's Unconscious

Reading is a social skill, and the stuff that texts are made of is the disciplined use of symbols. In scholarship, theories of semiotics focus in detail on rules to which texts and reading communities wish to socialize us. Introduced by Umberto Eco, the concept of the model reader refers to an ideal audience that the literary text anticipates and tries to create. A textual feature, the model reader represents the sum

total of appropriate readerly operations encoded in the structure of a
given text (Eco, 1979, 1994).

While it is instructions and strategies *in the text* that are the focus,
each model reader also hooks onto a particular moment in time and
space. The model reader of Dante's *Divine Comedy* is a medieval reader,
whereas the model reader of Mark's Gospel is first-century Greco-
Roman (Eco, 1994, 66). To imitate the model reader requires that you
learn and adapt to the language, culture, and literary conventions of a
particular reading community. From the critic's point of view, then,
literary and historical approaches are equally indispensable if we are
to obtain a full picture of the expressive potential of a particular text.

But do literary analysis and historical investigation suffice? What
incites me to ask this question is the suggestion made by Jacques Lacan
that language and the unconscious always go together. This implies
that there is more to the model reader, too, than the text may be
aware of.

(Very) roughly, the Lacanian line of argumentation goes as follows
(Lacan, 1977; cf. Richardson, 1983; Wright, 1984, 107–132; Easthope,
1999; MacCabe, 2002, xiii–xiv). First, the rule of language is of conventional rather than a natural order. Linguistic signs are arbitrary;
there is no particular reason for a particular word-sound (signifier) to
mean what we take it to mean, except that there is supposed to be
agreement on that. A cat is a cat and not a bat because the rules of the
symbolic system say so and for no other reason. We submit to that
rule when we cease to be infants and first assume language.

By doing that, we are also forced to renounce the infant's illusion of
immediate and guaranteed access to pleasure and satisfaction. In the
small infant's world, bodily *needs*, such as hunger, more or less automatically unleash the cry as a biological signal to the mother.[1] With
the advent of the symbolic, the cry is no more bound to the need, nor
is it conceived of as automatically producing the mother and the breast.
It has become a *sign*, which also means that the child now recognizes
the mother as another person and the breast as a separate object. Having left the world of need, the child enters the world of *demand*.
Demand is something that can be addressed to other persons, concerns
external objects, and can be produced independently of need.

After this point, there is no return to the original unquestioned
presence of the mother. A stand-in for the real thing, symbolic meaning introduces *lack* into the human subject. The child will understand that language is common property: instead of giving the child
exclusive power to call forth any potential object at will, symbols exist

independently of the child and signify everybody's longings. So the demand for loving presence gives way to a *desire* for something that is permanently lacking. This is the Lacanian linguistic version of the Freudian incest taboo and the Oedipus complex. The Father's role is played by what Lacan calls the *Name-of-the-Father* (Nom-du-Père), the "paternal metaphor," which supports the symbolic system and embodies the law that the external world will be available for your enjoyment only if you first renounce the mother.[2]

However, a part of the psyche will always refuse the linguistic contract. As a result, the unconscious emerges to host a longing after that lost, unattainable object of desire. It will make itself known by constantly checking language, the original tool of repression, for loopholes allowing for pleasure. We can track its presence through traces of its success in jokes, Freudian slips, and the metaphorical and metonymic use of language in art—that is, in all of those forms of expression that break the original agreement and effectively disrupt the illusion of one, fixed, unambiguous sense. For an illusion it is: wherever there is language, there is a potential surplus of meaning and the capacity for the unconscious to make itself felt. "Cat" may always mean something else. The repressed always returns—which makes literary texts "forms of persuasion whereby bodies are speaking to bodies, not merely minds to minds" (Wright, 1984, 4). We read not only for discipline but also for pleasure.

Lacan's reading of Freud has had a tremendous influence on literary and cultural studies. Establishing a link between language and the unconscious, it has provided critics with a way to make psychoanalytic criticism textual and rhetorical. This will, I think, benefit semiotic and psychoanalytic studies alike. It will enhance semiotic approaches by including the psychodynamic, pleasure-driven workings of the text and the reader (Kille, 2001, 16), on the other hand, it will make psychoanalytic criticism less speculative by grounding it on concrete formal features of material documents (as opposed to hypotheses concerning some historical author's psychic disposition, some fictive character's psychological profile, or the dynamics of some collective mind set behind a myth of unknown origin [cf. Brooks, 1987, 1–2; Kille, 2001, 133]). This would be especially useful in the study of ancient documents, in which the gaps in our historical knowledge make the temptation to speculate strong, although the only analysand available is the text.

Moreover, Lacan's work opens up the possibility of addressing the link between language and power in society. For Lacan, the (Name-of-the-) Father is not so much the actual family member as the implicit cultural authority who sanctions the use of symbols; similarly, the *phallus* does not refer to the male sexual organ but rather to having discursive power, that is, being mandated to name things in society.[3] This aspect of Lacan's theory adds to social and ideological criticism. Again, we need not speculate about the actual social situation behind the text and could rather look at the linguistic, narrative, and rhetorical features of the text itself.

To illustrate my case, I will now move on to the Gospel of Mark. My focus is on what I see as the fantasy-like structure of the Gospel.

The Fantastic Gospel

What links the text with the unconscious and makes it pleasurable is fantasy. As expressed in the imaginary scenes and narratives in dreams and art, fantasies allow us to grope for wish fulfillment in a disguised form, without our knowing it. In the private fantasies of our dreams, we are personally present. In art, we participate through identification, accepting the desire presented by the work. As a model reader, I "come to care about what the text cares about. Its lack becomes my lack, its desires my desire" (Easthope, 1999, 130).

For Freud, the wish always comes first, and every fantasy represents the fulfillment of a wish. This means that, in principle, there is one correct psychoanalytic interpretation for every dream and for every work of art, indicating exactly what wish the fantasy fulfills. For Lacan, on the other hand, fantasy rather stages desire, not expressing it but introducing the lack that makes it desirable. Fantasy comes first, and desire is only created by it, which means that there are multiple points of identification. No one wish explains everything, but different readers may read different desires[4] (cf. Easthope, 1999, 125–127).

In the Gospels, I would argue, fantasies are effective on the levels of both content and form. The good news the Gospels proclaim, as well as their actual narrative composition, have a fantasy structure. In fact, it seems that these two structures are codependent. This would be in accordance with Paul Ricoeur's idea of the gospels as *interpretative narratives* in which "the ideological interpretation these narratives wish to convey is not superimposed on the narrative by the narrator but is, instead, incorporated into the very strategy of narrative," so that the result is an "indissociable union of the kerygmatic and the narrative aspects" (Ricoeur, 1990, 237, 239). The Gospel narrative repeats the "original" fantasy of the kerygma so that the original is *refound* in the text (this would be the Freudian reading); on the other hand (and

I now bring in Lacan), it is only through this refinding that we first realize that something has been lost—that there once was a living kerygma that we now, in the presence of the text, lack.

Werner Kelber indeed noted that the very presence of the narrative Gospels bears witness to Jesus' absence: the living, immediate presence of Jesus in the (oral) kerygma is substituted by the distant, objectifiable Jesus of the text, so that the latter effectively marks the lack of the former. On the other hand, it is only through this lack that the lost living Jesus first becomes desirable. As the first narrative Gospel, Mark would have been instrumental in this change (Kelber, 1983).[5]

In Mark's story, Jesus looks very desirable indeed: an unfailing source of nourishment and integration, he attracts followers and draws crowds to the extent that he has almost no room to move about or time to rest and eat. Moreover, he neglects conventional social boundaries (of purity and holiness) that would rather have satisfaction postponed: he will not wait until the Sabbath is over or hands are clean to feed and heal people. Not surprisingly, people keep coming to him, while his enemies become so jealous they could kill.

However, although Jesus provides for people's needs, he will not treat their desires. A man who constantly hides his identity, he dismisses the possibility that his healing and feeding presence could be called forth by the power of the symbol.[6] The secret of the kingdom of heaven is only for the select few; for outsiders, the message is so disguised that

> they may indeed look, but not perceive,
> and may indeed listen, but not understand;
> so that they may not turn again and be forgiven.
> (Mark 4:12)

"The royal road" leads astray: like dreams, the parables want to remain not understood. Their *raison d'être* is not so much to reveal as to conceal the divine source of authority that properly belongs to the father only—that is, the divine phallus. Proclaiming the father's rule, the parables of the kingdom of heaven are equal to the Name-of-the-Father: as his symbolic representations, they too presuppose—and constitute—his actual absence. (The idea that it is the absent father who produces and guarantees symbolic order originates in Freud's *Totem and Taboo* [1953–1974a]. I will return to this below.)

Who are the select few, then? Who are to benefit from the kingdom? Jesus' disciples would be—if only they had what it takes. But the disciples will have none of the father's rule: their fantasy (the true content of which is apparently disguised from them) is to join Jesus in what would be the overthrowing of that rule, to assume the thrones on his left and right, and make the father's subjects their own. Although corrected by Jesus, the fantasy keeps returning (as fantasies do): first comes the argument on who is the greatest (Mark 9:33–34), then the request of the Boanerges boys (Mark 10:35–40).

The point the disciples are missing is *renunciation*. Notably, Mark's idea of renunciation is of a specific kind. As Mary Ann Tolbert points out, it comprises "giving up conventional social standing, power, wealth, and even family relationships . . . in order to follow the way of the Cross." This *status asceticism*, in fact, "stands in some contrast to Jesus' views on the more conventional bodily asceticisms related to eating, sexuality, comfort, and so on. Mark presents Jesus' relationship to food, for example, in a very positive, almost gluttonous, light . . . [and] what little Mark does have to say about sexuality is basically positive or at least affirmative of its value" (Tolbert, 1999, 40).

The Markan phallus definitely seems to be not the sexual organ but the symbol of power. With respect to that symbol, the disciples are challenged to face "castration anxiety." Only through that would they become like the model that Jesus more than once points out for them to follow: *the child* (9:35–37, 10:13–16). As the ultimate model, Jesus himself is childlike. He is the good son of the father, obedient to the point of death—even death on the cross. In Gethsemane he renounces his own desire and succumbs to the father's rule (14:36); on Golgotha, he faces the threat of ultimate destruction. His followers are expected to take after him:

> If any want to become my followers, let them deny themselves and take up their cross and follow me. For those who want to save their life will lose it, and those who lose their life for my sake, and for the sake of the gospel, will save it. (Mark 8:34–35)

So it is the child reader who is the model reader when it comes to the role of the unconscious in the text. It could hardly be otherwise: the unconscious is childish, the wish it repeats is infantile. In bluntest Freudian terms, it aspires to take the father's place; it is told it must not (let them deny themselves); it is tortured by the fear of castration (the cross); and it survives to lead a new life of its own (those who lose their life will save it). In the dynamics of Mark's narrative, it is the disciples who facilitate the reader's coming of age, first by providing a natural point of identification as followers of Jesus, but soon by turning into foils for the model reader, forcing him or her to take distance and, unlike the disciples, to assume a course of personal growth (cf. Tannehill, 1977).

In the Father's Presence

As religious fantasy, the Gospel can be both therapeutic and pathogenic. As in the story, so in real life should crises of maturation be gone through so that a new, advanced mode of life may follow. At best, the Gospel story could be taken to repeat, in a therapeutic manner, standard developmental processes that every person needs to endure in order to become a self-sustained individual, equal to the father. In terms of classic Freudian analysis, this would involve accepting, experiencing, and surviving the Oedipal trauma of being denied one's object of desire and feeling threatened on account of that. For Lacan, that experience is rooted in language: the human subject is founded on the perpetual renouncement of linguistic signifiers as appropriate objects of satisfaction (cf. the role of parables in Mark), and symbols mark the lack of what they stand for. In Christian mythology and ritual, the believer participates in this inevitable act of renunciation by participating in the death of Christ through baptism, "so that, just as Christ was raised from the dead by the glory of the Father, so we too might walk in newness of life" (Rom. 6:4). Read this way, the Gospel fantasy would actually support the development of the mature, realistic attitude to external reality that is necessary for a true sense of independence and personal identity to emerge.[7]

Unfortunately, however, wholly other types of reading are also possible. Instead of an inevitable confrontation with the realities of life, renunciation and childlike subordination could also be taken as permanent repressive ideals that hinder accepting and coping with actual reality.[8] In Freudian terms, the original fantasy of omnipotence would not then be negotiated with actual reality but would rather be defended by fixating to another fantasy, namely that of *voluntary castration*. What results is essentially a regressive and, in a sense, psychotic mode of reading.

At this point, the Freudian critic would ground his or her reading on what Freud called the "inverted" or "passive" variant of the Oedipus complex. The idea is that the boy child, instead of hoping to defeat the father, wishes to replace the mother as the object of the father's desire. If this phase of development is not passed through, first to autoeroticism or narcissism and then to the boy's successful identification with the father, psychic disorders are likely to follow. As a case in point, Freud discusses a certain Daniel Paul Schreber's paranoid symptoms as documented in his *Memoirs of a Nervous Illness* (Freud, 2002)—a central text for the psychoanalytic theory of psychosis.

Schreber was an honored judge who, during his mental illness, became convinced that he was going through a process of emasculation in order to become God's female partner. In Freud's interpretation, this was caused by his latent homosexual feelings toward his father; these were suppressed and transferred in a reversed form first to his doctor (whom he at first believed to be behind the plot of his unmanning) and then to God, a—or perhaps better, *the*—male figure. Unable to cope with the fact that he loved men, Schreber externalized this feeling and imagined that God wished to transform him into a woman.

As pointed out by Roland Boer, it is not incidental that Schreber's symptoms were distinctively religious; rather, "the language of psychosis is unavoidably theological" (Boer, 2002, 135–136; cf. Eilberg-Schwartz, 1994, 18, 34–35, 37). This is especially so in the light of Lacan's reading of Freud. In terms of Freud's theory, Schreber's psychosis resulted from a paradoxical attempt to avoid castration anxiety by means of making castration desirable: since the pursuit of the mother involves the risk of castration, it is better to seek the sexual favor of the father—which requires castration. What brings in the religious aspect is that in Lacan's psychodynamics, castration anxiety and the symbolic system go together. Denying unlimited access to objects of desire, it is castration anxiety that pushes the infant into the realm of the symbolic. The source of castration anxiety is represented within the symbolic system by the Name-of-the-Father—which, like all symbols, marks the absence of what it stands for. It is the absent father who produces and guarantees symbolic order. This was a point originally illustrated in Freud's *Totem and Taboo* and *Moses and Monotheism* (1953–1974a, 1953–1974b): the dead father is turned into a godlike source of law and order. What Freud took as primal history is interpreted by Lacan as "a myth of symbolic necessity": it is not real but fantasized parricide that constitutes civilization (Boer, 2002, 135). None of this, however, ever occurs in the case of psychosis. In the psychotic landscape, the absent father, the source of castration anxiety, is avoided by accepting castration—which produces an enduring sense of the father's actual presence, indeed, a sense of God revealed. Hence, the typically religious features of psychosis.

Voluntary castration is an extreme, yet possible, response to the call to take up one's cross. It comes with a reading that has the reader's desire for Jesus fulfilled, as the symbolic textual Savior transforms into a promised material presence. What would seem an ultimate act of renunciation—one has to give up one's whole life—is appreciated as a way of avoiding an equally complete loss and rejection. In Mark's words,

For what will it profit them to gain the whole world and forfeit their life? Indeed, what can they give in return for their life? Those who are ashamed of me and of my words in this adulterous and sinful generation, of them the Son of Man will also be ashamed when he comes in the glory of his Father with the holy angels. (Mark 8:36–38)

"Me and my words," that is, the obedient Son of God of the story, the symbol of absence, gives way to an omnipotent Son of Man, no longer a model of masculine identification but a masculine object of (psychotic) desire—a divine *bridegroom* whose glorified presence (parousi/a) fully exposes the glory of the Father. To be chosen by and joined with the bridegroom, the believer needs to be emasculated, transformed into *a bride of Christ.*

Divine Manhood

The manliness of God the Father is an issue in itself in psychoanalysis, although discussion of divinity and masculinity in early Christian religion is not restricted to psychoanalytic discourse: it is rather one of the points at which psychological criticism, historical criticism, and cultural criticism meet.

Several scholars have surveyed New Testament Christologies against the background of ancient Greco-Roman views on masculinity and femininity (see Moore & Anderson, 2003). They have pointed out that, in the ancient world, "manhood was not a state simply to be definitely achieved, but something always under construction and constantly open to scrutiny" (Gleason, 1995, xxii; cf. Conway, 2003, 164). In the cosmic order of things, the ideal man would be an image of perfection. All living beings related themselves to that ideal, some falling more short of it than others. Thus, there were not really two opposite sexes but rather a single mode of being—manhood—that men represented in a more advanced way than women; following Thomas Laqueur (1990), scholars speak of the *one-sex model of humanity.* This view was rooted in the physiological conceptions (of authors such as Aristotle and Galen) that regarded the female body as an incomplete, unfinished ("underheated," as they put it) version of the male body.

A relative quantity, manliness was never secure but in a constant state of crisis. You would need to demonstrate it, lest you fall in rank (cf. Conway, 2003, 165–166). It is a distinctive "culture of castration anxiety" that is the issue here—which also tells us (to look at things the other way around) something of the culture that psychoanalytic discourse apparently presumes is real. After all, emasculation is to be feared only if masculinity is perceived as a universal human value. In that respect, "ancient" and "modern" views may not be that different after all.

In their original cultural context, New Testament writings seem to offer two different kinds of response to the crisis of masculinity (which, as one might expect, correspond with the theory of psychoanalysis in a rather interesting way). Both start from the same presupposition: under natural conditions, you would have to give in. In a monotheistic one-sex model of the cosmos, God the Father is the absolute supreme crown of manliness. You cannot outman God: even the manliest man looks feminine in his presence. In this sense, monotheism brought the crisis of masculinity to an entirely new level (cf. Eilberg-Schwartz, 1994, 137).

In Christ, however, things are changed. A perfect Son of Man, Christ is the masculine, fatherly ego ideal in the flesh: the Father and the Son are one, and the Father's absent glory is fully and uniquely exposed in the Son's presence. With Christ, the masculine ego ideal first became approachable through the union of faith.

Apparently, this union has two dimensions. The first, more overt one is identification. The masculine ego ideal is within reach, because "natural," patriarchal differences in identity are no longer valid and identification with the Father is open to all: "there is no longer Jew or Greek, there is no longer slave or free, there is no longer male and female; for all of you are one in Christ Jesus" (Gal. 3:28). The Gospel of Thomas points out the consequences even more clearly: even women, such as Mary Magdalene, can be included in perfect manhood.[9]

The second dimension of being-in-Christ—and this corresponds to Freud's "inverted" version of the Oedipus complex—is devotion. The Father's full presence in the Son opens up the possibility of having a direct relationship with him as an object of his desire. While you still cannot outman God, you can at least pass everybody else in rank and seize the second prize as the bride of Christ. This is actually modeled (indeed by way of typology) in the frequent imagery of Israel as the Lord's spouse in the Hebrew Bible.

While the dimension of identification conforms well to ancient ideals of normative masculinity (everybody wants to be and, by God's grace, can be an image of man), the dimension of devotion comes with a rather strong feminine undercurrent.[10] Both dimensions deal with castration anxiety—although again it is not so much the physical body or sexual behavior as social order and structures of power that are at stake. The key issue is not masculinity or femininity as such but whether you belong to the ruling or the ruled, the dominant or the submissive (cf. Brakke, 1998; Conway, 2003, 167). Whether you actually have a penis or not, you will fear for your share of the phallus.

What Do Women Want?

Whether in the standard or the inverted version, the original Oedipus complex is essentially a male issue, occurring in an inherently androcentric universe. In the light of a classic psychoanalytic reading, the biblical text turns out to be a male patient whose early life setting is transferred intact to the interpretive model used and met with fully developed countertransference there. As to patriarchalism, the ancient setting and the modern method shake hands.[11]

Would there be any room for an element of feminine fantasy in the Gospels? What would the female element be like? To repeat Freud's question, what do women want?

Building upon Freud's theory of vaginal and clitoral satisfaction, Lacan suggests that a woman may have two objects. She may take her pleasure (or enjoyment—Lacan's original term, *jouissance*, has a wide range of connotations [cf. Lacan, 1977, x]) either in the desire to be what the man wants[12] (the phallic *jouissance* of being lacked) or in a particular desire of her own (the feminine *jouissance* that is not determined by the masculine desire from the outside but takes place entirely within the boundaries of the feminine). What exactly is desired in this latter case is enigmatic—for the reason that, being nonphallic, it transcends human language. It is no coincidence that Lacan characterizes this uniquely feminine type of bliss in terms of religious ecstasy (Lacan, 1982; cf. Easthope, 1999, 102–108).

In Mark's Gospel, Jesus' female followers do not share the male disciples' fantasy of power. Their own fantasy—which is repeated in the few short scenes in which Jesus' feminine followership comes into view—is *to take care of Jesus' body*. Simon's mother-in-law serves (diakonein) Jesus (1:31). In Simon the leper's house at Bethany, a woman comes and "performs a good service for Jesus" by anointing his body "beforehand for its burial" (14:3–9; an act the desirability of which could not be more completely missed by the male disciples: "What a waste!"). At the very end of the Gospel, when the male followers have fled for good, the women who "followed and served" Jesus in Galilee (15:41) come to anoint his body after the burial—only to find out that this violated, pierced body that has completed the service it came for (cf. 10:45 and 14:22–24) is absent. Experiencing an angelic vision, the women are seized by nothing less than *tromos* and *extasis*, a trembling ecstasy (16:8).

From the female point of view, the cross comes not as a threat: it is rather experienced as an accomplished fact—just like the little girl experiences castration as an accomplished fact according to Freudian theory. (Juliet Mitchell [1975] would indeed say that, even in the original Freudian framework, the recognition of this "fact" derives from patriarchy rather than from anatomy.) In a patriarchal culture, the self-denial and servility presented as a challenge to the male disciples are everyday realities to Jesus' female followers. Culturally, the reader is not made any more feminine than she already is, and it is rather Jesus who turns out to be feminine. Instead of proposing to others a future masculine model for identification, Jesus himself assumes an existing feminine one. In terms of the dominant ideology of masculinity, his passion and crucifixion crown his unmanning, as they expose his inability to protect the boundaries of his body from violation—that is, to keep up his manly status as an "impenetrable penetrator" (cf. Walters, 1997; Frilingos, 2003, 302; Glancy, 2003, 262–263; Gleason, 2003, 326). At the end of the Gospel, Jesus does not appear as a perfected male presence but provides the absence, the lack in the realm of the feminine, that makes the mute and nameless female desire possible.

According to this Lacanian reading, Mark would write both sexes (as has been said of Shakespeare). In the male language, there is the quest for the hidden (or, alternatively, revealed) glory of the Christian Father-God. In the female language, there is the peculiar coexistence of two desires: one for serving the alien desire, the other for a mystical joy in a world positively beyond sense. Jesus participates in both. As the Crucified One, he is the ultimate servant, "the slave of all" who "gives his life a ransom for many" (Mark 10:44, 10:45). As the Risen One, he is the transcendent object whose absence makes the mystic feminine bliss possible.

Notes

1. In *Écrits: A Selection*, Lacan's concepts of *besoin*, *demande*, and *désir* were translated into English as "need," "demand," and "desire"; see the Translator's Note (Lacan, 1977, viii).

2. As noted by Juliet Mitchell, the Father's role as the (metaphorical) embodiment of law is a cultural rather than a biological fact. The need for something or someone to "break the asocial dyadic unit of mother and child" and to provide the child with an entrance to human culture may be universal,

but that something or someone need not be the father. That it is the father is a historical effect of the patriarchal society (Mitchell, 1982, 23).

3. Note, however, that because language is common property, no individual can possess the phallus. As the prerequisite of symbolic exchange relations, the phallus rules over everybody. As a signifier, it has no given content: the association of the function of the phallus with the penis is arbitrary. (Yet the relationship between Lacan's work and patriarchal power relations—whether he conspires with them or merely describes them—remains a matter of debate among feminist scholars [see Grosz, 1990].)

4. *Wish* and *désir* are the standard English and French equivalents to Freud's *Wunsch*; see the Translator's Note in *Écrits: A Selection*: "The crucial distinction between '*Wunsch*' and 'wish,' on the one hand, and '*désir*,' on the other, is that the German and English words are limited to individual, isolated acts of wishing, while the French has a much stronger implication of a continuous force. It is this implication that Lacan has elaborated and placed at the centre of his psychoanalytic theory" (Lacan, 1977, viii).

5. Kelber's view was later challenged, and he has toned down his original thesis (see Uro, 2003, 106–133; cf. Kelber, 1994). Yet I think the narrative form does make a difference, even if the actual divide between orality and literacy were not that great after all. Reproducing a sequence of events that took place "once upon a time" in the world of the story, a narrative is an act of repetition—which implies that the original reality as such has become inaccessible. Blocked beyond representation, it constitutes the object of the narrative's textual desire.

6. For a comprehensive analysis of the secrecy theme in Mark, see Räisänen (1990). That the divine will be available as a source of care but not as a desired object of knowing (the sexual overtones of the Hebrew word for to "know" *yāda*, and its LXX Greek equivalent, *ginōskō*, considered) is, in fact, a recurring theme in the Jewish and Christian Bibles (as well as a classic topic in psychoanalytic treatises on the Bible). Another prominent case, of course, is Moses, who wished to know God (Exod. 33:13, 33:18) but could only see God's back (Exod. 33:12–23; cf. Eilberg-Schwartz, 1994, 103–105).

7. A different, yet similarly developmental, interpretation could be arrived at from the point of view of object relations theory—although in that case it is the destruction and survival of the mother as the loved object that is fantasized. Renouncing power and embracing suffering, Jesus emerges as an *imago matris* in the Gospels. In Brooke Hopkins's words: "The story of Jesus' death and resurrection mirrors fundamental developmental processes . . . whereby the infant and, later, the adult, comes to acknowledge his or her own destructive impulses and, as a consequence of that acknowledgement, comes to discover the otherness, the reality of the object whose destruction was desired" (Hopkins, 1994, 251). See also Douglas Geyer's astute object relations theoretical reading of the Gospel of Mark in its original historical setting (Geyer, 2001).

8. Compare Lyn M. Bechtel's comments on the interpretation of the story of the Garden of Eden. According to Bechtel, readings that entertain the theme of "sin and fall" may be psychologically dangerous, as they support an ideal of a perfect(ly asexual) world and human nature from which humanity has "fallen" and still falls short. Essentially a childish fantasy, such an interpretation of life "places people under the tyranny of an ego ideal" (Bechtel, 1994; cf. Kille, 2001, 109, 114).

9. Logion 114 reads: "Simon Peter said to them: 'Let Mary leave us, for women are not worthy of life.' Jesus said: 'I myself shall lead her in order to make her male, so that she too may become a living spirit resembling you males. For every woman who will make herself male will enter the kingdom of heaven.'" Mary's condition looks like Schreber's, except that transformation takes place from female to male and not the other way around. Regarding what "being made/making oneself male" actually means, Antti Marjanen (1998, 99–104) discusses three options—all of which are psychologically pertinent. First, the logion might refer to concrete male impersonation as part of the radical female ascetic's way of life. She would cut her hair, accept male dress, and reject all sexual life. Second, "becoming male" could imply a return to a pre-Fall (read: presexual) state before the gender division. This would be in harmony with logion 22, which speaks of "making the two one . . . so that the male not be male nor the female female." According to the third line of interpretation, becoming male would mean becoming spiritual instead of womanly (i.e., mundane).

10. Compare Moore (2001, 5, 146–168). According to Moore, the apostle Paul resorted to a peculiar theology of "soteriological sex change" (164) in order to reconcile this ambiguity: as an extraordinary act of self-mastery (the supreme masculine virtue of the time), the Pauline Jesus' absolute, "feminine" submission to God is "simultaneously and paradoxically a demonstration of his masculinity" (158). Similarly, although a right relation to Paul's (hyper)masculine God means assuming feminine submissiveness, mastery over sin (the supreme mastering and enslaving power in the world) through identification with Jesus (who overcame sin in a unique way) exemplifies supreme masculinity, "to which all human beings can now aspire, whether or not they have been blessed with male genitalia" (162).

11. In Freud's defense, it can be said that "psychoanalysis is not a recommendation *for* a patriarchal society, but an analysis *of* one" (Mitchell, 1975, xiii).

12. What the man wants is *to have* the phallus (which promises him the power to satisfy the insatiable *desire*)—which is impossible (cf. note 2 above). Responding to the male desire and "rejecting an essential part of femininity," the woman wants *to be* the phallus for him—which is equally impossible. For Lacan, love is wanting what you cannot get and giving what you do not have (Lacan, 1977, 289–290).

References

Bechtel, L. M. (1994). A Psychological Approach to Genesis 2:4b–3:24. Paper presented at the Society of Biblical Literature Annual Meeting, Chicago.

Boer, R. (2002). Non-sense: *Total Recall*, Paul, and the Possibility of Psychosis. *Screening Scripture: Intertextual Connections Between Scripture and Film*, George Aichele & Richard Walsh, eds. Harrisburg: Trinity Press International, 120–154.

Brakke, D. (1998). The Passions and the Social Construction of Masculinity. Paper presented at the Society of Biblical Literature Annual Meeting, Orlando.

Brooks, P. (1987). The Idea of Psychoanalytic Literary Criticism. *Discourse in Psychoanalysis and Literature*, Shlomith Rimmon-Kenan, ed. London: Methuen, 1–18.

Conway, C. M. (2003). "Behold the Man!" Masculine Christology and the Fourth Gospel. *New Testament Masculinities*, Stephen D. Moore & Janice Capel Anderson, eds. Atlanta: Society of Biblical Literature, 163–180.

Easthope, A. (1999). *The Unconscious*. London and New York: Routledge.

Eco, U. (1979). *The Role of the Reader*. Bloomington: Indiana University Press.

Eco, U. (1994). *Six Walks in the Fictional Woods*. Cambridge, MA and London: Harvard University Press.

Eilberg-Schwartz, H. (1994). *God's Phallus and Other Problems for Men and Monotheism*. Boston: Beacon Press.

Freud, S. (1953–1974a). Totem and Taboo. *The Standard Edition of the Complete Psychological Works of Sigmund Freud*, vol. 13. London: Hogarth Press, 1–161.

Freud, S. (1953–1974b). Moses and Monotheism. *The Standard Edition of the Complete Psychological Works of Sigmund Freud*, vol. 13. London: Hogarth Press, 211–236.

Freud, S. (2002). *The Schreber Case (Psychoanalytic Remarks on an Autobiographically Described Case of Paranoia [Dementia Paranoides])*. London: Penguin Books.

Frilingos, C. (2003). Sexing the Lamb. *New Testament Masculinities*, Stephen D. Moore & Janice Capel Anderson, eds. Atlanta: Society of Biblical Literature, 297–317.

Geyer, D. (2001). Disavowing the Gospel While Believing It. Paper presented at the Society of Biblical Literature Annual Meeting, Chicago.

Glancy, J. A. (2003). Protocols of Masculinity in the Pastoral Epistles, *New Testament Masculinities*, Stephen D. Moore & Janice Capel Anderson, eds. Atlanta: Society of Biblical Literature, 235–264.

Gleason, M. W. (1995). *Making Men: Sophists and Self-Representation in Ancient Rome*. Princeton: Princeton University Press.

Gleason, M. W. (2003). By Whose Gender Standards (If Anybody's) Was

Jesus a Real Man? *New Testament Masculinities*, Stephen D. Moore & Janice
Capel Anderson, eds. Atlanta: Society of Biblical Literature, 325–327.

Grosz, E. (1990). *Jacques Lacan: A Feminist Introduction*. London and New
York: Routledge.

Hopkins, B. (1994). Jesus and Object-Use: A Winnicottian Account of the
Resurrection Myth. *Transitional Objects and Potential Spaces: Literary Uses of
D. W. Winnicott*, Peter L. Rudnytsky, ed. New York: Columbia University
Press, 249–259.

Kelber, W. (1983). *The Oral and the Written Gospel: The Hermeneutics of Speaking and Writing in the Synoptic Tradition, Mark, Paul, and Q*. Philadelphia:
Fortress Press.

Kelber, W. (1994). Jesus and Tradition: Words in Time, Words in Space.
Semeia, 65, 139–167.

Kille, D. A. (2001). *Psychological Biblical Criticism*. Minneapolis: Fortress
Press.

Lacan, J. (1977). *Écrits: A Selection*. New York: W. W. Norton & Company.

Lacan, J. (1982). God and the *Jouissance* of Woman. *Feminine Sexuality:
Jacques Lacan and the 'École Freudienne,'* Juliet Mitchell & Jacqueline Rose,
eds. London: Macmillan, 137–148.

Laqueur, T. (1990). *Making Sex: Body and Gender from the Greek to Freud*.
Cambridge: Harvard University Press.

MacCabe, C. (2002). Introduction. *The Schreber Case (Psychoanalytic Remarks
on an Autobiographically Described Case of Paranoia [Dementia Paranoides])*.
London: Penguin Books, vi–xxii.

Marjanen, A. (1998). Woman Disciples in The Gospel of Thomas. *Thomas at
the Crossroads: Essays on the Gospel of Thomas*, Risto Uro, ed. Edinburgh:
T&T Clark, 89–106.

Mitchell, J. (1975). *Psychoanalysis and Feminism*. New York: Vintage
Books.

Mitchell, J. (1982). Introduction, *Feminine Sexuality: Jacques Lacan and the
'École Freudienne,'* Juliet Mitchell & Jacqueline Rose, eds. London: Macmillan, 1–29.

Moore, S. D. (1989). *Literary Criticism and the Gospels: The Theoretical Challenge*. New Haven: Yale University Press.

Moore, S. D. (2001). *God's Beauty Parlor and Other Queer Spaces in and around
the Bible*. Stanford: Stanford University Press.

Moore, S. D., & Anderson, J. C., eds. (2003). *New Testament Masculinities*.
Atlanta: Society of Biblical Literature.

Räisänen, H. (1990). *The 'Messianic Secret' in Mark*. Edinburgh: T&T
Clark.

Richardson, W. J. (1983). Lacan and the Subject of Psychoanalysis. *Interpreting Lacan*, J. H. Smith & W. Kerrigan, eds. New Haven: Yale University
Press, 51–74.

Ricoeur, P. (1990). Interpretative Narrative. *The Book and the Text: The Bible and Literary Theory,* R. M. Schwartz, ed. Cambridge and Oxford: Basil Blackwell, 237–257.

Tannehill, R. C. (1977). The Disciples in Mark: The Function of a Narrative Role. *Journal of Religion, 57,* 386–405.

Tolbert, M. A. (1999). Asceticism and Mark's Gospel. *Asceticism and the New Testament,* Leif E. Vaage & Vincent L. Wimbush, eds. New York: Routledge, 29–48.

Uro, R. (2003). *Thomas: The Gospel of Thomas in Historical Context.* New York: T&T Clark.

Walters, J. (1997). Invading the Roman Body: Manliness and Impenetrability in Roman Thought. *Roman Sexualities,* Judith P. Hallett & Marilyn B. Skinner, eds. Princeton: Princeton University Press, 29–43.

Wright, E. (1984). *Psychoanalytic Criticism: Theory in Practice.* London: Methuen.

CHAPTER 7

THE PSYCHOLOGY OF
JOHANNINE SYMBOLISM

Michael Willett Newheart

The symbol that shines brightest in the Gospel of John is that of light. Indeed, it appears in the opening section of the Gospel: "In the beginning was the Word. . . . In him was light, and that light was the light of humanity. The light shines in the darkness, and the darkness has not overcome it" (John 1:1, 1:4–5). This language alludes to the opening verses of Genesis, where in the beginning of creation God says, "Let there be light," thus separating light and darkness (Gen. 1:1, 1:3–4). In this essay, I attempt to allow some light to shine on the dark, mysterious, yet attractive subject of Johannine symbolism. To do so, I first survey recent developments in the interpretation of Johannine symbolism. I then suggest how psychology might be useful in the interpretation of the symbols. Next, I discuss the approach to symbols used by the analytical psychology of C. G. Jung. Finally, I sketch a Jungian reading of the Johannine symbols.[1]

Preliminary to the task, though, are a few definitions. "Johannine symbolism" refers to the symbolism in the Gospel of John, which is also referred to as "the Fourth Gospel" or, in this essay, simply "the Gospel." It is distinguished from the synoptic Gospels, which consist of Matthew, Mark, and Luke. The Epistles of John are considered only in a side glance, and the Revelation of John is not considered at all. The "Johannine community" refers to the group of Christians from which came the documents known as the Gospel and Epistles of John.

"The evangelist" or "the fourth evangelist" refers to the author of the Gospel of John; no further attempt at identification will be made.

Recent Discussion of Johannine Symbolism

Johannine symbolism has been a subject of considerable interest among New Testament scholars in the last decade or so. Indeed, their concerns reflect those of biblical critics at large. In the first section of this essay, then, I discuss recent studies of Johannine symbolism, especially those of a historical or literary nature, and then I offer a critique from a psychological perspective.

From the Enlightenment until very recently, critical biblical scholarship has been dominated by historical interests, so that the reigning paradigm has been historical criticism. These historical interests have been evident in treatments of Johannine symbolism. For example, in the 1980 presidential address to the Society for New Testament Studies, Xavier Leon-Dufour attempted a "symbolic reading" of the Fourth Gospel that was thoroughly grounded in history. The word "symbol" literally means "put together," and he attempted to "put together" the surface meaning of the symbols in the Gospel text and the deeper reality to which they point. The "symbolic operation," then, sets up an "analogical relationship" between two realities, which in the Fourth Gospel are the Jewish cultural milieu in which Jesus lived and the Christian cultural milieu in which the evangelist wrote. A symbolic reading "discovers the relationship between the present reality of the Spirit and the times past of Jesus of Nazareth" (Leon-Dufour, 1980–1981, 440–441).

New Testament scholars, though, have never been satisfied with just history; they have always sought to supplement their historical investigations with tools from other disciplines. For example, Rudolf Bultmann, the premier New Testament scholar of the twentieth century, used the existentialist philosophy of Martin Heidegger to interpret the biblical text. In his monumental commentary on the Fourth Gospel, he wrote that light is the "illumined condition of existence, of my own existence" (Bultmann, 1971, 41). This existentialist approach to Johannine symbolism was continued by John Painter. The symbols, he wrote, are objects from this world but "point beyond this realm to that which makes human existence authentic" (Painter, 1979, 40). Painter also attempted to set the symbols in the context of the conflict between the Johannine community and the synagogue. The evangelist held that "synagogue Jews" had a "false understanding of the symbols" while believers in his community had "the new authentic understanding" in Jesus (34). The evangelist took symbols that synagogue Jews would have understood in terms of the Jewish law and gave them a new point of reference in Jesus.

In the last decade or so, however, the existentialist approach has been criticized because it interprets history as a history of ideas of the early church and neglects the concrete social settings out of which the texts emerged. New Testament scholars, therefore, have turned to the social sciences to help explicate the social milieu of first-century Christianity (see Malina, 1981; Holmberg, 1990). Robin Scroggs noted that the use of social sciences in the study of the New Testament is an attempt to "put body and soul together again" (1980, 166). Studies using a social scientific approach to Johannine symbolism have focused on the social function of the symbols. For example, George MacRae (1970) noted that many of the symbols in the Fourth Gospel were paralleled in the Hellenistic literature of the day. He suggested that the evangelist incorporated a diversity of symbols in the Gospel to emphasize the universality of Jesus. On the other hand, Wayne Meeks (1972) maintained that the images in the Gospel depicted Jesus as an alien in this world in order to give legitimacy to the Johannine community of Christians who, because of their separation from their Jewish origins, felt alienated from society. Craig Koester (1989), however, emphasized both the universality and the particularity of Johannine symbolism.[2] Koester contended that the symbols strengthened the community's distinct social identity by evoking various associations in the minds of the Jews, Gentiles, and Samaritans who made up the Johannine community. Yet the symbols were transformed Christologically so that Jesus himself became the unifying center of the community.

New Testament scholarship in general, and studies of Johannine symbolism in particular, have been dominated by historical concerns, clarified in recent years by social science perspectives. Another important recent movement, however, has focused on literary concerns— that is, an emphasis on the text itself rather than the community or social milieu out of which the text came. The difference between historical criticism and literary criticism in New Testament scholarship is often phrased in terms of "window and mirror." Historical critics see the text as a "window" through which they can "view" the early Christian community and the world in which it lived. Literary critics, however, view the text as a "mirror" in which readers can "see" the world in which they live. Meaning is found in the interaction between text and reader (Krieger, 1964, 3–4).

Biblical literary critics have principally employed in their investigations narrative criticism and reader-response theory (see Moore, 1989).
Alan Culpepper discussed Johannine symbolism in his major study of
the Fourth Gospel from a narrative-critical perspective. His section
on symbols appears in the chapter on implicit commentary (Culpepper, 1983, 180–198). Culpepper maintained that any treatment of
Johannine symbolism must be based on adequate definitions, be sensitive to movement and development in the Gospel, relate the metaphors, symbols, and motifs to one another, and analyze their function
within the Gospel as a literary whole (188–189). He then focused on
"core symbols" or "expanding symbols," such as light, water, and bread,
which serve by repetition balanced by variation, and this variation
progressively discloses to us a sphere that is of great concern. Robert
Kysar looked at Johannine metaphors using reader-response criticism.
He contended that the reader's experience of the metaphors is affective as well as cognitive, for they elicit "emotional instability" for the
reader (Kysar, 1991, 95–96). Kysar also talked about the metaphors'
"participatory feature," "shock," and "decisional character" (98, 100).

Recent works in Johannine symbolism have been dominated by historical and literary concerns. Yet, it seems that studies from both perspectives have been unconsciously groaning and straining toward
a psychological perspective. For example, Painter's existentialist-
historical study said that the symbols "point beyond this realm to that
which makes human existence authentic" (1979, 40). From a literary
standpoint, Culpepper wrote that the core symbols in the Gospel dis-
close a sphere that is of great concern. Depth psychologists would add
that the realm "which makes human existence authentic" or the "sphere
which is of great concern" is the unconscious and that symbols serve
as mediators between consciousness and the unconscious. Meeks, looking at the symbols from a social-historical perspective, spoke of how
the Gospel's symbolic universe helped the Johannine community deal
with the alienation that it felt from society. Yet alienation is a psychological as well as a social phenomenon: it wounds the psyche of group
members and allows the individual to separate from the collective and
move toward wholeness. How did the symbols in the Fourth Gospel
help the Johannine community members do this? Social history, therefore, must be supplemented by psychological history. Koester seemed
to be taking an unwitting step in this direction when he wrote that the
Gospel's symbols evoked various associations in the minds of the Jews,
Gentiles, and Samaritans who made up the Johannine community.
What kinds of associations were evoked, and why were they evoked at

all? Might one say that these symbols arose out of the collective unconscious and that their use in the Fourth Gospel activated the archetypes in the minds of the readers or listeners?

Reader-response criticism also seems to be knocking on the door of psychology. Kysar spoke about the reader's "affective" experience of the metaphors in the Fourth Gospel and the "emotional instability" they elicit (1991, 95–96). What is the nature of this affective experience and this emotional instability? Is it not the metaphors bringing unconscious issues into the reader's consciousness? Writing in the same volume on literary approaches to the Fourth Gospel in which Kysar's essay appears, Wilhelm Wuellner called for the rehabilitation of psychological exegesis to supplement the new literary approaches (1991, 119). Stephen Moore, in his book on the use of literary criticism in the study of the Gospels, charged that New Testament reader-critics' readings were "ineluctably cerebral" and "emotionally retarded" (1989, 95–98, 106–107). Indeed, I think that such readings are the results of the insensitivity biblical literary critics have to the unconscious issues that the symbols raise in the reading experience. I might go so far as to suggest that critics' "ineluctably cerebral" readings are a defense against the unconscious issues that the symbols raise for them. Perhaps depth psychology can help "emotionally retarded" biblical scholars recover their feeling function.

The Relevance of Psychology

It is time, therefore, for psychology to take its rightful place alongside historical and literary criticism in the study of biblical texts and, specifically, Johannine symbols. This section of the essay briefly discusses the kinds of questions psychology raises for the study of the New Testament in general and Johannine symbolism in particular and then notes recent studies by New Testament scholars that have used psychological approaches, especially Jungian approaches. Psychology has much to add to both historical and literary perspectives. It can illuminate what we see through the window and in the mirror of the text—that is, it can help us to understand the mind of the person and the community that produced the text and it can help us to plumb the mind of contemporary readers as they encounter the text. Psychology is after all "the study of the soul" (psyche + logos), and of what does the New Testament consist but "soul books" written by, about, and for persons who, through their relationship with the Ultimate, were transformed in the depths of their being? Psychology can help us analyze these transformations in behavior, in feeling, and in relationship (see Scroggs, 1982). Indeed, it was noted above that other social sciences are said to help keep "body and soul" together, with social structures identified as the body and ideology as the soul. Would it not be more appropriate, however, to consider ideology as mind and psyche as soul? Psychology works alongside social sciences and literary criticism in the investigation of New Testament texts to keep body, mind, and soul together.

Indeed, psychology raises a host of questions for the interpreter to ask of New Testament texts in general and of Johannine symbolism in particular. Not only must one ask about the historical, existential, social, and narrative function of the Johannine symbols, one also needs to ask, What is the psychological function of these symbols? How did they function in the psyche of the first-century Johannine Christian, and how do they function in the psyche of the twentieth-first-century reader? Whether we look at the Fourth Gospel as a window or as a mirror, the symbols must be considered psychologically in order to get a full perspective.

In the last ten years two major works have been produced by New Testament scholars that utilize psychological approaches. Indeed, they represent two different ways to use psychology in New Testament studies. The first of these works was Gerd Theissen's *Psychological Aspects of Pauline Theology* (1987). Theissen is perhaps best known for his pioneering work in the social scientific study of the New Testament, but in this book he broke new ground in the psychological study. His definition of psychological exegesis was particularly instructive: it "seeks to describe and explain, as far as possible, human behavior and experience in ancient Christianity.... Under the rubric of psychological exegesis, we include all attempts to interpret texts as expression and occurrence of human experience and behavior" (Theissen, 1987, 1). For Theissen, psychological exegesis allowed the text to serve as a window onto the psyche of the first-century Christian. To this end, he gave attention to behavioral, cognitive, and psychodynamic perspectives.

The second important work in this area was Walter Wink's three-volume study of the Powers in the New Testament, in which he takes a psychological, as well as socio-ethical, approach to the Powers. Even before the appearance of this work, however, Wink had begun to make a case for the use of psychology in biblical study. In his controversial 1973 tract *The Bible in Human Transformation*, Wink wrote that historical biblical criticism was "bankrupt" of possibilities for personal and social transformation, and he turned to psychology to restore its solvency. For Wink, psychology allowed the New Testament text to serve as a mirror onto the reader's psyche. In an article on the use of psychological insights in biblical study, he wrote, "We have analyzed the text; now we may wish to find ways to let it analyze us" (1978, 141; cf. Wink, 1989).

Both Theissen and Wink used the analytical psychology of C. G. Jung in their work. For Theissen, Jung was one of several psychologists whose methods he used. Wink's early work in the psychological study of the New Testament was almost exclusively Jungian, but his more recent work on the Powers has supplemented that emphasis with the work of social psychologists. Other biblical scholars have employed Jung in their investigations. Wayne Rollins has written extensively on the relevance of Jungian psychology for the interpretation of the Bible (1983, 1985, 1986). Schuyler Brown has produced Jungian analyses of aspects of the Gospels of Matthew and John (1989, 1990), and I have written on Jung and John (Willett, 1988).

Psychology has some important perspectives to bring to bear on the New Testament text in general and on Johannine symbolism in particular. Some New Testament scholars are beginning to recognize this potential and to use psychological insights. Indeed, a number of them are looking to the work of Jung.

Excursus on Diel and Symbolism in the Fourth Gospel

Before looking at Jung, however, it seems appropriate to comment on a book that seemingly does what this paper is seeking to do, that is, to give a psychological analysis of Johannine symbols. Written by psychologist Paul Diel, the book is entitled *Symbolism in the Gospel of John* (Diel & Solotareff, 1988; see Diel, 1986a, 1986b).[3] Unfortunately, it is a model of how not to do psychological analyses of biblical texts! First, the book contains no dialogue with either biblical critics or other psychologists. Diel maintained that biblical critics pursue "dogmatic exegesis," which is concerned with supporting the dogmas of the church (Diel & Solotareff, 1988, 1). (Such a statement betrays an amazing ignorance of the history of modern biblical criticism, which is littered with controversy between the church and biblical scholars [see Neill, 1964, 1–32].) Diel's lack of dialogue with other psychologists is particularly curious, for his work is similar in many ways to that of Freud and Jung. (The back cover of the book identifies Diel as a "post-Jungian.") Furthermore, Diel was plagued by an ahistorical bias. He wrote in one place, "It is really not that important whether

Jesus actually lived or not" (Diel & Solotareff, 1988, 25). And in his interpretation of the prologue he wrote, "God does not exist, the Word does not exist, the beginning does not exist, Christ is not a person, spirit and flesh are not entities. All these words are only symbols, 'figures of speech'" (52). As a result, he engaged in a kind of allegorical interpretation using his own idiosyncratic "psychology of motivation." For example, in interpreting John 1:48–51, Nathanael's initial encounter with Jesus, Diel wrote that the fig tree symbolizes the "vital impulse," the open sky represents "inner joy," and the angels are Jesus' superconscious (77–78). Such allegorization reduces the Gospel's evocative symbols to signs that have a one-to-one correspondence with their meaning. Additionally, such an approach does not consider the literary function of the symbols within the Gospel narrative itself, nor does it attempt to locate the symbols in the cultural milieu of the Johannine community. Any reading of the symbols in the Fourth Gospel, whether it be sociological, narratological, or psychological, must respect the Gospel text itself and the milieu that gave it birth.

Jung's Approach to Symbols

The analytical psychology of C. G. Jung has much to add to the study of Johannine symbolism, for the study of myth and symbol was at the heart of his work. Indeed, the book that led to Jung's break with Sigmund Freud was entitled *Symbols of Transformation*, and his last book, which he edited, was called *Man and His Symbols* (1964). This section briefly summarizes Jung's approach to symbols, looking at the function of symbols in the psyche and their appearance in dreams and in art and literature.

In order for a person to move to maturity, or what Jung called "individuation," one must bring consciousness into dialogue with the unconscious. These opposites can be brought together only through symbols, which arise spontaneously out of the unconscious and are amplified through the conscious mind (Jung, 1953–1979, 11.746[4]). Symbols have a uniting quality: they unite opposites within the psyche, such as the conscious and the unconscious. Jung called this uniting function of symbols their "transcendent function" (see 8.131–193).

Jung distinguished sharply between signs and symbols. Signs are invented and are thus products of the conscious mind. Jung used the example of abbreviations such as UN and NATO. Symbols, however, are not invented but arise out of the unconscious and thus have numinous power. Jung wrote, "A sign is always less than the thing it points to, and a symbol is always more than we can understand at first. Therefore, we never stop at the sign but go on to the goal it indicates; but we remain with the symbol because it promises more than it reveals" (18.482).[5]

Symbols are formed by certain tendencies or patterns in the collective unconscious that Jung called "archetypes" (9.i.1–86). Archetypes include the shadow, anima/animus, and the Self. The shadow is the sum total of what one refuses to acknowledge about oneself (9.ii.13–19). Anima is the feminine principle in the male, and animus is the masculine principle in the female (9.ii.20–42). The Self facilitates the reconciliation between the conscious and the unconscious (9.ii.43–67). It is the archetype of wholeness, the ordering and unifying center of the psyche, what Jung called the "God-image" within us (11.757).

Jung believed that dreams were the chief source of all our knowledge about symbolism (18.431). Dream analysis held an important place in Jung's approach to symbols. He pursued a twofold approach in interpreting dream symbols: association and amplification. First, he encouraged the dreamer to list all of the personal associations that a symbol evoked for him or her. Second, Jung "amplified" the symbol by bringing to bear the various meanings that the symbol carried in religious traditions, mythologies, folklore, and fairy tales. Interpretation of the dream symbol was done at both the personal and general levels. Jung also often had the dreamer respond to the symbol in a personal way, such as through fantasy, art, drama, or poetry, in a process known as "active imagination" (18.391–415).

In all of his work with dream symbolism, Jung always led the dreamer back to the dream itself. He believed that only the material that was clearly and visibly part of the dream should be used in interpreting it. For example, Jung distinguished sharply his method of dream interpretation from Sigmund Freud's method, known as "free association," in which the dreamer made a chain of associations and one association led to another. For Jung, the dreamer was to return continually to the symbol itself to make associations. While he compared free association with a "zigzag line" that leads away from the dream itself, Jung compared his method to "a circumambulation, the centre of which is the dream-image" (18.434). Jung, therefore, paid close attention to both the form and the content of the dream. He was fond of telling his students, "Learn as much as you can about symbolism; then forget it all when you are analyzing a dream" (483).

Jung maintained that the general function of dreams was to restore psychological balance. The psyche is a self-regulating system, he said, which reestablishes psychic equilibrium through dream material. Dreams, therefore, have a complementary or compensatory function (521). Jung viewed this idea of compensation as a "law of psychic happening," and when he set out to interpret a dream he always asked, What conscious attitude does this dream compensate? (16.330)

Jung's approach to art and literature paralleled his approach to dreams, for he believed that the human psyche not only produced dreams but also was "the womb of all sciences and art" (15.133; also 97–132). Jung contended that there were two modes of artistic creation: the psychological and the visionary. The psychological mode deals with materials drawn from the realm of human consciousness, such as romance novels, murder mysteries, didactic poetry, and tragic and comic drama. The visionary mode, however, arises from the collective unconscious; it expresses the "primordial vision," that is, "true symbolic expression." Examples that Jung cited include Dante, William Blake's paintings and poetry, and Richard Wagner's operas (15.140–144). Literature in the visionary mode is, like dreams, compensatory to the conscious attitude of the artist or author. Jung described theater as "an institution for working out private complexes in public" (5.48). Art and literature, however, also exercise a compensatory function for people of the day. Jung wrote, "Whenever the collective unconscious becomes a living experience and is brought to bear upon the conscious outlook of an age, this event is a creative act which is of importance to everyone living in that age. A work of art is produced that contains what may truthfully be called a message to generations of [people]" (15.153).

Symbols held an important place in the work of C. G. Jung. They perform a transcendent function in the psyche, uniting conscious and unconscious. Jung's approach to dream analysis gave significant attention to the symbols in the dreams, using association and amplification to bring the meaning of the symbol to light. Just as symbols in dreams perform a compensatory function in the psyche of the dreamer, symbols in art and literature perform a compensatory function in the individual psyche of the artist or author and in the collective psyche of people of that day.

Johannine Symbolism in Jungian Perspective

With all this in mind, how can one read Johannine symbolism from a Jungian perspective, informed by various historical and literary approaches? The final section of this chapter sketches the broad outline of such a reading. I first give attention to the Johannine symbolic universe, with its dualistic nature and its symbols of the Self, anima/animus, and shadow. Then I try to locate the symbols in the experience of the Johannine community and evaluate them in terms of the experience of readers today.

The Johannine symbolic universe is dualistic in nature for it is dominated by opposites, such as light and darkness, spirit and flesh, life and death. Scholars, therefore, speak of "Johannine dualism" (see Willett, 1992, 57–58, 100). The primary dualism in the Gospel, however, is spatial, the dualism between the world above and the world below (see John 3:31, 8:23). Jesus has come into this world from above so that people might believe in him and be born from above (1:1–18, 3:1–21). The symbols are phenomena in this world that point to the world above, so that those in this world might, like Jesus, have their point of origin in the world above. The symbols bring together the world above and the world below. In Jungian language, the world above is the world within, the unconscious, while the world below is the outer world of ego-consciousness.[6] The symbols enter consciousness from the unconscious; they are manifested in the world below but they come from the world above. They are expressed in terms of consciousness but they point beyond themselves to the unconscious, so that the two may be integrated and the individual might experience wholeness. John Painter said it well in his existentialist interpretation of the symbols: "The symbols, derived from the world of sense experience, are used to communicate that which transcends the world in order that the transcendent might be experienced" (1979, 35). The transcendent becomes immanent, eternal life is experienced in this life; unconscious is made conscious as the opposites are reconciled in the human psyche. Thus, the Johannine symbols exercise their transcendent function and become symbols of transformation.

The symbols of transformation in the Gospel include water (John 4:10–15, 7:38), bread (6:35–58), and light (8:12, 9:5), but the central symbol, the symbol of the Self, the organizing principle of the psyche, is Jesus himself (Jung, 1953–1979, 9.ii.68–126). In no other Gospel does Jesus dominate the narrative as he does in the Fourth Gospel. He is the word become flesh who comes down from above to work miracles and to speak in long discourses, and he returns to the world above through death, resurrection, and ascension. His miracles are not just altruistic deeds but "signs" that reveal his glory and indicate that he is from above (John 2:11). These signs—turning water into wine (2:1–11), healing a man born blind (9:1–7), raising Lazarus from the dead

(11:1–44), dying, rising, and ascending (chapters 18–21)—indicate
that Jesus is a numinous figure, a messenger from above, or, psychologically, a figure from the unconscious.

The discourses of Jesus in the Fourth Gospel differ significantly
from his teaching in the synoptic Gospels, in which he teaches about
the reign of God through parables. In the Fourth Gospel, the subject
of the discourses is Jesus himself and the revelation he brings. Jesus
points to himself through "I am" sayings, such as "I am the light of the
world" (8:12), "I am the resurrection and the life" (11:25), and "Before
Abraham was, I am" (8:58). Jesus' "I am" is the "I" of the Self breaking
into consciousness, summoning persons to relationship with him. To
interpret this "I," the central symbol, Jesus, takes various other symbols such as light, bread, vine, and shepherd and identifies himself with
those. Through the "I am" sayings, the symbols are concentrated in
Jesus, so they derive their energy from this symbol of the Self.

In discussing a social historical approach to the Johannine symbols,
it was noted above that Koester maintained that the symbols unified
the Johannine community because they evoked associations within the
minds of the various community members. To use Jungian language,
these symbols were performing a "transcendent function" in the psyche
of community members before they entered the community, and when
the symbols were applied to Christ they were brought under the
power of the new symbol of the Self, Jesus. To take an example that
Koester used, the image of the shepherd was familiar from Hebrew
Scripture and Hellenistic writings as a symbol for leaders, both human
and divine, who ruled, protected, and cared for the people. The father,
the masculine principle, is projected onto an external figure. The
human or divine leader becomes that father figure who cares for the
individual like a child. In the Fourth Gospel Jesus says, "I am the good
shepherd. The good shepherd lays down his life for the sheep. . . . I
know my own and my own know me" (10:11, 10:14). Jesus is that nurturing father figure, even to the point of death. The symbol of the
shepherd comes under the sway of the symbol of the Self, so that
Jesus is defined as the nurturing Self and the shepherd is now defined
in Jesus.

A Jungian reading of the Johannine symbols, therefore, surveys the
appearance of symbols in the literature of the ancient Mediterranean
world. This process is very similar to the method of dream interpretation that Jung called amplification. When a particular symbol in the
Gospel is considered, it is important to understand how that symbol
functioned in the literature of the day, both Jewish and Hellenistic.

This is not to try to prove some sort of dependence, as was the tendency of previous generations of scholars, but to understand the first-century psyche and the role the symbols played within that psyche. For example, in another "I am" saying, Jesus says, "I am the bread of life" (6:35, 6:48). To those from a Jewish background the symbol of bread would have evoked numerous associations: the Passover meal, which celebrated the liberation from slavery in Egypt; the manna that God gave the Israelites as they wandered in the wilderness after liberation; the bread that Lady Wisdom served to those who would submit to her instruction; and finally, the Law, which was symbolized as bread by the rabbis. Therefore, the symbol of bread was a feminine symbol that spoke of the nourishment that God provides to the people, the nourishment that the Self supplies to consciousness from the unconscious. When Jesus says that he is the bread of life, the bread that comes down from heaven, he becomes that nourishment from the unconscious. Furthermore, this image is also associated with death, for Jesus says that the bread that he gives is his flesh (6:51). The symbol of the Self redefines and is redefined by another symbol, so that the transforming function of the symbol of bread is now applied to Christ.

It is important to note that both of these symbols, shepherd and bread, are connected in the Fourth Gospel with death: Jesus is the good shepherd because he lays down his life for his flock, and he is the bread of life in that he gives his flesh for the life of the world. The defining symbol of the symbol of the Self is the cross. The Johannine view of Jesus' death, however, is different from that of the synoptics and Paul, for in the Fourth Gospel the cross is a lifting up and glorification (3:14, 8:28, 12:23, 12:32, 13:31–32, 17:1, 17:5), it is the way in which Jesus returns to God (7:33, 14:12, 14:28, 16:5, 16:9, 16:16). Death, resurrection, and ascension are not separated as they are in other New Testament works, but together they form one "hour," the hour of Jesus' exaltation. The cross thus casts its shadow over all of the other symbols. All of the other symbols are killed, crucified between the opposites. But it is only then that they, like Jesus, are glorified. Only through association with death are the symbols given numinous power, returning to the unconscious from which they came.

In the Fourth Gospel, therefore, Jesus is the symbol of the Self, and that symbol is interpreted by other symbols in the "I am" sayings. Other personal symbols appear in the narrative in the form of various male and female characters, that is, anima/animus figures. The male characters have the determinative roles in the Gospel: Peter confesses Jesus as the holy one of God (6:69), later denies him (18:15–18, 18:25–27), but is given the task of shepherding the flock after Jesus' return to God (21:15–19); the Beloved Disciple has an intimate relationship with Jesus (13:23) and is the authoritative witness behind the Gospel (19:35, 21:24); Thomas initially refuses to believe reports of the resurrection but then confesses the risen Jesus as Lord and God (20:24–29); and John the Baptist serves as witness to Jesus (1:6–8, 1:15, 1:29–35).

Female characters have important roles as well: the Samaritan woman brings her entire village to faith in Jesus (4:7–42); Martha confesses Jesus as the Christ, the Son of God (11:27); Mary anoints Jesus (12:3); and Mary Magdalene is the first to see the empty tomb and the risen Jesus (20:11–18). At points in the narrative, the actions of women surpass those of men, for the story of the Samaritan woman is told immediately after the story of the misunderstanding Nicodemus (3:1–21), and the confession of Martha is greater than that of Peter (see Schüssler Fiorenza, 1984, 323–333; Willett, 1992, 145–147). The masculine principle is dominant in the narrative, but the feminine also has an important place. One might say that the narrative is "animus-driven," but the anima still has a place. Nevertheless, all of the characters, both male and female, are defined by their responses to Jesus, whether those responses are misunderstanding or commitment (see Culpepper, 1983, 146–148). The anima and animus figures are leading the reader toward the symbol of the Self.

In addition to symbols of the Self and anima/animus, shadow figures also appear in the Gospel, such as Satan, Judas, and Pilate. The darkest shadow, however, falls on a collective character, the Jews. No distinction is made between Pharisees, scribes, chief priests, and Sadducees, as in the synoptic Gospels, but all of these groups are collapsed into "the Jews." They are the primary enemies of Jesus: they continually debate with him (John 2:18–20, 5:16–18) and they seek to kill him (5:18, 7:1). The Jews are in conflict with Jesus because they are blind (9:40–41); their allegiance is to Caesar rather than to God (19:15); they are children of the devil (8:44; see Willett, 1992, 102–103). In other words, the Jews are oriented completely to this world, the world of ego-consciousness, and they struggle against Jesus, who is the messenger from the unconscious. Therefore, Jesus, the symbol of the Self, is clothed in pure light, while the Jews, the shadow figures, are painted in the darkest of colors.

The symbolic world of the Fourth Gospel, therefore, is dualistic in nature and consists of Jesus the symbol of the Self, who defines himself further through various symbols such as water, light, and bread; various anima/animus figures such as Peter, the Beloved Disciple, the mother of Jesus, and Mary Magdalene; and the shadow figures, principally the Jews. The question arises: What "compensatory function" were these symbols exercising within the Johannine community when the Gospel was written? Jung said that works of literature, like dreams, perform a compensatory function in the psyche of the author and the people of that day. What attitude, then, was this Gospel compensating? The Gospel text seems to indicate that community members had recently experienced expulsion from the Jewish community. The community's situation appears to be symbolized in the experience of the blind man who, after being healed by Jesus, is put out of the synagogue by the Jewish authorities (John 9:1–41). Furthermore, secret believers in Jesus are afraid to make their faith public for fear they too might be expelled (12:42; see also 9:22). Jesus tells his disciples that after his death they will be put out of the synagogue (16:2). These references in the Gospel to being put out of the synagogue seem to reflect the situation of the Johannine community: originally a sect within Judaism, it had been expelled from the synagogue because of its confession that Jesus was the Messiah.[7] David Rensberger summarized well the crisis the community would have experienced:

> The Christians who were expelled would have been cut off from much that had given identity and structure to their lives. Expulsion would have meant social ostracism and thus the loss of relationship with family and friends, and perhaps economic dislocation as well. It would certainly have meant religious dislocation. The synagogue meetings, the public liturgy, the festivals, and the observances were all now denied them, and the authoritative interpretation of the sacred scripture itself was in the hands of their opponents. What was threatened was thus the entire universe of shared perceptions, assumptions, beliefs, ideals, and hopes that had given meaning to their world within Judaism. (Rensberger, 1987, 26–27)

Through the Gospel narrative, the Johannine community was trying to maintain psychic equilibrium in the face of expulsion from the synagogue. The symbols in the Fourth Gospel were an important way in which they did this. The evangelist reclaimed symbols of transformation from the Jewish heritage, in which they referred to the Law, and refocused them on Jesus, so that the stabilizing effect that these symbols had were brought to bear on their situation of crisis. The symbols provided psychic grounding for the Johannine Christians in the alienation that they felt from the synagogue. The living water, the bread of life, the light of the world was not found in the Law but in Jesus, the Johannine community's symbol of the Self.

It is particularly interesting to see how the evangelist uses the symbols of light and darkness. These symbols express perhaps better than any other the "Johannine dualism": light is a universal symbol, representing truth, revelation, or consciousness. The Hebrew Scripture associated light with both Israel and the Law. Isaiah said that Israel was a light to the nations (49:6), and Psalm 119 said that the law was a lamp and a light (verse 105). This identification of the law and light was further elaborated by the rabbis, as the word "light" is occasionally replaced by "law." For example, where Isaiah 2:5 reads, "Let us walk in the light of Yahweh," the Targum on it reads, "Let us walk in the study of the Law." First-century Judaism associated itself completely with light; it was the light and it had the light in the Law. In identifying itself so completely with light, though, it failed to deal with its own darkness. When one does not "own" one's darkness or shadow, it is projected onto others (Jung, 1953–1979, 9.ii.16–17). Synagogue authorities projected their shadow onto the Johannine Christians, who held a "deviant belief"—that is, a new revelation of God in Jesus. The authorities held that they were in the light and the Johannine Christians were in darkness. Therefore, the believers in Jesus were expelled from the synagogue, suppressed into the unconscious.

How were the Johannine Christians to cope with the trauma of expulsion, in which they were alienated from the collective, separated from the mother? To deal with this trauma, the community reversed the symbols of light and darkness. They maintained that they had the light in Jesus and that the synagogue authorities were in darkness because they had rejected Jesus by casting believers out of the community. The Johannine believers projected their own shadow onto the synagogue authorities. This projection is given shape in narrative form in the Gospel: the Jews, representing the synagogue authorities, are the shadow figures, whereas Jesus, standing for the Johannine community, is the light. The consciousness of the Johannine Christians, then, was split: they had the light of consciousness, but the synagogue authorities were totally in the darkness of the unconscious, the recipients of the community's projected shadow. Such projection was the only way the community could maintain psychic equilibrium in the aftermath of the trauma of expulsion.

Apparently, the community's psyche remained split, for the Johannine Epistles, written about a decade after the Fourth Gospel, indicate that the community itself eventually split. The author of the first Epistle of John wrote concerning those who have left the community, "They went out from us, but they did not belong to us; for if they had belonged to us, they would have remained with us. But by going out they made it plain that none of them belongs to us" (1 John 2:19; see Brown, 1979, 103–109; Brown, 1981, 69–115). Some of the same language that the Gospel used for the Jews was now used for the members who left the community: they are in darkness (1 John 2:9–11), they are children of the devil (3:8); they are Antichrists (2:18, 2:22, 4:3).

The split in consciousness was realized in the split in the body; that is, the social body, the Johannine community. After the split, the community seems to have disappeared. Those loyal to the author were integrated into the larger church, and those who had left the community found a place in Christian Gnosticism (Brown, 1979, 145–167).

Up to this point, we have been interpreting the Gospel as a window onto the psyche of the Johannine community as it struggled with life after expulsion from the synagogue. However, the Gospel can also be approached as a mirror of the psyche of the modern reader. It is at this point that psychological criticism can join forces with some of the newer literary approaches, such as narrative criticism and reader-response criticism. The literary approaches note the participatory nature of the Johannine symbols. To use Jungian language, the symbols stir the depths of the human psyche because of their archetypal nature. One problem, however, with biblical reader-response criticism is that when the critic talks about the reader, it is actually a reflection of the critic himself or herself. The reader is usually a white, male, well-educated, middle-class academic (Tolbert, 1991, 206). Such an approach does not respect the diversity of readers that encounter the text. Fernando Segovia has contended that biblical reader-response critics were not sufficiently critical of their social location, for a person's race, class, gender, religion, and politics will affect one's reading of the text (Segovia, 1991a, 1–22). Furthermore, one must be critical of one's psychological location as well. Unconscious issues will determine one's conscious reading of the text. Just as an author attempts to resolve complexes through writing a piece of literature, a reader attempts to resolve his or her own complexes through reading, especially when the reader considers that piece of literature to be Scripture. The key question, then, is this: How do the Johannine symbols function in the modern psyche?

Perhaps the answer depends on the reader's social and psychological location. What does the reader bring to the text? To determine that, perhaps the reader could describe associations that are stirred in the psyche by the Johannine symbols. Then the reader could use active imagination with the symbols. The Johannine symbols can still serve as symbols of transformation, in that the Gospel's dualistic symbolic structure vividly indicates that there is another world besides this world, another realm other than ego-consciousness. There is the world above or the unconscious, and that realm reveals itself to us and confronts us for a response. The Gospel can lead to transformation those who are oriented to ego-consciousness, opening up to them the realm of the transcendent. In addition, for those in situations of evil, in which persons are totally possessed by personal or collective unconscious, Johannine symbolism can ensure them that the light of consciousness can be brought to bear. Furthermore, those who are in analogical situations to that of the Johannine community—that is, personal or social alienation from the collective—will draw sustenance from the Gospel's symbols.

Nevertheless, there are limitations, and I would like to mention some cautions. Jung argued that Christ was not an appropriate symbol of the Self for the modern age because of the lack of darkness in him (Jung, 1953–1979, 9.ii.74–75; see also 11.232). Indeed, this criticism weighs heaviest against the Fourth Gospel because alone in this Gospel does Jesus say, "I am the light of the world. Whoever follows me will never walk in darkness but will have the light of life" (John 8:12). We must have the light of life so that we might not be swallowed up in the darkness of the unconscious. However, if we identify so completely with the light, we lose touch with our own darkness and project it onto others, particularly those of a different race, gender, religion, socio-economic class, or political party.

We see the literary remains of such a psychological process in the Fourth Gospel itself. The Johannine community identified with Jesus as the light and projected their darkness onto the Jews. Moreover, frankly, the church has been the worse ever since, for the Gospel has fueled antisemitism. It is important to remember, though, that the picture of the Jews in the Fourth Gospel is a counterprojection. The Johannine community projected its shadow onto the synagogue authorities because that is what the synagogue authorities had done to the community. Perhaps the figure of the Jews in the Fourth Gospel can help the modern reader become conscious of—and withdraw—his or her own projections that are made onto others. Through reading about the shadow figure of the Jews in the Gospel, the reader can become conscious of the darkness within himself or herself.

We also need to evaluate the transformative possibilities of the symbols that are identified with Jesus, the symbol of the Self in the Gospel. The symbol of the shepherd comes to mind. Segovia criticized the use of this particular image because it has been used oppressively in missionary situations. The first-world missionary becomes the shepherd, and the third-world believers are the sheep, thus legitimating the authority of the missionary over the nationals (Segovia, 1991b, 187–188). David Miller has made a similar critique. He argued that the image of the shepherd is perfectionistic and that it places the believer in an infantile position (Miller, 1981, 11–19). He went on to supplement the image of Christ as the good shepherd with images from mythology such as the ram and the cyclops (28–43).

Perhaps this is the way we need to move. The Johannine Jesus can only be a symbol of the Self if he is amplified with other images that can include darkness as well as light, evil as well as goodness. In doing so I think that we are in the spirit of the Fourth Gospel, in which Jesus says that God will send a Paraclete, the spirit of truth, that will lead us into all truth (14:16, 16:13). This spirit is with us and in us, emerging from the unconscious to bring us to wholeness.

Therefore, a symbolic reading of the Fourth Gospel from the Jungian perspective would see the Johannine symbols as symbols of transcendence, which reconcile unconscious and conscious, the world above and the world below. The Johannine symbolic world includes Jesus as the symbol of the Self, which is elaborated with various other symbols, female and male characters serving as anima and animus figures and the Jews as the shadow figures. In the context of the Johannine community, these symbols functioned as compensation for the trauma of expulsion from the synagogue, so that the symbols of Judaism were reappropriated in terms of the new symbol of the Self, Jesus. Johannine symbols can still be transformative in the modern world, but limitations exist. Therefore, Jungian psychology gives a needed perspective on Johannine symbolism.

The Fourth Gospel ends with the following words: "But there are also many other things that Jesus did; if every one of them were written down, I suppose that the world itself could not contain the books that would be written" (John 21:25). The Gospel begins with the Word and ends with the inadequacy of words. So, in the end, the reader is left with no more words, only experience—of God, of Christ, of truth, of glory, but also of Satan, of Antichrist, of falsehood, of suffering. One might say, then, that along with light, let there be darkness.

Notes

From Michael Willett Newheart (1994). The Psychology of Johannine Symbolism. In *Jung and the Interpretation of the Bible*, D. Miller, ed. New York: Continuum, 71–91. Reprinted with permission of the publisher.

1. For my more recent interpretation of the Gospel of John, see Willett Newheart (2001).

2. I am indebted to Dr. Koester for graciously sharing a copy of this paper with me. He is pursuing this kind of approach in a forthcoming book on the symbols in the Fourth Gospel to be published by Fortress.

3. Diel died in 1972, and the book was prepared by his student Jeannine Solotareff, based on manuscripts written by Diel over forty years ago. Diel's interest in biblical symbolism is evident in his other books (Diel, 1986a, 1986b).

4. These works by Jung are cited by volume number and paragraph (rather than page) number.

5. In this respect, Jung's conception of symbols was very similar to that of Paul Tillich. For a study of the two, see Dourley (1981, especially pages 31–47 on symbols).

6. For a similar approach, see Wink (1984), where he wrote, "Heaven is the transcendent 'Within' of material reality" (118). See also Jung's own interpretation of the Gnostic myths, in which he equated divinity with the unconscious and matter with the ego (Jung, 1953–1979: 9.ii.287–346).

7. The important study in this regard is that of Martyn (1979). Martyn contended that the Johannine Christians were expelled from the synagogue based on the Benediction Against Heretics, which had recently been introduced in the synagogue liturgy. The Gospel, then, was written as a "two-level" drama, in which Jesus' struggle against the Jews reflected the struggle of the Johannine community against the synagogue authorities. Recently, scholars have questioned whether the Benediction Against Heretics was the specific instrument by which Johannine Christians were excluded from the synagogue. There is, however, widespread agreement that whatever the instrument, the group was in fact excluded (see Rensberger, 1987, 26).

References

Brown, R. E. (1979). *The Community of the Beloved Disciple.* New York: Paulist.

Brown, R. E. (1981). *The Epistles of John.* Anchor Bible. Garden City: Doubleday.

Brown, S. (1989). Universalism and Particularism in Matthew's Gospel, *Society of Biblical Literature Seminar Papers,* D. J. Lull, ed. Atlanta: Scholars Press.

Brown, S. (1990). The Beloved Disciple: A Jungian View, *The Conversation Continues: Studies in Paul and John in Honor of J. Louis Martyn,* R. T. Fortna & B. R. Gaventa, eds. Nashville: Abingdon.

Bultmann, R. (1971). *The Gospel of John: A Commentary,* G. R. Beasley-Murray, trans. Philadelphia: Westminster.

Culpepper, R. A. (1983). *Anatomy of the Fourth Gospel: A Study in Literary Design.* Philadelphia: Fortress.

Diel, P. (1986a). *The God-Symbol.* San Francisco: Harper and Row.

Diel, P. (1986b). *Symbolism in the Bible.* San Francisco: Harper and Row.

Diel, P. & Solotareff, J. (1988). *Symbolism in the Gospel of John.* San Francisco: Harper and Row.

Dourley, J. P. (1981). *The Psyche as Sacrament: A Comparative Study of C. G. Jung and Paul Tillich.* Toronto, Canada: Inner City Books.

Holmberg, B. (1990). *Sociology and the New Testament: An Appraisal.* Minneapolis: Fortress.

Jung, C. G. (1953–1978). In G. Adler et al., eds. *The Collected Works of C. G. Jung,* R. F. C. Hull, trans. (Vols. 1–20) Princeton: Princeton University Press.

Jung, C. G. (1964). *Man and His Symbols.* New York: Dell.

Koester, C. (1989). Symbol and Unity in the Fourth Gospel. Paper presented at the annual meetings of the Upper Midwest Society of Biblical Literature, St. Paul; and the Catholic Biblical Association, Syracuse, NY.

Krieger, M. (1964). *A Window to Criticism: Shakespeare's Sonnets and Modern Poetics.* Princeton: Princeton University Press.

Kysar, R. (1991). Johannine Metaphor—Meaning and Function: A Literary Case Study of John 10:1–8. *Semeia, 53,* 81–111.

Leon-Dufour, X. (1980–1981). Towards a Symbolic Reading of the Fourth Gospel. *New Testament Studies, 27,* 439–456.

MacRae, G. (1970). The Fourth Gospel and Religionsgeschichte. *Catholic Biblical Quarterly, 32,* 13–24.

Malina, B. (1981). *The New Testament World: A Cultural Anthropological Approach.* Atlanta: John Knox.

Martyn, J. L. (1979). *History and Theology in the Fourth Gospel.* Nashville: Abingdon.

Meeks, W. (1972). The Man from Heaven in Johannine Sectarianism. *Journal of Biblical Literature, 91,* 44–72.

Miller, D., ed. (1994). *Jung and the Interpretation of the Bible.* New York: Continuum.

Miller, D. L. (1981). *Christs: Meditations on Archetypal Images in Christian Theology.* New York: Seabury.

Moore, S. D. (1989). *Literary Criticism and the Gospels: The Theoretical Challenge.* New Haven: Yale University Press.

Neill, S. (1964). *The Interpretation of the New Testament 1861–1961.* London: Oxford University Press.

Neyrey, J. R. (1988). *An Ideology of Revolt: Johannine Christology in Social-Science Perspective.* Philadelphia: Fortress.

Painter, J. (1979). Johannine Symbols: A Case Study in Epistemology. *Journal of Theology for Southern Africa, 27,* 26–41.

Rensberger, D. (1987). *Johannine Faith and Liberating Community.* Philadelphia: Westminster.

Rollins, W. (1983). *Jung and the Bible.* Atlanta: John Knox.

Rollins, W. (1985). Jung on Scripture and Hermeneutics: Retrospect and

Project, *Essays on Jung and the Study of Religion*, L. H. Martin & J. Goss, eds. New York: University Press of America, 81–94.

Rollins, W. (1986). Jung's Challenge to Biblical Hermeneutics, *Jung's Challenge to Contemporary Religion*, M. Stein & R. Moore, eds. Wilmette: Chiron Publications, 107–125.

Schüssler Fiorenza, E. (1984). *In Memory of Her: A Feminist Theological Reconstruction*. New York: Crossroad.

Scroggs, R. (1980). The Sociological Interpretation of the New Testament: The Present State of Research. *New Testament Studies, 26,* 164–179.

Scroggs, R. (1982, March). Psychology as a Tool to Interpret the Text. *Christian Century, 24,* 335–336.

Segovia, F. F. (1991a). Towards a New Direction in Johannine Scholarship: The Fourth Gospel from a Literary Perspective. *Semeia, 53,* 1–12.

Segovia, F. F. (1991b). The Final Farewell of Jesus: A Reading of John 20:30–25. *Semeia, 53,* 167–190.

Theissen, G. (1987). *Psychological Aspects of Pauline Theology.* Philadelphia: Fortress.

Tolbert, M. A. (1991). A Response from a Literary Perspective. *Semeia, 53,* 206.

Willett, M. E. (1988, Fall). Jung and John. *Explorations, 77,* 77–92.

Willett, M. E. (1992). *Wisdom Christology in the Fourth Gospel.* San Francisco: Mellen Research University Press.

Willett Newheart, M. (2001). *Word and Soul: A Psychological, Literary and Cultural Reading of the Fourth Gospel.* Collegeville: Liturgical Press.

Wink, W. (1973). *The Bible in Human Transformation: Toward a New Paradigm for Biblical Study.* Philadelphia: Fortress.

Wink, W. (1978). On Wrestling with God: Using Psychological Insights in Biblical Study. *Religion in Life, 47,* 141.

Wink, W. (1984). *Naming the Powers: The Language of Power in the New Testament.* Philadelphia: Fortress.

Wink, W. (1986). *Unmasking the Powers: The Invisible Forces That Determine Human Existence.* Philadelphia: Fortress.

Wink, W. (1989). *Transforming Bible Study: A Leader's Guide.* Nashville: Abingdon.

Wink, W. (1992). *Engaging the Powers: Discernment and Resistance in a World of Domination.* Minneapolis: Fortress.

Wuellner, W. (1991). Putting Life Back into the Lazarus Story. *Semeia, 53,* 113–132.

CHAPTER 8

THE COGNITIVE ORIGINS OF JOHN'S UNITIVE AND DISUNITIVE CHRISTOLOGY

Paul N. Anderson

The most distinctive aspect of John's Christology is not that it is the highest in the New Testament, nor that it is the lowest; that the Son is one with the Father or subordinate to the Father; that eschatology is present or futuristic; that Jesus knows what is going to happen or that he anguishes in pathos; that the signs are embellished or that they are existentialized. The most distinctive aspect of John's Christology is that *both* parts of these polarities, and others, are held together in dynamic tension within the Johannine narrative. This is the most salient and characteristic of John's provocative Christology. Not only has it been the primary source of classic Christological debates,[1] but it has also been the prevalent interest of most modern literary, historical, and theological investigations of the Fourth Gospel.[2]

A primary strategy for addressing John's Christological unity and disunity has been posing a diachronic history of composition involving the conflation of earlier sources and later editions. In other words, John's perplexities might be addressed by assuming multiple sources, authors, and contexts of the material's origins. Such approaches are indeed attractive, as several of John's perplexities are addressed through them. However, because conclusive evidence for such sources is itself in doubt, other attempts to understand the origin of these tensions must be explored. They cannot be ignored or simply harmonized away. My earlier work (Anderson, 1996) identifies four major sources of John's Christological unity and disunity, but this essay is concerned with only one of those: namely, the degree to which John's Christolog-ical tensions may be attributed to cognitive factors in the thinking and experience of the evangelist.[3]

Diachronic Solutions to John's Theological Tensions

One reason for the enduring influence of Bultmann's commentary on John is that not only did he claim to identify three major sources underlying the work of the evangelist and the work of an ecclesiastical redactor overlaying it, but each of his hypothetical sources addresses at least one of John's historical, literary, or theological puzzles.[4] This also is the probable reason why criticisms of his source-critical work on John have been only partially successful. They have pointed out the fact of John's stylistic unity (despite significant *aporias*—rough tran-sitions and perplexities in the text) but have not addressed adequately the hermeneutical value of Bultmann's (and other diachronic schol-ars') identification of other sources being in theological tension with the fourth evangelist's contribution. The interpretive value of identi-fying such sources and the evangelist's dialectical employment of them is illustrated magnificently in Robert Fortna's second book on John's hypothetical "Signs Gospel."[5] Here Fortna identifies the origin of much of John's theological tension as being what I call a "literary dialogue" between the evangelist and his source. Regarding the *aporia* of John 4:48, for example, Fortna says, "The most natural explanation for these phenomena, then, is that the narrative stems from more than one author: it consists of an older and a younger layer. In short, redaction has taken place" (1988, 5).

While Fortna's work stands on its own, it also builds on Bultmann's work, so that the hermeneutical implications of Bultmann's source-critical work must be highlighted, albeit briefly. (a) Bultmann attributes at least one aspect of John's high/low Christological tension to the lit-erary dialogue between the exalted motifs in an inferred revelation sayings source (including most of the Prologue and the "I am" say-ings) and the incarnational Christology of the evangelist. (b) Bult-mann attributes the tension between the glorious Johannine signs (as well as their origin) and the existentializing work of the evangelist to his dialectical employment of a signs source, as he comments upon the signs' revelational significance while deemphasizing their thaumatur-gic and sensationalistic value. (c) "Solved" by the redaction hypothesis are the apparent tensions between present and futuristic eschatologies and between instrumentalistic and Christocentric sacramentologies.

The disordering/reordering aspect of this hypothesis also allows Bultmann to solve some transition and sequence aporias; but most tellingly, it affords him the opportunity to restore the "original order" of the text, which interestingly enough reveals Gnostic-type poetic verses thought to represent the sayings source employed by the evangelist. (d) The passion source theory simply "explains" the origin of distinctive Johannine passion material (a derivation-critical requirement if it is accepted that the evangelist cannot have been among the eyewitness generation) as it shows no stylistic or ideological contrast to the work of the evangelist.

Fortna, of course, includes most of this material in his version of the Signs Gospel, and that move is a more plausible one. A mistake made by Bultmann, however, is that while he successfully casts many of the Johannine dialectical tensions into sharp relief, he only allows for literary explanations of those tensions. Ironically, Bultmann elsewhere describes lucidly the kind of dialectical reflection that modern biblical exegetes and theologians exhibit, but he fails to allow this first-century biblical writer/thinker—the fourth evangelist—to have been such. In his 1927 Eisenach address,[6] Bultmann asked:

> What, then, is meant by *dialectic*? Undeniably it is a *specific way of speaking* which recognizes that there exists no ultimate knowledge which can be encompassed and preserved in a single statement.
>
> The dialectical method in philosophy depends on the conviction that every truth expressed is a partial truth and that the whole truth which is its basis can best be found by first setting beside it the contrary statement. For the contrary statement . . . must also contain a portion of the truth. By setting the two partial truths against each other and combining them, it may be possible to grasp the underlying principle. (Bultmann, 1969, 146)

What Bultmann is here describing is a cognitive and reflective dialogue, but he apparently rules out this sort of dialogue as a potential source of John's Christological tensions. Conversely, C. K. Barrett has argued convincingly that a "dialectical theologian" is precisely the sort of thinker the fourth evangelist must have been. In his compelling essay "The Dialectical Theology of St. John" (1972),[7] Barrett connects the theological style of the fourth evangelist with the Socratic practice of dialectical thought (see *Theatetus* 189–190). *Thinking* is "the conversation which the soul holds with herself in considering anything." Says Barrett,

> In Socratic dialogue—and dialogue (*dialegesthai*) is dialectic—concepts are looked at first from one side then from another, definitions are

proposed, attacked, defended, abandoned, or improved, opposite points
of view are canvassed and, sometimes at least, combined. And the process of thought itself is conceived as fundamentally unspoken dialogue.
(Barrett, 1972, 49)

Again, the present interest is to explore the degree to which the
epistemological origin of John's Christological unity and disunity is
attributable to cognitive-reflective origins rather than literary-correc-
tive ones. This is especially needed, as literary-critical evaluations of
Bultmann's diachronic theory of John's composition are finally uncon-
vincing. As C. K. Barrett declared about John, "*Someone* published it
substantially as it now stands; and I continue to make the assumption
that he knew his business, and that it is the first duty of a commentator
to bring out this person's meaning" (Barrett, 1978, 22).[8] Upon inves-
tigating the epistemological origin of the Fourth Gospel's dialectical
tensions, two in particular seem attributable to the cognitive dialectic
of the evangelist: the evangelist's apparent ambivalence toward Jesus'
signs and the evangelist's pervasive juxtaposing of the flesh and glory
of Jesus.[9] These two analyses explore this possibility, drawing upon
two research-based models of cognitive analysis: the developmental
model of James Fowler's stages of faith development and James Loder's
transformational (crisis) model assessing the anatomy of any knowing
event.[10] Attempts are made to evaluate the cognitive origins of these
two sets of Christological tensions in John and then to apply the findings toward meaningful interpretation.

The Evangelist's Ambivalence toward Jesus' Signs

In none of the four canonical Gospels is there any evidence that
Jesus' miracles were understood clearly, free from ambiguity. Especially in Mark and John, Jesus' followers display a good deal of confusion over the meaning of Jesus' signs. Divergent between Mark and
John, however, is the *valuation* of the signs as explained by Jesus. In
Mark 8:14–21, Jesus declares the import of the feeding to be that the
disciples need not worry about bread to eat. Jesus had fed the 5,000
and the 4,000, so his disciples should put aside their hunger, replacing
it with faith in Jesus' ability to do miracles any time he chose. Likewise, the result of the sea crossing in Mark 4:35–41 is described in
equally thaumaturgic tones: "What sort of man is this that the wind
and the waves obey him!" And the Markan Jesus again calms the storm
in Mark 6:45–52.

In John 6:26, however, the valuation of the miracles is diametrically opposite: "You seek me not because you saw the signs, but because you ate the loaves and were satisfied!" declares the Johannine Jesus. Likewise, in the Johannine sea crossing, it is the disciples who are calmed, not the forces of nature (John 6:20f.). Obviously, John existentializes the value of Jesus' miracles, and whether the evangelist has co-opted a signs source with which he disagrees, or is simply correcting the prevalent interpretation of Jesus' miracles,[11] the epistemological origin of this posture was likely to have involved the evangelist's cognitive dialogue between earlier perceptions and later experiences. In the synoptics, faith leads to miracles; in John, while some of this is also true, more characteristically faith is their resultant goal.

In both traditions, the interpretive valuation of miracles involves notions about their original significance and explanations about their subsequent continuation and nonoccurrence. The apparent dearth of miracles, perceived or otherwise, in spite of belief in their value and availability, must have produced the pre-Markan judgment: "The reason miracles do and do not happen *hinges upon our faith*. Jesus declared numerous times, 'Your faith has made you well,' and in Nazareth, even Jesus could do no miracles because of their lack of faith. If you don't see the miracles you hope for, it's not God's fault. *You* did not believe strongly enough. If you would have faith—even the size of a mustard seed—you could command that mountain to jump into the sea . . . and it would!"

Conversely, John interprets the value of miracles in the light of their relative dearth accordingly: "The reason Jesus performed signs was to lead humanity to a saving faith in God. He never intended the miracles to be the center of Christian experience; they were done to signify the spiritual realities in Christ which they prefigure. Whether people are born blind or loved ones fail to be spared from premature death, the promise is the same: God can and will be glorified in the experiences of those who believe in Christ. Blessed are those who have *not seen* and yet *believe!*"

The common issue addressed by the pre-Markan and the Johannine traditions alike is *theodicy*. Why do signs not happen as often as anticipated, despite the belief that they should? While both traditions address the same issue, they pose different answers. The former attributes the problem to human lack of faith; the latter explains the function of signs as divinely initiated vehicles of revelation—means of glorifying God. Obviously, each of these approaches involved particular kinds of theological reflection within the Gospel traditions themselves. As the Markan and Johannine narrators commented on the value of Jesus' miracles, those appraisals of value must have been affected by the experiences of early interpreters and their reflections upon those experiences in the light of growing understandings of the ministry of Jesus. This involved cognitive dialogues between perceptions and experiences, and to analyze them appropriately, Fowler's stages of faith development deserve to be explored. First, however, consider a summary of his approach.

Patterned after the developmental research of Kohlberg, Piaget, Erikson, and Levinson, Fowler's theory of faith development nonetheless establishes its own voice of authority. Based on hundreds of extensive interviews, Fowler poses six stages through which one's faith may develop. Assuming that all humans begin with at least some sort of undifferentiated, *primal faith* (ages 0–4), the first stage of faith is *intuitive-projective* faith (stage 1) according to Fowler.[12] Characterized by the preschool child's (ages 3/4–7/8) understanding of God as the projection of one's needs, during this stage of faith the child perceives God as serving the primary task of taking care of him or her. Stage 2 (*mythic-literal*) faith involves the junior's (ages 6/7–11/12) distinguishing of the "real" world from make-believe stories. During this stage the child shows considerable concern for fairness and belonging within a group. God often is perceived as a God of rules, and life is understood in connection with cause/effect relationships. *Synthetic-conventional* faith (stage 3), according to Fowler, is precipitated by the breakdown of literalistic constructs in the presence of implicit clashes between stories. For the adolescent (ages 11/12–17/18), authority tends to shift from traditional authority roles to individuals commanding personal authority and respect, as well as one's peer group. It is "synthetic" in that values and beliefs are being synthesized into a working whole; it is "conventional" in that the individual values fit in with one's religious group of peers. Stage 4 (*individuative-reflective*) faith involves a shift in authority from one's faith group or leaders toward establishing one's autonomous system of beliefs reflectively. Precipitated by contradictions in authorities' opinions on important matters, or clashes between "what they say" tenets and "how it is" observations, the young to middle-age adult is driven to establish his or her opinion on matters of faith. Here, "ownership" is key. Previously held views are demythologized, and one comes to distinguish between one's authentic self and societal roles. An important consideration presents itself regarding stage 4 faith. According to Fowler, while nearly all adults reach a synthetic-conventional stage of faith and most reach the individuative-reflective stage, fewer reach stages 5 and 6.

Movement to a *conjunctive* (stage 5) level of faith is precipitated by contradictions not between external sources of authority but between one's autonomously held convictions and/or one's experiences. Here, one's awareness of life's complexities threatens the adequacy of owned faith systems, and yet, neither can one deny his or her experiences or convictions. In contrast to the disjunctive (either/or) choices that establish stage 4 autonomous faith, stage 5 faith is conjunctive (both/and). It brings together dialectically glimpses of truth that must be held together in tension. Not all contradictions can be "solved" in this stage of faith, but neither can their component parts be ignored or denied. At times they come to be embraced as genuinely paradoxical, and God's truth becomes appreciated as finally beyond one's abilities to organize and define it. This leads to *universal* faith (stage 6). On this level of faith, conventional concerns for safety, provision, and survival give way to ultimate concerns, which lead one to sacrifice—at times greatly—for one's vision of universal principle. Fowler does not recommend this level of faith as a desired norm, as society itself would be strained to the point of breaking if all people operated postconventionally. Nor do those who reach stage 6 faith operate on this level consistently. Rather, it represents one's response to ultimate truth whereby it ceases to represent convictions one holds, and one becomes held by conviction as a captive of universal truth.

Obviously, Fowler's theory fits well within the religious situation of twenty-first-century Western society, but can it also apply to a first-century Jewish/Christian thinker operating within a Hellenistic context? One of the weaknesses of Fowler's theory is that it claims adequacy regardless of theological content. It represents only the structures of faith. This, however, is also its strength as it relates to the present study. If indeed the religious quest—across time and culture—involves the movement from self-centered faith (stages 1 and 2) to societally accepted religious views and norms (stage 3) to autonomous convictions (stage 4) to conjunctive appreciations of paradox and variant aspects of truth held in tension (stage 5) to universal principle (stage 6), Fowler's theory becomes extremely relevant to analyzing the epistemological structures (and perhaps origins) of Gospel traditions.[13] In particular, movement between stages 3, 4, and 5 applies to the present study. Where such religious authorities as leaders of the local synagogue in a first-century Asia Minor (or Antioch, Palestine, or Alexandria) context must have appealed to the traditions of Judaism and the authority of the Scriptures, the tensions experienced by Johannine Christians would have been indeed parallel to ones analyzed by Fowler in modern religious contexts. This sort of struggle can be identified throughout the progressive conversion of the man born blind in John 9 and in Jesus' debates with the Jewish religious leaders in John 5–10. Furthermore, it is inconceivable that the evangelist, who so clearly describes the rejection of Jesus as the refusal to move from a stage 3 level of religious faith to a stage 4 level of belief in Jesus ("they loved the praise of men more than the praise of God" [John 12:43]) and who describes autonomous yet monological Christian beliefs (John 6:68–70, 16:29f.) as being only partially adequate, should not have made similar faith-stage transitions himself. The operative question is not whether Fowler's work applies to analyses of Gospel traditions, but how.

At this point it becomes clear that these insights apply to the development of the synoptic traditions as well as the Johannine. In terms of Fowler's stages of faith development, the above pre-Markan view of miracles operates on either a stage 3 (synthetic-conventional) or a stage 4 (individuative-reflective) level of faith.[14] The Johannine valuation of signs, however, is clearly operating on a stage 5 (conjunctive) level of faith. On the one hand, the signs in John are embellished. Jesus begins his ministry with a "luxury miracle" (John 2:1–11) and a healing that is done from afar (John 4:45–54); the middle signs become central platforms on which to construct major Christocentric dialogues and discourses (chapters 5, 6, and 9); and the raising of Lazarus is the most glorious miracle of the New Testament (chapter 11). Signs confirm Jesus' messiahship (John 2:18f., 3:2, 7:31, 10:41f.) and evoke belief within the narrative (John 2:11, 4:53, 6:2, 11:15, 11:45, 11:48, 12:11, 12:18f., 20:24–29). Sometimes a prediction is made by Jesus to facilitate belief (John 12:32f., 14:29, 16:4, 18:32), and in two cases a voice is sounded from heaven for the "faith" benefit of those who are present (John 11:41f., 12:28f.). Jesus' signs in John are indeed employed centrally as revealers of Jesus' glory and provokers of human faith (John 20:30f.).

On the other hand, John clearly betrays an antipathy toward faith that depends mainly on miraculous signs. Belief on the basis of the miracles themselves is encouraged, although finally considered an incomplete kind of faith (John 10:37f., 14:11). The Johannine Jesus declares his disgust regarding those who require signs and wonders before they will believe (John 4:48), and he rebukes the crowd for following him, not because they had seen the revelational significance of the feeding but because they had eaten of the loaves and were satisfied (John 6:26). People misunderstand Jesus' identity and mission on the basis of their signs-faith and want to rush him off and make him their king (John 6:14). They even play the role of the tempter, offering their belief in exchange for another sign (John 6:30f.). At every turn, the Johannine Jesus existentializes the import of the signs, and they become pointers to who Jesus is: the one to whom the Scriptures point and of whom Moses wrote (chapter 5), the true bread of life coming down from heaven (chapter 6), the one who opens the eyes of the blind and exposes the blindness of those who claim to see (chapter 9), the resurrection and the life (chapter 11). Indeed, blessed are *those who have not* seen . . . and yet believe (John 20:29).

Clearly at work in the Johannine tradition is a cognitive dialogue within the thought and experience of the evangelist. Earlier impressions of the value of Jesus' miracles give way to new understandings in the light of confirming and challenging experiences. A central question is whether the evangelist, or his signs narrative, *ever* embraced a pre-Markan thaumaturgical view of Jesus as a *Theios Aner* (a God-Man). There is no evidence that John's miracles ever employed solely a wonder-attestation proper or that discourse and interpretation were ever truncated from the Johannine signs. Neither is there any hard evidence that lends itself to favoring an alien source over the evangelist's interaction with his own traditional material or at least with the prevalent (oral) interpretation. Again, one would be happy to believe in a signs source if there were any evidence that pointed convincingly to an alien narrative source rather than the evangelist's dialectical interacting with his own tradition. The numeration of the first two signs, the distinctiveness of the Johannine signs, their intrinsic connectedness to the Johannine discourses, and the central place of John 20:30f., however, can all be explained just as well by regarding John's signs as simply having been part and parcel of the pervasively independent Johannine tradition.

Fortna and Bultmann believe, in Fowler's terms, that the fourth evangelist is operating on an individuative-reflective (stage 4) level of faith, correcting a synthetic-conventional (stage 3) interpretation of Jesus' miracles. John's perspective has little elasticity to it and is demythologizing (perhaps even showing some characteristics of stage 2 faith). This view, however, does not account for the largely dialectical treatment of Jesus' signs in John, despite the fact that synoptic-like wonder attestations are missing. To assume that these ever were present in the Johannine miracle narratives moves beyond empirical evidence to conjecture, ironically solving the presence of a Johannine wonder by appealing to another. To de-Johannify the ending of a miracle narrative, however, only to re-Markanize it, does not a signs source demonstrate. The fourth evangelist often appears to be operating on a conjunctive (stage 5) level of faith, and the theories of diachronic scholars often overlook that fact. While the evangelist deemphasizes the wondrous value of Jesus' miracles, nowhere does he deny their centrality to Jesus' ministry, and he employs them strategically as platforms upon which to construct his Gospel narrative. The structure of his thought here is pervasively dialectical, and this is the way the reader is meant to understand Jesus' ministry as well.

Nonetheless, diachronic advocates invoke a literary-source dialogue to account for this theological tension in John, but in doing so the evangelist's own dialectical pattern of thought is obfuscated. What is clearly suggested by the Johannine text is the existential tension between the belief that miracles (or at least answers to prayer [John 14:12–14]) ought to have followed the ministry of Jesus and the fact that the community has apparently also experienced the bewilderment of unfulfilled hopes. These experiential crises are the stuff of which the evangelist's existentialization of Jesus' miracles is made. Here we have a cognitive dialogue, moving from an individuative-reflective (stage 4) appraisal of Jesus' miracles to their conjunctive (stage 5) valuation as revelatory signs. Movement from stage 4 (individuative-reflective) faith to stage 5 (conjunctive) faith is precipitated by the crisis of one's autonomously held convictions being challenged by one's subsequent contravening experiences. One cannot deny either one's convictions or one's experiences, however, and the reflective theologian must hold together the truth of both in dialectical tension.

The individuated[15] appraisal of Jesus' miracles in John apparently included the following convictions: (a) Jesus did miracles and they were wondrous. Jesus' signs attest that he has been sent from God, fulfilling the typologies of Moses and Elijah, and they mark the dawning of the new age (John 11:27, 20:30–31). (b) Jesus' miracles also enhance the well-being of humans, the objects of God's love, and they provide a foretaste of God's saving/healing work done through Jesus as the Messiah/Christ. Illness exists not as the penalty of fault but as a platform upon which to demonstrate the work of God (John 9:1–3). (c) Miracles will continue through believers who ask their requests in Jesus' name, and even greater things (whatever that means) will be done in the postresurrection community of faith (John 14:12–14, 16:23–26). These high valuations of miracles are similar to the synoptic, prevalent view, but they are also different enough to be considered independently Johannine, as opposed to being derivative from another tradition.

On the other hand, one detects clear tones of disappointment and frustration in John, which suggest that the evangelist's convictions have been tempered by contradictory experience. (a) The grieving of Mary and Martha still seems fresh in the Lazarus narrative. *Both* women exclaim, "Lord, if you had been here my brother would not have died!" (John 11:21, 11:32). The death of Peter (and the Beloved Disciple)[16] is also foretold (John 21:18–23). (b) Persecution and suffering are predicted by the Johannine Jesus in ways that suggest that Johannine Christianity must have experienced hardship from external sources (John 6:51–66, 15:18–25, 16:1–4, 17:14–21). (c) The true source of blessing lies neither in seeing the miraculous transpire nor in being a member of the eyewitness generation: "Blessed are those who have not seen, and yet have believed," declares the Johannine Jesus (John 20:29).

The cognitive tension between authentic conviction and contravening experience must have moved the evangelist to a conjunctive (stage 5) level of faith. Neither could he deemphasize the miracles of Jesus— so central to his understanding of God's eschatological initiative—nor could he deny his experiences and those of others, which modified his own understandings of Jesus' miracles and which certainly challenged prevalent notions of Jesus' ministry as a miracle worker. As the prevalent (synoptic) interpretation continued to place the blame for the relative dearth of miracles upon the individual's lack of faith, it never moved far beyond a synthetic-conventional (stage 3) mode of operation.[17] On the other hand, the Johannine tradition had begun to reconsider the significance of Jesus' signs, given the subsequent, relative dearth of miracles, and it came to view the synoptic approach as woefully inadequate. It also clarifies Jesus' original intentionality. Thus, the Johannine Jesus takes pains to declare the prevalent evaluation of the feeding (as presented in all five of the synoptic feeding narratives: "they ate and were satisfied") flawed and likely to contribute to a misunderstanding of Jesus' central mission. Likewise, the significance of Jesus' miracles is not that the blind see and the dead are raised. Rather, they bespeak the kerygmatic conviction that Jesus is the light of the world—the resurrection and the life. The one who believes in him, though he or she were dead, will never die (John 11:25f.).

The Flesh and Glory of Jesus

In contrast to a developmental model of cognitive reflection, a crisis model suggesting the anatomy of any event of knowing is also helpful

for assessing one of John's Christological tensions: the flesh and glory
of Jesus. Again, diachronic analyses come quickly to rescue John from
its ideological tensions,[18] but the evangelist's Christology is both high
and low. It is arguable that emphases upon the messianic deity of
Christ played an important rhetorical function during the community's
debates with the local synagogue (during the 70s and 80s C.E.) and
that emphases upon the fleshly humanity of Jesus served antidocetic
functions in the 80s and 90s (see Appendix), but as a contrast to the
monological (either/or) Christology of the Elder, the fourth evangelist's is thoroughly dialogical. The best explanation for this difference
is the contrast between the creative genius of first-generation dialogical thought and the more systematized and monological character of
second-generation constructs. The former explores the truth creatively,
posing an ongoing reflective dialogue between earlier perceptions and
later experiences; the latter defines the "correct answers" according to
a given authority and uses them as standards by which to judge later
expressions of faith. This difference in the cognitive structuring of
Christological views is the most convincing evidence suggesting that
the author of the Johannine epistles was a leader other than the evangelist. Says Judith Lieu:[19]

> The Gospel balances realised eschatology with more traditional state-
> ments of future hope, a strong sense of election with an emphasis on the
> individual's responsibility to respond, predeterminism with the univer-
> sal scope of God's salvation, the world as opposition with the world as
> the sphere and goal of the mission of the Son, tradition with the creativ-
> ity of the Spirit, God as the one whom Jesus makes known with Jesus as
> the only way by which God can be known. In each case it might seem
> that I John holds on to the first member of those partnerships far more
> firmly than he does the second, that a creative dialectic has been surren-
> dered in the interests of the security of dogmatism and exclusivism.
> (Lieu, 1986, 205f.)

One reason for this fact is that the evangelist embraces an agency
Christology (based on Deuteronomy 18:15–22; again, see Appendix)
that employs seemingly egalitarian and subordinationist motifs as two
sides of the same coin.[20] Another is the evangelist's encounter theology. Put simply, not all of John's high Christological material can be
explained on the basis of assuming a movement from lower to higher
appraisals of Jesus; nor can all of the evangelist's use of humanizing
detail be accounted for on the basis of inferring antidocetic correctives
or novelizing additions by the evangelist. John's tradition is thorough-
goingly independent from the synoptics', and the epistemological

origin of John's encounter theology must have been an experiential one.[21] According to Loder (1981, 39–44), any knowing event will have at least five steps to it. These are (1) a sense of *conflict*. We are confronted by an unusual experience that requires interpretation. (2) This leads us into an *interlude for scanning*. One searches one's frame of reference for interpretive helps. (3) One's working "hypothesis" becomes cast in the form of a *constructive act of the imagination*. (4) As this hypothesis is tested, a sense of *release and opening* emerges as it seems to fit. (5) This is followed by *interpretation*, which reflects backward on the event and applies its meaning to future situations. While Loder's work is not based upon empirical research in the way that Fowler's is, he nonetheless has drawn significantly from a century or more of theoretical work on the thinking process, and his work is worthy of scientific consideration and application.

John's encounter theology is reflected by several instances in which a theophanic encounter with God through the man Jesus is narrated, as Jesus is highly exalted in John. (a) The Johannine sea-crossing narrative is rendered as a *theophany* rather than the pre-Markan epiphany (John 6:19f.). Rather than floating past the boat like a phantasm (Mark 6:48–50), Jesus comes to the disciples and addresses them in ways reminiscent of Exodus 3:14 (see Anderson, 1996, 167–193, for a full development of the distinctively Markan and Johannine "eikonic" impressions). (b) People experience themselves as being known intimately by Jesus—a characteristic of spiritual encounter. From Nathanael (John 1:47–50), to the Samaritan woman (John 4:17f., 4:39), to Mary Magdalene's "Aha! experience" in the garden (John 20:10–18), the transforming encounter is intrinsic to the Johannine independent tradition. The Johannine Jesus even knows what is in the human heart as well as what will happen to him (John 1:48, 4:3, 4:16–19, 5:6, 5:42, 6:15, 6:64, 13:1, 24:24f.). (c) To encounter the Son is to encounter the Father in John (John 14:6–10). These motifs are embedded in all levels of the Johannine witness.

On the other hand, the Johannine Jesus is portrayed in starkly human ways. (a) Jesus' suffering is described in fleshly terms. On the cross Jesus thirsts (John 19:28), out of his pierced side flow physical blood and water (John 19:34), Thomas places his finger and hand into the flesh wounds of Jesus (John 20:27), and the "bread" offered by Jesus is his flesh—given for the life of the world (John 6:51c). (b) Jesus is filled with *pathos*. He groans (John 11:33, 11:38), he weeps (John 11:35), his heart is deeply troubled (John 11:33, 12:27, 13:21), and he loves his own unto the end (John 11:1, 11:3, 11:36, 12:23, 13:1, 14:21,

15:9f., 19:26f.). (c) The love motif continues within the community of faith as the last will and testament of the departed savior. The love of the Father for the Son (John 3:35, 10:17, 15:9, 17:23f.) and Jesus' love for his disciples (John 11:5, 13:1, 13:34) now become the model for their loving of Christ and one another (John 13:34f., 14:23, 15:9f., 15:12, 15:17, 17:20–26, 21:15–17). Once again, proximity to the man, Jesus, is suggested by the structure of this content, rather than distance from him.

Obviously, the primary epistemological question regarding this content asks whether John's peculiarities reflect later departures from a singular tradition or an independent trajectory from the early stages of the Gospel traditions. Given the fact that of forty-five similarities between John 6 and corollaries in Mark there are no identical ones,[22] John cannot possibly be considered derivative from Mark. This is even less likely regarding John's relation to Matthew and Luke. The implications of this probability are highly significant. There may *never* have been a time when there was a singular Gospel tradition that diverged into synoptic and Johannine traditions. From the earliest stages of Jesus' ministry, it appears that valuations of his work were at least dual: pre-Markan and Johannine. Furthermore, given the fact that the fleshly and glorious portrayals of Jesus are inextricably connected within John's dialectical style of thought, we probably have something more like a creative first generation of thought than a more categorizing second- or third-generation structure of thought. By the time the Elder writes the Johannine Epistles, he quite readily poses the apostolic faith in terms of right answers versus wrong answers. He even employs the eyewitness motif to bolster its authority.[23] Unless one believes Jesus is the Christ, that one is the "Antichrist" (1 John 2:18–25); and, unless one believes Jesus came in the flesh, that person embodies the spirit of the "Antichrist" (1 John 4:1–3). The component parts of the evangelist's Christology are there, but the dialectical structure is missing, thus suggesting an author other than the evangelist— probably the Gospel's compiler/redactor.

This is where cognitive analysis becomes extremely helpful to the historical-critical method. It helps in assessing the epistemological origin of the dialectical tension between the flesh and glory of Jesus in John. One clear result of recent analyses of John 1:14 is that neither Bultmann nor Käsemann is correct in forcing John's Christology into an incarnational mode or an exalted one.[24] The Word became flesh, and we beheld his glory, declares the evangelist. Not only is his a theology of encounter, but its epistemological origin is most likely to have been a tradition that stemmed from Christocentric encounters with the divine. It is indeed likely that some of these encounters were mystical, reflecting spiritual encounters with the *Parakletos*, but the interwovenness between the fleshly and the glorious motifs as they pertain to the man, Jesus, suggests proximity to the actual ministry of Jesus rather than distance from it alone. Such a view is highly problematic given the vast discrepancies between the synoptic and the Johannine traditions, but the cognitive structure of John's independent witness suggests it. Some of John's independent insights may even be due to divergent first impressions within the earliest stages of the Gospel traditions. Thus, between the witnesses leading up to and following Mark and the developing witness of John, we may have two "bi-optic" traditions that were in dialogue with each other for over half a century before John was finalized in its present form.

Conclusions and Implications

In conclusion, cognitive analysis[25] is extremely helpful in assessing the epistemological origins of John's distinctively unitive and disunitive Christology. In the Fourth Gospel we have a remarkable combination of encounter material, perhaps going back to the earliest stages of Gospel traditions, and we also have extended, reflective developments of the significance of Jesus' words and works for later audiences as they faced new crises and situations. The evangelist builds on original insights dialectically, at times finding new relevance in earlier perceptions and at times modifying preconceptions to be more adequate for subsequent experiences. Finally, it must be remembered that Gospel "traditions" were not disembodied sets of ideas floating docetically from place to place within the early Christian movement. "Gospel traditions" were *persons*—living human beings—who thought about, perceived, experienced, and reflected upon God's saving activity through Jesus Christ. These involve matters of cognition, not just *religionsgeschichtlich* dialogues with alien traditions or sources,[26] and they deserve to be assessed by means of the best cognitive-critical tools available. In that creative venture, the paradigms of Fowler and Loder give us a start, although they are by no means the only paradigms worthy of employing within such investigations.

The implications for interpretation in this new venue of critical analysis are extensive. Rather than reading John's Christological unity and disunity as the result of abstract speculation or the production of a novelized drama, it must be seen as a theological reflection, engaged thoroughly, as all theological work is, with human experience. In that sense, the fourth evangelist—whoever he may have been—was an astute dialectical theologian. While embracing the best of the past, he integrated it with later experiences belonging to himself and members of his community.[27] And this is precisely what we do as modern exegetes and theologians. As we read his testimony, we find ourselves drawn into the narrative and connected with the subject he bespeaks. His transforming encounters become ours, and even as we reflect on the words ". . . blessed are those who have not seen . . ." we find ourselves included in the company of the original audience. In that sense, Christocentric encounters with God through the man, Jesus, cease to be a significant—although partial—source of the Johannine narrative alone; they become its product as well.

Appendix

Sources of John's Unitive and Disunitive Christology

While the above essay outlines the cognitive origins of John's Christological unity and disunity, its explorations must be understood within the scope of the larger study. The evangelist's cognitive and reflective tensions influenced, and were influenced by, other levels of "dialogue," and this should be kept in mind. Relevant conclusions in Anderson (1996, especially Table 22, 262) are that John's Christological tensions are due to at least four kinds of "dialogue" (dialectic) as follows.

1. Theological schemas used by the evangelist. (a) An agency Christology based on Deuteronomy 18:15–22 accounts for the apparent subordinationism and egalitarianism in the Father/Son relationship in John. (b) Jewish manna eschatology (exemplified by 2 Bar. 28–30) accounts for at least some of the tension between present and futuristic eschatologies, as these are intertwined in the messianic anticipation of one who imparts heavenly manna as the inauguration of the new age. (c) Divine/human dialectic, interpreting the history of salvation as a series of divine initiatives, calling forth believing responses on the part of humanity, accounts for the apparent tension between free will and determinism in John. Therefore, history-of-religions analysis does play a role in interpreting the Johannine witness, but John's revealer theology was Jewish rather than Gnostic, and it was central to the evangelist's theology rather than alien to it.

2. Rhetorical correctives within the dialectical Johannine situation. (a) Tensions with the local Jewish synagogue prompted a cluster of

"high" Christological motifs, including preexistence and superiority motifs. (b) Slightly later tensions with docetizing Gentile Christians prompted a cluster of antidocetic emphases on the flesh-and-blood-ness of Jesus. (c) Tensions with the centralizing church prompt a series of correctives, including the revelational value of miracles, an incarnational view of sacramentology, and finally the expanded doctrine of apostolicity. The latter finally called forth a Johannine corrective to institutionalizing tendencies within the late first-century church, and this may reflect something of a Johannine-synoptic sort of dialogue manifesting a fourth tension. (d) Corrections of synoptic thaumaturgical valuations of the feeding and other aspects of Jesus' ministry. "They ate and were satisfied" is not a backwater engagement of an alien source; it is the prevalent valuation of the feeding rendered in all five synoptic feeding narratives that the Johannine Jesus rejects (John 6:26).

3. The dialectical theology of the fourth evangelist. (a) Theodicy within the experience of the evangelist and/or his community produces an existentializing interpretation of miracles' "significance." (b) Theophanic or numinous experiences produce an interwovenness between Christocentric encounters with God and graphic, nonsymbolic portrayals of Jesus' humanity. (c) The "surprise" of openness to the Gospel among the nations produces a tension between the particularity and universality of his Christocentric soteriology (John 1:9). (d) New meanings regarding the story of Jesus find their way into the evangelist's retelling it in the light of evolving situations and community needs.

4. The dialogical function of the Fourth Gospel as a written communication. (a) The signs, the witnesses, and the fulfilled word are designed to lead people into a saving response of faith to God's initiative in Jesus. (b) Dialogues with Jesus are crafted so as to place the reader in the place of the discussant, thereby facilitating an imaginary conversation with the Johannine Jesus. (c) Earlier material suggests interests in evangelizing (especially the Jews), whereas later material (John 1:1–18; chapters 6, 15–17, 21, the Beloved Disciple and eyewitness references, etc.) suggests interests in maintaining group cohesion in the presence of persecution and schismatic tensions (especially docetizing threats). Within this later context, the leading, guiding, convicting, and comforting work of the Holy Spirit is emphasized as the original intentionality of Jesus for his ongoing ministry to the Christian community of faith.

Therefore, the dialectical origins of John's Christological tensions were diverse rather than singular, and this is one of the reasons their analysis has been somewhat elusive. They reflect several kinds of dialogue, each of which deserves its proper analysis in interdisciplinary ways. Cognitive criticism, however, is vital to understanding the sort of thinking involved in maintaining or appropriating Christological schemas, addressing concerns within the historical development of the Johannine situation, and evoking the literary means by which the Johannine hearer/reader was addressed. In that sense, the evangelist seeks to engage later audiences in the same transformative realities he and his contemporaries had themselves engaged. In understanding those realities and how they developed, considering the cognitive origins of John's Christological tensions provides a helpful step forward.

Notes

From Paul N. Anderson (1995). The Cognitive Origins of John's Christological Unity and Disunity. *Horizons in Biblical Theology, 17*, 1–24. Reprinted with permission of the publisher.

1. Consider for instance the Christological debates leading up to and continuing though the seven Ecumenical Councils of the patristic era. The relation of the Son to the Father, the dual nature of the Son, Trinitarian, and *Filioque* debates (to name just a few) had as the origin of both sides in the debates the unitive and disunitive Christology of the Fourth Gospel.

2. See Paul N. Anderson (1996), where over one hundred of the most significant treatments of John's Christology are organized into five major categories and thirteen subcategories (17–32). In each of these categories and subcategories, issues pertaining to John's Christological unity and disunity are central. See also Bibliography I for about 250 titles (278–286).

3. The other three are the evangelist's agency Christology rooted in Deuteronomy 18:15–22, his responding to contemporary crises in the evolving Johannine context, and the use of narrative and discourse as a means of engaging the reader in an imaginary dialogue with Jesus; these are described more fully in the Appendix in this chapter. The first issue is developed more fully in my "Having-Sent-Me Father" essay (Anderson, 1999), and the second and third are developed by means of using John 6 as a case study in my longer "*Sitz im Leben*" essay (Anderson, 1997). The latter attempts with John 6 something parallel to what J. Louis Martyn achieved with John 9.

4. Indeed, some of his most enduring judgments addressed all three issues. See Rudolf Bultmann (1971) for the most significant New Testament work of the twentieth century.

5. See especially Fortna's excursus and his section entitled "The Theological Development from Source to Present Gospel" in his second monograph (1988, 205–220).

6. Later titled "The Significance of 'Dialectical Theology' for the Scientific Study of the New Testament" (1969), this essay provides an important way forward, but Bultmann himself does not make the connection.

7. The present work is largely an extended footnote to Barrett's fine essay on John's dialectical theology (1972), which I believe is the most significant, and nonetheless neglected, single essay on either John 6 or John's Christology.

8. Barrett's judgment here is worth considering. When the twenty or so stylistic characteristics of Bultmann's signs source, the revelation-sayings source, and the work of the evangelist (the redactor "imitated" the style of the evangelist) are all measured within John 6, they tend to be distributed evenly throughout the entire chapter (see Anderson, 1996, 72–136).

9. See the Appendix in this chapter for how these two investigations fit into an overall analysis of John's unitive and disunitive Christology. Other tensions attributable to the evangelist's dialectical thought include John's soteriological universalism/particularity, treatment of the *Ioudaioi*, sacramentalism, and dualism (on the latter, see Kysar, 1993, 78–96).

10. James Fowler's research-based 1981 monograph is the primary source used here; see James Loder's text (1981) for an excellent treatment of cognitive factors elemental within any knowing event.

11. Robert Fortna is on target when he describes the primary motivation for inferring a Signs Gospel as being the fact of theological tension in John, rather than stylistic or contextual evidence (1988, 213). The question is whether theological tension, in itself, justifies the extensive speculation employed by diachronic scholars and whether inferences of the kind of corrective deduced by Fortna and others really does justice to the phenomenological structure and character (and thus the epistemological origin) of the evangelist's thought. It is a fact, for instance, that the valuation of the feeding in all five synoptic feeding narratives is that the crowd ate the food and were satisfied. A more plausible understanding of John 6:26 is that here the Johannine Jesus is portrayed as correcting the prevalent synoptic-related valuation of Jesus' feeding miracle rather than a backwater literary text alone.

12. The following discussion summarizes the main points in Fowler's books (1981, 119–213; 1984, 48–76).

13. Further discussions of Fowler's theory may be consulted in Anderson (1996, 137–193), Dykstra and Parks (1986), and Astley and Francis (1992). Carol Gilligan's work (1982) may qualify some of Fowler's work as it relates to women, but it does not diminish it. Fowler already incorporates some of the best of her insights into his work (1984), and as women were included as subjects of his research, his paradigm does not suffer the vulnerabilities that Gilligan has pointed out in Kohlberg's work.

14. We probably have a movement from a synthetic-conventional (stage 3) approach to miracles (represented by Jewish thaumaturgy) that has been co-opted by the pre-Markan tradition and melded into an individuative-reflective (stage 4) interpretation of Jesus' ministry. Whether or not Peter, or

someone like him, was indeed a prevalent source for Mark (as Papias testi-
fied), a conspicuous connection exists between the thaumaturgical thrust of
Jesus' miracles in Mark and the presentation of Peter's ministry in Acts. In
every sermon attributed to Peter in Acts, a wondrous act of God plays a central rhetorical role, and Peter himself is presented as performing wonders.
John, however, does not. Eventually, the "Petrine" interpretation of Jesus'
miracles becomes the prevalent one and thus assumes a synthetic-conventional
(stage 3) structure as the prevalent view of the mainline church. In the presentation of Jesus' rejecting synoptic thaumaturgical themes in John 6:26 and
6:70, we do have a dialogical engagement with traditional perspectives
reflected in the synoptics, making the inference of a hypothetical source
unnecessary.

15. By individuated I mean that the evangelist has come up with a view of
Jesus' miracles that is parallel to the prevalent view of the synoptics but that
is not identical to it. In that sense, it operates on an individuative-reflective
(stage 4) level of faith development. There is no evidence that the individuated valuation of miracles in the pre-Markan tradition was ever identical to
the Johannine. We may indeed have two "bi-optic" trajectories underlying
the synoptic and Johannine accounts. See Anderson (2001, 175–188), and for
a comprehensive analysis of John's relation to all four (including Q) synoptic
traditions, see Anderson (2002).

16. In John 21:22f. the compiler implies that the Beloved Disciple has died,
and it is explained that Jesus never promised that he would not die, he only
said to Peter, "What is it to you if he remains alive until I come?"

17. By this I mean that hard, critical questions tending to challenge prevalent notions appear not to have been posed too intensely to the synoptic
view that miracles happen as a result of human faith. In fact, by the time Matthew was written, the motif seems even more embellished. Then again, it
could reflect a stage 4 individuated (Petrine?) connecting of human faith with
the seeing of wondrous results, which emerged into a more conventional,
stage 3 stance.

18. One of the main advantages of Bultmann's revelation sayings source is
that it "explains" the tension between John's elevated Christological discourses and the incarnational Christology of the evangelist. Once more, however, a cognitive dialogue is mistakenly identified as a literary one.

19. Judith Lieu's analysis here is incisive.

20. The Son is equal to (to be equated identically with) the Father precisely because he does nothing on his own and does only what the Father
tells him to do. See Anderson (1996, 252–265) for further development of
this view.

21. Despite the problematic implications of this view, the dialectical character of John's Christology suggests proximity to, and distance from, the
actual ministry of Jesus, rather than distance from it alone. This is where epistemology and theology meet. Do we have as the original source of John's

encounter theology someone's transforming encounters with Jesus? If not, whence the origin and why the motif? To once again invoke the catch-all justification for eisegetical interpretive moves—"It must be due to the theologizing license of the evangelist"—is overly speculative and imprecise. It begs the analytical question, "Why?" And that leads again to experiential and cognitive questions regarding the epistemological origins of John's distinctive material.

22. These may be observed in Anderson (1996, Tables 7 and 8, 98–102). P. Gardner-Smith (1938) identified four significant differences between John 6 and Mark in his study; whereas Anderson's tables identify forty-five differences in terms of detail.

23. See 1 John 1:1–3. Given the fact that the eyewitness motif in the Gospel of John represents the work of the compiler (clearly John 21:24, and probably 19:35), as well as several other confirming factors, it is indeed arguable that the compiler of the Gospel was also the author of the Epistles of John.

24. See for instance Marianne Meye Thompson (1988, 33–52). Previously (Anderson, 1996, 137–166), I developed the view that John 1:14 must be seen as an intentionally conjunctive statement: "The Word became flesh . . . and we have beheld his glory." Significantly, these two motifs are connected by an experiential clause: "and dwelt among us."

25. While Professor Ellens has pointed out to me helpfully that Fowler's work is a structuralist model employing psychoanalytic and psychodynamic theory and that Loder's work is largely a transpersonal psychological model, I use the word "cognitive" in the broad sense. I do not mean to suggest that either of these are models of "cognitive psychology" proper; rather, they are both analyses of *cognition*—one describing a developmental and reflective approach, the other describing the crisis of any knowing event.

26. Yes, *religionsgeschichtlich* connections are helpful, but when one asks why did the evangelist co-opt an agency motif or a Logos Christology, one is returned once more to experiential and cognitive issues, an overlooked field in the historical-critical method and *traditionsgeschichtlich* investigations overall.

27. This is also the conclusion of Franz Mussner (1967), and sustained work deserves to be performed on the historical and theological character of the Johannine tradition. It is neither one nor the other—it is both.

References

Anderson, P. N. (1996). *The Christology of the Fourth Gospel; Its Unity and Disunity in the Light of John 6.* Wissenschaftliche Monographien zum Alten und Neuen Testament II #78. Tübingen, Germany: J.C.B. Mohr (Paul Siebeck).

Anderson, P. N. (1997). The *Sitz im Leben* of the Johannine *Bread of Life Discourse and Its Evolving Context, Critical Readings of John 6*, A. Culpepper, ed. Biblical Interpretation Supplemental Series #22. Leiden: E. J. Brill, 1–59.

Anderson, P. N. (1999). The Having-Sent-Me Father—Aspects of Agency, Irony, and Encounter in the Johannine Father-Son Relationship. *Semeia*, *85*, 33–57.

Anderson, P. N. (2001). John and Mark—the Bi-Optic Gospels, *Jesus in Johannine Tradition*, R. Fortna & T. Thatcher, eds. Philadelphia: Westminster/John Knox Press, 175–188.

Anderson, P. N. (2002). Interfluential, Formative, and Dialectical—A Theory of John's Relation to the Synoptics, *Für und wider die Priorität des Johannesevangeliums*, P. Hofrichter, ed. Theologische Texte und Studien #9. Hildesheim, Germany: Georg Olms Verlag, 19–58.

Astley, J., & Francis, L., eds. (1992). *Christian Perspectives on Faith Development: A Reader*. Grand Rapids: Eerdmans.

Barrett, C. K. (1972). The Dialectical Theology of St. John, *New Testament Essays*. London: SPCK, 49–69.

Barrett, C. K. (1978). *The Gospel According to John* (2nd ed.). Philadelphia: Westminster.

Bultmann, R. (1969). The Significance of "Dialectical Theology" for the Scientific Study of the New Testament, *Faith and Understanding* (Vol. 1), R. Funk, ed., L. P. Smith, trans. London: SCM, 145–164.

Bultmann, R. (1971). *The Gospel of John*, G. R. Beasley-Murray, R. N. W. Hoare, & J. K. Riches, trans. Philadelphia: Fortress Press.

Dykstra, C., & Parks, S., eds. (1986). *Faith Development and Fowler*. Birmingham: Religious Education Press.

Fortna, R. (1988). *The Fourth Gospel and Its Predecessor: From Narrative Source to Present Gospel*. Philadelphia: Fortress Press.

Fowler, J. W. (1981). *Stages of Faith Development: The Psychology of Human Development and the Quest for Meaning*. San Francisco: Harper & Row.

Fowler, J. W. (1984). *Becoming Adult, Becoming Christian*. San Francisco: Harper & Row.

Gardner-Smith, P. (1938). *Saint John and the Synoptic Gospels*. Cambridge: Cambridge University Press.

Gilligan, C. (1982). *In a Different Voice*. Cambridge: Harvard University Press.

Kysar, R. (1993). *John: The Maverick Gospel* (2nd ed). Philadelphia: Fortress Press.

Lieu, J. (1986). *The Second and Third Epistles of John*. Edinburgh: T&T Clark.

Loder, J. (1981). *The Transforming Moment: Understanding Convictional Experiences*. San Francisco: Harper & Row.

Mussner, F. (1967). *The Historical Jesus in the Gospel of John*. New York: Herder and Herder.

Thompson, M. M. (1988). *The Humanity of Jesus in the Fourth Gospel*. Philadelphia: Fortress Press.

CHAPTER 9

A PSYCHODYNAMIC APPROACH TO 2 CORINTHIANS 10–13

Anthony Bash

Why Another New Approach to Biblical Studies?

The last thirty years have seen an explosion of new methods of reading Scripture. To the established disciplines of historical, literary, and redaction criticism have been added rhetorical criticism, feminist criticism, structuralist criticism, social scientific criticism, reader-response criticism, and others. So why the need for another approach to reading the biblical text, using models drawn from the world of psychology and psychotherapy? Should we not heed J. H. Neyrey's warning, "It is always tempting for modern readers to psychologize biblical characters, often imposing on them modern notions of the self or motivations and strategies typical of the modern world" (Neyrey, 1994, 137; see also Pilch, 1997; Dominian, 1998)?

In one sense, Neyrey is correct. As N. T. Wright properly acknowledges, with Jesus (or for that matter any New Testament person) one cannot engage in "the scientific study, via Freud or Jung or whoever, of that which lies behind conscious thought and action, in the 'psyche' so called" (1998, 108; see also Theissen, 1987, 1) because we cannot interview Jesus or his family, take a case history, or ask supplementary questions. What we have is in the biblical record—and any attempt at a psychological reading of the text about a person must, at best, be inferential and speculative.

However, to ask whether a particular form of behavior by a person in the Bible might at least be *affected* by psychological processes (if not

explicable by them) is a wholly different question from seeking to
explain the psychology of that biblical character or to explain the text
on wholly psychological grounds. Scholars have for a long time been
asking questions of biblical texts based on known paradigms of psychological behavior and established patterns of psychodynamic interaction. As long ago as 1935, for example, R. H. Strachan (1935, 106)
asked whether Paul's behavior in 2 Corinthians 5:13 might show signs
of megalomania. Well known in Europe is G. Theissen's *Psychological
Aspects of Pauline Theology* (1987). Theissen's method was to use a pas-
tiche of psychological models (in particular, learning theory, psychodynamic models, and cognitive models) to interpret "religious experience and behavior" (1987, 3). J. H. Ellens summed up the argument for
a psychologically based approach as a component to the interpretation
of Scripture:

> [I]n addition to all the other text-critical paradigms which are legiti-
> mately applied to the text of scripture, surely we must apply the para-
> digms for understanding how humans function, what they tend to say,
> why they say what they say[,] the way they say it, and what messages
> mean as seen through standardized psychological paradigms when
> applied in a given context. Psychology is another lens through which it
> is possible to see any text and understand dimensions of it . . . which
> could not be understood if one did not employ this lens. (Ellens, 1997,
> 206–207)

The idea of asking psychological questions of a text is not, therefore,
new (see Rollins [1996, 153–160; 1999, 3–32] for a history of research
on this question), but the idea remains to be more fully explored and
applied.

An important step forward in the application of psychological models of interpretation to Scripture has occurred as a result of the Society
of Biblical Literature Psychology and Biblical Studies Group founded
in 1991 and currently convened by Wayne Rollins. Rollins (1996, 160)
has issued a powerful plea for what he terms "a psychological-critical
approach to scripture." The aim should be, he argues, "to examine
texts . . . as expressions of structure, processes, and habits of the
human psyche, both in individual and collective manifestations, past
and present." Rollins sets out five areas for research, of which one is
"the contribution of psychological-criticism to biblical exegesis." This
area of research presupposes that biblical texts are the result of conscious or unconscious processes in, among others, the minds of the
authors of the texts. He highlights four principal aspects of such exegesis (biblical symbols and archetypal images, psychodynamic factors,

biblical personality portraits, and the psychological analysis of religious phenomena) and also suggests a fifth: "the unconscious factors at work in the history of the text, its authors and the community in which the text has emerged" (Rollins, 1996, 164).

This chapter applies one subbranch of Rollins' psychological-critical approach to Scripture. It explores some of the possible psychodynamic processes at work in the mind of Paul when he wrote 2 Corinthians 10–13. As a subbranch of the psychological-critical approach, this task may conveniently be labeled "psychodynamic criticism."

To clarify, "psychodynamics" is the technical term given to models of interactive human behavior and presupposes that what people do may be affected by unconscious responses and drives. Many of these responses and drives have been identified and explored principally in the twentieth century. Some of the terms associated with such responses and drives have passed into common speech: extraversion and introversion are common examples. Other terms may be less well known: they include defenses (or defense mechanisms), projection, transference, projective identification, repression, acting out, regression, and so on. Psychodynamic models do not explain human behavior but they do contribute some understanding of how and why people said and did what they did. When applied to Scripture they are a critical tool to be used in conjunction with other critical tools and are designed to enhance understanding and to enrich existing critical methods.

A Question of Method

In keeping with the views of an increasing number of scholars, I assume that some of the psychological responses and drives that have been carefully explored and researched in the twentieth century are applicable both transculturally and diachronically.

Underlying this assumption are two related questions. The first is, To what extent is the human psyche, as described and understood in modern psychological theory, principally a construct of nineteenth and twentieth century social realities? The second question is, To what extent have the psychological processes of the human psyche remained unchanged during the course of recorded human history? These questions are difficult to answer—and in seeking to do so, one must heed warnings (for example, Malina, 1993) against reading texts anachronistically and ethnocentrically.

It is generally true that historians, anthropologists, and sociologists have "kept their distance from psychology" (Burke, 1992, 115). As long ago as 1958, it was said that the "next assignment" for historians was to take psychological factors into account in their work (Lange, 1958), although this call remains largely unheeded except in relation to collective psychology (i.e., how groups, rather than individuals, respond). Nevertheless, in the view of Peter Burke, psychological theory does have a contribution to the reading of texts. He writes: "To make proper use of an autobiography or diary as historical evidence . . . it is necessary . . . to consider not only the culture in which the text was written and the literary conventions of the genre, but also the age of the author . . . [and] his or her position in the life-cycle" (Burke, 1992, 116; see Erikson, 1968, 701–702).

It is likely that it will be impossible to prove that the psychological processes identified in the nineteenth and twentieth centuries are applicable diachronically. The method of psychologists has been developed with the living—not the dead—in mind, and with people—not documents—as the primary focus of attention. Nevertheless, cultural anthropologists are carrying out work that seeks to show that some aspects of human self-expression are not culture specific but universally found (Ekman, 1973; Ekman, 1999, 301–320). If those aspects of human self-expression are synchronically *and* universally found, then it is also possible that they may be found universally *and* diachronically.

This approach by cultural anthropologists is already well tried in the field of biblical studies: for example, a recent study on food offered to idols in 1 Corinthians interprets the text of 1 Corinthians 8–10 with insights from the dilemmas faced by the Torajanese Christians in twentieth-century Indonesia, who apparently face the same issues (Newton, 1998). Clearly, there will not be precise correspondence between different contemporary cultures; neither will there be precise correspondence between modern and ancient cultures. Nevertheless, in both cases there will be some points of correspondence; if there were not, it would be very difficult to read texts meaningfully at all.

In addition, there seems to be a growing awareness that psychological processes evident in relationships among people today are also evident in people of the first century. Downing, for example, concludes that "[t]he ability of people back then [in the first century] . . . to deploy complex first, second and third person language, singular and plural, indicates that their social formation and sustenance as individual persons in relation have much in common with our own" (Downing, 2000, 61).

This chapter extends the approach that has been taken in the past and explores one aspect of supposed correspondence between modern and ancient cultures when it comes to psychological methods of defense. It is a first attempt, as far as the writer knows, to interpret 2 Corinthians 10–13 in the light of the idea of "defense mechanisms" developed by modern psychologists. Its usefulness will in part be determined both by its consistency with other findings and by the new insights on old findings that it may offer. There is room for much further work using this method. If a body of useful work develops, then the method may become self-authenticating, as is the case with other methods used in the critical reading of texts.

Defense Mechanisms: Displacement and Denial

Consider a typical situation that many of us may have faced. A has had a bad day at work because his employer has been unreasonable. On return from work, A, who is sometimes given to outbursts of anger, is irritable with B, his spouse. B then overcorrects her six-year-old daughter, C, for a trivial misdemeanor. C is angry with her mother, B, and on her way out—and when no one is looking—kicks the family cat, D.

In psychodynamic terms, what is going on in the family I have described? Quite simply, we are seeing A, B, and C unconsciously defending themselves from an unpleasant truth or situation by taking it out on another member of the family. Each has been provoked but is either unable or unwilling to confront the person who has provoked him or her. Instead, the family members have redirected the feelings of anger or frustration they have onto someone or something else.

The processes I have described are formally called "defense mechanisms"—that is, they are unconscious ways of defending ourselves from having to face and address unpleasant feelings or circumstances (Freud, 1953–1974, 45–56 [a reprint of an article of 1894]). Defense mechanisms are for self-protection, to help us avoid what we do not want to face. They often arise as a result of conflict between people or within one's internal life, and they are the ways that people adapt to such conflict (Bateman & Holmes, 1995, 76). In one textbook, the term is described as follows: "*Defense* is a general term describing the ego's active struggle to protect against dangers . . . and their attendant unpleasant affects . . . throughout life. . . . Painful feelings of anxiety, depression, shame, or guilt ensue as signal affects, impelling the ego to ward off the wish or drive. Defense operates unconsciously; the individual does not recognize the defense mechanisms he or she uses to ward off dangerous drives or wishes. The operation of defense mechanisms may delete or distort aspects of reality" (Moore & Fine, 1990, 48).

The principal defense mechanism we see in the scenario I described is called "displacement," that is, the way people deflect onto others what they are themselves feeling in relation to another or others in a situation of conflict. Displacement typically arises when a person is provoked but is "unable or unwilling" to resist the attack, with the result that the person displaces his or her anger or aggression onto someone else, sometimes called the "scapegoat" (Berkowitz, 1993, 77). Reasons for being unable or unwilling to resist the attack may arise, for example, from fear (for example, B may fear an angry outburst from A), a perception that power is unequally distributed (for example, A may fear losing his job if he confronts his employer about the employer's unreasonable behavior), or lack of maturity to deal with conflict (for example, C is too young to engage with B about being overcorrected). Displacement "[s]hifts the focus or emphasis in . . . behavior, generally by diverting the interest of intensity (cathexis) attached to one idea onto another idea that is associatively related but more acceptable to the ego" (Moore & Fine, 1990, 48; Baron & Richardson, 1994, 24–26). The purpose of displacement is to help adapt to and minimize conflict and to "reduce tension, maintain intrapsychic equilibrium, regulate self-esteem and play a central role in dealing with anxiety, whether it arises from internal or external sources" (Bateman & Holmes, 1995, 76).

In the example I set out, A's anger arose from a situation at work, but A expressed his anger as arising from B's behavior or actions. Likewise, B's excessive correction of C arose from her anger with A but used the pretext of C's misbehavior to express her anger with A not to A but to C.

Closely related to the defense called displacement is a defense called "denial." Denial may involve cognitive acceptance of a painful event, but the associated painful emotions are repudiated. Anna Freud describes this defense as involving a denial of "the existence of objective sources of anxiety and 'pain'" and calls the defense "so simple and so supremely efficacious" (A. Freud, 1948, 85). If, in the example I gave, A or B or C were asked why he or she were angry with B, C, or D, respectively, probably none would admit that it was because he or she were angry with the person who had first provoked him or her.

"Splitting," an idea developed by Melanie Klein (see Khan, 1975, vols. 2, 3, and 4), is also often closely associated with denial. Splitting is a process whereby a person divides an object into "good" or "bad."

The result is that the object can be separated mentally and so ambivalence avoided. Bateman and Holmes say, "Denial involves splitting in which there is cognitive acceptance of a painful event while the associated painful emotions are repudiated" (1995, 88).

How, then, do these principles apply to 2 Corinthians 10–13?

2 Corinthians 10–13

It is widely accepted that chapters 10–13 of 2 Corinthians chronologically follow chapters 1–9 and were written separately on another occasion. Chapters 1–9 express Paul's relief that the Corinthians have heeded his appeals in earlier correspondence. In contrast, in chapters 10–13, Paul seems once again under attack and vehemently defends himself before the Corinthians, perhaps even making himself look a fool (2 Cor. 11:16–12:10) in their eyes for doing so.

The Corinthians had raised specific issues with Paul. These issues appear to have been Paul's worldly approach (10:2), the tone of Paul's earlier letters (10:10), and accusations of his being manipulative (12:16). 2 Corinthians 11:16 and 12:19 are probably Paul's defense of what he anticipates would be the Corinthians' objections to his letter. The Corinthians had also raised other issues that seem to reflect their agreement with the opinions and criticisms of others to whom Paul was vehemently opposed. The issues seem to concern Paul himself and, by extension, the integrity and legitimacy of both his apostolate and the gospel he preached. In particular, Paul had been unfavorably compared to certain other emissaries who had visited the Corinthians. These emissaries are dismissively called by Paul "false apostles" (2 Cor. 11:13) and "superlative apostles" (2 Cor. 11:5, 12:11). I follow the widely held view that these were one group of people. To put the issue in modern language, he upbraids the Corinthians in general terms for readily submitting to "someone" whose Christology, pneumatology, and soteriology (2 Cor. 11:4) are different from his own.

Beyond this, however, it is difficult to tell precisely what the Corinthians had raised with Paul. In comparison with 1 Corinthians, where Paul responds systematically to a letter that had been written to him and where it is possible to reconstruct with a fair degree of certainty at least parts of the letter to Paul, it is exceedingly difficult in 2 Corinthians 10–13 to identify what the Corinthians had said (or perhaps written). It is also difficult to identify and separate out what Paul chooses to address at his own initiative. Although the point cannot be proved, it seems likely that Paul chooses to address a broader range of questions than the Corinthians had perhaps in fact raised.

In addition, who are the people whom Paul so allusively refers to when defending himself? Scholarly debate continues but has reached no widely accepted conclusions. In my view, the people are unlikely to include Peter and James because Paul does not name either Peter or James; in contrast, Paul names James and names—and condemns—Peter in Galatians 2:11 for compromising what Paul saw as "the truth of the gospel" (verse 14) (but cf. Gal. 5:7). Clearly, Paul was unafraid to refer specifically to identifiable individuals when he could. More likely to be the case in 2 Corinthians 10–13 is that those Paul refers to are members of a group rather than particular individuals. I suggest that Paul does not know the names of the individual members of the group, nor has he met them (but cf. Furnish, 1984, 49ff.).

I suspect also that Paul is probably uncertain about what theological views the group holds. A careful reading of 2 Corinthians 10–13 discloses very little about the group's theology—except that Paul thought he disagreed with it. Compare, for example, 1 Corinthians, where Paul systematically addresses clearly identifiable theological issues with the church; compare also, for example, Galatians, where Paul does appear to have a clear idea of what the Judaizers believe—and as a result he cogently engages with the theology of the Judaizers. I have already referred to 2 Corinthians 11:4, which is probably the only example of a clear statement of theological difference—but Paul's disagreement is expressed so generally as to reveal very little and suggests that Paul in fact knew very little about the substance of the group's theology. In 2 Corinthians 10–13, the primary issues concern the basis of apostolic authority (10:7, 10:8, 11:12, 11:13, 11:21–12:13), different practices when it came to material support (11:7–11, 12:14–18), and doubts about Paul's own attributes and abilities—his supposed weakness (10:1), that he was a bully (10:8–10), his speaking abilities (11:6), his status (11:22, 11:23), his spirituality (12:1–6), his deception (12:17, 12:18), and perhaps even that he was a failure (13:6, 13:7). Although these issues have theological implications and are rooted in theological questions, the way that Paul deals with them is primarily pragmatic, utilitarian, and ad hoc, adding weight to the suggestion that Paul did not know the theology of the group whose influence on the Corinthians he regarded as so disruptive.

And what of Paul in this situation? He felt attacked and criticized. In Paul's view, he was being defamed and falsely accused by a group whose members were not known to him, whose theology was obliquely mediated through what the Corinthians were saying, and who were intruding into Paul's legitimate area for work (2 Cor. 10:13–11:2). On almost any reading of the text, Paul comes across as exceedingly angry with the Corinthians, aggressive, threatening, confrontational, and combative. This is so, notwithstanding that Paul may be using "a style of writing parallel with the devices used by the philosophers in their debate with the sophists" (Martin, 1986, 300). Paul's language is sometimes military (2 Cor. 10:3–5), disciplinarian (2 Cor. 10:6, 13:2), and authoritarian (2 Cor. 10:8, 13:10). Paul has abandoned his irenic stance in chapters 1–9, and despite his protestations of love (11:11, 12:15) he proceeds with an excoriating indictment of what he sees as Corinthian error.

How could Paul go about restoring the confidence of the Corinthians in his ministry and integrity? The obvious approach, as in Galatians, is to substantively engage with the theology of the members of the visiting group and also with the members of that group. But as I have shown, Paul could not do that in this case. He did not really know what the group stood for, or why it stood for what it did, or who its members were. So instead he turns his anger on the Corinthians. To use the technical language from psychodynamics I introduced above, he shows evidence that he displaced his anger—that is, he deflected onto the Corinthians themselves the anger he felt toward the shadowy visitors to the Corinthians and the situation they had created for the church. I have already argued that it is probable that the letter Paul wrote to the Corinthians addressed far more than the Corinthians had raised; in my view, Paul probably did so because of his anger and frustration at being unable to identify and respond directly to those who were, to his mind, misleading the Corinthians.

It seems to have escaped many commentators that it is surely pastorally inept to blame the Corinthians, an apparently young church, for failing properly to understand Paul's gospel and for heeding the teaching of others. The true target for blame is those who intruded into an area of ministry that Paul regarded as being legitimately and exclusively his own (2 Cor. 10:13–16). But instead of directing his anger at those who have misled and distracted the Corinthians, Paul "scapegoats" the Corinthians and blames them with a fury and passion that is, in the circumstances, probably wholly out of proportion to the supposed offense. Paul may have felt unable to express his anger to those who had misled the Corinthians if he knew or suspected that the group had connections with the "pillars" in Jerusalem (James, Cephas, and John; see Gal. 2:9), either because he was afraid to do so or because of his perception of his unequal power vis-à-vis the Jerusalem apostles. In contrast, in Galatians 2:11, he did personally engage with Cephas about an issue of theological disagreement.

There is, in addition, an untypical reaction by Paul to what he sees as the errors of the Corinthians. Sometimes, Paul blamed others for leading astray his churches (for example, Gal. 3:1; Phil. 3:2, 3:18; Rom. 16:17, 16:18), although as in the case of the Galatian churches he recognizes also that the churches have a share of the blame. The idea that others are to blame *is* in 2 Corinthians 11:3, 11:14, 11:15, where Paul fears that "the serpent" and the "servants" of Satan will lead astray the Corinthians (and the same dualistic language occurs in 1 Thess. 2:14–16 and 3:5, but in this case the church had successfully resisted Satan), but Paul does not take up that idea in 2 Corinthians except in passing. Instead, in 2 Corinthians 10–13 Paul appears almost entirely to blame the Corinthians for being led astray; and even though he refers to those who had misled them (for example, 11:15, 11:13, and 12:11), he condemns only the Corinthians. It was apparently the fault of the Corinthians that they had submitted to another spirit and to another gospel (11:4) and that they had time for those who opposed Paul and who, in Paul's view, oppressed the Corinthians (11:19, 11:20). This unbalanced and untypical reaction corroborates my suggestion that, as Paul did not know the identity of those who were misleading the Corinthians, he displaced his anger toward them onto the Corinthians.

There is also a deeper underlying issue for Paul. The fact that the Corinthians have heeded the teaching of the group that visited them reflects badly on Paul's own failure to instruct the Corinthians properly. Perhaps Paul's inability to see any good in the group that had visited the Corinthians is also evidence of splitting; that is, for psychological reasons Paul denies that the group is anything except wholly bad. In an earlier letter to the Thessalonians, Paul forewarned that church of difficulties in his absence (1 Thess. 3:4); either he failed to do so with the Corinthian church or he did not do so adequately. If he had stopped to reflect, surely an expression of personal failure with the Corinthian church would have been in order. Acknowledgment of failure or mistakes seems to have been difficult for Paul, at least in relation to the Corinthian church. For example, it is difficult to avoid the impression that he *had* vacillated about revisiting the Corinthians, despite his protestations to the contrary (2 Cor. 1:15–2:1). Instead of acknowledging failure or mistakes, Paul chooses to blame the Corinthians rather than himself. In psychodynamic terms, this is a classic expression of denial.

Paul did, of course, live in a culture in which to admit personal failure would result in a loss of honor (Malina, 1993, 25–50). He had been challenged and, by contemporary standards, he had to answer the challenge to preserve his honor. It could be argued that in failing (because refusing) to acknowledge personal failure, Paul was simply following the social conventions of the agonistic culture in which he lived.

It is too simplistic to think that Paul lived uncritically in his own culture. The shame of the cross—but the honor God had bestowed by it—had confronted Paul and his contemporaries with a paradox that showed that the social conventions of shame and honor did not always hold good. Within Paul's own thought, there is a nascent critique of contemporary culture that is evident even in 2 Corinthians 10–13. Otherwise, why would Paul insist that, although he lived in the world, he was not carrying on a worldly war (10:3)? Otherwise, why would he insist he was being a fool in the *Narrenrede* (Discourse of Fools; 11:1–12:11)? Otherwise, how could he have been perceptive enough to realize that the shame of his own weakness as a human being was the point of entry for the power and grace of God in his life (12:9)? Paul could and did critically appraise aspects of his culture at times; in the case of the failure of his ministry among the Corinthians, the psychological defense of denial precluded him from engaging critically with that failure and with the influence of his own culture on his actions and reactions.

The question of Paul's actions and reactions is, of course, also bound up with the question of Paul's apostolic power and authority. He forewarns the Corinthians that when he returns he will "show boldness with . . . confidence" (10:2) and that he expects them to obey and intends to punish disobedience (10:6). He reminds them of his "authority" (10:8, 13:10) and intends to be "weighty and strong" (10:10)—but, he trusts, not "severe" (13:10)—in the exercise of that authority in person. But how realistic are these hopes? He had once before made a "painful visit" (2:1) at which his authority seems to have been spurned, and as a result he had decided to refrain from a further visit (1:23). Why should Paul think that a third visit, following 2 Corinthians 10–13, should result in a better outcome (13:1, 13:2, 13:10)? Is not this perhaps further evidence of denial on the part of Paul—denial that his pastoral relations with the Corinthians were irretrievably damaged and that his threatening, blustering letter that restated his claim to the very authority the Corinthians were repudiating was reinforcing, not ameliorating, that damage?

Paul seems to have had two approaches to reasserting his apostolic power and authority among the Corinthians. The first involves a reaffirmation and restatement of his apostolic credentials (10:8, 10:11–18, 11:1, 11:2, 11:21b–12:13, 12:19, 13:2, 13:3, 13:10). But to do this among people who already doubt them would probably only serve to reinforce the disagreement that exists. Such an action is characteristic of someone who is showing denial. It is as if Paul were thinking: "If I restate my views and convictions with greater clarity and vigor, the Corinthians will respond favorably and accede." In my view, Paul has missed—and is unconsciously denying—the point. It is not that the Corinthians had misunderstood. I suspect they had understood very clearly. It is that they *disagreed* with Paul and had *rejected* his apostolic authority.

The second approach on one level shows clarity and insight on Paul's part. For Paul feels compelled to argue ad hominem, taking on his opponents on their own terms as best he can (and so contradicting his claim in 10:3–12 not to be acting in the way his opponents were or comparing himself with them), in order to undermine their claim to authority. The *Narrenrede* (11:1–12:11) is Paul's self-acknowledged indulgence in foolishness, an indulgence he claims the Corinthians have forced him into (11:1, 12:11). He is aware that what he says is "not with the Lord's authority" (11:17) and that in so doing he is foolish (11:1, 11:17, 11:21, 12:11), boastful (11:16, 11:18, 12:1), and even mad (11:23). But after completing the discourse, Paul denies what he has previously acknowledged: he says he has not been defending himself before the Corinthians and, even though in 11:17 he said he spoke "not with the Lord's authority," he now says he has been speaking "in the sight of God" (12:19)! If further evidence of Paul's denial in 2 Corinthians 10–13 were needed, it is surely to be found at this point.

Conclusion and Further Reflections

This study has interpreted Paul's behavior disclosed in what he wrote in 2 Corinthians 10–13 using known models of psychodynamic interaction. The application of these psychodynamic models to 2 Corinthians 10–13 has yielded useful results, not only confirming the value—and weakness—of generally accepted findings but also contributing a measure of new understanding. The principal drawback to this method of engaging with the text is that the only data we have are what are contained in the text; we are not able to probe further or ask questions of Paul, as one would normally seek to do when interpreting behavior psychoanalytically. However, in the case of any method of interpretation of a New Testament text, we are faced with this same limitation: the text is all that we have. Nevertheless, in the text there is evidence, as I have shown, that Paul did consistently deny the reality of the situation in which he found himself and that that denial resulted in statements, an approach, and a style that probably would reinforce—not resolve—his difficulties with the Corinthians. The very fit of the approach I have been taking and the useful results it has yielded are evidence of the value of reading biblical texts psychodynamically, and they support the view I have put forward that the psychological processes evident in human beings probably show continuity across the centuries.

I have argued that the reasons for Paul's failure either to name the leading members of the group who had visited the Corinthians or to engage substantively with their theology have not been adequately explored. This study offers some reasons for that failure and for the particular ways that Paul dealt with the situation of powerlessness and ignorance in which he found himself.

Such powerlessness and ignorance are, of course, a form of weakness—and a form that clearly Paul did not relish. Certain other types of weakness Paul apparently rejoiced in, for by them God's power was demonstrated (2 Cor. 12:9, 12:10). This particular form of weakness was one that Paul did not seem to be able to rejoice in, notwithstanding that it is described in the same context in which Paul *is* referring to other weaknesses of which he could boast and with which he could be content.

Paul seems to have been selective about which weaknesses he welcomed and which he did not. One might go further and say that there exists, in Paul's notion of the apostolate, ambivalence about weakness. On the one hand, certain weaknesses in Paul's view modeled the dying of Christ so that in those weaknesses the life of Jesus was manifested to a watching world (2 Cor. 4:7–12). But Paul did not apply this principle in the case of all weaknesses. For example, as I have pointed out elsewhere (Bash, 1997, 110–116, 158–164), Paul did not believe that the Corinthians were free to reject his appeal to them when he spoke to them as Christ's (weak) suppliant, thereby contradicting the idea that he *was* a suppliant. And in the case of 2 Corinthians 10–13, we see evidence of a similar inconsistency: the weakness arising from ignorance about the group visiting the Corinthians and their theology led to threats, bluster, anger, and hostility. These reactions are explicable on psychodynamic grounds but they are inexplicable on the basis of Paul's own theological convictions about weakness—and his own previous experience of weakness—expressed elsewhere in 2 Corinthians. There is in logic, surely, no difference between weakness arising from the apostolic sufferings listed in 2 Corinthians 4:7–10 and the weaknesses and sufferings alluded to in 2 Corinthians 10–13 that arose from the Corinthians rejecting his apostolate. The difference rests in Paul's attitude to the weaknesses and sufferings; in the case of 2 Corinthians 10–13, Paul does not appear to demonstrate the "spirit of faith" to which he refers in 2 Corinthians 4:13 and that was so transformative of his experiences there. I suggest that his failure to engage with his sufferings and weaknesses in 2 Corinthians 10–13 with the "spirit of faith" arose from the displacement and denial I have explored in this chapter.

Note

From A. Bash (2001). A Psychodynamic Approach to 2 Corinthians 10–13. *Journal for the Study of the New Testament, 83,* 51–67. Reprinted with permission of T&T Clark/Continuum.

References

Baron, R. A., & Richardson, D. R. (1994). *Human Aggression.* New York and London: Plenum Press.

Bash, A. (1997). *Ambassadors for Christ: An Exploration of Ambassadorial Communication in the New Testament.* Tübingen, Germany: Mohr-Siebeck.

Bateman, A., & Holmes, J. (1995). *Introduction to Psychoanalysis. Contemporary Theory and Practice.* London and New York: Routledge.

Berkowitz, L. (1993). *Aggression. Its Causes, Consequences and Control.* New York: McGraw-Hill.

Burke, P. (1992). *History and Social Theory.* Cambridge: Polity Press.

Dominian, J. (1998). *One Like Us: A Psychological Interpretation of Jesus.* London: Dartman, Longman & Todd.

Downing, F. G. (2000). *Making Sense in (and of) the First Christian Century.* Sheffield, England: Sheffield Academic Press.

Ekman, P. (1973). Universal Facial Expressions in Emotion. *Studia Psychologica, 15,* 140–147.

Ekman, P. (1999). *Handbook of Cognition and Emotion,* T. Dalgleish & M. Power, eds. London: Wiley, 316–318.

Ellens, J. H. (1997). The Bible and Psychology, an Interdisciplinary Pilgrimage. *Pastoral Psychology, 45,* 193–208.

Erikson, E. (1968). On the Nature of Psychohistorical Evidence. *Daedalus, 97,* 695–730.

Freud, A. (1948). *The Ego and the Mechanisms of Defence*. London: The Hogarth Press and the Institute of Psycho-Analysis.

Freud, S. (1953–1974). The Neuro-Psychoses of Defence. In *The Standard Edition of the Complete Psychological Works of Sigmund Freud*, vol. 3, J. Strachey, ed. London: The Hogarth Press and the Institute of Psycho-Analysis, 45–61.

Furnish, V. P. (1984). *II Corinthians: A New Translation with Introduction and Commentary*. New York: Doubleday.

Khan, M. M. R., ed. (1975). *The Writings of Melanie Klein*. London: The Hogarth Press and The Institute of Psycho-Analysis.

Lange, W. L. (1958). The Next Assignment. *American Historical Review, 63*, 283–304.

Malina, B. J. (1993). *The New Testament World: Insights from Cultural Anthropology*. Nashville: Westminster/John Knox Press.

Martin, R. P. (1986). *2 Corinthians*. Waco: Word Books.

Moore, B. E., and Fine, B. D., eds. (1990). *Psychoanalytic Terms and Concepts*. New Haven and London: The American Psychoanalytic Association and Yale University Press.

Newton, D. (1998). *Deity and Diet: The Dilemma of Sacrificial Food at Corinth*. Sheffield, England: Sheffield Academic Press.

Neyrey, J. H. (1994). "Despising the Shame of the Cross": Honor and Shame in the Johannine Passion Narrative. *Semeia, 68*, 13–137.

Pilch, J. J. (1997). BTB Reader's Guide: Psychological and Psychoanalytical Approaches to Interpreting the Bible in Social Scientific Context. *Biblical Theology Bulletin, 27*, 112–116.

Rollins, W. G. (1996). Rationale and Agenda for a Psychological-Critical Approach to the Bible and Its Interpretation. In *Biblical and Humane*, D. Barr, L. B. Elder, & E. S. Malbon, eds. Atlanta: Scholars Press, 153–171.

Rollins, W. G. (1999). *Soul and Psyche: The Bible in Psychological Perspective*. Minneapolis: Fortress Press.

Strachan, R. H. (1935). *The Second Epistle of Paul to the Corinthians*. London: Hodder & Stoughton.

Theissen, G. (1987). *Psychological Aspects of Pauline Theology*. Edinburgh: T&T Clark.

Wright, N. T. (1998). Theology, History and Jesus: A Response to Maurice Casey and Clive Marsh. *Journal for the Study of the New Testament, 69*, 105–112.

CHAPTER 10

DIFFERENTIATION IN THE FAMILY OF FAITH: THE PRODIGAL SON AND GALATIANS 1–2

Kamila Blessing

Introduction: Differentiation and the Family as System

Psychiatrist Murray Bowen (1985a, 1985b) was the first to create a self-consistent theory of the relationships within the family.[1] He also showed that society generally manifests the attributes of the family. The family system, as it is called, exhibits certain characteristics—the first of which is that it is a system. No one person in the relationship is truly independent. When one person "moves" within the relationship, he pulls the others along, albeit in some unexpected ways. A grandmother dies; the grown grandchildren feel their parents' need for something to fill their grieving hearts; soon there is a great grandchild ("Too bad Grandma didn't get to see her!"). Coincidence? Not really. In families, the system does not just influence the members' decisions; it influences the members' basic emotional style, the health of their relationships, and the emotional style of their future families. The system determines its members' identity in more than name.

Applying this knowledge to interpretation, the first thing we might expect from family systems theory is insight into the many family situations in the Bible. But immediately, it brings us to the heart of the Scriptures. "Family situations" in the Bible include the religious family because religious groups often function emotionally as family systems—and as determinants of identity—for their members. Religious groups and their interactions in many ways drive the text. Examples occur in John (Jews and the emergent Jewish-Christian church) and in Galatians and Romans (Jews, Gentile Christians, and the question of what constitutes religious identity). Furthermore, these groups are presented explicitly in terms associated with the family. For example, John says that believers are given the power to become the children of God (John 1:12; cf. Rom. 8:21). Here, the metaphorical language is not merely metaphor; it virtually invites the use of family systems theory in interpreting the Bible.

Below, we review the concepts of differentiation of self and the triangle and then introduce the fugue. All of these elements will be useful in understanding the family—and the message—of the Prodigal Son.

Differentiation

In Bowen theory, differentiation of self is a spectrum—a spectrum that Bowen regards as universal across culture, time, and place. "Differentiation" refers to the degree to which the person's intellectual system is in control of the feeling system. If the dominance of feelings is high, reason and principle take a back seat to social pressure and to raw emotion. If the intellect is dominant, the person still participates in emotional life but emotion is in balance with well-considered life principles. Figure 10.1 shows the continuum.

A person's place on the spectrum is determined by several things. First, the basic level of differentiation in the parents influences the individual child's level. Each person is "located" at some point on the spectrum most of the time. Second, the level of anxiety in the system influences the day-to-day functioning of the person. A highly differentiated person will react to a sudden increase in anxiety by temporarily going lower on the spectrum but will later recover. A less differentiated

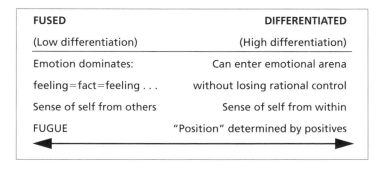

FUSED	DIFFERENTIATED
(Low differentiation)	(High differentiation)
Emotion dominates:	Can enter emotional arena
feeling=fact=feeling . . .	without losing rational control
Sense of self from others	Sense of self from within
FUGUE	"Position" determined by positives

Figure 10.1. The differentiation continuum

person will react in the same way but will have more difficulty recovering. For this reason, continual anxiety often causes the less differentiated person to succumb to emotional or physical illness. Finally, a person can move permanently along the spectrum in response to a life crisis or other defining moment. The story of the Prodigal Son will illustrate such an event.

The Triangle

According to Bowen, the most stable relationships are triangles (as a three-legged stool is more stable than a two-legged one). In fact, any relationship, however extended, tends to coalesce into triangles. The "corners" of a triangle are not necessarily people, however. A religious group—or God or a deceased relative—may form one corner of the triangle. However, the corners always exert a controlling influence upon relationships and upon the person's sense of identity. The main function of a triangle is to alleviate the tension between two people; the two, being unable to resolve issues between them, refocus their anxiety onto a third person. For instance, divorcing parents may use their child as a locus to work out their differences, giving the child conflicting rules or competing for the child's affection. Such triangles tend to be pathogenic—perpetuating anxiety (and perhaps illness) among their members as time goes on.

Some triangles, however, are therapeutic, providing a healthy shock absorber for the anxiety. They increase the health of the person and keep that health in place. A stable marriage, for instance, helps the partners to deal with the stresses of life and tends to increase its own stability over time, as the shock-absorbing function proves its great value for both. Such a couple might attend religious services together and share the value that God is helping them through even quite severe problems. The couple and God form a very stable triangle.

Achieving such a triangle is in fact one of the major objectives of religious premarital counseling. With a couple in marriage counseling, a therapist can become the third corner, helping them to regain and keep the health of the marriage. Jesus often took on just such a healing role. In fact, the triangle is a powerful way to understand his works because they are all pointedly done in relationship—Jesus with the sick person and with God, whose works he was doing. (The analysis of John 9 in volume 1, chapter 10 illustrates Jesus' therapeutic triangles.)

Fugue or Emotional Cutoff

Sometimes people who are too close to a situation for comfort shut down emotionally, and sometimes they leave physically. For instance, I went to public high school in a very white Protestant area. In that school, there was a group of advanced students who continually played an emotional game with the teachers, making the curtains "mysteriously" tie themselves in knots and other minor but irritating things. I always wondered why the smartest and in some ways most privileged kids would do such things. In our senior year, I finally asked one of them why. What he said surprised me. It turned out that he and the other Catholic students felt badly disparaged by the teachers. Being unable physically to leave the public school, they began to do things that were not severe enough to be destructive but just bad (and funny) enough to give themselves an emotional "break." Another student became depressed because of a teacher's punitive attitude toward the students and made excuses to stay home from school. Both are types of fugue—flight from an anxious emotional situation.

Bowen's term for fugue was "emotional cutoff"; "fugue" (flight) will be used here because of its descriptive value. In families, fugue is often a means to escape from family tensions and begin life over again. What makes it a fugue, rather than a simple departure, is that it is always an unsuccessful attempt to resolve unhealthy emotional attachments— most often, attachments to parents. In Bowen theory, a fugue "predicts" that some such unresolved attachment has been determinative for the person.

There are two types of fugue. First, there is the geographic form, which involves physical flight—like the student who stayed home. In the second type, intrapsychic fugue, the subject remains on the scene physically but only at the expense of dysfunction within—in the form of physical illness, depression, or episodic irresponsibility toward others (like the prankster students). The higher the anxiety, the more the person attempts to achieve emotional isolation from others (Bowen, 1985b). However, the isolation is a fiction. According to Bowen, "The person who runs away from his family of origin is as emotionally dependent as the one who never leaves home. They both need emotional closeness, but they are allergic to it" (1985a, 382). Thus, the flight is not really voluntary in the sense of striving toward something positive. It is determined by family stresses.

In the Bible, both types of fugue can be seen. In Genesis 16, Hagar, Sarah's maidservant, becomes pregnant by Abram (by Sarah's design);

then there is friction between the two women and Hagar runs away. Hagar's flight is a geographic fugue because she remains intensely connected emotionally to Abram, whose child she is carrying. The triangle (Hagar, child, Abram) remains even though she has removed herself physically. In contrast, Hagar has another journey away from the family in Genesis 21 that is not a fugue: Hagar and her son Ishmael are sent away for good because of continued tensions between the two women over their sons. She is not running away in this case. However, the ill will between the women has evidently persisted for some (possibly) seventeen years. That ill will tells us something about another possible fugue. One wonders how Hagar dealt with being in close proximity to Sarah for all those years, dependent as she was on her mistress for her sustenance. If Hagar found emotional means of distancing herself from Sarah in that time, that may have been an intrapsychic fugue.

Fugue and the Triangle

Triangles are related in a significant way to fugue. In either type of fugue, the person does not escape the triangle; he merely stretches the "sides" of the triangle. When Hagar fled from Sarah in Genesis 16, she stretched the sides of the triangle Hagar, child, Sarah (or, Hagar, child, Abram); but the triangle remained intact emotionally. The question is, If flight does not accomplish the desired freedom, how can a person be liberated?

Bowen's goals for therapy address this very issue. They are "to take [the individual] a microscopic step toward a better level of differentiation" (1985a, 371)—a move along the continuum—and to convert what begins as fugue into healthy independence. The latter is really a conversion of a pathogenic triangle to a therapeutic one. Such a change often results from a crisis situation. In crisis, some people disintegrate. Others go on to health but must "grow up" to do so. In Hagar's fugue in Genesis 16, an angel appears and tells her to go back and submit to Sarah and her son will prosper. She returns with a view toward fulfilling God's purpose thus announced, which may indicate a positive move along the continuum. In what may be another such move, when she is sent away, a second angel tells her that God has heard her distress and will make the boy into a great nation (21:17–18). Hagar sees a spring and is saved from dying of thirst and seeing her son die.

It is noteworthy that in both cases Hagar takes responsibility for her life, deliberately returning in the first case and providing for her son in the second. It may be that this story is a rudimentary account of a woman's progressive move toward greater differentiation. In this case, religious experience gives her perspective and courage, and God's grace helps her both to live and to develop emotionally. So there is a psychological adjustment that would probably only have taken place out of dire necessity. Also there is the work of the Spirit giving her not only an uplift but an anchor for her life—a stable, therapeutic triangle with God at its pinnacle.

The Task

The concepts of differentiation, triangles, and fugue can provide insight into the Bible beyond the stories of patriarchal families, however. They can aid in interpretation even beyond the religious "family systems" mentioned above. To show this, we have chosen the parable of the Prodigal Son because it contains a family story but also because it contains something else—a structure that is intended specifically to put the reader in relationship with the storyteller. In this text, there are actually not one but two systems to consider: the system of the people within the text, and the system that connects the reader with the story and the storyteller.

We now turn to the analysis of the story of the Prodigal Son in Luke 15. Here, two events will be demonstrated:[2] (1) the Prodigal and his family moving along Bowen's continuum of differentiation; and (2) the way such a story invites and prompts the reader to move along an analogous continuum. This and the analysis of Galatians 1–2 will serve to demonstrate the versatility of Bowen theory as hermeneutic.

Bowen Theory Analysis of the Narrative of the Prodigal (Luke 15)

Triangles in the Story of the Prodigal

In the text, we can identify triangles simply by noting the people and "significant others" who are mentioned in relation to each other. The parable of the Prodigal begins (Luke 15:11, NRSV): "There was a man who had two sons." So the first triangle is: *Father, Son1, Son2.* There is also another triangle implicit in the situation: *Son2, Family, Judaism (religious practice).* This triangle is significant because the son's familial and religious identity cannot be separated out and both are about to be challenged together. The narrative continues (verse

12): "The younger of them said to his father, 'Father, give me the share of the property that will belong to me.' So he divided his property between them." Now we have: *Father, Son1, Inheritance1* and *Father, Son2, Inheritance2*.

The next event is the first "fugue" in the story (verse 13a): "A few days later the younger son gathered all he had and traveled to a distant country." (There is a second fugue, but it is not yet evident in the text.) A critical point is that the younger son's level of differentiation can be inferred from what he is said to have done. According to Bowen, level of differentiation is largely determined by the time a person attempts a life of his own. It is in the nature of fugue that the person who engages in such flight—here the Prodigal—is inclined to impulsive behavior; running away from parents is a prime example. (Note that it is not necessary that he leave secretly or quickly to be engaged in this kind of "running away.") The younger son's action fits Bowen's definition of the geographic fugue. The fugue predicts a low level of differentiation in the Prodigal as well as an unresolved attachment, evidently to the father.

The fugue stretches the triangle in relation to his family:

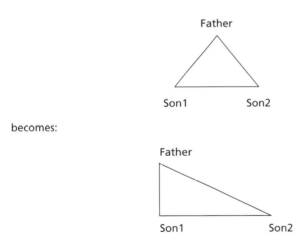

Thus, the younger son has fled the family but not his connection (triangle) with it, as the remainder of the story demonstrates.

The Crisis

In verses 13–14, the anxiety level is raised by the addition of two physical stressors, poverty and famine: "He squandered his property in dissolute living. When he had spent everything, a severe famine took place throughout that country, and he began to be in need." The question is whether increased anxiety will drive the younger son further toward the low end of the differentiation continuum. Alternatively, he may begin to use reason in lieu of emotion-driven reaction. If reason prevails, it may lead to a fundamental change to a higher level of differentiation. The text shows that at first, the Prodigal's efforts to supply his needs are ineffectual, and lower differentiation is a distinct possibility (verses 15–16): "So he went and hired himself out to one of the citizens of that country, who sent him to his fields to feed the pigs. He would gladly have filled himself with the pods that the pigs were eating; and no one gave him anything." The text does not say that he does not eat the pigs' food, or that something happens to make it unnecessary. He is still considering it.

There is another source of stress as well. Religious practice must, in this context, be a controlling factor in his willingness to accept certain solutions. This element seems small to the modern reader, but to the original audience of the parable it is an obvious identity determinant. The Old Testament makes clear the Jews' revulsion toward anything that had come into contact with pigs. Such things were ritually unclean, and a person who was so unclean could not come into contact with others without making them unclean as well. (Of course, in the narrative, it is assumed that the father and sons are Jews.[3]) This matter of eating is therefore a significant element of the narrative of the Prodigal—so religiously significant that it does not need to be stated for the first-century audience.

The Move Along the Continuum

At this point in the text, the Prodigal arrives at the defining moment of his life. Verses 17–20a begin: "But when he came to himself . . ." According to Derrett (1967, 65), "came to himself" means he has "grown up." Is this an increase in differentiation? The text continues, ". . . he said, 'How many of my father's hired hands have bread enough and to spare, but here I am dying of hunger! I will get up and go to my father, and I will say to him, "Father, I have sinned against heaven and before you; I am no longer worthy to be called your son; treat me like one of your hired hands."' So he set off and went to his father." (Note the acknowledged triangle: *Son2, Father, [Father in] Heaven*.)

This decision does in fact represent an increase in self differentiation. Look at the way Bowen spins out the nature of the change: at the moment of positive movement along the continuum, long-term gain begins to be deemed worth the effort. The person uses his convictions to overrule the emotional system in situations of anxiety and panic. He is able to evaluate himself more accurately in relation to others without the pretend postures that result in overvaluing or undervaluing himself. In this case, the Prodigal becomes free to go back, despite all that it might cost him in humiliation, because he has weighed the effects of staying or leaving physically (and religiously). He has set aside his former arrogance; he does so because he is otherwise literally faced with death.

For the Prodigal, the situation in which his emotions dominate is inherently unstable and leads to starvation, but when he lets his conviction dominate, he moves to an inherently stable position—not just because he is going to be fed but because he has resolved his emotional dis-ease with the father. The fugue is over and the toxic emotional sides of the triangle are now just the positive connection between father, son, and heaven. Starvation is replaced by nurture in several senses:

Inheritance

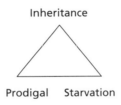

Prodigal   Starvation

becomes:

Guarantee of a different type:

Heaven

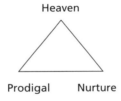

Prodigal   Nurture

This is the conversion of fugue into healthy distance that Bowen holds as the object of the therapeutic triangle.

A New Crisis

His return, however, leads to a new crisis. According to Bowen, when one family member comes to a better level of differentiation, then other family members take steps in reaction to this development. Family members' individual reactions may be either positive or negative. As the text continues, it illustrates both. In verse 20b: "While he was still far off, his father saw him and was filled with compassion; he ran and put his arms around him and kissed him." Thus, the father physically demonstrates his acceptance of the Prodigal. His welcome is followed by the Prodigal's confession (verse 21) and the father's gifts to him (verses 22–24). As a result, one of the original triangles is restored— the father, the Prodigal, and the Prodigal's spent inheritance. The last element of this triangle is indeed spiritually and psychologically present; its physical absence dominates the action in the narrative. This restored triangle is effectively noted, in past tense, in verse 27, when a servant tells the older brother: "Your brother has come, and your father has killed the fatted calf, because he has got him back safe and sound."

Father, Son2, Missing Inheritance and *Father, Son1, Inheritance1* should now resolve to a primary pattern of *Father, Son1, Son2*. Physically, the family is back together, or so it seems. However, there is a complication, predicted by Bowen. In any such family group, the inertia against even healthy change is so strong "that any small step toward differentiation is met with vigorous disapproval" (1985a, 371). Such "vigorous disapproval" is manifest in verses 29–30 when the older son says, "Listen! For all these years I have been working like a slave for you, and I have never disobeyed. . . . But when this son of yours . . ." "Yours" is an explicit disavowal of the older son's apparent closeness in the triangle with the father and younger son.[4]

Thus, there is a new dilemma. The obvious triangle representing resolution—the one the narrative has led the reader to expect—is not to be (verse 28): "Then [the older son] . . . became angry and refused to go in." The father acknowledges one triangle that he believes to be in a healthy degree of closeness (verse 31): "Son, you are always with me, and all that is mine is yours" (that is, the triangle *Father, Son1, Inheritance1*). He pleads for restoration with the younger son. He also contradicts the older son's disavowal with the pointed phrase, "this brother of yours" (verses 28 and 32): "His father came out and began to plead with him . . . 'this brother of yours was dead and has come to life; he was lost and has been found'."

However, the older son has himself been engaged in fugue, only now manifested. There must have been an emotional distance between brothers before the story began; it was converted by the fugue into a physical distance, but that is now gone. The distance remains, although it is now converted again into an emotional distance—in the form of a sharp discomfort with the renewed closeness. The emotional distance quickly converts to a physical distance again as the older son— despite his father's pleas—keeps himself apart. With this, the narrative ends—that is, it ends on the surface.

The Reader as Part of the Story

There is, however, a larger system that must be taken into account—
that of narrator, story, and reader:

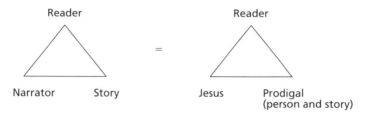

Reader   Reader

=

Narrator   Story   Jesus   Prodigal
                                                (person and story)

Considering this wider relationship in systems terms yields an
insight into the text that is of some importance to Bible scholars. That
is, whether the story was intended to end in this way or whether it is
a fragment. As the narrative "ends" without a satisfying ending, the
reader feels a sharp emotional cutoff (to return to Bowen's term).
Although it is an artifact of the text—or, perhaps, the art of the writer—
it is as if the narrator has fled from the reader, leaving unresolved tensions. Because the reader cannot know what would have happened
next in the narrative, there is neither literary nor emotional resolution. This felt lack has led many Bible commentators to the assumption that something is actually missing from the text.

Another way to express the sense of absence is that the narrative
itself forms a triangle. The first corner is the Prodigal's fugue. The
second is the Prodigal's return and the older son's fugue. The implication is that there is a third corner—a resolution narrative, withheld
by the narrator. It exerts emotional pressure on the reader until the
reader supplies it. If this view is correct, the older son's fugue is not
the final ending. How can such an assumption be justified? In this
case, the absence of resolution has a clear function. This is one of the
parables of Jesus, intended to create a change of heart in the reader.
The reader is to distance himself from the pseudo-faithful older son
and identify with the ultimately faithful Prodigal. The third corner of
the triangle can be supplied, along with a sense of resolution, as the
reader himself resolves to be more like the younger son. A moment of
crisis (the sense of something missing—a hunger!) thus produces in
the reader a situation analogous to the Prodigal's crisis. The reader
has been set up potentially to be propelled along the continuum to a
higher level of differentiation.

This type of resolution for the narrative correlates with a number of
significant interpretations of this text (for example, Derrett, 1967; Sanders, 1969, 433–438). These scholars see the older son as a metaphor for

ancient Judaism and the younger one for the Gentiles (pagans) who were seen as unworthy of inheriting the kingdom of God. They suggest that the message of this text is that even the unworthy and ungodly can be welcomed into the kingdom by the Father in heaven, just as if they were God's own honored children. Reading this, Gentiles would then know that they were acceptable to God and Jews would know that they should honor the Gentile believers when they come to God's house. The text in effect then *creates communion* among God's different children—making them one by virtue of God—instead of a collection of very different classes or races.

What is interesting to the scholar is this: if this is the intent of the narrative, then Luke must have intended the unfinished triangle that propels the reader into commitment to the Lord. Thus, the "incompleteness" itself is the proof that what we have here is the original form of the text. This would be an important discovery and an extraordinary view into the text and its author. Therefore, Bowen's systems approach to the family—extended to the family of faith—substantiates one important interpretation of this text and further empowers the reader and the scholar in understanding the Scriptures.

Bowen theory has also articulated some of the earthly means by which the text draws the reader into relationship with the storyteller Jesus. It does so by telling him the story, then by prompting him to identify with the Prodigal, then by providing the fertile ground for the reader to choose relationship with the Father in heaven as a resolution to the story. If the reader remains in the triangle with Jesus long enough, he has thereby added to the communion of saints.

Galatians 1–2: The Christian as Differentiated Self

Bowen Theory: The Conforming Disciple

We now turn to an analysis of Galatians 1–2. We first describe a concept that will prove central to this text: that of the conforming disciple. The summary of the concept of the pseudoself and the solid self that leads into it may be supplemented by reference to Volume 1, Chapter 10.

In a "fused" person, the feeling system dominates the intellectual and life decisions and relationships are emotion driven. Bowen calls this the dominance of the *pseudoself.* The healthy balance of the intellectual system with emotion—differentiation—is evidence of the dominance of the *solid self.* The pseudoself and the solid self are both aspects of every individual. The person who is governed more by the solid self is more independent of the emotionality of others even in highly charged situations but is still free to participate in the emotional. This person's goals, therefore, are determined from within rather than by social pressure—often a characteristic of a leader in the community. The chief characteristics of the person who is dominated by the solid self include a set of clearly defined beliefs, arrived at by careful consideration and deliberate choice, and consistent with one another, that enable the person to take responsibility for the self and for the consequences of his beliefs.

A notable manifestation of "fusion" (domination by the pseudoself) is the "conforming disciple." Under pressure from the group of which he is a member, in a moment of anxiety, a person tends to move lower on the continuum. The conforming disciple goes further in his reaction; he takes refuge in statements such as "the rule says . . ." The group's rules will prevail, even to the extent that the individual reverses a position of conviction. Such reversals reflect "relationship-oriented energy that goes back and forth on the same point" (Bowen, 1985a, 342), offering no constructive alternative.

At the same time, as anxiety increases, the parties will withdraw from relationships outside of the system (or perceived to be so). The result is maximum pressure on the group members who are least differentiated and ever stricter boundaries defining the group. In the analysis that follows, Peter is portrayed as a conforming disciple. The Galatians are urged not to be like him.

Analysis of the Passage:[5] Introduction

The Players

In Galatians, there are at least three sets of "players." Paul, the author, was a Jew of high religious pedigree who was converted to belief in Jesus. In Galatians 1, he tells how God commissioned him to preach the Gospel of Jesus Christ. (Other accounts of his conversion experience on the road to Damascus can be found at Acts 9:1–19, 22:3–21, and 26:12–18.) In the middle of the first century, believers in Jesus were mostly Jews and did not necessarily cease Jewish religious practice. For instance, Acts 21 tells us that Paul continued to purify himself ritually so that he could make offerings in the temple in Jerusalem.

The second "player" is the Galatians, Greek-speaking Gentiles (pagans who had never been Jews) whom Paul has converted to Christianity. The third is a group of Jewish missionaries who have come after Paul and taught a "different gospel" (Gal. 1:6).[6] The purpose of the letter is to deny this counterfeit message and urge the Galatians to follow the Gospel they received from Paul—recalling the gift of the Holy Spirit they received with it.

The Positions

According to the other missionaries, to be saved as Christians the Gentiles must also adopt practices that specifically define Jews as Jews. These practices included particularly the law against Jews eating with Gentiles (converted or not!) and circumcision. In other words, the Gentiles would have to be circumcised, and thus become Jews, so that they could have fellowship with other Jews who believed in Jesus. Since, like Paul, the first Christians continued their Jewish customs, such practices made sense to those missionaries. What constitutes Christian faith and practice for Gentiles, however, was a new question that the church was confronting at the time of the letter.

Paul's basic contention was that all are one in Christ (Gal. 3:28, 5:6, 6:15), and so such divisions are set aside—a proposition that had apparently been accepted by some Jewish Christians, particularly Peter, who ate with the Gentiles (Gal. 2:12; cf. Acts 10). For Paul, a Gentile could become a Christian without becoming a Jew first. God now had two "children"—the circumcision and the uncircumcision. They were equal in the Spirit and in salvation and should have fellowship together. Paul's stance was evidently not easily understood by the original groups of Gentiles and Jews, however, and continues as a source of misunderstanding in Bible interpretation today.

At stake for the first-century reader is one's very ability to relate to God. For instance, the ability to participate in the temple worship depended upon such observances. Who exactly is God's child? (Hence the statement in John 1:12 that the reader has power to become the child of God through belief in Jesus.) Thus, the principal issue is one of religious belonging or identity. That Paul's purpose is indeed one of achieving a new type of religious identity is made unambiguous in the resounding conclusion of Galatians 1 (verses 20–21): "I have been crucified with Christ and I no longer live, but Christ lives in me. The life I live in the body, I live by faith in the Son of God" (cf. 6:15).

The particular argument Paul uses is interesting from Bowen's point of view: he says that if social pressure is the only reason for such observances, they are hypocritical (for example, 2:4, 11–13). In fact, the necessity of religious practice being self- and God-directed is stated in Galatians 1:10–2:15 no fewer than twenty-five times. Self-directedness (and Christ-directedness) must therefore be central—a fact that has received little or no attention in the scholarly literature.[7]

The Approach

In Galatians 1:10–2:15, Paul uses himself and Peter as examples of appropriate versus inappropriate Christian identity-related behavior. This text sets the tone for the entire letter and reverberates particularly in Paul's direct instruction to the Galatians (3:1–5; cf. 5:1–6) and in the conclusion of the letter (particularly 6:11–15). In the course of the argument, his descriptions of genuineness (himself) versus hypocrisy (Peter) bear striking resemblance to Bowen's solid self versus pseudoself. Analyzing these verses in Bowen's terms provides insight into Paul's purpose. It also demonstrates the way in which these characteristics of family systems function in a religious setting. If it can be shown that Galatians 1–2 is in fact central to the purpose of the entire letter, our argument will contribute to the solution of a long-standing problem of interpretation.[8]

A Caution

One caution: Paul is not propounding a modern concept of individualism. Rather, the premise is that the message of faith in Christ may be known directly from God by many people and that this direct connection is the appropriate source of religious identity. It is most important to realize that what is known directly is tested against the Gospel of Christ crucified and risen, the Gospel shared by the main body of the believers. This is why Paul can so vigorously defend what he received directly from Christ and also claim that his Gospel was deemed acceptable by the Jerusalem church. His Gospel and theirs are the same. There is no cult forming here. The "different gospel" is rejected for this very reason.

Most of all, this analysis shows what, for Paul, constitutes a faith life that is true to self and God. Notice that while Bowen does not address issues of relationship with God, inner guidance, or mystical experience, these aspects of spirituality enter into the way the self directs its decisions, actions, and relationships. For this reason, we can use Bowen theory to talk about Paul's self-direction—self-direction to remain under the dominion of the Christ who appeared to him.

A Threefold Structure, and a Negative Example

In his instruction to the Galatians, Paul illustrates healthy identity in Christ three times over, supplemented by one striking negative example. The three examples of healthy functioning come from three aspects of Paul's call, all discussed in Galatians 1–2: the way in which the call came (1:10–24) and Paul's self-directedness; the deliberateness of his choice between religious identities (1:13–14, 1:23); and the relationship between his call and that of the Jerusalem apostles (2:1–10).

Paul's Self-Directedness

The first part begins as Galatians 1:10a,b announces the point upon which the argument will turn. We regard seeking to please God rather than people as evidence of self-directedness. Self-directed actions, their sources, and results are italicized to clarify the structure of the argument:

1. (10a) Am I now seeking human approval,
2. (10b) or God's approval?

The verse goes on to give the significance of the opposition—that serving Christ hangs upon it—and also states the negative pole of the opposition twice for emphasis. Verse 10c,d,e parallels 10a,b, a form of emphasis:

3. (10c) Or am I trying to please people?
4. (10d) If I were still pleasing people,
5. (10e) I would not be *a servant of Christ.*

The issue, stated in Bowen's terms, is as follows: am I directed more by the solid self or more by the pseudoself? Verses 11–12 answer the question:

6. (11) . . . the gospel that was proclaimed by me is not of human origin
7. (12a) for I did not receive it from a human source
8. (12b) nor was I taught it,
9. (12c) but I received it through a revelation of Jesus Christ.

In verses 15–17, Paul reverses the order, restating God's call as opposed to people's bidding:

10. (15a) But when God, who had set me apart before I was born
11. (15b) and called me through his grace,
12. (16a) was pleased to reveal his Son to me,
13. (16b) so that I might proclaim him among the Gentiles,
14. (16c) I did not confer with any human being,
15. (17) nor did I go up to Jerusalem to those who were already apostles before me . . .

Thus, God has acted in three ways (set apart, called, revealed) to create in Paul the ability and purpose of proclaiming his new faith in

Christ—involving no earthly person's influence. Verse 17 concludes with Paul going to Arabia and returning to Damascus—literally, going his own way. Finally, in verses 18–19, Paul acknowledges one connection with other Christian leaders, accompanied by heavy reservations: "Then after three years I did go up to Jerusalem to visit Cephas . . . but I did not see any other apostle except James . . ." The whole passage concludes with one of Paul's rare but pointed personal attestations, verse 20 (cf. 6:11): "In what I am writing to you, before God, I do not lie!"

Paul's Deliberate Choice

The entire section concerning the actual call (verses 15–20) is bracketed by verses 13–14 and 23, which contain three references to his (former) life in traditional Judaism and three phrases describing his former attitude toward Christians:

Traditional Judaism:

16. (13a) You have heard, no doubt, of my earlier life in Judaism . . .
17. (14a) I advanced in Judaism beyond many among my people of the same age,
18. (14b) for I was more zealous for the traditions of my ancestors.

Former attitude toward Christianity:

19. (13b) I was violently persecuting the church of God and was trying to destroy it.
20. (23) [Other churches of Judea] only heard it said, "The one who formerly was persecuting us is now proclaiming the faith he once tried to destroy."

Thus, Paul has made a decisive choice between two sets of religious life principles and has taken responsibility for his beliefs—two of the characteristics of Bowenian differentiation. Whether he actually moved along the differentiation continuum at this juncture cannot be known solely from a text. However, his already deep level of conviction and ability to act upon it were unchanged. Only the direction of his commitment changed (albeit dramatically). It is possible that the experience on the road to Damascus, which brought about this change, was in its human aspect a manifestation of an already highly integrated personality.

Relation to the Jerusalem Apostles' Call

On the third aspect of his call, Paul writes (2:2), "I went up [to Jerusalem] in response to a revelation" and laid out "the gospel that I proclaim to the Gentiles"—but only privately, to the inner circle of "acknowledged leaders." Verse 2:6 continues the theme of Paul's independence: "those leaders contributed nothing to me."

Why, then, did he go to Jerusalem at all? He went (verse 2) "in order to make sure that I was not running, or had not run, in vain." According to Martyn (1997, 192–193), this was an attempt to show that the church was not fragmented but was greater than the divisions created by traditional religious boundaries. In other words, Martyn supports the idea that the issue is one of identity and of what we might call family boundaries. The Jerusalem apostles validated Paul's call and thereby incorporated it (and his mission to the Gentiles) into the church at its original center. This part of the letter thus goes further than Galatians 1, stating that his call has won affirmation by the authorities of the original family of faith.

Now Paul makes four separate statements (Gal. 2:7–9) that are remarkable. They assert that God had endorsed two different but equal Christian missions—different specifically in the religious practices they deemed acceptable. In the verses describing these, those describing Paul's mission are underlined:

21. (7) . . . when they saw that *I had been entrusted with the gospel for the uncircumcised,* just as Peter had been entrusted with the gospel for the circumcised

22. (8) (for he who worked through Peter making him an apostle to the circumcised *also worked through me in sending me to the Gentiles*),

23. (9a) and when James and Cephas [i.e., Peter] and John, who were acknowledged pillars, *recognized the grace that had been given to me* [i.e., by God],

24. (9b) they gave . . . the right hand of fellowship, agreeing that *we should go to the Gentiles* and they to the circumcised.

The equality-cum-independence of his call allows him then to assert that he need not require Jewish practice or initiation rites of his Gentile converts. He further escalates this aspect of his argument (verses 3–5), pointing out that he did not submit "even for a moment" to any "false believers," that is, those who tried to force Gentiles to follow Jewish law (specifically his Greek Gentile companion Titus). So finally the independence of his call is seen to provide for a specifically non-Jewish Christian mission. He has thereby drawn a new boundary among religious identities.

The Decision about Religious Identity

This brings us to a question that is of great interest to Bible scholars. Acts 15 records the Council of Jerusalem, in which Paul, Peter, and the disciples deal with the same problem as that of Galatians: some missionaries have claimed that no one can be saved unless they are circumcised. The apostles finally decide that the Gentiles do not have to be circumcised. They are asked only to refrain from sexual immorality and from eating meat sacrificed to idols, blood, and animals that have been strangled. No other Jewish cultic practices are necessary for them to be saved as Christians. Some scholars think that the meeting recorded in Galatians 2 is this same council; but if so, then why is the issue of Jewish observance still in dispute? If not, then Paul fights the same battle in two places.

This raises another issue of interest to our study, however. Acts 15 and Galatians 2 both articulate these new religious "family" boundaries. If Galatians was written first, this text represents the first time that religious authorities officially recognized the new religious identity groups. If Acts was written first, Galatians is the earliest textual evidence of the application of these new boundaries. In this historical context, the issue of differentiation by Paul and by his family of followers is of extraordinary importance. We are seeing a process of differentiation, in various senses, taking place before our eyes, as it were. In it, Paul is urging a high degree of personal psychological differentiation in the believers—enough to withstand a very strident social and cultural resistance from Jewish Christians and possibly from Gentiles as well.

The Place of Jewish Observance

The theological underpinnings of his argument are not new, however. Paul justifies his stance on the issue of the Gentiles' salvation, paradoxically, on the basis of Judaism itself (Gal. 2:15–16): "We ourselves are Jews by birth and not Gentile sinners; yet we know that a person is justified not by the works of the law . . . because no one will be justified by the works of the law." Under Judaism, one is justified by faith. Following the law is the response of the (Jewish) faithful to God; hence Paul's frequent quote of Habakkuk 2:4 (for example, Gal. 3:11). The argument is that for everyone (Jewish and Gentile), salvation is by faith.

He thus reduces the use of the identity-defining Jewish laws—for Gentiles—to human convention. Observance of them is not hypocritical for someone who was born to the Law of Moses; they are free to remain in the station in which God had put them. But for Gentiles, and for Jewish Christians who are doing these observances specifically because of pressure to conform to the ways of people, it is nothing more than hypocrisy and a denial of the power of Christ in their lives. Christ himself is sufficient for their salvation.

In Bowen's terms, Paul is condemning religious practice that demonstrates the dominance of the pseudoself.

The Negative Example: Peter's Hypocrisy

All Paul needs now to make his point is a short, sharp contrast, and for that purpose he provides the example of Peter ("Cephas" in Hebrew). Here Paul refers to an earlier incident that had occurred in Antioch—another primarily Gentile city where there was a thriving new Christian community under the influence of Jewish Christian missionaries. He refers here to James, the leader of the Jewish Christians in Jerusalem. Some of the Jerusalem Christians were referred to as the "circumcision faction" because of their conservative stand on Jewish law. Galatians 2:11–14 says:

> But when Cephas came to Antioch, I opposed him to his face, because he stood self-condemned; for until certain people came from James, he used to eat with the Gentiles. But after they came, he drew back and kept himself separate for fear of the circumcision faction. And the other Jews joined him in this hypocrisy, so that even Barnabas was led astray by their hypocrisy.

Paul's point is that Peter was not acting from a consistent reference point, a position of conscience. Peter was being undifferentiated! Incidentally, nothing in the letter indicates that Peter could not have kept to the usual Jewish custom of eating apart from Gentiles—provided that it was his consistent position. Such was not the case, however. Like Bowen's conforming disciple, he is implicitly citing the Jewish group's law, and he is evidently going back and forth under the prevailing social pressure. The pseudoself took precedence in Peter and others as soon as a situation of conflict (and increased anxiety) arose.

The terms "hypocrisy" (used twice), "fear," "not acting consistently," and "self-condemned" make it clear that Paul equates Peter's actions essentially with the opposite of God's call. Paul could not have made clearer that the religious position that withstands social pressure—the one dominated by the solid self—is the one to which his converts are called. He is challenging them to a healthy faith and religious life—albeit at the cost of intense social and political pressure such as Peter faced.

Paul's Challenge to the Galatians

In the challenge to the Galatians that follows (3:1–5), Paul asks the Galatians to choose the newly defined religious identity as Christians and reject the boundary of Jew versus non-Jew (cf. 3:28, "there is . . . neither Jew nor Greek . . . for you are all one in Christ"). He therefore applies to their situation the dichotomy between "works of the [Jewish] law" (now equated with social pressure) and the self-directed (Spirit-directed) position. In quoting the challenge, we have italicized the self-directed behavior to highlight their alternatives:

> You foolish Galatians! Who has bewitched you? . . . The only thing I want to learn from you is this: Did you receive the Spirit by doing the works of the law or *by believing what you heard?* Are you so foolish? *Having started with the Spirit,* are you now ending with the flesh? Did you experience so much for nothing?. . . Well then, does God supply you with the Spirit and work miracles among you by your doing the works of the law, or *by your believing what you heard?*

Paul even makes the point (6:12–13) that those who are compelling the Galatians to follow Jewish law are doing it only because of social pressure (persecution, on the one hand, and commendation from their fellow missionaries, on the other). They are as hypocritical as Peter because they do not even value the law for itself or from the heart.

In the chapters between 3:5 and the conclusion, Paul goes on to several arguments about the relative place of faith versus law; the many issues raised there are outside the scope of this chapter. However, he makes clear that wherever obedience to the law is a slavery (i.e., imposed from outside, by human social pressure) it is the opposite of the Spirit (or Christ) living within the believer. He writes, for example, "This persuasion [to be circumcised] is not from him who calls you [i.e., Christ]" (5:8). Hence his summary: "In Christ Jesus neither circumcision not uncircumcision is of any avail, but faith working through love" (5:6). The conclusion of the entire letter reinforces 5:6: "For neither circumcision nor uncircumcision is anything; but a new creation is everything!" (6:15).

Paul is not, of course, doing therapy with the Galatians. He is telling them that, in the situation of increased religious-social pressure (and increased anxiety), they must not succumb to fear and conformity as

Peter had. They must rely on their God-given sense of themselves as a wholly new creation and then live in the new religious identity. Hence, the entire letter centers upon the direction of the self, as opposed to socially imposed custom.

Galatians 1–2 is thus far more than a defense of Paul's status; indeed, it forms a powerful basis for the rest of the letter—supporting arguments made by Gaventa (1986) and Dunn (1997). In Bowen's terms, Paul has composed a substantial argument in favor of religious practice that comes primarily from the solid self rather than from the pseudoself.

Paul and the Reader

In the challenge to the Galatians, Paul is of course appealing directly to his reader—ancient and modern. Here is where the concept of the triangle becomes useful. Look what Paul has said so far. Superficially, Paul is caught between two sets of believers:

Paul

Galatians   Missionaries

This is an anxious system and Paul's emotion in it is very evident (for example, in 5:12). However, his principles remain and he is undaunted in his zeal for the one Gospel. Where does his consistency and his strength come from? The answer is that the triangles really look like this:

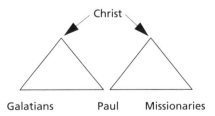

Christ

Galatians   Paul   Missionaries

Paul displaces his anxiety onto Christ, and being thus in touch with his source of strength, he remains in a very stable triangle with Christ and his believers, the Galatians. Even though there is a great deal of insistence and therefore apparent defensiveness in Paul's argument, the ultimate stability of the relationship is shown by the very fact of this epistle. Paul won the argument and kept his disciples.

Christ in the triangle is the Christ who saves without demanding religious observances (see 2:21, 3:4; if salvation depends upon these things, your faith and Christ's sacrifice are for nothing). Building on this, Paul has shown how unstable, indeed toxic, is the triangle that does not include this Christ. Look what happened to Peter:

The anxiety created by the missionaries from James had to be displaced, and he displaced it onto the Gentiles by separating from them rudely and leaving the relationship unresolved. It has resulted in a fugue:

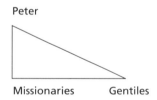

and consequently another fugue:

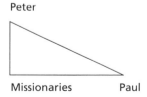

The reader can feel the tension in the unresolved relationships with the Gentiles and with Paul, particularly when Paul has named the cause of the tension as hypocrisy. Therefore, Paul is saying to the reader, do not be like Peter and others who have put themselves in this unstable and unfaithful position. Be like me, in the triangle with the

Christ of my own conversion; you are already in it, because he has spoken to you through me and now also through the Spirit:

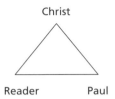

The anxiety you feel is created in you by these missionaries (that is, by human pressure). Displace it to Christ, who already gave himself for our pain (1:3–4). This is the dependable relationship that cannot fail you. You have seen by my example just how effective and powerful it is.

This message he gives almost by osmosis as he demonstrates that that is what his relationship with Christ has been for him. Thus, there is an emotional appeal to the reader that is not contained solely in emotional wording but is inherent in the triangles represented by the text. For all of this, however, the argument is highly intellectual compared with a text like the parable. Paul appeals to the reader to see how eminently reasonable is faith in Christ and how unreasonable is anyone who adds to it for his own power or prestige or other attempted gain. He bids the reader to take responsibility to stay in that stable triangle with himself and Christ.

He thus urges the reader to a highly differentiated position in two ways. He tells the reader how to be differentiated in this situation. And he treats the reader as a differentiated person, already possessing the capacity (in the power of the Spirit) to make a considered choice and be consistent in keeping it.

In conclusion, Bible scholars have traditionally contended that in Galatians, Paul makes a simple choice against Judaism and for Christianity. In contrast, Martyn (1990) contends that the letter is not about Judaism per se at all but is about two ways of birthing a new Christian family (community). The Bowenian view of the text is consistent with the latter. The two ways are through (manmade) observances or through conviction about Jesus only. More than one-third of the letter is deliberately constructed to make his point about the necessity of acting out of conviction. In his argument, he uses three kinds of examples: (1) a call strictly from God (not people); (2) a call (affirmation) ultimately from God but coming through the Jerusalem apostles; (3)

a "call" (Peter's) arising from people only. These represent a continuum from best to worst and clearly, by example, suggest ways to a healthy Gentile Christian church (or any healthy family of faith).

This then also implies that anyone can hear and be faithful to God's call. The human contribution to the action of the Spirit in guiding one's life is not one's social "worthiness" but rather an increasingly healthy balance of emotion and intellect—movement toward Bowen's solid self.

Conclusion

In what way has Bowen theory contributed to our understanding of the Prodigal Son and of Galatians? When we speak of the text as communion, we mean that the text is an earthly and spiritual instrument by which a reader is brought into relationship with Jesus and with the body of believers. The psychological structures of the text help to bring about an ever self-replicating triangle: the text, the reader, and the Lord; the text, the reader, and the next reader, and the next . . . with the Lord. It shapes a community not only around itself but through its internal dynamics and through the person of Christ who is always meant to be the head of the triangle—and whose very nature is to be one of the corners of a triangle that is the Trinity. We have in the end a theory of interpretation that is incarnational—because it embodies the work of Christ, drawing the reader to himself—and that is also Trinitarian in its very essence. Bowen might not have approved. But then, he did say that all relationships embody these structures. Why should we begin now to exclude the relationship with the head of the family himself?

Notes

1. In Volume 1, Chapter 10, Bowen theory was introduced with reference to several Bible texts, culminating with John 9. In this chapter, we look further at the power of Bowen theory as hermeneutic, addressing two kinds of texts that we did not use in the previous chapter: a parable and a hortatory text urging the reader to right Christian faith.

This chapter goes deeper into Bowen theory to explore the central concept of differentiation of self among the family of faith. The introduction recapitulates briefly the basics of Bowen theory given there. Then, we present further material on the psychological fugue in preparation for the analysis of

Luke 15. An analysis of Galatians 1–2 follows, applying the concept of the "conforming disciple" to Peter's "hypocritical" behavior.

2. Derrett (1967) makes explicit many of the family interactions put here in Bowen's terms. He spends a great deal of time on, particularly, the effect of sibling position without any apparent knowledge of Bowen.

3. There is not space here to go into detail; but, for example, in the two centuries just before the writing of the narrative of the Prodigal, an identity-determining event for the entire Jewish people was recorded in 2 Maccabees 7. In that account, taken to be historical, a mother and her seven sons were tortured and killed because they would not eat pork or transgress the food laws in any way. These eating practices, along with circumcision, were the ways in which Jews defined themselves as Jews and as separate from the pagans. Therefore, these very laws were the points at which the pagan rulers of Palestine attacked the Jews to gain control over them.

4. Jeremias (1972) and Derrett (1967) both write that the older son's phrase "this son of yours" is a family-distancing move. Derrett (1967) notes that this was recognized by some ancient interpreters as well.

5. This analysis must of course be limited in scope. For instance, we address issues of religious identity (Jewish Christians vs. Gentile Christians); research on the relations between the Jews and Gentiles in the New Testament is so abundant that it cannot be addressed here. We are also limited to Paul's (human) behavior, including his description of Christ's action in his life. However, God's action in the life of a believer is taken to be an objective reality, occurring alongside the person's behavior. We also cannot address whether Paul represents himself and Peter with historical accuracy. The analysis here deals solely with his text as it stands. It follows one strand of Paul's argument that has to date been addressed only in passing by Bible scholars. Its object is to discern Paul's intended message and its implications for a healthy religious identity, using a framework based upon Bowen theory.

6. One identity group Paul never addresses in Galatians—unlike the later letter to the Romans—is non-Christian Jews. Thus, in interpreting its statements concerning religious practice, the reader cannot simply assign Paul's criticisms to Judaism per se. For example, Paul's attribution of hypocrisy (twice in 2:13) is made specifically against Jewish Christians, not against Jewish practice in itself. Thus, Paul is not in fact writing about Judaism at all but about how to achieve a healthy Christian identity—a point that bears upon the interpretation of the entire letter.

7. However, this conclusion is consistent with the work of a small number of important New Testament scholars (for example, Gaventa, 1986).

8. Traditionally, Paul's conversion as represented in Galatians 1–2 has been regarded as tangential to the purpose of the letter, serving only to defend Paul's status as an apostle before he attempts to persuade the Galatians of his own Gospel. However, recent scholarship (for example, Gaventa, 1986; Dunn, 1997) shows that it is in fact paradigmatic for the entire text

References

Betz, H. D. (1979). *Galatians, a Commentary on Paul's Letter to the Churches in Galatia*, H. Koester, H. W. Attridge, A. Y. Collins, E. J. Epp, & J. M. Robinson, eds. Hermeneia Series. Philadelphia: Fortress Press.

Bowen, M. (1985a). Theory in the Practice of Psychotherapy. In *Family Therapy in Clinical Practice*. Northvale: Jason Aronson, 337–387.

Bowen, M. (1985b). Toward the Differentiation of Self in One's Family of Origin. In *Family Therapy in Clinical Practice*. Northvale: Jason Aronson, 529–547.

Derrett, J. D. M. (1967). Law in the New Testament: The Parable of the Prodigal Son. *New Testament Studies, 14*, 56–74.

Dunn, J. D. G. (1997). Paul's Conversion—a Light to Twentieth Century Disputes. In *Evangelium Schriftauslegung Kirche, Festschrift für Peter Stuhlmacher zum 65. Geburtstag*, J. Adna & S. J. Hafemann, eds. Göttingen, Germany: Vandenhoeck and Ruprecht, 77–93.

Gaventa, B. R. (1986). Galatians 1 and 2: Autobiography as Paradigm. *Novum Testamentum XXVIII*(4), 309–326.

Jensen, C. A. (2003). Toward Pastoral Counseling Integration: One Bowen Oriented Approach. *The Journal of Pastoral Care and Counseling, 57*(2), 117–129.

Jeremias, J. (1972). *The Parables of Jesus* (2nd rev. ed.). New York: Charles Scribner's Sons.

Martyn, J. L. (1990). The Covenants of Hagar and Sarah. In *Faith and History, Essays in Honor of Paul W. Meyer*, John T. Carroll, Charles H. Cosgrove, & E. Elizabeth Johnson, eds. Atlanta: Scholars Press, 160–192.

Martyn, J. L. (1997). *Galatians, a New Translation with Introduction and Commentary*, W. F. Albright & David N. Freedman, eds. *The Anchor Bible, 33A*. New York: Doubleday.

Rollins, W. G. (1993). Rationale and Agenda for a Psychological-Critical Approach to the Bible and Its Interpretation. Paper presented at the Society of Biblical Literature, Psychology and Biblical Studies Group, Washington, DC.

Sanders, J. T. (1969). Tradition of Redaction in Luke XV.11–32. *New Testament Studies, 15*, 433–438.

CHAPTER 11

Paul's Letter to the Galatians in Social-Psychological Perspective

Dieter Mitternacht

This study focuses on socio-religious contexts using a combination of epistolary-rhetorical and social-psychological analyses to shed some light on the crisis between Paul and his converts in Galatia.

From the very first lines of the letter to the Galatians, the reader senses Paul's strong need to expose and correct a serious deviation from the truth of the Gospel that he perceives at work subversively among the Galatian Christians. He appears agonized and enraged over their readiness to accept a different message and goes so far as to threaten them with loss of salvation.

Paul issues a sharp reprimand, fully aware that there will be extensive opposition to his corrective appeal. In fact, in what appears to be a well-designed rhetorical strategy, he tries, on the one hand, to demolish the addressees' resistance by denigrating their ability to discern what is best for them and accusing them of foolishness and of being bewitched (Gal. 3:1). On the positive side, he tries to change their cognition of what is best for them by appealing to the quality of their initial experiences as followers of the crucified Christ, reminding them of their mutual affection (4:12–21). In addition, throughout the letter, Paul inserts a series of reproaches against some people who are not among the addressees but who, from Paul's point of view, have deceived the Gentile Christ-believers in Galatia.

From the foregoing, it is clear that the letter to the Galatians provides an example of powerful communication dynamics. The dynamics are reflected both in conflicting cognitions within the letter and in its epistolary-rhetorical design. Having advanced himself as the only unwavering apostle of Jesus Christ, commissioned with the truth of the Gospel to the Gentiles (chapters 1 and 2), Paul proceeds with great rhetorical skill to expose their conflicting cognitions, reinforcing his argument with promises and threats that allow for only one reasonable and safe response: namely, to yield to his way of seeing things.

The rhetorical strategy of the letter is to compel the reader to agree that the turn of events in Galatia is incredible. How could this group of Christ-believers in Galatia choose or be advised to accept such an opposing point of view? What went on in their minds, indeed, what went on in their *lives* that would lead them to show such disregard for the truth of the Gospel (2:14)? On the other hand, one might ask whether the danger Paul perceived and portrayed so graphically was really so great. Both Peter and Barnabas seem to have chosen a course of action that is condemned by Paul (2:11–14), but neither in their case nor in that of the Galatians is there reason to assume that they had any intention of abandoning their faith in Christ. It appears that their choices did not seem as problematic from their perspectives as they did from Paul's. How could versions of faith in Christ be so different? What models or roles determined the self-perception of these different parties?

My quest for answers to these questions led me to investigate theories from social psychology that deal with incompatible social cognition based on schematic preferences, such as causal schemata and role schemata. Such theories may further our insights into the causes and motivations behind the arguments of the letter.

However, before such an investigation can be successfully pursued, the letter's epistolary-rhetorical design has to be examined. Thus, I begin with an analysis of the rhetorical strategy (communication psychology, if you wish) to establish an informed reading of the dynamics of the text.

The Crisis in Galatia: Epistolary-Rhetorical Analysis

The Gentile addressees[1] in Galatia, who had recently come to believe in Christ, are described as having abandoned the one who had called them. The phrase with which the charge is introduced (*thaumazo oti*; 1:6) is usually translated as "I am astonished that . . ." Such a translation is literally correct, but from the perspective of epistolary analysis the phrase is a conventional expression of ironic rebuke (Mullins, 1972, 385–386).[2]

Studies of ancient letter writing have shown that there are a number of recurring expressions that can be classified as letter formulae. A fundamental presupposition for such identification is that both sender and receiver are aware that certain wordings are used in letters for particular purposes (Mullins, 1972, 388f.).[3] In some cases, epistolary formulae, such as greetings or farewell wishes, are easily identified. One of the signals of epistolary formulae is that they "show the writer's attitude toward the *audience* to which he is writing, not his attitude toward the *material* he is presenting" (Mullins, 1972, 388).

In addition to such functional signals, epistolary formulae can be identified according to position and wording (Mitternacht, 1999, 174–176). With regard to position, some formulae, such as the superscription, always occur in the beginning of the letter opening (which is obvious from the label attributed to the formula); others belong to the letter closing.

Formulae that occur in the body of the letter tend to be less stable with regard to position and are not always easily detected. At least two "body formulae" have been identified. I am thinking of the *rebuke formula*, which occurs usually somewhere near the beginning of the letter body, and the *request formula*, which often occurs at the structural center of a letter.[4] Both of these formulae are present in Galatians: (1) the expression of rebuke epitomizes the tone of the whole letter. The reader is put in a state of alert that is reinforced with expressions such as: "What fools you are, you Galatians! Who has bewitched you?" (3:1). Farther into the letter, the addressees are informed that failure to comply with the author's demand is tantamount to falling from grace (5:4). (2) The request formulae in 4:12 ("Become as I, for I [am] as you, brethren I beg you") epitomizes the letter's concern and functions as the structural center of the letter.[5] These initial epistolary-rhetorical observations indicate that the crisis in Galatia, as Paul perceived it, was closely linked to his own person, namely, the Galatians' lack of eagerness to imitate him, or—to use social psychological terminology—to adopt the *role schema* he had presented to them by way of living it before them (3:1).

Identifying Motives and Purposes

Traditional interpretation of Galatians, influenced by Lutheran theology, finds the theme of grace verses works at the heart of the epistle, with Paul's special animus directed specifically against circumcision as an example of "works" by which one seeks to "save" oneself. It describes Paul's opponents as a conscience-laden, law-centered group searching for peace with God through works of the law.

According to the so-called "new perspective on Paul" that tries to correct the traditional interpretation, Paul does not address a problem of humanity in general but the specific issue that concerns the status of Gentiles in the first Christian communities and circumcision as an identity marker. It is not works righteousness that Paul is opposing but the claim that Gentiles can only become Abraham's heirs if they become Jews. Both perspectives, of course, share the view that the crisis in Galatia had to do with the Gentile Christ-believers' uncertainty about their salvation.

But there is no evidence in the text that the addressees' conscience was heavy and that therefore they were tempted to complement Christ faith with works of the law or improved identity status. The rhetorical intensity with which their mistake is described—a mistake that is said to lead back to a state of "spiritual" slavery (4:10, 5:1), including the loss of Christ and grace (5:4)—reveals an unambiguous position on the part of the author. It says nothing, however, about the addressees' motives, except that they apparently acted without knowledge of the spiritual dangers of which they are now informed.

A survey of those few passages in which the author specifically refers to action taken by the addressees shows that no single motive or purpose is articulated. In Galatians 4:21 we read: "Tell me, you who desire to be under law, do you not hear the law?" This sentence states that the addressees want to be under the law, but it says nothing about motives and purposes. Galatians 3:1–5 tells us that the Spirit is given apart from the law. But again, nothing is said about why Gentiles were trying to embrace the law.

In Galatians 4:9, Paul asks: ". . . how can you turn back again to the weak and beggarly elemental spirits, whose slaves you want to be once more?" And in 1:6 he asserted: "I am astonished that you are so quickly deserting him who called you in the grace of Christ—and turning to a different gospel . . ." That these statements are polemical exaggerations seems evident, especially in view of the fact that Paul can speak in very conciliatory tones to this same audience. For example, Paul calls the addressees "brethren" (3:15), "sons of God," "baptized into Christ," and affirms that they "have put on Christ" (3:26–27). It is apparent, therefore, that he did not "really" mean to imply that they had abandoned Christ. Likewise, he can hardly have imagined that they *wanted* to be slaves to weak and beggarly spirits. In other words, the polemic distortion is intended and obvious to everyone; the motives and purposes described as self-destructive cannot be taken to reflect the addressees' own position or expectations.

Another allusion to the situation in Galatia is found in 5:15: "But if you bite and devour one another, take heed that you are not consumed by one another." Apparently the problem is not that there is too much law obedience but, rather, just the opposite.

Again, any information about motives or purposes is lacking, but a vital clue about the conditions in the Galatian communities is provided: conflicts existed with potentially devastating effects. This in turn fits well with 4:29, where the various situations of the Galatian congregations are equated with the persecution of "him who was born according to the Spirit" in Isaac's time. It also accords with the information provided about the situation in Antioch (2:11–14), where the *fear* of the rest of the Jews seems an essential concern. In 2:15–21, which may be a virtual continuation of the dispute with Peter in Antioch, Paul argues for faithfulness to Christ Jesus and claims that works of the law do not make anyone righteous (2:16, 2:21). Again, it is far from apparent that the issue at stake was the Gentile addressees' fear of loss of salvation. The one thing stated explicitly is that Peter and the other *Jewish* Christ-believers acted hypocritically[6] for fear of other Jews in Antioch (2:12), a fear that most likely was motivated socio-politically.

The theme of social hardship and even persecution[7] surfaces as a major issue throughout the letter. It recurs in connection with the description of the "opponents," whom I prefer to call "advisers" or "counselors" since that may in fact mirror the addressees' point of view.[8] These references are especially important because it is probably here that the clearest information about underlying motives and purposes is given. In mentioning the advisers' troubling and bewitching of the congregations, three motives are supplied: (1) they care only because (*hina*) they themselves want to be cared about (4:17); (2) they want to gain status in order to (*hina*) avoid persecution (6:12); and (3) they act this way in order to (*hina*) "glory in . . . [their] flesh." Obviously, the socio-political self-interest of the advisers is being put on display.

Since, toward the end of the letter, the advisers are accused of having no real interest in the law (6:13), the case seems clear. The assumption that these people could have propagated what has been labeled "legalism" or some other kind of complementary soteriology[9] is not specified in the text. Instead, their attempts to improve their own situation at the expense of the congregations are Paul's central concern. In light of his aggravation over having lost the Galatians' friendship (4:15ff.), Paul's own self-interest may of course have prejudiced his denigration of the advisers' motives. At any rate, a conflict of personal interest can be detected.

Someone may wish to respond: All right, perhaps we do not have access to the addressees' motives, and the presentation of the motives of the advisers may be prejudiced, but we do know definitely that circumcision was practiced among the Gentiles and that *that* is what Paul opposes. Agreed! But what can we conclude from this? Is it not just as apparent that Paul considers both circumcision and noncircumcision to be of no significance compared to steadfast faith or the new creation (5:6, 6:15)? And is it not at the same time obvious to him that Jewish men who believe in Christ are circumcised and obligated to keep the entire law (5:3) (Nanos, 2000, 156)? Circumcision in itself can hardly be the reason for Paul's very strong reaction to the activities of the Galatians as shown in this letter. Therefore, we are back to the question of motives and purposes. Why would Gentile Christ-believers in Galatia want to be circumcised and what is the advice that they followed?

The Real Issue: A Calling to Imitate the Crucified Christ

In Galatians 4:12–15, Paul describes his first visit to Galatia and reminds the Galatians of the kindness and hospitality shown him. Despite his precarious situation and difficult condition ("and though my condition was a trial to you, you did not scorn or despise me" [4:14]),[10] they received him "as Christ Jesus" and with overwhelming solidarity (4:15). That Paul suffered from an eye disease should probably be considered a misinterpretation of both 4:13 and 4:15b. The expression "if possible, you would have plucked out your eyes" (4:15b) indicates the highest degree of loyalty.[11] Had the weakness Paul refers to been a physical illness, he would have probably not used the phrase "weakness of the flesh" in 4:13 but either just "weakness" or "weakness of the body" (Martin, 1999b, 69–70).[12] Instead of physical illness, the text seems to indicate that Paul's visit put both him and the Gentiles who chose to be loyal to him and his message under social pressure and affliction.

In Galatians 3:1, Paul describes his first visit to Galatia as a public manifestation of Jesus Christ as crucified. Here again, eyes are mentioned as well as evil eye imagery (*ebaskanen*)[13] and also the suffering of the addressees (3:4).[14] Both these reminders of their first meeting support the letter's central testimony and plea: "Brethren, I beseech you, become as I [am], for I also [have become] as you [are]" (4:12). What it means to become like him Paul explicates in the ego statements in 5:11 (persecuted for the sake of the offensive cross), 6:17 ("I bear on my body the stigmata of Jesus"), and 2:19b–20 (". . . crucified with Christ; . . . and the life I now live in the flesh I live in faithfulness to the son of God, who loved me and gave himself for me"[15]). To this Christ he relates as a slave (1:10)? "Become as I" means thus: become as one who follows in the footsteps of him who was crucified.

Crucifixion was perhaps the most humiliating punishment a person could be sentenced to in antiquity. A person sentenced to be crucified was not considered a victim but rather a dangerous criminal or agitator (Hengel, 1977, 83; see also Gal. 3:13). One might therefore consider a public portrayal of Jesus Christ as crucified to be a rather poor proselytizing strategy. Even so, that is how the Gospel was presented and received in Galatia (3:1).[16] In Galatians 1:4, Christ is described as the one "who gave himself for our sins to deliver us from the present evil age." It is quite possible that this verse stems from a pre-Pauline tradition (Synofzik, 1977, 17; Witherington, 1998, 76f.). But the fact that Paul would use a text in which Christ's sacrificial death is not associated with forgiveness but with deliverance from the present age indicates that he wanted to emphasize the dynamic (and not the forensic) aspects of crucifixion from the start. Like Christ, who was not swayed by suffering and a violent death but rather resisted this evil age, should those who believed in him live their lives.

Accepting that Paul in this letter is advocating uncompromising loyalty to the suffering, crucified Christ as both savior and role model, it seems natural to interpret the genitive construction *pistis Christou* subjectively. It is Christ's faithfulness that is contrasted with works of the law, and it is "in [this] Christ we endeavor to be justified," that is, become partakers of God's gift and power (2:17).[17] Therefore, Christ for Paul can never be just the object of receiving faith. He is the subject of faithfulness, a faithfulness in which even "I live" (2:20).[18] He is redeemer *and* paradigm, he is the life in which all else becomes reality. The addressees of the letter are therefore encouraged to realize that their social and political expectations and way of life should be based on their identification with the crucified Christ.

In light of this reading of Galatians, a correlation between the purpose of the letter and the advisers' motives and purposes can be seen. Looking beyond the rhetorical overtones of the accusations, it is possible to confirm that the advisers were trying to reduce suffering by positively inducing group identity (pro friendship) and social status (versus persecution). Paul, however, saw the advice as a betrayal of the fundamental premise in the call to Christ and therefore pleaded with the addressees: "Brothers, I beseech you, become as I" (4:12). The Gentile Christ-believers in Galatia are called to participate in a Pauline discipleship that can be summarized with the words: *imitatio Christi crucifixi*. Paul's complaint is that they had known this from the very beginning but have never quite embraced the commitment fully.

How Much Must One Endure?

Among the Gentile Christ-believers in Galatia there were those who wanted to be circumcised in order to be part of a religiously, socially, and politically functional structure. For Gentiles, to become Christ-believers meant marginalization in society and estrangement from their families. By their confession to Christ as Lord they had become excluded from participation in essential societal functions that they would still have performed as "God-fearers" (i.e., friends of some sort of the synagogue).[19] Their claim to a status that went beyond friendly affiliation now also excluded them from the context in which confession to Christ and societal coexistence was possible: the Jewish community, the diaspora synagogue.[20] To be sure, they had placed their trust in Christ for the assurance of salvation. Their current problem, however, was not peace with the one and only God but peace with their fellow men.

Paul's uncompromising reaction of strong indignation quite likely struck them like a hailstorm out of a blue sky. Why shouldn't they also be allowed to be like him and many others: circumcised Christ-believers sharing Jewish societal status? "That which is good enough for him should be good enough for us!" they may have thought to themselves. Besides, probably there were proselytes among them who had come to believe in Christ through Paul. The only difference between them and uncircumcised Christ-believers was that they had been circumcised (maybe shortly) before Paul came to Galatia.

As if that was not complex enough, it was also known in Galatia that Paul, as a Christ-believer, had preached that Gentiles should be circumcised. When he denies the rumor that he was *still* encouraging circumcision by asserting that it was *no longer* so (5:11), he confirms that he actually had been circumcising Gentiles at some earlier point in his apostolic career.[21] The reason he gives for his change of mind is that he will no longer avoid the offensiveness of the cross (*skandalon tou staurou*). The grotesque suggestion that follows: ("I wish those who unsettle you would mutilate themselves!" [5:12]) appears like a sarcastic compensation for the embarrassment about the rumor of incongruity. Important for this study is the fact that Paul affirms a direct correlation between persecution and noncircumcision and that he will no longer participate in the aversion of persecution of Gentile Christ-believers by admitting them to the rite of circumcision.

In Galatia, of course, it was remembered vividly how gratefully Paul had accepted the hospitality shown him when he was in need of it. That the suffering of these long-time friends now seems to leave him unmoved may have come as a surprise to them. Why not let people alleviate a difficult situation, especially when a solution that should be satisfactory to all parties seems to exist (or at least had existed recently)?

The intensity with which the solution is rejected by Paul demonstrates that two different views of the Christlike life are in collision with each other, views that seem to have less to do with differences about law and grace than with the everyday consequences of following a crucified Messiah.

Causal Schemata and Perceptions of Performance Levels: Social-Psychological Reflections

Having set forth my epistolary-rhetorical reading of the text, I now turn to social psychology for help in exploring the motives and purposes embedded in the dynamic of the argumentation, hoping to elucidate the overall understanding of the Galatian crisis.

One of the focuses of social psychology is on how one's self-perception and view of reality influences the perception of others, how experiences, expectations, self-interest, belief and misunderstanding, success and failure, preference and personality type inspire attributions of causes to peoples' behaviors and interactions. "Each of us, in our experiences with cause-effect relations in the world, develops certain abstract conceptions about how causes work together to yield effects" (Fiske & Taylor, 1991, 39), that is, consciously or unconsciously, we identify *causal schemata*.[22] H. H. Kelley (1972) has distinguished two types of causal schemata, those relating to tasks that demand high-level performance and those relating to tasks in which average-level performance suffices. In other words, people recognize that to successfully complete a high-level performance task, a number of causes have to be present, whereas any one of several causes can suffice to complete an average-level performance task. Kelley has summarized the two types of causal schemata under the headings (1) the multiple necessary causes schema and (2) the multiple sufficient causes schema.

For instance, a student who scores ninety percent on a multiple choice test may have simply been lucky. Or maybe she was able to eliminate the wrong answers. Maybe, in fact, she knew the right answers. In any case, the successful completion of the task is not very informative about causes because it is not dependent on a definite set of causes. A successfully completed high-level performance task, on the other hand, such as the laudable completion of a cuisine contest or a marathon race, confirms the presence of multiple causes, because a definite set of causes is necessary for success. Therefore, a successful completion will inform the perceiver that a definite set of causes has been present and active.

A precondition for the attribution of causes to a task is, of course, that the perceiver first determines the performance level of the task. In the above cases, the choices seem obvious. If one transfers the principle of causal schemata to tasks that are performance level ambivalent, however, considerable potential for incongruent determinations develops. In addition, if one applies the principle to religiously determined tasks, neither success nor failure (salvation or condemnation; the crown of life or shame) can be measured empirically, since the outcome is determined by projections in the mind of the perceiver. This may complicate the attribution procedure but it does not invalidate it; causal attribution to religious experience is still being performed.

In a socio-religious context such as the one in Galatia, where teachings of unconditional grace and of categorical demands are united in a message of justification in and through a crucified Christ, any attribution of causes, however firmly secured in the mind of the perceiver, must by definition be dependent on subjective presuppositions. In religious contexts, presuppositions may of course pass as revelatory propositions.

If one's primary focal point is on a gracious God, one may think of the religious walk of life in terms of an average-level performance task. The assurance of the Spirit's testimony in one's heart confirms that God is "Abba, father" (4:7). With such confidence, a petty matter like the circumcision of some Gentile Christ-believers in Galatia can only play a minor role, especially since all seem to be agreed that circumcision as such is of no concern (5:6, 6:15). Compliance either way would certainly not thwart God's plan for his children. Instead, since the circumcised identity secures the only realistic prospect of coping as Christ-believers in Galatia, circumcision becomes a desirable cause for the successful accomplishment of the appointed task.

If, however, one focuses on the call to *imitate* the crucified Christ, the religious walk of life profiles as a high-level performance task, a race with winners and losers and no time for compromise or detours. Failure to accomplish just one necessary cause constitutes a threat to the success of the whole. Thus, once success is defined as the unyielding imitation of the crucified Christ, getting circumcised to avoid persecution is a breach of a necessary cause (cf. Gal. 5:2–4).

It is apparent that Paul measured his calling in terms of a competitive race, most clearly articulated in 1 Corinthians 9:24–27. Using the imagery of a tournament, he states that one is not in the competition for the sake of participation but in order to win: "Do you not know that in a race all the runners compete, but only one receives the prize? So run that you may obtain it. Every athlete exercises self-control in all things" (verses 24–25a). Forty-seven of fifty-three instances where the Greek word root *kauch* (part of words like "praise," "boast," or "pride") occurs in the New Testament, it is found in the authentic Pauline letters (the rest are found one each in Ephesians, 2 Thessalonians, and Hebrews and three in James). Paul may reject self-praise in references to the law or for inclusion in the Jewish people, but with regard to his sufferings he does not hesitate to boast (Rom. 5:3). He believes in praise for having refrained from rightful privileges (1 Cor. 9:15), devotion (2 Cor. 1:12, 11:10; Gal. 6:4, 6:14), and for the successful establishment of churches (1 Thess. 2:19; 1 Cor. 15:31; 2 Cor. 1:14, 7:4, 7:14, 8:24, 9:2–3, 10:13, 10:15, 10:16). For Paul, high-level performance, reward, and praise are part of the religious walk of life. No one should be satisfied with mediocre, ordinary performance. Only complete dedication entitles one to acclaim and the imperishable wreath (1 Cor. 9:25).[23]

Importantly, Paul does not distinguish his duty as an apostle from his basic confidence in the mercy of God. But, as can be seen from his assertion in Philippians 3:8–11, in the end the two cannot be separated. Sharing in the sufferings of Christ is tantamount to attaining to the resurrection from the dead. Thus, the Galatians' failure to heed the call to imitate the crucified Christ was tantamount to failure to attain to salvation.

To be sure, Paul attests that the Gentiles in Galatia were neither licentious nor indifferent. They had shown compassion and solidarity with the weak and victimized for the sake of Christ—especially toward

Paul—as he acknowledges (Gal. 4:14). Contrary to Paul, however, they do not seem to consider hardship and persecution necessary to the task. Instead, experience may have taught them that when your brother is in need, you assist by alleviating his suffering. And as marginalization had become insufferable and the temptation to go back to the religious practices of family and friends had become imminent (Gal. 4:10–11), they contemplated joining the one environment in which confession to Christ was feasible religiously, socially, and politically.

Role Adoption and Zeal: Social Psychology and Mythical Role Theory

Theories about causal schemata have contributed to making the cognitive incongruence in the argumentation of Galatians transparent. Yet, there remains the question of how such contrary perceptions of the religious walk of life may have come about. Here, I combine insights from social psychology and psychology of religion. Social schema research has produced a number of typologies of schemata, among them *role schemata*. Whereas causal schemata focus upon the perception of single events or tasks, role schemata are cognitive structures that organize one's knowledge about a set of behavior expected of a person in a particular social position (Fiske & Taylor, 1991, 119). Roles can be achieved by effort and intent (job, club membership, etc.) or ascribed, that is, acquired at birth or automatically (age, race, sex).

A third category of roles has been introduced by Hjalmar Sundén's religion-psychological role theory (Sundén, 1959; cf. Wikström, 1987; Holm, 1995). Sundén argued that there are mythical textual roles that encode religious man for specific role experiences. These roles are actually more important than socially given roles since they have the potential of shaping role patterns over successive generations and of achieving, with time, internally stable common features.[24] They are socially determined, however, inasmuch as all reality is perceived reality based on social agreement (Sundén, 1959, 47–48). They are ethnological in that they are group specific, and it is the group's perspective that legitimates and maintains the perceptual "set." They are individual in that they constitute the result of individually accumulated states of readiness (see below).

Mythical roles, then, comprise a dual interplay, since they belong to both God and humans. Nils G. Holm summarizes Sundén's mythical role experience as follows:

> If there is a stimulus and a motivation of a particular kind, the search and discovery of a model can occur in the individual mind, with the result that the mythical roles structure that individual field of perception. What then occurs is that the individual *takes the role* of the human party in a mythical role play, and simultaneously *adopts* God's role, which unconsciously structures perception so that what happens in or around the individual is actually experienced as the action of God. For a brief instant, the person can quite concretely experience the action of God. A *phase shift* has taken place, and the individual field of perception has become structured by a mythical role. (Holm, 1995, 409)

After a while, the individual may shift back to a more secular and everyday perception. But the mythical role remains in the mind as a latent structure of experience and will be activated as soon as a relevant stimulus occurs.[25] As Gerd Theissen has pointed out, Sundén's role theory overcomes a false dichotomy between tradition and experience. Through the proposal of roles, religious tradition shapes religious experience and vice versa. By adopting the roles of Abraham and Christ, Paul restructures his perception of himself and the world (Theissen, 1983, 48). At the same time, the mythical role is not unconditional but interrelates with the personality of the person who adopts the role. And as the role is activated, it becomes the activity of God. "Through the role of God, the individual makes contact with a role which allows the experience of a living, active, and eternal God" (Holm, 1995, 416).

Finally, Sundén argued, in contrast to Otto and Schleiermacher, that religious experience is not something like a "raw" core that is interpreted. There is no "intermediate space" between the stimulus and the interpretation. Rather, religious experience is the consequence of the "perceptual cycle," capturing all of a person's mental qualities. As a person interacts with specific role situations in religious texts, "frames of reference" begin to emerge and accumulate into a "state of readiness." In a crisis situation that is structurally close to a specific role situation in a religious text, the state of readiness may then generate a role-adoption process (cf. Wikström, 1987, 394–395; Holm, 1995, 405). The actual religious role experience triggers an individual amalgamation, a mixture of dominating and assisting role concepts into a role adoption.

Application of these ideas to the letter to the Galatians seems rather simple. We can first of all note Paul's own record of his mythical role adoption: "But when God who had set me apart in my mother's womb

and had called me through his grace, was pleased to reveal his Son in
me . . ." (Gal. 1:15). Paul's identification with Christ takes place in a
moment of crisis (cf. 1:23). His reflection on what happened provides
insights into the individual accumulation process. The role of the servant of God in Isaiah 49 is invoked in the reference to "being set apart
in the mother's womb" and incorporated into the affirmation of the
Son of God being revealed within. This in turn connects with 2:20 ("I
have been crucified with Christ. It is no longer I who live, but Christ
who lives in me.") and 6:17 ("I bear in my body the stigmata of Christ").
In addition, we note Paul's affirmation of being a zealous person from
his youth on (1:14). The achieved role of which Paul does not hesitate
to boast even as he looks back on it, his effort to be a scholar among
the Pharisees, suggests what sort of personal traits affected the accumulation process. The role model Christ could have prompted other
states of readiness. But in Paul's case it is an assimilation of the Christ
model with models such as the athlete, the zealot, and the servant of
God of Isaiah 49 (Theissen, 1983, 254). Thus, his identification centers on the relentless imitation of the crucified Christ.

"Become as I . . . ," Paul admonishes the addressees and laments the
fact that so far they had not had the mythical role experience of the crucified Christ. They had suffered (3:4) and they had demonstrated exceptional dedication (4:14), but they had not internalized the role that was
so graphically portrayed before their eyes (3:1). The reference to evil
eye sorcery at this point in the argument highlights Paul's bewilderment about the lack of role transfer. It may even be a way of counter-
balancing the cognitive dissonance of success/failure. Only a malicious
counteractivity could have prevented his vivid presentation from
catching on.[26]

The roles the Galatians did internalize (so it would appear, since
Paul bases his affirmative arguments on them) are "children of God"
(3:26), Abraham's children and heirs (3:29), sons who call God "Abba,
father" (4:6), even Paul's children (4:19), children of the promise, and
children of the free woman (4:28, 31).

Conclusions

This study has tried to shed some light on the situation in Galatia,
aiming at correcting the traditional misconception that Paul and his
mission were under attack from intolerant and exclusivist opponents of Paul[27] demanding of the Galatian Christ-believers that they
be circumcised lest they lose salvation. Instead, it has been asserted

that the circumcision activities in Galatia were the result of societal pressures, conventions, and laws that regulated peoples' lives in Galatia. No agitators were needed to demand that the Gentile Christ-believers be circumcised. Maybe help and advice were requested, but not to defeat Paul. Instead, there may have been a need for guidance regarding how the statement "We should not trouble those of the Gentiles who turn to God" (Acts 15:19) should be applied in this critical situation.

Already before these Galatian Gentiles met Paul, they probably had close contact with the synagogue communities in the area, some of them as liminals[28] to Judaism. Through Paul's inspirational presence accompanied by manifestations of the Spirit (Gal. 3:1–5) and overwhelming enthusiasm (4:14–15) they had come to entrust their lives to Jesus the Messiah who sacrificed himself to save them from the present evil age (1:4). They had been baptized as "God's sons in Christ Jesus" and accepted him as Lord of their lives (3:26, 3:27). They had understood: no more incense on home altars, no more sacrificial meals at business repasts, no more participation in cultic activities of either city or state. They had realized that in principle they were excluded from vital social and family contexts. In their initial enthusiastic state, they had been willing to make any sacrifice (4:15).

Perhaps they had hoped or even been promised that in some way they would acquire the Jewish community's socio-political and religious privileges. At least Paul would have assured them that in Christ they were to be counted among the righteous without being circumcised. But this assurance did not alleviate their situation—at least not in this world—and as time went by they were forced to admit that it had become unbearable.

From the text we cannot deduce where the advisers came from. That there was some sort of authorization from the leadership in Jerusalem is implied by the depreciating references to Jerusalem in the letter's introductory chapter. At any rate, the Gentile Christ-believers in Galatia were encouraged to abide by their faith in Christ.

Causal schemata and role-adoption theories have contributed to making the incongruence of cognitions plausible and understandable. Role-adoption dynamics have been seen to impute a determination and a fervor that would not be easily swayed and that may account for Paul's persistence despite the danger of losing the Galatians' friendship completely. However, the Gentile Christ-believers in Galatia had not had an experience similar to Paul's. They were in fact strangely resistant to the challenge. And so, as Paul's plea "Become as I" (4:12)

resounds his initial appeal (3:1), the reader is made aware of the importance of role adoption as a vital motivator for religious enthusiasm.

Notes

1. I am referring to the "encoded addressees," not the "empirical readers"
(for a discussion of the distinction between "empirical reader," "encoded
explicit reader," and "encoded implicit reader," see Stowers (1994, 21–22). It
is the encoded reader that we find in the text; the empirical readers we know
nothing about in this case. There is no information about the reception of the
letter. In fact, we do not even know whether this letter ever reached its
addressees.

2. N. A. Dahl confirmed Mullins's observation already in 1973. His article has now been published (Dahl, 2002, 117–142). See Nanos (2002, 32–61)
for a detailed analysis of the formula. Nanos considers irony to be the key to
the interpretation of the letter as a whole (see especially 51–61).

3. Similar conventions occur today. For example, if a letter begins with
"Dear John," the "dear" has a weaker connotation than if the same expression
is used in a phrase like "What would I do without you, dear John?"

4. The request formula contains a verb of request that corresponds to the
social roles indicated by the superscription.

5. For a detailed analysis of the request formula in Galatians, see Mitternacht (1999, 215–232). For an alternative reading, see Martin (1999a, 123–
138).

6. A rhetorical critical analysis must note that the accusation of hypocrisy reflects what the author wishes to convey as part of his rhetorical strategy. Whether or not Peter and Barnabas would have agreed with Paul's
assessment remains undecided. There are a number of additional rhetorical
issues that need to be considered in order to come to terms with this passage
(see Mitternacht, 2002, 412–419).

7. For details, see Baasland (1984) and Mitternacht (2002, 427–430).

8. For details on this issue, see Mitternacht (2002, 412–416, 433). I do
not use the designations "opponents" or "agitators" because these terms
entail submission by the interpreter to the rhetoric of the medium to be
examined. Mark Nanos, whose position on this issue coincides with mine, has
suggested that we use the designation "influencers" (Nanos, 2002, 193–199).

9. Robert Jewett has drawn the conclusion that the agitators' nomism
was only apparent. What the Galatian *pneumatics* were really aspiring to was
mystical perfection (Jewett, 1971, 207–208). According to Howard (1979,
11), the "agitators" conceived of themselves as allies of Paul and thus were
not a little surprised at his massive opposition.

10. Probably these expressions resound social exclusion through separation curses and evil eye magic (Longenecker, 1998, 156).

11. For references to ancient authors, see Betz (1979, 227f.).

12. References to 2 Corinthians 12:7 in support of Galatians 4:13–15 to confirm bodily sickness are irrelevant. Mullins (1957, 299–303) was the first to my knowledge who has argued against such a comparison. Contra Hafemann (2000, 169–170).

13. On this and other allusions to evil eye imagery in this letter, see Nanos (2002, 184–188).

14. Regrettably, translations of this passage often render the word *pascho* as "to experience," although the word's plain meaning in both the New Testament and the Septuagint is "to suffer" (Michaelis, 1979, 912).

15. This translation may seem unusual. It corresponds, however, with the self-image apparent in other texts (cf. 2 Cor. 4:11): "For while we live we are always being given up to death for Jesus' sake, so that the life of Jesus may manifest in our mortal flesh."

16. To be sure, the reference to "Christ being put forward as crucified," and thus a transgressor of the law, is important for the theological-soteriological discussion in 3:10–14 (cf. Borgen, 2000, 352). But in my view, it is the social consequences of the transgressions of law by Christ and his followers that are focused upon primarily here.

17. For Paul, Christ personifies the righteousness of God; for Paul, righteousness always is both gift and power. This has been emphasized but with different implications by Käsemann (1964, 190) and Stuhlmacher (1965, 222).

18. The well-know slogan concerning Paul's soteriology by E. P. Sanders ("getting in by grace, staying in by works") should in my opinion be modified for Galatians to: "getting in by faith in Christ's faithfulness, staying in by a faithfulness that is in accord with his faithfulness."

19. Shaye Cohen's investigation into the ways by which a Gentile in antiquity became less a Gentile and more a Jew led him to propose seven categories (Cohen, 1999, 140–174). Based on implications from Galatians 4.8–11, I conclude that the former association of the Galatian addressees with Judaism would have been closer to category 4, "practicing some or many rituals of the Jews," than to category 5, "venerating the god of the Jews and denying or ignoring all other gods."

20. A presupposition of this assertion is, of course, that the first Christ-believers in Galatia, Jews and Gentiles, considered their religious homestead to be the larger Jewish community (cf. Nanos, 2000, 157–159). The separation of Christianity from Judaism does not occur in Paul's lifetime, in my opinion.

21. The logic of the argument suggests the presupposition of Paul's previous activities as a Christ-believer among Gentiles (Mitternacht, 2002, 427f.; see also Munck, 1959, 91). Most exegetes reject such an inference as unacceptable (taking Timothy's circumcision as an exception) and claim either (1) that the text must refer to Paul's pre-Christian activities (Witherington, 1998, 372), (2) that the verse must refer to the circumcision of Jews (Dunn, 1993, 279), or (3) that the reference is hypothetical altogether (Howard, 1979, 9, 11).

22. "A causal schema is a general conception the person has about how certain kinds of causes interact to produce a specific kind of effect" (Kelley, 1972, 151; see also Kelley, 1973; Fiske & Taylor, 1991, 32–41). F. Heider, the inventor of attribution theories, had taken his point of departure with the simple observation that humans want to control their lives. They want to be able to feel safe in their environment and plan their future. For those reasons, they use their common sense to attribute causes to the actions of other people (Heider, 1958; cf. Fiske & Taylor, 1991, 24–26).

23. The prevailing impact of this outlook is confirmed by the pastoral letters (cf. 2 Tim. 2:3–7).

24. Sundén's role theory combines elements from social psychology, socio-cultural perspectives (what later came to be known as sociology of knowledge), and perception psychology (Wikström, 1987, 391).

25. Sundén's role theory has prompted a number of studies, primarily in Scandinavia, not the least on how biblically attested divine acts such as spirit baptism and glossolalia initiate role taking (for references, see Holm, 1995, 411–412).

26. I hasten to add that in my view this assertion tells us nothing about the actual activities of the advisers (contrary to many commentators, who indulge in identifying the "ghastly" opponents). The reference to evil eye sorcery is a rhetorical countermeasure that fits the overall one-sided portrait of the advisers throughout the letter, as I have tried to demonstrate above.

27. In a number of articles and a monograph, this position has been opposed with fervor by Nanos (2002, 6–8, 264–266).

28. The term "liminals" (Lat. *limen* = threshold) is used of persons who have begun the *rite de passage* to become proselytes (see Cohen, 1999, 198–238).

References

Baasland, E. (1984). Persecution: A Neglected Feature in the Letter to the Galatians. *Studia Theologica, 38,* 135–150.

Barclay, J. M. G. (1987). Mirror-Reading a Polemical Letter: Galatians as a Test Case. *Journal for the Study of the New Testament, 31,* 73–93.

Berger, K. (1980). Die impliziten Gegner. Zur Methode des Erschließens von 'Gegnern' in neutestamentlichen Texten." In *Kirche. Festschrift für Günther Bornkamm zum 75. Geburtstag,* D. Lührmann & G. Strecker, eds. Tübingen, Germany: Mohr Siebeck, 372–400.

Betz, H. D. (1979). *Galatians.* Philadelphia: Fortress.

Borgen, P. (2000). Openly Portrayed as Crucified: Some Observations on Gal 3:1–14. In *Christology, Controversy and Community: New Testament Essays in Honour of David R. Catchpole,* D. G. Horrell & C. M. Tuckett, eds. Leiden, The Netherlands: Brill, 345–353.

Cohen, S. J. D. (1999). *The Beginnings of Jewishness: Boundaries, Varieties, Uncertainties.* Berkeley: University of California Press.

Dahl, N. A. (2002). Paul's Letter to the Galatians. Epistolary Genre, Content and Structure. In *The Galatians Debate: Contemporary Issues in Rhetorical and Historical Interpretation*, M. D. Nanos, ed. Peabody: Hendrickson, 117–142.

Dunn, J. D. G. (1993). *A Commentary on the Epistle to the Galatians.* London: A&C Black.

Fiske, S. T., & Taylor, S. E. (1991). *Social Cognition* (2nd ed.). McGraw-Hill Series in Social Psychology. New York: McGraw-Hill.

Hafemann, S. (2000). The Role of Suffering in the Mission of Paul. In *The Mission of the Early Church to Jews and Gentiles*, J. Ådna & H. Kvalbein, eds. Tübingen, Germany: Mohr Siebeck, 165–184.

Heider, F. (1958). *The Psychology of Interpersonal Relations.* New York: Wiley.

Hengel, M.. (1977). *Crucifixion.* London: SCM.

Holm, N. G. (1995) Role Theory and Religious Experience. In *Handbook of Religious Experience*, R. W. Hood, ed. Birmingham: Religious Education Press, 397–420.

Howard, G. E. (1979). *Paul: Crisis in Galatia: A Study in Early Christian Theology.* Society of New Testament Studies, Monograph Series 35. Cambridge: Cambridge University Press.

Jewett, R. (1971). The Agitators and the Galatian Congregation. *New Testament Studies, 17*, 198–212.

Käsemann, E. (1964). Gottesgerechtigkeit bei Paulus, In *Exegetische Versuche und Besinnungen* (2nd ed.). Göttingen: Vandenhoeck & Ruprecht, 1964, 181–193.

Kelley, H. H. (1972). Causal Schemata and the Attribution Process. In *Attribution: Perceiving the Causes of Behavior*, E. E. Jones, D. E. Kanouse, H. H. Kelley, R. Nisbett, S. Valins, & B. Weiner, eds. Morristown: General Learning Press, 151–174.

Kelley, H. H. (1973) The Process of Causal Attribution. *American Psychologist, 28*, 107–128.

Longenecker, B. W. (1998). *The Triumph of Abraham's God: The Transformation of Identity in Galatians.* Edinburgh: T&T Clark.

Lyons, G. (1985). *Pauline Autobiography: Toward a New Understanding.* SBLDS 73. Atlanta: Scholars.

Martin, T. W. (1999a). The Ambiguities of a "Baffling Expression" (Gal 4:12). *Filologica Neotestamentaria, 12*, 123–138.

Martin, T. W. (1999b) Whose Flesh? What Temptation? (Galatians 4.13–14). *Journal for the Study of the New Testament, 74*, 65–91.

Michaelis, W. (1979). *pascho, ktl.* In *Theological Dictionary of the New Testament*, vol. 5. Grand Rapids: Eerdmans, 896–939.

Mitternacht, D. (1999). *Forum für Sprachlose: Eine kommunikationspsychologische und epistolär-rhetorische Analyse des Galaterbriefs.* Coniectanea Biblical New Testament Series 30. Stockholm: Almqvist & Wiksell International.

Mitternacht, D. (2002). Foolish Galatians? A Recipient-Oriented Assessment of Paul's Letter. In *The Galatians Debate: Contemporary Issues in Rhe-*

torical and Historical Interpretation, M. D. Nanos, ed. Peabody: Hendrickson, 408–433.

Mullins, T. Y. (1957) Paul's Thorn in the Flesh. *Journal of Biblical Literature*, 76, 299–303.

Mullins, T. Y. (1972). Formulas in New Testament Epistles. *Journal of Biblical Literature*, 91, 380–390.

Munck, J. (1959). *Paul and the Salvation of Mankind*. Atlanta: John Knox.

Nanos, M. D. (2000). The Inter- and Intra-Jewish Context of Paul's Letter to the Galatians. In *Paul and Politics: Ekklesia, Israel, Imperium, Interpretation*, R. A. Horsley, ed. Harrisburg: Trinity, 146–159. Reprint (2002). In *The Galatians Debate: Contemporary Issues in Rhetorical and Historical Interpretation*, M. D. Nanos, ed. Peabody: Hendrickson, 396–407.

Nanos, M. D. (2002). *The Irony of Galatians: Paul's Letter in First Century Context*. Minneapolis: Fortress.

Stendahl, K. (1976). The Apostle Paul and the Introspective Conscience of the West. *HTR* 56 (1963) 199–215. Reprint pages 78–96 in Stendahl, K. *Paul Among Jews and Gentiles*. Philadelphia: Fortress Press.

Stowers, S. K. (1994). *A Rereading of Romans: Justice, Jews and Gentiles*. New Haven and London: Yale University Press.

Stuhlmacher, P. (1965). *Gottes Gerechtikeit bei Paulus*. Göttingen, Germany: Vandenhoeck & Ruprecht.

Sumney, J. L. (1999). *"Servants of Satan," "False Brothers," and Other Opponents of Paul*. Journal for the Study of the New Testament Supplement Series 188. Sheffield: Sheffield Academic Press.

Sundén, H. (1959). *Religionen och rollerna. Ett psykologiskt studium av fromheten*. Stockholm: Diakonistyrelsen.

Synofzik, E. (1977). *Gerichts- und Vergeltungsaussagen bei Paulus*. Göttingen, Germany: Vandenhoeck & Ruprecht.

Theissen, G. (1983). *Psychologische Aspekte paulinischer Theologie*. Göttingen, Germany, Vandenhoeck & Ruprecht. (English edition 1987)

Wikström, O. (1987) Attribution, Roles and Religion: A Theoretical Analysis of Sundén's Role Theory of Religion and the Attributional Approach to Religious Experience. *Journal for the Scientific Study of Religion*, 26, 390–400.

Witherington, B., III (1998). *Grace in Galatia: A Commentary on Paul's Letter to the Galatians*. Grand Rapids: Eerdmans.

CHAPTER 12

REVELATION 17: THE APOCALYPSE AS PSYCHIC DRAMA

Charles T. Davis III

The "end of the world" story is a psychic drama that is spontaneously projected on the world. Consequently, the repeated empirical failures of predictions for the end do nothing to discourage further speculation and eschatological faith. The Christ–Antichrist story as an end of the world drama has endured through two millennia because it arises from the unconscious and expresses the deepest fears, desires, and needs of our hearts. This vision is deeply embedded in our tradition and is often difficult to detect. Like Proteus, the Christ–Antichrist story shifts its forms. In this respect, the story functions as a repressed neurotic symptom that needs to be brought to consciousness by critical analysis. Positively, the story appears in our culture when there is a need for a savior to balance a society that is in some sense "out of control."

The Christ–Antichrist Story

The term "Antichrist" is found only in 1 John 2:18, 2:22, and 4:3 and 2 John verse 7, but it is traditionally associated with the Beast of the Apocalypse. In 2 Thessalonians 2:3, 2:8, and 2:9, the "Lawless One" is described as an anti-Christ, a heretic who will do battle with Christ and be destroyed. It is an easy transition from the Lawless One to the Imperial Beast, since a similar scene depicts the destruction of the Beast in Revelation 19:11–21. The narrative elements from these texts were, over time, linked in the Christian imagination.

In Revelation 11:7, the Beast ascends from the mythical bottomless pit into history to kill the two prophets in Jerusalem. Revelation 12 follows with a cosmic drama. The Red Dragon, Satan, seeks in vain to devour the child of the Celestial Woman. The child who will "rule all the nations with an iron rod" (Rev. 12:5; all citations are from New Revised Standard Version) ascends into Heaven. The Celestial Woman descends into the wilderness and escapes (12:6). War erupts in Heaven. Satan is cast down to earth along with his angels (12:7–9). The cosmic conflict ends. Heaven is perfected by the expulsion of evil. The primordial, cosmic battle between good and evil shifts into the historical realm.

The Beast from the Sea with seven heads (13:1), which are the hills of Rome and seven kings as well (17:9), embodies the power of Satan on earth. Having one head that was killed but healed, this beast bears a caricature of Christ. The world, which is composed of those whose names are not written in the primordial Book of Life (13:8), worships this beast—the Roman Empire—which wages war upon the saints (13:7). The king or head that is a parody of the risen Jesus is Nero. As in a dream with multiples of the same image, he now appears as the second beast arising "out of the earth" (13:11). His name is "666" (13:18)—*Neron Caesar*. Nero is a pseudo-Lamb that speaks with the voice of the Dragon and founds a false worship of the first beast, the Roman Empire, through deceptive miracles (13:13–15). The members of the false church of the Lamb are marked on their foreheads, or right hand, by the Beast (13:16), who apes the marking of the saints on the forehead with a seal, probably the blood of the Lamb (7:3). This is the Christian church that accommodates itself to Rome.

When the dramatic action shifts to the wilderness in Revelation 17:3, the Celestial Woman has been replaced by the Whore of Babylon (17:3–6), drunk with the blood of the saints. She is seated upon the Beast from the Sea—now identified symbolically as Nero (17:8–11), the emperor who was raised from the dead in parody of Jesus.

Christ appears in Revelation 19:11 as the warrior on the white horse descending to earth to lead the "armies of heaven" to war (19:11–16). He is identical to the child who would rule with an iron rod (17:15). He is the Messiah of David. The two imperial beasts are captured and thrown alive into the lake of fire (19:20). Satan, who only recently was cast from heaven to earth, is bound in the mythical pit for 1,000 years (20:2–3) while the martyr church sealed by God rules the earth with Christ. Satan is then released to lead his armies against Jerusalem. Fire from heaven consumes his army, and he is cast into the lake of fire (20:9 10).

The Christ–Antichrist Story as a Challenge
to Critical Scholarship

There is an understandable temptation to dismiss this story as a neurotic vision. We must, however, reject Freud's contention that religion (and art) is *only* a garbage dump for repressed desires and hostilities. Paul Ricoeur observes in *A Philosophical Interpretation of Freud* that "man is capable of neurosis as he is capable of religion, and vice versa" as he responds to the "triple suffering dealt the individual by nature, his body, and other men" (1970, 533). Certainly, Christian communities have used this story to focus the desires of the neurotic and to direct repressed hatreds, sadistic tendencies, and violent impulses toward the enemies of their religious group (Ricoeur, 1970, 532; McGinn, 1994, 3). We may also discover more creative possibilities if we remember with Ricoeur that "one and the same fantasy can carry two opposed vectors: a regressive vector which subjects the fantasy to the past"—the violent primal scene of Freud, for example—"and a progressive vector which makes it an indicator of meaning"—as it is linked, for example, to faith and the kerygma of love (Ricoeur, 1970, 539).

Since "the Antichrist legend can be seen as a projection, or perhaps better as a mirror, for conceptions and fears about ultimate human evil" (McGinn, 1994, 2), our critical consciousness must purge the story of the end of its archaic literal or descriptive (historical) projections (Ricoeur, 1970, 542). We may then explore its archetypal symbols and the trajectory of hope that arises from its orientation to future human possibilities. Beyond the destructive movement of criticism, a positive hermeneutic will allow us to encounter "symbolic forms [that] conceal from everyday consciousness more than they reveal" as we seek to recover through interpretation the "repressed aspects of our being" (Mudge, 1980, 14).

If unchallenged by a critical hermeneutic, the Christ–Antichrist story invites an eisegesis that justifies violence against both Christians and non-Christians. Kenneth G. C. Newport in *Apocalypse and Millennium: Studies in Biblical Eisegesis* is certainly correct in his observation that "the history of *popular* exegesis and the interaction between the biblical text and the *non*-critical interpreter of it . . . is an area that has been much neglected" (2000, 3) While critical scholarship has a relatively minor impact on society, Newport continues, "the history of millennialism . . . bears . . . testimony to the way in which non-critical interpretations of the same text have affected the lives of millions" (3). When an American General Officer characterizes the "war" in Afghanistan and Iraq as a battle against Satan (Thompson, Dickerson, &

Waller, 2003), he is implicitly speaking from two millennia of Christian apocalyptic eisegesis and can expect to draw a large following. The eisegetical tradition is deeply embedded in popular culture and continues to energize hope, while academic interpretation fails to do so. It is imperative in a volatile world that critical scholarship rise to the challenge of eisegesis and offer more constructive alternatives that also speak to the needs of the heart.

The Dynamics of a Psychic Drama

A myth is a psychic drama driven by an archetypal plot that arises spontaneously from the unconscious. It expresses the life of the soul (Jung, 1959, 6). From a literary perspective, Bernard McGinn in *Antichrist: Two Thousand Years of the Human Fascination with Evil* characterizes apocalyptic material as "future" or "apocalyptic legends" that present history in terms of "mythic language and symbols" (1994, 19). Apocalyptic writers interpret history through psychic projections that reveal the unconscious life of the soul. The Christ–Antichrist story requires a psychic interpretation to supplement cultural investigations of the Apocalypse. Schuyler Brown observes in *Text and Psyche* that "whatever the author's conscious intention may have been, a religious text arises out of a world of archetypal imagery" and speaks to the reader as it powerfully engages "his or her unconscious feelings" (1998, 26).

Carl G. Jung defines archetypes as structuring influences arising from the unconscious "which, independently of tradition, guarantee in every single individual a similarity and even a sameness of experience, and also of the way it is represented imaginatively" (1959, 58). In more pedestrian terms, an archetypal plot is a spontaneous template that normally functions below the level of consciousness. Consider the sports cheer: "Two bits, four bits, six bits, a dollar / Everyone for ___, stand up and hollar." One need only fill in the blank with one's team name for this "boilerplate" to work. The Christ–Antichrist story is a psychic boilerplate that can be projected as a cultural drama in which the Antichrist is pitted in battle against Christ, or his representative. As social conditions change, the Antichrist is identified with the person or movement that is perceived as the Christian enemy: Nero, the Jews, Muhammad, Islam, the Pope, heretics, Luther, America—to name some major figures.

An analogous and complementary case for the psychic drama can be made from a Freudian perspective. In *Psychoanalysis and Storytelling,*

Peter Brooks views a story's plot as a dynamic "desire machine designed and intended to adapt itself to the tensions inherent in the human condition, caught as we are between an often obscure yet powerful past wherein the origins of desire are buried, and a desired future that takes its shape from the past and the present" (Rickard & Schweizer, 1994, 3). Positively, the reader is motivated by the "desire to understand origins and the need to find a workable 'truth,' an explanation that . . . will allow the 'plot'—of one's life or one's fiction— to resume its movement into the future and toward its desired end" (Rickard & Schweizer, 1994, 7). This interpretive move shifts our attention to the realm of "as if" (Brooks, 1994, 42), to the realm of future alternatives that give rise to hope for the satisfaction of desires.

Like Jung, Brooks recognizes that human stories tend to be constructed upon a common template. He observes:

> Freud works from the premise that all that appears is a sign, that all signs are subject to interpretation, and that they speak of messages that ultimately tell stories that contain the same *dramatis personae* and the same narrative functions for all of us. (Brooks, 1994, 23)

The transfer of the Freudian theory to literary texts is based upon the assumption that "the structure of literature *is* in some sense the structure of the mind . . . a term which designates the economic and dynamic organization of the psyche" (Brooks, 1994, 24–25).

Brooks observes that our fictions, personal and literary, serve us as analogical models guiding us in "discovery procedures" and are not simply illustrations or moments of color in our lives (40). "Psychoanalysis," says Brooks, "matters to us as literary critics because it stands as a constant reminder that the attention to form" is one more attempt to draw the symbolic and fictional map of our place in existence (44).

Carol Pearson states in *Six Archetypes We Live By: The Hero Within* that an archetype "carries with it a way of seeing the world" that we project, with the result that "the external world tends to oblige us by reinforcing our beliefs about it" (1989, xxi). Archetypal plots are dangerous because they are self-validating. To the uncritical mind, the map of reality defined by the archetype simply appears as "the way things really are." There is no awareness of the psychic projection of the archetypal plot upon the world. Analysis changes the situation by naming the plots and thus withdrawing the projection. Pearson warns that when we do not name the archetypes "we are hostages to them and can do nothing else but live out their plots to the end. When we name them, we have a choice about our response" (xx).

Archetypal plots can neither be created consciously nor destroyed, only recognized. When we disown such plots, they merely assume a disguise. Upon careful examination, archetypes can be found lurking under our cultural stereotypes, such as the "Antichrist." "Stereotypes are laundered, domesticated versions of the *archetypes* from which they derive their power" (Pearson, 1989, xix).

The term "Antichrist" is a stereotype in contemporary culture. McGinn notes that Protestant appeals to the Antichrist story, on the one hand, deteriorated "into a monotonous insistence on the pope Antichrist motif" (1994, 7) from the seventeenth century to the present. On the other hand, the term was "directed against so many foes, both real and imagined, that it lost much of its invective power," with the result that the Antichrist plot suffered a severe decline and exists largely in "repetitious forms" (7).

The Christ–Antichrist stereotypes are not without power. Newport cautions us that "the eighty or so charred bodies at Waco are an unwelcome and sobering reminder of the fact that when placed in the hands of certain readers, certain texts can and do become volatile and potentially explosive" (2000, 199–200). Newport's study reveals that David Koresh was not an eccentric or a demented individual but the exponent of a Seventh Day Adventist tradition that can be traced back to William Miller's failed prediction that Jesus would return on October 22, 1844.

According to Newport, the Seventh Day Adventists inherited the stereotypical equation of the Roman Catholic Church with the Antichrist, but they "added a new dimension" by arguing that the second beast of Revelation 13, the False Lamb, "was none other than the United States of America" (2000, 198). At Waco, true believers understood themselves to be doing battle with Satan and his Beast, the United States. Such is the power of a stereotype. Archetypal plots can surface to take over our lives at any time. Denying their existence only increases their corrosive influence by allowing it to remain unconscious.

The Dragon–Hero Psychic Drama Underlying the Christ–Antichrist Story

Humans harbor a deep desire to understand origins. The regressive tendency that Eliade calls the nostalgia for paradise, "the perfection of beginnings" (1959, 92), speaks to our desire to abolish time and recover the innocence of paradise, our original home. Apocalyptic literature reorients the search for paradise by prophetically projecting it into the future, as McGinn (1979, 1994) demonstrates. The New Jerusalem of

Revelation 21:9–27 will transcend the paradise of our origin because it offers us an innocence that is the consummation of historical experience.

The end as a psychic event introduces a cycle into linear time. Although we may repudiate the cyclic view of history philosophically, we cannot escape the psychic need to periodically abolish past time and revitalize the cosmos. The terror of time—experienced as failure, death, defeat, and evils of all sorts— leads us into despair. Hope is renewed as sin is ritually and mythically abolished and social balance reestablished. In the ancient world, historical leaders were assimilated to the "archetypal action performed *in illo tempore* (before 'history' began) by ancestors or by gods" (Eliade, 1970, 32). The myth of the primordial cosmic struggle of the hero and the dragon (serpent, monster) reconnects a society with the energy of the pretemporal moment of creation. History is transfigured into myth, into conformity with an eternal archetype, overcoming the terror of time (Eliade, 1965, 37).

In the Apocalypse, the cosmic aspect of the hero–dragon psychic drama is introduced with the appearance of Satan as the enemy of the Celestial Woman in chapter 12. Satan is unable to capture the Divine Child, the Celestial Woman, or those who confess the name of Jesus. He reappears, however, in chapter 13 as he confers his powers upon the Beast from the Sea (Rev. 13:2) for the purpose of dominating the world (13:4) and making "war on the saints and to conquer them" (13:7). This is an important juncture in the development of the Apocalypse. The battle has shifted from the cosmic dimension into the historical dimension. Satan has been cast from heaven to earth even as Jesus has ascended into heaven to take Satan's place (12:5, 7–9), and Rome is the symbol that evokes the presence of the dragon on earth. The ancient myth of the struggle between the dragon and the king/god is historicized with the result that it now has a future referent to the "Man of the end-time" (Ricoeur, 1967, 202)—Jesus, the heavenly king who will come again to free the world of evil.

Thompson observes in *The Book of Revelation* that the identities of the various beasts are blended so that there are no hard and fast boundaries among them (1990, 80). Thompson also observes that the Celestial Woman flees into the wilderness to escape the Dragon but that in the very next reference to wilderness we meet the Whore of Babylon as the woman in the wilderness. He comments, "if the wilderness passages are taken strictly sequentially, the good woman has been transformed . . . into the evil woman on the beast" (82). Jung makes a complementary observation in *Psychology and Religion: West and East*: "the Whore is the chthonic equivalent of the sun-woman,

Sophia, with, however, a reversal in moral character" (1958, 446). The Whore is the dark shadow aspect of the Celestial Woman, just as Satan is the shadow of the Son of Man.

If we imagine the Celestial Woman to be the embodiment of holy wisdom (Sophia) in the true church that descended from heaven to earth, then the transformation of the Celestial Woman into the Whore of Babylon follows. Through the action of Satan and his Antichrist, the true church has been perverted into the Whore of Babylon, a fallen Celestial Woman that serves the interest of Rome.

In Christianity, the historicized myth of the Christ/hero versus the Antichrist/dragon provides a mechanism for the abolition and renewal of time through the anticipation of the future victory of Christ the King over Satan (Rev. 19). Successive time periods are experienced as dominated by historical figures who can be assimilated to the archetypes of the Christ/hero or the Antichrist/villain.

This mechanism is already evident in 1 John. The world is divided into two communities: the children of God and the children of Satan (1 John 3:9–10). The antichrists, following the Antichrist who is already in the world, have left the Johannine community to join the children of the devil (2:18–19). These former brothers, who dared to disagree with the community, are envisioned as the enemies of the Son of God who was sent to destroy the works of the devil (3:8).

The Johannine community demonstrates a deeply felt psychic need to abolish the old time with its worn-out institutions and to embrace the hope of a new creation. Unfortunately, this real psychic need, which can appear in any community, most often goes unacknowledged and is projected onto historical events and persons, as in this case where the antichrists are former members of the community. The psychic need to abolish and recreate the world can only be satisfied by an inward journey that leads to a transformation of the symbols by means of which we construct our map of reality.

The Assimilation of Jesus and Nero to an Archetypal Plot

Historical personages persist in the collective memory only if they are assimilated into archetypes. Eliade notes in *Cosmos and History: The Myth of the Eternal Return* that an historical figure endures in the popular memory for no more than two or three centuries without being assimilated to the heroic archetype (1965, 43). Persons capable of imitation by later generations lose their historical particularity as they become universal, timeless images available for storytelling. Celtic Arthur won long-forgotten battles; King Arthur, the archetypal Christian king, has moved the souls of millions for a millennium.

Nero, the emperor, and Jesus, the peasant, represent the extreme poles of the social continuum. They had no significant historical relationship. Their association in the Apocalypse is the result of their being appropriated by the collective memory as the opposing images of the human tyrant and the true human king. Throughout Christian literature, they stand like Siamese twins: Nero—the Antichrist, the very embodiment of ego, Satan, and cosmic evil; Christ—the embodiment of the Logos and light, self, and the god-man of the end time.

As the symbols of the primordial struggle are reoriented to the end and are embodied in a quasi-historical drama, their focus shifts from the cosmic perspective to the inner, psychic perspective. This inner referent of the hero battle was not immediately recognized; the material was projected. McGinn identifies Origen as the first to seek the meaning of the Antichrist in the inner life of individuals (1994, 64–65). The projection is most fully withdrawn by Augustine, who argued that the Apocalypse is "a message about the perennial struggle between good and evil in the souls of men" (McGinn, 1979, 26). Augustine's principle is "go not outside, return into thyself: Truth dwells in the inward man" (Jung, 1958, 107; translated from *Liber de Vera Religione*, *xxix*, 72). In effect, Augustine recognizes that the Christ–Antichrist story is a psychic drama.

The introspective interpretation of the Christ–Antichrist story exercised a strong influence in the West through the twelfth century (McGinn, 1994, 79). It is this line of interpretation that needs to be revived today as criticism withdraws projection by stripping away the literal-historical aspects of the story.

Jesus and Nero as Polarities in the Image of the Self

The Self archetype coincides with the God archetype. As Jesus was assimilated to the Christ, the hero, and the god-man, he became an archetypal image of the Self for Christian culture. In *Symbols of Transformation*, Jung writes, "In the Christ-figure the opposites which are united in the archetypes are polarized into the 'light' son of God on the one hand and the devil on the other. . . . Christ and the dragon of the Antichrist lie very close together so far as their historical development and cosmic significance are concerned" (Jung, 1956, 368).

The result of the cultural projection of the Self archetype upon

Jesus is a split in the cultural image of the Self/God. All the good is projected on God's Christ; all the bad is projected on Satan's agent, the Antichrist. This split prevents human/divine wholeness and encourages the projection of human evil upon our enemies as the Shadow archetype—the repudiated and thus unconscious aspects of our own life. The expulsion of Satan from heaven (Rev. 12) splits the God archetype as well. All that is evil in heaven is projected first upon the earth (Rev. 12) and then upon the underworld (Rev. 19). The perfect God with his perfect Son are counterbalanced by the evil Satan and the Nero Antichrist. So long as the God/Self archetype is split by projection, Christian man will be dogged by his pagan shadow, Christ by the Antichrist, God by Satan, heaven by earth and underearth. The Christ cannot exist without the Antichrist once this split in the Self archetype is made. McGinn makes a similar point from a theological perspective when he observes that "the early Church's rapidly evolving Christology seems to have stimulated the development of an obverse 'Antichristology,' that is, a more detailed and inflated account of the career and person of the final enemy" (1979, 17). The myth of the dragon-king fight projected through prophecy into a future historical event was an ideal narrative container for this new psychic orientation.

The ancient leader, who is assimilated by his culture to the God-man hero archetype, is always vulnerable to an ego inflation that deceives him into claiming the powers of divinity for himself, as emperor worship demonstrates. This ego inflation lays the groundwork for the emperor to be portrayed negatively as the monster who as "the giant of self-achieved independence is the world's messenger of disaster, even though, in his mind, he may entertain himself with humane intentions" (Campbell, 1973, 15). The true hero, by contrast, is one who has achieved the submission of his role to the higher powers of the inner world. Hero and dragon/Antichrist are the two roles that leaders may play in the psychic drama as aspects of the Self.

The popular legend of the resurrected Nero held that the mortally wounded Nero was alive in Parthia waiting to return to liberate the Roman Empire (Warmington, 1969, 168). At least three pretenders appeared during the first century claiming power as the resurrected Nero. Nero's biography was written by poets, Tacitus and Suetonius predominantly, who demonized him while the popular imagination linked him with the invincible hero. Nero is eventually constellated in the collective imagination as both poles of the Self archetype. Black Nero, the monster, is complemented by Light Nero, the hero risen from the dead to return and destroy the enemies of Roman society.

For Christians, the image of Nero the savior was an abomination. The emperor believed to have persecuted Christians could only be an archetypal villain, an Antichrist.

In Revelation 13 and 17, the Nero of popular culture is assimilated to the image of the Antichrist, the enemy of Jesus, the Jewish Messiah. John paints the image of two Christian communities in bold colors: one dominated by Rome, the other by Christ. In short, the existence of the Christian community itself, like Jesus and Nero, has been assimilated to the Hero–Dragon archetypal plot. Life is understood quasihistorically as a battle between a false, Roman-sanctioned Christianity deriving from Satan and a true Christian community of martyrs led by the Son of God. This image of the Christian community as the embodiment of the hero slaying the dragon is an abiding legacy of the Apocalypse. It has provided a firm foundation for Christian eschatological and apocalyptic activity from Patmos to Waco.

The Transformation of the Archetypal Plot in the Middle Ages

Constantine resolved the division between a false "Roman" church and a true "martyr" church through the person of the emperor as he made Christianity his religion. The archetypal plot was not abandoned. It was a template Christianity needed. From a theological perspective, McGinn observes:

> Antichrist was not an accident or a superfluous addition to Christian faith. It resulted logically from the opposition between good and evil implied in the acceptance of Jesus as divine Son of Man, Christ, and later, Word of God. . . . Christians need the legend of the Antichrist. (McGinn, 1994, 33)

The archetypal story continues in altered form as the legend of the godly Last Emperor, the representative of Christ.

In *The Influence of Prophecy in the Later Middle Ages: A Study in Joachimism*, Marjorie Reeves observes the operation of this transformed hero myth in the sibylline prophecy as early as the mid-fourth century in Europe (1993, 299). The story runs as follows. A mighty Greek emperor, Constans, would appear to reign for a century or more over an age of prosperity in which the triumph of Christianity would be consummated. The heathen would be converted or destroyed. Jews would convert to Christianity, and Gog and Magog would be defeated. At the end of this century, the emperor, in imitation of Christ, would go to Golgotha and lay down his crown and robe, surrendering them to God. Then, the Antichrist would appear in "the final fury of evil to reign in the Temple at Jerusalem. Here human agencies would be of no avail: the Archangel Michael would appear to destroy him and, immediately after, history would be wound up at the Second Coming" (300).

According to Reeves, the seventh-century tract *Pseudo-Methodius* was composed in the East; during the eighth century, it was circulated in Charlemagne's court, popularizing the Last World Emperor legend in both East and West (300). It is of utmost contemporary interest that the rise of Islam was assimilated to the archetypal drama for the first time in this document (McGinn, 1994, 90). In the tenth century, the Burgundian Abbot Adso again popularized the legend. Most importantly, "the promise of a last emperor gave scope for racial aspirations and there quickly developed, first, a French tradition of a Second Charlemagne, and then a German tradition of a Last Emperor" (Reeves, 1993, 301).

The First Crusade brought renewed interest in the legend. By the end of the eleventh century, there was the hope of a resurrected Charlemagne who would lead Christians to a victory over the Muslim infidels. The Nero/Christ antithesis is transfigured into the infidel/resurrected Charlemagne antithesis. Christianity unified in the person of the godly last emperor constitutes the positive pole of the Self archetype, while the community of the infidel constitutes the negative pole through projection. But this state did not long continue.

Constantinople fell to the Muslim Turks in 1453. The Emperor Constantine Palaiologos was killed and, in the popular imagination, assimilated to the hero. The legend arose that "the last Emperor . . . would come back to rescue them. He was not really dead. He was merely asleep and waiting a call from heaven" (Nicol, 1992, 98). The archetypal plot that centuries earlier created the legend of the resurrected Nero is applied to the last emperor of Constantinople.

Further development of the Last Emperor legend was made possible by the historical vision of Joachim of Fiore. He interpreted the Apocalypse in light of three states of Christianity: the Time of the Father, the Time of the Son, and the Time of the Holy Spirit. Latter-day Joachimists understood themselves to be poised on the transition between the Age of the Son and the Age of the Spirit. The new Age of the Spirit would be ushered in by a good pastor of the church, the angelic pope, who would champion monastic spirituality. Indeed, Celestine V was assimilated to this archetypal story. As this eighty-year-old hermit pope rode "from the wilderness meekly riding upon an ass to take up" the papal office, he was hailed along the way by the crowds in messianic terms (Reeves, 1993, 401). Celestine V entered popular mythology as the prototype of the angel-pontiff yet to come.

Celestine's resignation after five months, under the guidance of the man who would succeed him as Boniface VIII, made it easy to assimilate this event to the myth that the Antichrist would seize the papacy. The subsequent persecution of the spiritual Franciscans further suggested the presence of the power of evil. On the one hand, we have the true pope backed by the true Franciscans; on the other, the carnal church and the pseudopope. Reeves writes that they reasoned as follows: just "as the Jewish synagogue was rejected when the 'new man' Christ established His new Law, so the sixth age of the carnal church would be rejected when the 'new man' Francis has established his Rule" (Reeves, 1993, 408). The final step in this new myth was the identification of the church under Boniface VIII as the church of Babylon.

We have come full circle. As in the Apocalypse, the church is split into archetypal poles. The story, however, has been amplified. By the fourteenth century, there was the expectation of two Antichrists. "An 'oriental' Antichrist . . . would preach in Jerusalem and seduce the Jews; an 'occidental' Antichrist . . . would be a heretical Emperor, a new Nero" (Reeves, 1993, 323). The angelic pope would appear, initiating the Age of the Spirit. "The King of France . . . would be elected as Roman Emperor and the entire world would submit to him. The Emperor and the Pope together would carry out the final programme of reform" (Reeves, 1993, 323).

As in the case of Nero centuries earlier, the light/dark poles of the Self archetype are evident in the portrayal of both the emperor and the pope. The last emperor could take the form of the Antichrist destroying the Church or as its savior. Likewise, the pope could be portrayed as the dark force of Babylon or as the spiritual angelic pope sent to restore the church by the establishment of the holy practice of monastic poverty. The basic program was that church and state must be cleansed, the Muslim converted, and all mankind led into a true evangelical life. Together, the godly last emperor and the angelic pope would accomplish this task of healing the church and the world.

The Modern Apocalypse

Post–French Revolution culture has produced two contrasting secular heroes as transformations of the Christ–Antichrist. In England, Sherlock Holmes and Professor James Moriarty are antagonists representing good and evil in the post-Christian, scientific world. In

America, Batman, as portrayed in Tim Burton's *Batman Returns* (1992), does battle with Penguin in an America that is only superficially Christian and about to fall victim to terror. While Arthur Conan Doyle offers a vision of the form a Christ substitute might take in a world without deity, Burton's movie speaks from American popular culture calling upon America to prepare for Armageddon. Doyle reifies the Christ–Antichrist story into a detective–criminal antagonism, while Burton offers us a true psychic drama reflecting the unconscious life of the American psyche/soul. *Batman Returns* is an American apocalypse.

Sherlock Holmes

Derek Jarrett, in *The Sleep of Reason: Fantasy and Reality from the Victorian Age to the First World War*, places the Sherlock Holmes stories in the context of the collapse of the traditional Christian symbols of heaven and hell under the pressure of the French Revolution. Jarrett narrates the story of a Victorian England that was alive with Christ–Antichrist speculation. He suggests that Holmes "had come to remedy the situation and trade old myths for new ones" (Jarrett, 1989, 5).

The dynamics of the split in the Self archetype characteristic of the Christ–Antichrist story is illustrated by Brooks's 1994 analysis of Sherlock Holmes's death. In the episode "The Final Problem," written in 1893, Doyle intended to bring the Sherlock Holmes series to an end. Holmes encounters his diabolical twin, Moriarty. Brooks observes that "Moriarty comes into being, as it were, through Holmes's own deductive powers, as a kind of structural necessity of the interpretive work of detection" (Brooks, 1994, 62). Holmes and Moriarty are equal but opposite forces, each perfectly balancing the other as members of a duality. "The inevitable outcome is their mutual extinction at the Falls of Reichenbach" (63).

Jarrett observes that the life of Holmes as a Jungian archetype was established "pretty convincingly in 1894, when he came back to life after he had been sent to his death" (Jarrett, 1989, 4). Events proved that Holmes was not a conscious creation of Doyle to be manipulated at will. Poets dive deeply, at great personal risk, into the unconscious and articulate images that express the collective social mind. Jarrett observes that the massive popular protest over Holmes's death forced Doyle "to realize that the great detective had an existence outside that of his creator" just as literary critics recognize that the "text or structure of a piece of fiction" has "a reality which transcends the consciousness of its author and may even make a study of his or her intentions irrelevant" (1989, 4).

The image of Holmes and Moriarty clutching each other in death in "The Final Problem" would have been a happy ending. It unified the split Self/God archetype. The collective mind objected. The readers of Doyle's mysteries were not receptive to this resolution; they were not able to face the truth about the balance between Holmes (good) and Moriarty (evil) and unify the Self image. In this respect, the new secular myth was at heart as Christian as its predecessor.

Holmes, like the last emperor, is a warrior who gave enthusiastic support to World War I. Jarrett observes that the desire that underlay the great devotion of many to the archetypal Holmes, as to a real person, was the basic human need "to believe in heroism and self-sacrifice, in man's readiness to fight the good fight" (1989, 6). Under the pressure of rationalism, the archetypal Hero–Dragon plot assumed a disguise. A coolly rational detective using the scientific method is the new secular hero; an evil genius of the criminal underworld is the new dragon. The message is clear. Modern cultural life is constituted by the never-ending saga of "cops and robbers" or "cowboys and outlaws." Hope rests in having an intelligent police force. The detective story genre is Holmes' abiding legacy.

An American Apocalypse: *Batman Returns*

America has not yet suffered the disillusionment that swept Victorian England. In *American Apocalypses*, Douglas Robinson writes:

> the very idea of America in history *is* apocalyptic, arising as it did out of the historicizing of apocalyptic hopes in the Protestant Reformation. . . . America was conceived as mankind's last great hope, the Western site of the millennium . . . its future destiny was firmly and prophetically linked with God's plan for the world, and the national dream of an American Age, a great paradisal future to be ushered in by America remains strong even in our time. (Robinson, 1985, xi)

In *Batman Returns*, Tim Burton (1992) creates a comprehensive American apocalypse that challenges this optimistic assumption. Unlike its Christian predecessors, the story is not reified through projection. It is a pure psychic drama, a cultural dream.

In this movie, there is an interesting twist. We see American popular culture speaking prophetically to American Christianity about the Antichrist (Penguin) and Armageddon, the destruction of the forces

of Gog and Magog at the Gotham City Zoo by Batman, an outworn
messiah who says to Catwoman, "We are the same; split right down
the center." The destruction of Gotham City by the forces released from
the sewer is only narrowly averted, and one feels that Batman will be
a poor defense in the future. The American messiah must soon give way
to the forces from the abyss. The movie calls for an American change
of direction in images worthy of an eighth century biblical prophet.

Biblical allusions abound. The movie opens at Christmas with Penguin cast upon the waters of the storm sewer as Moses was cast upon
the Nile. Thirty years later, like Jesus, Penguin makes his epiphany at
Christmas. His present to the world is a package delivered in the name
of the businessman Shreck (German *Schreck* = fear, terror). Hordes of
clowns and harlequins stream forth from the sewers through this
gigantic Christmas package to riddle Gotham City with death and
destruction. This is Penguin's answer to the city's wish for "unconditional love" and "world peace." Penguin's program as conveyed to
entrepreneur Shreck is simple, "What you hide, I discover." All that has
been forced into the underworld—the sewer system of Gotham City—
will now invade consciousness and demand recognition. The shadow
will take its toll. The message is clear: there is a heavy price to be paid for
irresponsible economic development and a religion that has lost its soul.

Penguin becomes the Antichrist by imitating Herod's massacre of
the innocents. Shreck, like an evil last emperor, conceives and manages
Penguin's campaign to become the mayor of Gotham City through a
recall election. The key to this event is this statement by Shreck during a campaign of terror that he is helping Penguin wage: "They [the
people of Gotham City] have lost faith in all symbols." Christianity
and the commercialized Christmas culture it spawned in America is
dead. It was killed by the simonistic entrepreneur manipulating a pop-
ulace that responds according to the whims of sentimentality rather
than through true virtue.

Conclusion

End of the world plots arise to consciousness when we have an inner
psychic need or desire to break free from an outmoded map of reality.
The Christ–Antichrist story specifically should alert us to an inner
warfare—within individuals and/or society—between the good self
and the bad self. A psychic problem cries out for a resolution that hon-
ors all aspects of the personality, all members of society.

The Christ–Antichrist archetypal plot is toxic when it is projected as political boilerplate upon one's enemies. Even Holmes' story is toxic insofar as it splits society into a respectable lawman-criminal dichotomy. The projection must be withdrawn and faced. Repressing the plot is counterproductive. Whether it is allowed an underground existence through theology, movies, or storytelling, or is tolerated as a stereotype, it continues to be toxic. Augustine correctly interpreted the story as a psychic drama that unfolds in the human heart. The Christ–Antichrist story tells us about repressed dimensions in our personal and social selves—as Tim Burton attempts to do in *Batman Returns*.

References

Brooks, P. (1994). *Psychoanalysis and Storytelling*. Cambridge: Blackwell Publishers.

Brown, S. (1998). *Text and Psyche*. New York: Continuum.

Burton, T., director (1992). *Batman Returns* [Film]. Warner Bros.

Campbell, J. (1973). *Hero with a Thousand Faces*. Princeton: Princeton University Press.

Eliade, M. (1959). *The Sacred and the Profane*, W. R. Trask, trans. New York: Harper and Row.

Eliade, M. (1965). *Cosmos and History: The Myth of the Eternal Return*, W. R. Trask, trans. New York: Pantheon.

Eliade, M. (1970). *Patterns in Comparative Religion*, R. Sheed, trans. New York: World Publishing Company.

Jarrett, D. (1989). *The Sleep of Reason: Fantasy and Reality from the Victorian Age to the First World War*. New York: Harper and Row.

Jung, C. G. (1956). *Symbols of Transformation*, R. F. C. Hull, trans. Princeton: Princeton University Press.

Jung, C. G. (1958). *Psychology and Religion: West and East*, R. F. C. Hull, trans. Princeton: Princeton University Press.

Jung, C. G. (1959). *The Archetypes and the Collective Unconscious*, R. F. C. Hull, trans. Princeton: Princeton University Press.

McGinn, B. (1979). *Visions of the End: Apocalyptic Traditions in the Middle Ages*. New York: Columbia University Press.

McGinn, B. (1994). *Antichrist: Two Thousand Years of the Human Fascination with Evil*. San Francisco: HarperSanFrancisco.

Mudge, L. S. (1980). Paul Ricoeur on Biblical Interpretation. In *Essays on Biblical Interpretation*, L. S. Mudge, ed. Philadelphia: Fortress Press, 1–40.

Newport, K. G. C. (2000). *Apocalypse and Millennium: Studies in Biblical Eisegesis*. New York: Cambridge University Press.

Nicol, D. M. (1992). *The Immortal Emperor: The Life and Legend of Constantine Palaiologos, Last Emperor of the Romans*. New York: Cambridge University Press.

Pearson, C. (1989). *Six Archetypes We Live By: The Hero Within.* San Francisco: HarperSanFrancisco.

Reeves, M. (1993). *The Influence of Prophecy in the Later Middle Ages: A Study in Joachimism.* Notre Dame: University of Notre Dame Press.

Rickard, J. S., & Schweizer, Harold (1994). Introduction. In *Psychoanalysis and Storytelling.* Cambridge: Blackwell Publishers, 1–19.

Ricoeur, P. (1967). *The Symbolism of Evil,* E. Buchanan, trans. Boston: Beacon.

Ricoeur, P. (1970). *A Philosophical Interpretation of Freud,* D. Savage, trans. New Haven: Yale University Press.

Robinson, D. (1985). *American Apocalypses: The Image of the End of the World in American Literature.* Baltimore: Johns Hopkins University Press.

Thompson, L. L. (1990). *The Book of Revelation.* New York: Oxford University Press.

Thompson, M., Dickerson, J. F., & Waller, D. (2003, November 3). The Boykin Affair: A Long Career of Marching with the Cross. *Time,* 30–31.

Warmington, B. H. (1969). *Nero: Reality and Legend.* New York: W. W. Norton & Company.

CHAPTER 13

PSYCHOLOGICAL ASPECTS OF BIBLICAL APOCALYPTICISM

J. Harold Ellens

In this chapter I shall develop and illustrate the role of psychological process in the development of the master stories of Judaism and Christianity. This formative process was shaped by the memory and interpretation of key historical events that seemed to the ancient Israelites to answer the main question driving the development of their faith, theology, and religious traditions. That question was, "How is God in history, and what does our history and experience, therefore, mean?" The trajectory of development in rabbinic Judaism seems to have been derived from the rational disciplines of the Pharisees, while Christianity arose from the other Judaism, namely, the apocalyptic stream and the Jesus movement that flowed from it. The consequence of these two different sources is the rise of twin religions with remarkably different original psychological tones, styles, objectives, and rationales.

Theological formulations, ritual processes, liturgies, and transcendental visions of reality are fixed upon by any given culture or community in large part because of the psychological need that these formulations and processes fill. They fill these needs by giving meaning, identity, and consolation to that community and its culture. These formulations and community visions derive their warrant from the degree to which they meet those psychological needs. This does not preclude the presence of genuine spiritual, transcendental, or transpersonal factors at work in these formulations. Indeed, quite the opposite! The theology and religion of any given community reflects the key formative psychological factors at work in the initial experience that gave rise to that particular theology and religion, such as the experience and memory of suffering, disempowerment, exile, or massive loss. They also reflect the central psychological factors at work in the habitual ways in which the human psyche gives voice to such experiences, such as in the metaphors and mythos, or master story, in which the memories of the initial experience are preserved.

Of the numerous kinds of religious perspectives that have been shaped in important ways by psychological dynamics, one of the more interesting and pervasive in biblical and extrabiblical literature is the apocalyptic tradition of postexilic Judaism. This apocalyptic tradition developed innovative ways of envisioning human encounters with the transcendental world and of conceptualizing the nature and presence of transcendental forces in the history and experience of human communities. These visionary perspectives are evident throughout the Bible. They are rooted mainly in the memory of divine interventions in the history of the believing community, particularly in the theology of the Exodus tradition, which shapes so much of the religious mainstream in the Hebrew Bible. I believe that this Exodus tradition is essentially a psychological perspective and that it seeded the eschatological and apocalyptic formulations of postexilic Judaism, including that form of it that became Christianity.

Exposition

Judaism

Apocalypticism represents one of two trajectories of postexilic Judaism. The other one is the form of Judaism that matured into the Pharisee-Sadducee and Talmudic traditions. These produced what we now know as rabbinic Judaism. The apocalyptic tradition developed, in large part, in terms of Daniel 7–9 and 1 Enoch 37–71. It led to cloistered and urban Essenism as well as to the preexistent and eschatologically exalted Son of Man imagery of the Jesus movement. The psychodynamics of this trajectory reflect the way in which the community processed the loss experiences of their exile in a drive toward a persistence of hope, vindicating the transcendental integrity of the faith community in the face of its temporal mundane devastation. That community accomplished this through psychologically significant metaphors, models, and eschatological, apocalyptic figures and trajectories that came to inform later Christian theology.

The Exodus tradition dominates the theology and psychology of the Hebrew Bible and became the primary grounding metaphor for both Jewish and Christian Scriptures and worldviews. As a result, protoapocalyptic ways of thinking about the God-human interface are evident throughout the Hebrew Bible and are rampant in the New Testament. Crucial psychological dynamics can be discerned as gathering continually increasing momentum throughout this long tradition of protoapocalypticism. By psychological factors I mean the full range of factors that have to do with the function of the psyche: all of that which we normally describe as psychology and spirituality. In my model, these two words are interchangeable, in that sense. So for something to be psychological does not reduce it from the spiritual or the transcendental or the transpersonal but merely means that the event is processed and formulated in terms of how the psyche needs to experience it and articulate that experience. The psychological dimension of that process includes, of course, all of the person-formative defensive constructions and growth dynamics set in motion by an event or experience.

Such psychological factors in both the cultural setting and in the faith tradition of the biblical and postexilic communities of Judaism are strongly evident. They can be seen, for example, in the metaphors of transcendental deliverance that form the mainstream of the Exodus narrative and its pervasive tradition. We note them as clearly in the theology of the remnant and its suffering servant. These constitute the backdrop for the community's longing for an ultimate eschatological consummation. They also become the warrant for the persistence or survival of the ancient faith community itself.

Faced with the ultimate depression and confusion of the exile in the era between 722 and 500 B.C.E., the persistence of hope and meaning, and the psychological survival of the community and its members, required a massive rerationalization of the perceived role of, and the transcendental forces operating in, the daily life and eschatological destiny of the faith community. Their memory and metaphors of the Exodus provided them the ready-made storehouse of resources for that rerationalization and for the persistence of hope and meaning.

In this trajectory of Judaism that produced the Pharisee-Sadducee and rabbinic worldview, transcendental presence or intervention in this world came through the ministry of divine wisdom (*Hokma*). This personified divine wisdom was initially represented as the source of the Torah. By the time of the Talmudim, the Torah was seen as preexistent and transcendent and the source of divine and human wisdom (*Hokma*). Life and destiny are, therefore, a mundane quest for wisdom, rational and responsible godly living on earth in the here and now. However, the apocalyptic tradition led from the eschatological world views of Daniel, 1 Enoch, and the like, to the Enochic tradition, to the urban and cloistered (Qumran) Essene movements, to Gnosticism, and to the Jesus movement. In these developments also, transcendental and divine presence manifested itself in history through the presence of divine wisdom (*Hokma* and *Sophia*). In these innovative traditions, however, divine wisdom was manifested in the Son of Man, the Torah being less central and eventually irrelevant. The Gospels have Jesus declaring that in the Son of Man one greater than Moses and superior to the Torah and to the temple is present in history.

It is interesting that in this apocalyptic tradition, also, divine wisdom starts out as preexistent and transcendent but manifests itself on earth in the Son of Man rather than in the Torah. Moreover, as in rabbinic perspective the Torah became preexistent and heavenly, the source of divine and human wisdom, in the end the Son of Man became transcendent and preexistent in the apocalyptic and hence the Christian tradition. Then the Son of Man became the source of the wisdom of both God and humankind. The much-discussed character of this Son of Man had at least the following qualities. He was a prophetic figure with a divine call to an earthly ministry. He anticipated a transcendental exaltation and a cataclysmic eschatological return. In that final *parousia* the world would be judged, history ended, and a new age of the divine kingdom once and for all introduced. This would constitute the consummation of transcendental and transpersonal destiny for humans. This was a rerationalization of loss into persistent hope and an ultimate vindication of the apocalyptic faith community.

The psychodynamics of this process involve the special experiences through which any given community and its individual members processed, and rationalized into an operational model, the following experiences. First, massive loss such as bondage in Egypt, exile in Babylon, and the death of "him whom we thought would be the one to deliver Israel." Second, meaninglessness resulting from a lack of a word from God and lack of a clear and consistent life of righteousness and prosperity in the community. Third, depression resulting from diaspora and exile, despair of trying "to sing the Lord's songs in an alien land." Fourth, anxiety, fear, guilt, and shame resulting from internalizing pain, in the form of those four emotions, as humans typically do. Fifth, efforts toward a persistence of hope against all hope. To process these driving psychological needs, master them in an operational model, and vindicate the transcendental faith and integrity of the faith community, these believers formulated apocalyptic metaphors, models, visions, and mythic ideations. They created eschatological apocalyptic figures, trajectories, and consummations, which became their faith visions and operational expectations.

Christianity

The enigma of Jesus, in this question of the psychodynamics of the apocalyptic faith tradition, is focused by the tension between the low Christology of the synoptics and the high Christology of the doxological hymns in Colossians 1 and Philippians 2, Johannine transcendental theology, and the second-century eucharistic theology of the church. The problem unfolds as follows.

1. The Son of Man sayings in the Gospels are generally understood to fall into three categories: Son of Man as earthly teacher and healer, Son of Man as suffering servant who dies and is exalted, and Son of Man returning on the clouds in judgment at the end of history. All of these sayings in the Gospels are always placed in the mouth and only in the mouth of Jesus, and he never uses or tolerates any other designation.

2. All three categories are in the Q source, if you grant that the "Son of Man hath not where to lay his head" is in the second category (i.e., *logia* about the suffering, dying, and resurrecting Son of Man).

3. The *Sitz im Leben* or "life setting" for all of these *logia* except those with obvious anachronisms can be found comfortably and authentically in the life and work of Jesus as depicted by the synoptics. This is a vulnerable point in the argument because the same community that gives us the report of Jesus' *logia* is the community that gives us the narrative presenting the *Sitz im Leben*. Therefore, the argument is persuasive only if the evidence for this model is internally consistent and in the end overwhelming.

4. The second-century church did away with the Son of Man title or phrase as it was used in the Gospels, never hung any doctrine or celebrated truth on it, and never identified with it in any way in its celebration of Jesus. Therefore, it is hard to believe that they would have claimed that this was his self-designation unless they could not avoid it because it really was his phrase and self-identity. It is internally consistent to assume or acknowledge that this really was Jesus' self-designation and that it represents a definitional notion he had about his person and role.

5. It seems likely, given the above, that the concept of the Son of Man progressed and developed in Jesus' self-consciousness over time

so that it came to include all three categories of *logia*: a man with a
ministry of teaching and healing on earth proclaiming the kingdom of
God; a man in this ministry suffering and dying and being exalted
by God; and a man exalted to transcendence in an apocalyptic and
eschatological role, descending at the end of history in a *parousia* of a
new age.

Category 1, the Son of Man as earthly teacher, could have been the
psycho-spiritual result of Jesus' consciousness from his early years,
focused by the drama of his baptism, that he had a special vocation to
proclaim the kingdom of God. This would have been clarified by the
temptations in the wilderness, in which he dissociated himself from
the Son of David messianism of the Jerusalem religious authorities,
reducing his messianic identity to that of the Son of Man. It is clear
from the narrative of the temptations that he struggled with messianic
ideas of nearly megalomaniacal proportions: solving the world's problems by feeding the poor with stones turned to bread, captivating
humankind with the spectacular psychological manipulation of miraculously jumping harmlessly from the temple parapet, and bowing down
to the secular powers to become the new Alexander the Great.

He may have moved psychologically to the second category, the suffering, dying, and exalted Son of Man, after the failure of the first mission of the disciples and the abandonment by the multitudes, when he
became aware of the fact that he was on a collision course with the
authorities in Jerusalem. This seems to be the scenario lurking behind
the language of Mark 8.

Assuming this model to be warranted, he would have moved psychologically to an apocalyptic and eschatological notion of his role and
destiny when he realized that his cause was destined to fail. The only
way to save himself and his cause, ideologically, would have been to
envision himself drawn up into the transcendent status of divine vindication, from which he would descend to bring in the kingdom after all.

This argument is vulnerable, of course, because it is impossible to
sequence the three categories of *logia* chronologically in the Gospels,
even if they can be accorded status as the kind of concepts Jesus held
regarding himself.

6. If this model is taken as our hypothesis, for the sake of testing it
against the data, it must be said at least that neither the Son of Man *logia*
nor the exalted eschatology in the Pauline and Deutero-Pauline literature in Colossians and Philippians is the mere product of liturgical
enthusiasm but reflects a thoughtfully crafted theological worldview.

7. If this was Jesus' psychological and theological worldview, and

therefore his self-concept, progressively developing through all three categories, where would he have gotten such a worldview that produced his own sense of himself as the synoptic Son of Man? Moreover, whence came the transcendental Christology of the Pauline literature, the Johannine literature, and the second- and third-century church?

According to Boccaccini's *Beyond the Essene Hypothesis* (1998), just such a worldview was available in Enochic Essene Judaism in its various forms. A review of his entire argument is genuinely worthwhile to the student or scholar with special interest in this issue.

According to the rubrics of Occam's Razor, this model hypothesis manages the data better than any of the others available; therefore, it is imperative to take it seriously. This would imply that inherent in Jesus' own developing self-concept, conceived in the context of Daniel 7:13 and 1 Enoch 37–71, were the seeds and warrants for the church's subsequent transcendental Christology.

Conclusion

Whereas Marcus Borg (1994) accounts for the psychological and spiritual issues I raise by means of his hypothesis that Jesus was a Galilean mystic, while others think he was a wandering Cynic, it seems to me much more persuasive to acknowledge that the historical data regarding Jesus' sense of self and of his role leads to a psychological understanding of the influence upon him of the apocalyptic perspective of the Enochic Essene tradition. In this perspective it is rather easy to account for the psychological motives and their sources that led Jesus and the Jesus movement to handle the community experience of loss and feared annihilation in the triumphalist manner that shaped Jesus' own self-concept, at least as reported in the Gospel narratives, and that ultimately designed the contours of Christian theology.

References

Bellinger, W. H., Jr., & Farmer, W. R., eds. (1998). *Jesus and the Suffering Servant, Isaiah 53 and Christian Origins.* Harrisburg: Trinity.

Boccaccini, G. (1998). *Beyond the Essene Hypothesis: The Parting of the Ways Between Qumran and Enochic Judaism.* Grand Rapids: Eerdmans.

Borg, M. J. (1994). *Meeting Jesus Again for the First Time.* San Francisco: HarperSanFrancisco.

Bultmann, R. (1951–1955). *Theology of the New Testament,* 2 vols, K. Groebel, trans. New York: Scribners.

Burkett, D. (1999). *The Son of Man Debate: A History and Evaluation.* Cambridge: Cambridge University Press.

Collins, J. J. (1997). *Apocalypticism in the Dead Sea Scrolls.* New York: Doubleday.

Eschel, E. (1999a). The Identification of the "Speaker" of the Self Glorification Hymn. In Escher, E. (1996). 4Q471b, A Self Glorification Hymn. RQ 17. *The Provo International Conference on the Dead Sea Scrolls,* D. W. Parry & E. Ulrich, eds. Leiden, The Netherlands: University of Leiden.

Eschel, E.(1999b). 471b:4Q Self-Glorification Hymn. DJD 29. Oxford.

Flint, P. W., & VanderKam, J. C., eds. (1999). *The Dead Sea Scrolls After Fifty Years,* 2 vols. Leiden, The Netherlands: Brill.

Garcia-Martinez, F. (1996). *The Dead Sea Scrolls Translated: The Qumran Texts in English* (2nd ed.). Grand Rapids: Eerdmans.

Knohl, I. (2000). *The Messiah Before Jesus: The Suffering Servant of the Dead Sea Scrolls.* Berkeley: University of California.

Nickelsburg, G. W. E. (1992). Son of Man. In *Anchor Bible Dictionary* (Vol. VI), D. N. Freedman, ed. New York: Doubleday.

Schuller, E. (1999). 431:4Q Hodayot. DJD 29, Oxford.

Toedt, H. E. (1965). *The Son of Man in the Synoptic Tradition.* Philadelphia: Westminster.

Wink, W. (2002). *The Human Being, Jesus and the Enigma of the Son of the Man.* Minneapolis: Fortress Augsburg.

CHAPTER 14

The Bible and the Psychology of Shame

Jill L. McNish

Therefore, . . . let us run with perseverance the race that is set before us, looking to Jesus the pioneer and perfecter of our faith, who for the sake of the joy that was set before him endured the cross, disregarding its shame, and has taken his seat at the right hand of the throne of God.

—Heb. 12:2

We read Thee best in him who came
to bear for us the cross of shame;
sent by the Father from on high
our life to live, our death to die.

—from Hymn 455, *Episcopal Hymnal*, 1982

The scarlet letter was her passport into regions where other women dared not tread. Shame, Despair, Solitude! These had been her teachers— stern and wild ones—and they had made her strong, but taught her much amiss.

—Hawthorne, 1999

When people asked me what my research was about and I said that it was about shame, it tended to stop the conversation. The response was typically a polite, "Oh, well, shame. That's nice." I discovered that shame is not a topic that evokes most peoples' lively enthusiasm. Nobody wants to talk about it. There is a sense in which to talk about shame is shaming. I confess that I came to this subject rather reluc- tantly myself. It was as if *it* came to *me*, and I finally had to accept that this is what I needed to be working on.

My perspective is that of a pastor in the institutional church and a spiritual director. I have taught students in college and seminary settings. I have worked as a chaplain in short-term psychiatric units. This issue of shame just kept hitting me between the eyes. It was not something I was looking for, but the fact is that virtually every depressed person I spoke with presented either directly or indirectly with issues that I came to identify as shame issues. And when I started reading more about it, I began to see it everywhere—in my patients, parishioners, students, friends, and, yes, in myself.

Around the same time as I was forming this insight about the ubiquity of shame as a primary element of psychic suffering, I was preaching on a weekly basis in the churches I was serving. When you are a solo pastor in a small church, it means that you preach just about every Sunday; you slog your way through the appointed lectionary readings week after week. As I worked through all those passages, I began to notice that not only were my parishioners, my directees, my students, patients, friends, and colleagues dealing with issues that could be seen directly or indirectly as shame issues, but that many of the events from the Gospel that I was preaching about—that is, events in the life, ministry, and death of Jesus of Nazareth—were most fundamentally about shame. When the lectionary passages did not directly suggest shameful circumstances for Jesus himself, they often implied something shameful in the lives and circumstances of people he was engaged with, ministering to, or speaking about in parables (see Wimberly, 1999).

I believe that understanding the psychic and spiritual phenomenon of shame, and its centrality in human life, is key to understanding the psychic power, meaning, and transformative potential of Christianity. The reason that I study psychology and religion is that I believe that understanding the psychological underpinnings of lived faith experience gives us courage. Working at the intersection of psychology and lived religious experience, I propose positive, life-giving potential for shame.

The great Rollo May once wrote that an important part of healing is "utilization of suffering." However, as May also noted, "a human being will not change his or her personality patterns, when all is said and done, until forced to do so by suffering. . . . Suffering is one of the most potentially creative forces in nature" (May, 1989, 123). Shame is a cause of great suffering in human life. It is also a recurrent biblical theme. The idea that suffering has creative, transformative potential is hopeful and optimistic. We live in a society in which it is generally assumed that a constant state of "happiness" is the ultimate (and a realistic) human value and that it is somehow neurotic not to feel "happy" most of the time. However, as theologian John Hick once said, "The capacity to find God in suffering and defeat as well as in triumph and joy is . . . the special genius of Christianity" (Hick & Goulder, 1983, 80). This is most particularly and obviously true with shame experience. The central figure of Christian faith experience suffered the worst imaginable shame—the public exposure and shame of the cross—and was transformed (i.e., "resurrected") in and through that experience. We too can be transformed—psychologically—by shame experience if we face it honestly.

The Phenomenon of Shame

What is shame? What is the difference between shame and guilt? People do not much mind talking about guilt. It is much easier to say "I feel guilty" about this or that than "I feel shame." Even in psychotherapy, people often use the word "guilt" when clearly what they are talking about is "shame," and I think that shame is at the root of most depression (see Bradshaw, 1988).

Guilt is a sense of remorse for things done or left undone. In guilt, we maintain some power and control. Sometimes we can go back and fix it. We can apologize. We can repent. Guilt does not have the self-reference that shame has. Shame is not so much about what has been wrongfully done or left undone. It is not so much about *actions* or *inactions.* Rather, it is a sense of being somehow flawed at the core of one's being. It is about self. Of course, shame and guilt are often fused. Shame is often triggered by reason of a wrongful act or omission. However, the affect of shame does not depend on doing something wrong—it just is. It is a worm at the core of human life.

The biblical examples that I think best illustrate the distinction between shame and guilt are the first two kings of Israel, Saul and David. Saul's downfall might be seen as a consequence of his unremitting and exaggerated sense of shame. Saul failed to obey God's supposed command in matters that would strike most of us as trivial, if not downright understandable (1 Sam. 15). When these infractions were pointed out to him by the prophet Samuel, Saul experienced a total collapse of self-worth (1 Sam. 16:14).

A biblical example of guilt would be King David's reaction to being shown by the prophet Nathan that his adulterous taking of Bathsheba and engineering the death of her husband was grievously wrong. When David's sin was pointed out to him, he atoned and fasted for seven days. Then he rose from the ground and returned to his life. In David we encounter a man who experienced and atoned for a grievous wrong he had committed—indeed, by most standards a much more grievous wrong than the ones Saul had committed. Having repented, however, David continued to experience God's love. He still experienced himself as a valuable person. He got on with it. What David experienced was guilt, guilt for which he repented. David, unlike Saul, who was driven mad by shame, was able to continue his life—chastened but with a continuing sense of his own self-worth (2 Sam. 12).

When you feel guilt you say, "How could I have *done that*. What a moral lapse *that act* was!" But when you feel shame you say, "What an ass I am! What an *uncontrolled person. I am a bad person. Everybody hates me*" (H. Lewis, 1971, 34–36). When one works with people suffering from major depression, one will hear this kind of litany of self-hate. It is almost an incantation. This is reminiscent of the self-hatred that Freud talks about in his well-known *Mourning and Melancholia*, which compares the experience of simple grieving with depression (in his day called "melancholia"). There he says, "In grief the world becomes poor and empty; in melancholia it is the ego itself. The patient represents himself to us as worthless, incapable of any effort and morally despicable; he reproaches himself, vilifies himself and expects to be cast out and chastised. He abases himself before everyone" (Freud, 1917, 246). Clearly, this is a description of a person experiencing shame.

At its most basic, shame arises out of life in the body and it often has reference, directly or indirectly, to the needs, desires, situation, limitations, or condition of the body. It arises out of the uniquely human experience of being a creature yet feeling somehow that one is spirit. One is helpless and powerless in so many ways, and it is experienced as humiliating. There are different shaming circumstances that occur at different developmental stages of life. In infancy and young childhood, there is the shame and mortification of complete powerlessness and dependency. In adolescence, there is shame associated with the developing body and unruly manifestations of sexuality. In adulthood, shame might arise when you discover that you are not going to be everything that you had hoped or expected. There are losses, abandonments, and rejections by lovers and spouses. In short, there are failures galore. As we grow older, we experience shame in the decline of our physical and mental powers, our sexual prowess, our physical attractiveness and youthful appearance, which we in this culture hold so dear. We are forced to confront our finitude and mortality. If we are born in a female body, we may occasionally be shamed by reason of its objectification. If we happen to have a lesbian or gay sexual orientation, we will be shamed. In general, sexuality is a very fertile ground for shame experience, and I think it would be fair to say that everyone has his or her particular shame issues around sex, either conscious or unconscious (see McClintock, 2001). If we do not have what our culture tells us is a perfect body type, we will at times feel shame. If we are not a member of the white race in a racist society, we experience shame. In fact, as Erving Goffman says in his now classic book *Stigma*:

> [T]here is only one completely unblushing . . . [person] in America: a young, fully employed, married, white, urban, northern, heterosexual Protestant father of college education, of good complexion, weight, and height, and a recent record in sports. Every American male tends to look upon the world from this perspective. . . . Any male who fails to qualify in any of these ways is likely to view himself, during moments at least, as unworthy, incomplete and inferior. (Goffman, 1963, 128)

Different cultures shame people for different things. The shame affect is there, cross-culturally, but in Eastern cultures, which have been called "we-cultures," for example, a person might feel more shame for letting down his group, his family, or even his employer than in this culture (M. Lewis, 1995, 215–216; Roland, 1996, 106). Elderly people in our culture who cannot live independently feel shame. This is not the case in Eastern cultures, where two, three, and four generations are expected to live together and people are never expected to be completely independent. In Eastern cultures in general, age is a source of pride and status, not shame, with great respect and deference being accorded to the wisdom and experience of elderly people.

What I am driving at is that the affect of shame exists in all human beings. There is what has been referred to as a "shame continuum" (Edelman, 1998, 31). The affect of shame is part of what defines us as human. It is just a matter of what gets dumped into it, how much gets dumped into it, and most importantly, what to do with it.

Obviously, shame can become pathological. It can hijack the entire personality. It can make us sick. This, I think, is fundamentally the situation for people suffering from depression, withdrawal, abuse of power, addiction, denial, scapegoating, blaming, violent rage, or killing perfectionism. These are all defenses to shame. Perfectionism is a shame defense that society loves—it makes for good children and productive employees. Paradoxically, shame is manifest in the great achievers of society in the form of killing perfectionism as well as in those who have been most defeated in society.

Righteousness is another defense to shame. Righteousness is a defense that the institutional church is very fond of: it uses this defense constantly. Clergy are deemed to be "set apart"—righteous. They are held to higher standards than others. Deviation from those standards can lead to being cast out of the church (see Pattison, 2000). The concept of being set apart means that clergy (and the church in general) tend to work even harder than the average person to deny or otherwise defend against that which is deemed shameful. We need only think of the pedophilia scandal that is now so pervasively and unremittingly vexing the Roman Catholic Church to see the most dramatic imaginable example of the cost of the shame defenses of righteousness, abuse of power, and denial (see Kennedy, 2001). And, once again, the shame has to do with the body and particularly with distortions in human sexuality that seem to be the almost inevitable result of theologies that view it with revulsion and fear.

When we convince ourselves that we are *right*, we circumvent the experience of shame. An example used by John Patton in his book *Is Human Forgiveness Possible?* is the situation of a woman whose husband left her for someone else. This woman was so fixated with the idea of being in the right that she could never let go of her bitterness, forgive, and move on. She averted the direct experience of shame, but at great cost to herself (Patton, 1985, 14).

Affect theorists following Sylvan Tomkins contend that "shame/humiliation" is one of six innate negative affects. An affect is an inborn propensity for feeling, a feeling human beings are hard-wired to experience. The other five inborn negative affects posited by Tomkins are fear/terror, distress/anguish, anger/rage, disgust, and dismell (which is a little-known affect consisting of the experience of revulsion triggered by smell). The positive affects are interest/excitement and enjoyment/joy. There is one neutral affect—surprise (Tomkins, 1963; Nathanson, 1992, 136). Tomkins and his followers contend that the affect of shame/humiliation includes as subsidiary experiences guilt, shyness, and embarrassment (Tomkins, 1963, 118).

Interestingly enough, human beings are the only creatures that experience shame. It is believed to be the last affect that has developed in evolution (Nathanson, 1992, 136). Mark Twain once noted that "human beings are the only animals that blush, or need to." Indeed, blushing is one of the physiological manifestations of shame. Other physiological manifestations include lowering of the head, sweating, and increased heart rate. People have been known to faint, even to die, of shame (Schneider, 1977, 78). Most of us have had the terrible experience at some time in our lives of feeling shame so profound that we actually feel dizzy. One feels the ground falling out from under. It feels like death, and it is no surprise that the word "mortification" has its etymology in death—total annihilation. The experience of shame can feel so intense and annihilating that it is sometimes described in terms of awe, dread, or the *tremendum*. It is the dread some people experience in the direct confrontation with the holy, as discussed in Rudolph Otto's classic book, *The Idea of the Holy* (1923/1958; see Edelman, 1998). In confronting Jesus' divinity, Peter falls at Christ's feet and exclaims, "Go way from me Lord, for I am a sinful man" (Luke 5:8; all Scriptural quotations are from the New Revised Standard Version). Indeed, throughout Scripture one finds that fear and dread is the response to direct confrontation with divinity. This, I think, is the experience of puniness in the presence of God. "It is a fearful thing to fall into the hands of the living God" (Heb. 10:31) because God is so ineffably, inscrutably *big* and infinite and we by comparison are so small. Meeting divinity confronts us with the limitations of our creaturely finitude.

Here is what Sylvan Tomkins says in his often-quoted description of shame:

> [S]hame is the affect of indignity, of transgression and alienation. Though terror speaks to life and death, and distress makes of the world a vale of tears, *yet shame strikes deepest into the heart of man. While terror and distress hurt, they are wounds inflicted from outside which penetrate the smooth surface of the ego; but shame is felt as an inner torment, a sickness of the soul.* (Tomkins, 1963, 118; emphasis added)

How telling it is that a secular psychological theorist would refer to the affect of shame as a "sickness of the soul."

The Revelatory Potential of Shame

When I tell people that my research is about shame, if they are willing to engage the subject at all they typically say, "Shame, what an awful thing! How do we get rid of it?" The answer is, we do not get rid of it, because it is part of the human condition. To shed all of our shame we would have to shed our histories, our families of origin, and our personalities. Attractive though this prospect may seem at times, aside from its patent impossibility, implicit in it is an unwillingness to embrace one's own unique life and destiny. To use a Christian metaphor, it is "Christ refusing to be crucified, or Jesus refusing to be Christ" (Edelman, 1998, 17). Shame has amazing transformative and revelatory potential. It is, I think, a gift from God that has the potential to draw us into ever-deeper relationship with God.

In its pathological forms, the boundaries that shame erects become too rigid. We may push people away and isolate ourselves because we would rather be alone than seem foolish. But having said this, even those who have been laid very low indeed by shame, people whom we might characterize as shame-bound individuals, can find great transformative potential in shame. Examples of this abound in Christian tradition. Some of the very greatest spiritual geniuses have, I think it can be argued, been tormented and transformed by shame. Saint Augustine, Saint Teresa of Avila, Saint John of the Cross, Saint Ignatius, to name just a few. Modern-day examples would include Teresa Liseaux, Bill W (the founder of Alcoholics Anonymous), Anton Boisen (the founder of Clinical Pastoral Education), and Simone Weil. These are all shame-bound individuals who transformed shame to find deep relationship with God on the other side.

Shame is a part of what impels us to seek relationship with God. If we have any doubt about that, we need only look at the Adam and Eve story. This is not really a story about "original sin." The story of the primal couple's expulsion from paradise is in fact a story of original shame. It is a myth that speaks profoundly to us, that carries great archetypal truth, because it is the story of the time when humankind first understood that it was separate from God. It is the end of what Tillich calls "dreaming innocence" (Tillich, 1957, 35). It is the story of humankind's first realization that it was made of spirit, in God's image, but yet was separate from God. Adam and Eve tried to hide their nakedness, because shame originates in the body, and it is the pain of exposure. Exposure is one of the most salient aspects of shame. The human couple began to wear clothing and left paradise. This is the pain of separation and individuation. When Adam and Eve left the paradisal garden, it was experienced as painful separation from God, but eating that fruit was also the beginning of human beings' individuation, of their inventiveness, curiosity, creativity. From this archetypal moment, human individuals began to experience the boundaries imposed by shame. "Then the lord God said, 'See, . . . [these humans] have become like one of us, knowing good and evil'" (Gen. 3:22). Leaving the paradisal garden set limits and gave shape, substance, and direction to human life. Adam and Eve lost their unthinking experience of unity with God and nature, but they began the process of finding themselves as human creatures. The unity that was lost is what individuals seek to regain their whole lives long—in their spirituality and in the most felicitous expressions of sexuality. The negotiation of the suffering involved in grasping and seizing that which was gained, while still holding onto a piece of the unity that was lost, is the challenge of human existence.

Shame is paradoxical. There are two distinct aspects to it. One aspect serves social adaptation and ensures membership in human society through conformity to basic norms of behavior. The other seemingly opposed aspect ensures that the collective does not violate the individual's boundaries and personal integrity (Hultberg, 1988, 117; Jacoby, 1996, 22). Shame separates us, creates boundaries, and this is not always a bad thing. We all need boundaries. Boundaries are what define us as individual human beings. They give shape and definition and limits to our lives. If we did not have the boundaries imposed by the shame affect, we would have no private inner reality that would impel us to do anything expressive of our individuality or creativity. Leon Wurmser sees shame as "the guardian of inner reality": "shame guards the separate private self with its boundaries and prevents intrusion and merger" (Wurmser, 1997, 65). The affect of shame permits primary process thinking:

[S]hame may be needed as a guard for the autonomy of the primary processes, the most intimate life we all have—our feelings, "the logic of the heart." On the other end of the developmental spectrum it means that shame fences in that field of life that allows creativity to blossom and insight to arise. *In one sentence then: Shame protects privacy: it functions as a guardian against any outer power that might exploit the weakness in the essential realms of the self and interfere with one's own inner struggle.* (Wurmser, 1997, 66; emphasis added)

The psychologist Helen Lynd did a groundbreaking study in 1958—*On Shame and the Search for Identity*. Before that, there had not been much serious work done on the subject of shame. In her book, Lynd talks about the revelatory and the transformative qualities of shame. Her primary premise is that when, as, and if we are able to confront our own places of shame, we have found the key to identity formation. Confronting the shadow of shame is part of the key to what Carl Jung would call individuation—the process of becoming whole. No other affect is as close to the experienced self as shame. None is closer to the sense of individual identity. Individuation requires bringing painful aspects of ourselves to the light of day. Confronting shame is painful. Lynd contends that some individuals exist more along what she calls a *guilt axis* and others on a *shame axis*. The following is reprinted from Lynd's analysis of the so-called guilt axis compared with the shame axis:[1]

Guilt Axis	Shame Axis
Concerned with each separate, discrete act	Concerned with the overall self
Involves transgression of a specific code, violation of a specific taboo	Involves a falling short, failure to reach an ideal
Involves an additive process; advance to healthy personality by deleting wrong acts and substituting right ones for them	Involves a total response that includes insight, something more than can be reached by addition
Involves competition, measurement on a scale, performing the acts prescribed as desirous	Involves acting in terms of the pervasive quality demands of oneself; more rigorous than external codes; each act partaking of the quality of the whole
Exposure of a specific misdemeanor, with emphasis on to whom exposed; exposure of something that should be hidden in a closet	Exposure of the quick of the self, most of all to oneself; exposure of something that can never be hidden in a closet, in the depths of the earth, or in the open sunlight
Concern about violation of social codes of cleanliness, politeness, and so on	Concern about unalterable features of one's body, way of moving, clumsiness, and so on
Feeling of wrongdoing for a specific harmful act toward someone one loves	Feeling that one may have loved the wrong person or may be inadequate for the person one loves
Being a good, loyal friend, husband, wife, parent	Feeling an overflowing feeling for friend, husband, wife, children, which makes goodness and loyalty a part of the whole experience with no need for separate emphasis
Trust built on the conception of no betrayal, no disloyal act, as a preliminary for giving affection	Trust that is a process of discovery that gradually eliminates fear of exposure, which is not the result of an act of will but unfolds with the unfolding experience
Feelings of anger, jealousy, meanness for certain socially recognized causes	Inwardly deep feelings of anger, jealousy, meanness in outwardly slight situations known to oneself only
Emphasis on decision making; any decision is better than none	Ability to live with some indecisiveness (multiple possibilities) even though it means living with some anxiety
Feeling of guilt toward someone who has denounced one for adequate or inadequate cause	Feeling of shame toward someone who trusts one if one is not meeting that trust
Emphasis on content of experience in work, leisure, personal relations	Emphasis on quality of experience, not only on content
Surmounting of guilt leads to righteousness	Transcending of shame may lead to a sense of identity, freedom

Of course, nobody exists only along one or the other of these axes. We all exist on the guilt axis as well as the shame axis, but most of us are more heavily tilted in one direction or the other. Recall that guilt is an aspect of the affect of shame. Guilt does not penetrate as deeply into the experienced self as shame, so when a person has a guilt axis orientation, chances are that he or she is not as inclined to go as deeply as a person with a shame axis orientation. He or she is prepared to lament and repent of wrongful acts and omissions but not to contemplate the deeper existential questions that the shame axis addresses: What is the meaning of my existence as a creature in the world? How does my adherence to societal norms compromise my individual integrity? What do my secret instinctual desires say about me as a spiritual being?

One could also see this analysis in terms of British psychoanalyst D. W. Winnicott's True Self versus False Self. Winnicott's False Self is the obedient and compliant self that unthinkingly follows rules, and the True Self represents creative living. Winnicott held that although children might be taught rules and codes to be obeyed, real morality is an inborn, internal morality to be found and nurtured within each developing individual. For example, he stated that "what is commonly called religion arises out of human nature, whereas there are some who think human nature is rescued from savagery by a revelation from outside human nature" (Winnicott, 1986, 143). He cautions parents that children can be taught rules but that the parent will "only succeed to the extent that the child has a capacity to believe in anything at all" (143). This capacity depends not upon the rules that are taught but rather upon the "experience of the person as a developing baby and child in the matter of care" (143). In one of Winnicott's many beguiling and enigmatic statements, he said, "Probably the greatest suffering in the human world is the suffering of the normal or healthy or mature person" (Winnicott, 1988, 80). This underscores Winnicott's contention that a person who is governed by True Self experience is more likely to wrestle with the rules that are handed down to him/her by society. In Lynd's language, True Self experience involves living more on the shame axis than on the guilt axis, because shame is closer to the experienced self than is guilt. Of course, True Self experience also requires relinquishment of shame defenses that block the transformation of shame.

One could also see this as applying to existence according to the Levitican law versus justification by faith. The apostle Paul and Martin Luther might be seen as having begun their faith journeys on the guilt axis and moved to the shame axis. Paul himself boasted of his former zeal for ancestral traditions (Gal. 1:14). Yet, after his conversion, Paul

exhorted Christian righteousness by faith, not adherence to the letter
of the law, "for the letter kills, but the Spirit gives life" (2 Cor. 3:6).
Luther later interpreted Paul as a theological opponent of Judaism. He
contrasted "justification by works of law"—i.e., life on the guilt axis—
with "justification by faith" in his indictment of Roman Catholic legalism. Although later scholars have questioned Luther's interpretation
of Paul, nevertheless, as Erik Erikson notes in *Young Man Luther*,
Luther's "basic contribution was a living reformation of faith. . . . The
relation of faith and law is, of course, an eternal human problem,
whether it appears in questions of church and state, mysticism and
daily morality, or existential aloneness" (Erikson, 1958, 257).

Individuals who are extremely orthodox in their religious belief
system—be they Christians, Orthodox Jews, or Moslems—tend to live
primarily on the guilt axis. They feel safe in following the rules, and
they feel guilty when they break the rules. Guilt may, indeed, be a kind
of defense to the deeper experience of shame. Huckleberry Finn felt
terrible guilt for breaching the moral code of his day in not turning in
the runaway slave Jim. Jim was, according to what Huckleberry had
been taught, the property of someone else. But he ultimately followed
his own inner code. He felt guilty for not turning Jim in, but he would
have felt shame had he turned Jim in. Shame in its broadest sense gen-
erates an internal, portable morality, and it is a much more difficult
way to live, but ultimately I think a more mature way to live, than
would be possible strictly on the guilt axis.

Lynd postulates that identity based more on the shame axis than on
the guilt axis goes deeper and is more of a continuous process of creation than identity based strictly on the guilt axis. This is because the
guilt axis leads individuals to find meaning and purpose in their lives
based upon what *others* have taught them to think, feel, and do. A person whose primary identity is on the guilt axis may, at relatively small
expense, fulfill the requirements that his society or religion makes of
him. He just needs to obey the rules. Shame, on the other hand, confronts one with unexpected, often undesirable aspects of self. To feel
shame is to experience the unexpected. Things are different from
what one thought, and not in a positive way. Your spouse has fallen in
love with someone else and wants a divorce. Or you had thought of
yourself as a good person but you have been unfaithful to your spouse.
Your child is using illegal drugs. Your body has been diagnosed with
cancer, or multiple sclerosis, or Parkinson's disease. Your boss says
that you are not performing well enough and will have to look elsewhere for a job. Or your country, which is supposed to be invincible,

is attacked, humiliated, and wounded by terrorists using your country's own airplanes loaded with your countrymen. All of these events are humiliating.

Shame invites reexamination of the whole meaning and purpose of society and oneself. Allowing shame experience without constant resort to shame defenses requires an ability to risk, to endure disappointment, frustration, and ridicule. Because shame experience is self-referential, it invites examination and exposure of the self. This is the key to the formation of a unique personal identity. As we shall see, this is the psychological truth that Christianity teaches.

What Does Scripture Have to Say about Shame?

How important a concept is shame in Scripture? This question is important because, as Wayne Rollins points out, the Bible may be seen "as a part and product, not only of a historical, literary and socio-anthropological process, but also of a psychological process" (Rollins, 1999, 92). This means that "conscious and unconscious processes are at work in the biblical authors and their communities, in the texts they have produced, in readers and interpreters of these texts and in their communities, and in the individual, communal and cultural effects of those interpretations" (92). Psychological biblical criticism examines texts and their interpretation "as expressions of the nature, structure, process, and habits of the human soul/psyche, both from individual and collective manifestations, past and present" (93).

The stories that make up the biblical witness—the stories that Christians have been reading and hearing read in church pews for 20 centuries—rose up from the collective and were preserved in oral and written tradition for hundreds of years. In religious life, life in the spirit, symbol and mythic truth is the truth that matters most. In *Answer to Job*, Carl Jung wrote:

> Christ would never have made the impression he did on his followers if he had not expressed something that was alive and at work in their unconscious. Christianity would never have spread through the pagan world with such astonishing rapidity had its ideas not found an analogous psychic readiness to receive them. (Jung, 1952a, 440)

Clearly, shame is an archetypal experience (Hultberg, 1988; Jacoby, 1996). Archetypes are factors "responsible for organization of unconscious psychic processes" or inherited "patterns of behavior" that are so powerfully charged as to "develop numinous effects" (Jung, 1952b, 436–437). One of the archetypes we first meet up with as we begin to acquaint ourselves with the contents of the unconscious is "the shadow" (Jung, 1950, 8). The shadow contains those aspects of the self that we would prefer to disassociate from—our sinful desires, our weaknesses, our aggressiveness, and other perceived character deficits. The Jungian Peer Hultberg contends that "shame is strongly connected with the shadow and persona; in other words, with . . . [humans] as social beings" (Hultberg, 1988, 109–110). He goes so far as to associate the experience of "eternal shame" with hell itself, "implying utter physical destruction while one is kept alive and conscious" (Hultberg, 1988, 115).

I believe that what the Christian story did was to constellate the human shame archetype—the inborn human shame propensity— around events in the life and ministry of Jesus of Nazareth. I believe that this is a primary explanation for the psychic/emotional power of the Christ event. The reason it can be salvific psychologically is that it is possible to see in Jesus a person who transformed and was transformed in shame, resurrected even to the Godhead. How did he do this? He refused to deploy the defenses to shame that the rest of us humans often deploy: rage, acting out, power abuse, violence, righteousness, depression, denial, addictions, withdrawal, contempt, blaming, scapegoating. Jesus stayed in the abyss of the shame vortex and refused to give in to it, and he helped others to do this too. The revelatory potential of shame means that it has profound religious, spiritual, and pastoral implications. It means that confrontation of shame issues can expand our relationships with each other, with self, and with God. This is key to understanding "resurrection" and the key to transformation of the shame experience. The result is a sense of peace, the feeling of being held and contained in and by the ground of being in spite of what you may experience as shameful about yourself.

With these premises in mind, let us then look at the biblical use of the word shame. The word "shame" and its direct derivatives (i.e., "ashamed," "shameful," "shamed," and "shameless") appear some 218 times in the New Revised Standard Version of the Old and New Testaments. In the Old Testament, uses of the word "shame" seem to be roughly grouped into the following categories: shame experienced in connection with exposure of bodily nakedness (Isa. 47:3); shame experienced in connection with failure of various sorts (Jer. 20:11); shame experienced in connection with defeat in war (Jer. 50:2); shame as the consequence of sin (Dan. 9:8); shame as an emotion attendant upon outcast status (Zeph. 3:19).

We thus see that the Scriptural uses of "shame" are in close accord with the phenomenology of shame already discussed in this article. In sum and substance, shame is about *exposure*—for example, of the body, which is irrefutable proof positive of our creatureliness. It is also about failure and defeat. Finally, it is about being isolated, rejected, and outcast, and it is often fused with guilt for perceived wrongdoing.

The word "guilt" as used in Scripture is almost exclusively associated with wrongdoing, breaking of the law and commandments. It appears approximately 135 times in the Old Testament and not at all in the New Testament. The emphasis shifts in the New Testament from guilt in consequence of transgressions in keeping the law to shame—an essential sense of unworthiness that is acknowledged, held, transformed, and expiated by God embodied in the man Jesus, who suffered ultimate shame in his conception, life, and death.

There are 150 psalms contained in the Old Testament—Hebrew poetry that gives voice to every human emotion. Within the 150 psalms, 50—fully one-third—are psalms of lament. In a typical Christian church service, a psalm is read or chanted by the congregation. Many of those psalms pull no punches in the anguish of shame they express. It sometimes strikes me as paradoxical to sit in a congregation of well-educated, well-dressed, well-fed, and, although perhaps only on the surface, self-satisfied worshippers saying words like this together: "All day long my disgrace is before me, and shame has covered my face" (Ps. 44:15); and "You know the insults I receive, and my shame and dishonor; my foes are all known to you" (Ps. 69:19).

In the 150 psalms, the word "shame" or "ashamed" appears some forty-five times, and I believe that the disproportionate number of appearances of the word is reflective of its centrality in religious feelings. There are 9 psalms that plead for God never to let the psalmist "be put to shame." There are 18 psalms in which God is exhorted to put the psalmist's *enemies* to shame. The picture emerges from reading the psalms that shame is the worst experience of anguish and suffering one can have. Psalmists plead with God not to experience it, and they wish it on their worst enemies. The desperate tone of this pleading does tend to corroborate Sandra Edelman's contention that deep shame experience is numinous in the horror and dread it evokes: "There they shall be in great terror, in terror such as has not been. For God will scatter the bones of the ungodly; *they will be put to shame, for God has rejected them*" (Ps. 53:5; emphasis added).

The psalms of lament often express our hurt and anger over our self-perceived foolishness and ridiculousness and/or anger over the ridicule and abuse we suffer at the hands of others. They help us to give

voice to our feelings about our unlovability and sense of shame, abandonment, rejection, and isolation. "The wisdom of the psalms of lament
is that deep feelings of frustration and agony cannot remain unex-
pressed without doing serious damage to the one who has them"
(Wimberly, 1999, 54).

When we reach the New Testament, it seems to me that we can discern a subtle shift in the meaning, the significance, and the consequences of shame experiences. There were many shameful events in
the life and death of Jesus of Nazareth: his irregular conception (which
would have made him "illegitimate" in a culture in which the chastity
of women in a man's clan was key to his honor), his birth in a manger,
his irregular itinerant lifestyle, his unmarried status, his shameful execution (Pilch & Malina, 1998, 106–113; Capps, 2000).

As for Jesus' earthly ministry, it is, of course, the stuff of count-
less Sunday school lessons, for generations past and present and generations yet unborn, that Jesus was kind and compassionate to outcasts and sinners and that we should be likewise. It behooves us,
however, to look closely at the people to whom Jesus ministered.
When we do, we see that most of them were individuals under clouds
of shame (McClintock, 2001, 142–144)—shame that isolated them
from and made them unacceptable in their community. Here are
some of the people whom Jesus healed, ministered to, and associated with:

- Zacchaeus, a tax collector despised by his people for his collaboration with the occupying Romans in exacting taxes from the
  Jews (Luke 19:1–9), and other "tax collectors and sinners" with
  whom Jesus ate and otherwise associated (Matt. 9:10–13);
- the woman with the hemorrhage who was ritually impure
  under Jewish law (Mark 5:25; Luke 8:43–48);
- the sinner woman—presumably a prostitute—who came unin-
  vited to the Pharisee Simon's dinner party and washed Jesus'
  feet with her tears (Luke: 7:36–50);
- various and sundry lepers, who were ritually impure and outcasts from the community (Mark 1:40–44; Luke 17:11–19)
  (Pilch & Malina, 1998, 104–106);
- women, such as the Samaritan woman at the well with whom
  Jesus engaged in conversation about matters of shame to her,
  and the Syrophoenician woman who pleaded with him on behalf
  of her daughter (Matt. 15: 21–28; John 4:7–30; Mark 7:24–30);
- the raving Gerasene demoniac (Mark 5:1–20);

- various other persons who were "possessed by demons" (Matt. 8:28–34, 17:14–20; Luke 8:1–2, 9:37–43, 11:14; Mark 1:23–27, 3:22);
- an adulteress who was about to be stoned to death (John 8:4);
- a blind man who was presumed to have sinned, or had parents who sinned, about whom Jesus announced that the blindness was not due to anyone's sins (John 9:1–3).

Jesus told parables about love and acceptance of shamed and defiled individuals, such as the prodigal son, whose behavior in demanding and then dissipating his inheritance in dissolute living before his father's death, sleeping with pigs, etc., would have been heard by his listeners as completely beyond the pale (Luke 15:11–32). Jesus tells those who are insulted by being slapped on the right cheek to turn the other as well (Matt. 5:39). In a culture in which an assault to the face or head was viewed as a great humiliation, this too was a radical directive. Jesus himself was shamed during his trial and passion when he was blindfolded, scourged, and insulted, his face was struck (Mark 14:65; Luke 22:65; John 18:22), and his head was mockingly crowned with thorns (Neyrey, 1981, 204–205).

Jesus repeatedly exhorted people that "the greatest among you must become like the youngest, and the leader like one who serves" (Matt. 18:2–5; Luke 9:46–47, 22:26–27), thereby exalting the humble at the expense of the prideful and the powerful. Even as he was believed to be, at the very least, a great teacher, he humbled himself by washing the feet of lesser men at the Last Supper and exhorting them to do likewise (John 13:1–8).

Jesus taught that the shamed and outcast tax collector who prostrated himself at the temple was exalted by God, but the prideful Pharisees who "trusted in themselves" and their righteousness and "regarded others with contempt" would be "humbled" (Luke 18:9–14).

As he himself hung on the cross half naked after being spat upon, whipped, ridiculed, and crowned with thorns, Jesus conversed lovingly with self-confessed criminals (Luke 23:39–44).

Jesus returned to his disciples after his crucifixion and death not in a glorified body but rather still bearing the wounds of his humiliating death. Indeed, it was these wounds in his hands and his side that he displayed to Thomas to clearly identify himself as the Christ (John 20:24–28). As Pilch and Malina put it, "honor and shame as they touch Jesus are best evidenced in the passion account, and this in a culture where crucifixion was the most humiliating of all possible forms of

death" (Pilch & Malina, 1998, 113). However, "God's raising Jesus
from the dead demonstrates God's vindication of Jesus and the ascrip-
tion of paramount honor to him. It equally underscores God's approval
of Jesus' standards for what is honorable and what is shameful" (Pilch
& Malina, 1998, 114).

Jesus turned shame on its head. We see it everywhere in the Gospels. In an honor/shame culture in which a male's honor was the most
fundamental core value (Pilch & Malina, 1998, 106–114), Jesus
allowed himself to be ridiculed. Jesus did not shame other people—
with the notable exception of those who shamed others. He seemed
particularly attracted to shamed outcasts and perhaps was not far from
being one himself (Pilch & Malina, 1998, 45–48), by reason of the
irregular circumstances of his conception and birth, his life and ministry, and his crucifixion and death. In fact, John Dominic Crossan has
contended that the "healing miracles" of Jesus recounted in Scripture
were not intended to be read as literal interventions in the physical
world but healing of a sense of rejection and isolation. Jesus "refused
to accept the disease's ritual uncleanness and social ostracization"
(Crossan, 1995, 82; Pilch & Malina, 1998, 102–106).

It is a great mistake, however, to limit our understanding of the
meaning of the Gospels to an exhortation to be kind and inclusive
with outcasts. Yes, of course we should be kind and inclusive with outcasts, but there is a much deeper meaning to be gleaned from the Gospels. The Gospels are truly chronicles of shame as inner experience.
They are about the outcast, the unlovable, the impure, the abandoned—
i.e., the shamed—*inside* all of us, not just *outside* of us. We do well to
take in this message, and not just the message that we should be kind
and compassionate to others. New Testament scholar Robin Scroggs
has written that "The psychological realities coming to expression in
the biblical texts may be either descriptions of the imprisonment of
the self needing release, or those of the liberated, transformed person"
(Scroggs, 1982, 336). The main point is that "God's acts of salvation,
insofar as they lead to transformation happen not outside us or to us,
but primarily *within* us. Salvation means *changes*. Changes in how we
think, in how we feel, in how we act" (336). Jesus' transformation of
shame—i.e., his resurrection—is a description of a "liberated, transformed person." He is, indeed, the "bearer of archetypal truths about
the human condition that are alive and at work in the conscious and
unconscious haunts of the human psyche or mind" (Rollins, 2001).

We, all of us, carry sexual shame, fear of abandonment and loss of
love, of exposure, dread of public shaming and ridicule, of disease,

physical, spiritual, emotional infirmity (call them "demons" if you will), horror regarding our finitude and physicality, our lust and greed. We are not just exhorted to be kind to outcasts. We—all of us to a greater or lesser extent—experience ourselves as outcasts.

To the extent that the Gospels are about being kind, generous, compassionate, and inclusive to *others* who are outcasts, I believe that they are most fundamentally about the shame defense of *projection*—projection of our own shame onto others. If and to the extent that we were honestly and courageously to confront our own shame, our own isolation and outcast status, we would not be tempted to treat others as outcasts and seek to isolate and stigmatize them.

Here is an example of how depth psychology is helpful in religious life. Jung taught us that the protagonists in dreams are none other than different aspects of the dreamer. He relates two dreams: one of a theologian dreaming of a drunken tramp; the other of a high-society lady dreaming of a dissolute prostitute. Jung related that "[b]oth of them were outraged and horrified, and absolutely refused to admit, that they had dreamed of themselves. . . . The other person we dream of is not our friend or neighbor, but the other in us, of whom we prefer to say: 'I thank the Lord, that I am not this publican or sinner'" (Jung, 1964, 151).

Depth psychology helps us to look for and own the publican, the sinner, the dissolute prostitute, the hypocrite—all of the shamed, exiled pieces of ourselves. Why do this? Nobody wants to see these things, but we are impelled toward psychic and spiritual growth, just as a child is impelled to walk and talk and otherwise achieve independence. Psychic and spiritual growth can be attained only in this process of owning the fragments of ourselves. This is the pursuit of wholeness, and there is a cost to it because seeking wholeness does not mean finding just the good parts of ourselves but all of ourselves. This is what is involved in the transformation of shame and integration of the shame experience. This may be the ultimate meaning of Jesus' insistence to his disciples, after feeding 5,000 people with two fishes and five loaves of bread, that they "Gather up the fragments . . . so that nothing may be lost" (John 6:4–15) (Yarbrough, 1999, 28).

Jesus seemed to see an inevitability to his final shaming, telling his followers, "The Son of Man must undergo great suffering, and be rejected by the elders, chief priests and scribes, and be killed, and on the third day be raised" (Luke 9:22). Why *must* this final shaming happen? Psychologically, the religious and spiritual power of Jesus' story derives precisely from the shaming followed by the resurrection.

Hebrews 12:2 is quite explicit in spelling out the Christian experience of Jesus' achievement:

> Therefore, since we are surrounded by a great cloud of witnesses, let us also lay aside every weight and the sin that clings so closely, and let us run with perseverance the race that is set before us, *looking* to Jesus the pioneer and perfecter of our faith, who for the sake of the joy that was set before him endured the cross, disregarding its shame, and has taken his seat at the right hand of the throne of God. (emphasis added)

In 1 Corinthians, Paul spells out what he appears to see as a central meaning of the Christ event:

> Consider your own call, brothers and sisters: not many of you were wise by human standards, not many were powerful, not many were of noble birth. *But God chose what is foolish in this world to shame the wise; God chose what is weak in this world to shame the strong; God chose what is low and despised in the world, things that are not, to reduce to nothing things that are, so that no one might boast in the presence of God.* He is the source of your life in Christ Jesus, who become for us wisdom from God, and righteousness and sanctification and redemption, in order that, as it is written, "Let the one who boasts, boast in the Lord." (1 Cor. 1: 26–30; emphasis added)

This theme of transforming weakness (i.e., shame) to strength that is so present in the Christ event is also seen in 2 Corinthians 12:6–10, where Paul explains how he appealed three times to God to remove from him an unspecified "thorn in the flesh." God did not grant the request but instead replied, "My grace is sufficient for you, for power is made perfect in weakness. So I will boast all the more gladly of my weaknesses, so that the power of Christ may dwell in me. Therefore I am content with weaknesses, insults, hardships, persecutions, and calamities for the sake of Christ; for whenever I am weak, I am strong."

To see how Jesus transformed weakness to power, let us briefly retrace some of the key aspects of the Gospel narrative of his ministry. First, he was faithful to his own call, regardless of the cost. He courageously accepted the terrible anguish and defeats that seem to have gone along with the triumphs. The Gospels of Matthew, Mark, Luke, and John proclaim the commencement of Jesus' earthly ministry at his triumphant baptism, at which time the heavens open up and God's spirit descends upon him (Matt. 3:13–17; Mark 1:9–11; Luke 3:21–22; John 1:29–34) with the pronouncement, "This is my Son, the Beloved, with whom I am well pleased." Immediately thereafter, however, according to the Gospels of Matthew (4:1–11), Mark (1:12–13), and Luke (4:1–13), Jesus is driven by the Spirit into the wilderness with wild beasts and is tempted there by Satan for forty days. Here we see a subtext that continues throughout the Gospels of triumph followed by anguish. The story of Jesus' anguish and temptations in the wilderness is typically seen and preached in the light of his ultimate triumph over those temptations, but it could not have been experienced at the time this isolated and famished individual was going through it as other than agonizing and most probably terrifying. This is an instance in which, in the words of Jung, Jesus confronts his shadow, which must necessarily include his own shame issues.

Next, the biblical text describes Jesus as sustaining an intentional, prayerful relationship with God. There are many other instances in the Gospels in which Jesus intentionally retreats from his encounters with crowds into prayerful communication with God (Luke 9:28–36; Matt. 14:13–14, 14:22–27; John 6:15). When in his journeys Jesus came to minister in his hometown of Nazareth, he was reminded that he was just a carpenter, the "son of Mary" (Mark 6:1–6)—and this last identification would have been shaming in a time, place, and culture in which one who was honorably conceived would be identified by his father's lineage. It has been suggested that "the question 'Where did this man get all this [wisdom and power]?' may imply a hostile answer. Perhaps his is the offspring of someone other than his father" (Perkins, 1995, 592). In an honor/shame culture in which the chastity of the women in a man's clan was of almost numinous significance, it is extremely likely that Jesus of Nazareth was viewed by his community as illegitimate. This would immediately have placed him outside proper "covenant status" in the house of Israel (Capps, 2000, 149).

It is not surprising, given the paralysis and self-negation that attends shame, that Jesus found himself unable to accomplish "deeds of power" in his hometown and said, "Prophets are not without honor, except in their hometown, and among their own kin, and in their own house" (Matt. 6:4). It is not much of a stretch to conclude that Jesus' impotence in Nazareth resulted from the shaming reminders he received there of his humble—and in at least one respect even shameful—origins. According to the Gospel of Luke, Jesus was actually driven by the townspeople out of town and led to the brow of the hill "so that they might hurl him off the cliff" (Luke 4:29–30).

Jesus' own family seems to have questioned his sanity: having heard (and evidently credited) news that he had lost his mind, his mother and siblings came at one point to collect him (Mark 3:21).

The final time that Jesus retreats to pray is in the garden immediately before his capture by Roman authorities, his passion, and death.

Here we find the most painful struggle of all—a struggle that includes sweating blood and terrible fear, anguish and an obvious sense of profound isolation, loneliness and betrayal—all essential elements of the shame experience. Jesus interrupts his prayer two or three times to beg his disciples to stay awake while he prays, but to no avail. They dissociate from the situation by sleeping.

Jürgen Moltmann stresses Jesus' rejection. He was rejected and abandoned by humanity, but this was not the worst of it: on the cross, he "was abandoned by his Father, whose immediate presence he proclaimed and experienced in his life" (Moltmann, 1993, 63). According to Mark 15:37, he died with a loud, inarticulate cry, just after remonstrating, "My God, my God, why have you forsaken me?"(Mark 15:34). Hebrews 5:7 says that he died with "loud cries and tears." However, "because, as the Christian tradition developed, this terrible cry of the dying Jesus was gradually weakened in the passion narratives and replaced by words of comfort and triumph, we can probably rely upon it as a kernel of historical truth. Jesus clearly died with every expression of the most profound horror" (Moltmann, 1993, 146).

Moltmann suggests that Jesus' worst "torment was his abandonment by God." Furthermore, "what happened on the cross" must be understood as "something that took place between Jesus and his God." Thus, "the origin of Christology . . . lies not in Jesus' understanding of himself or in his messianic consciousness, nor in the evaluation of him by his disciples. . . . It lies in what took place between Jesus and his God . . . in what was given expression in his preaching and his actions and was literally 'put to death' in his abandonment as he died" (Moltmann, 1993, 149).

Jesus was, indeed, "folly to the wise, a scandal to the devout and a disturber of the peace in the eyes of the mighty. That is why he was crucified" (Moltmann, 1993, 24). The earliest Christians were frequently called to task about the fact that, as an oracle of Apollo recorded by Porphyry wrote, they were "persisting in . . . vain delusions, lamenting in song a god who died in delusions, who was condemned by judges whose verdict was just, and executed in the prime of life by the worst of death, a death bound with iron" (Hengel, 1971, 4–5). This oracle asserted that "the one whom Christians claim as their God is a 'dead God'—a contradiction in itself. . . . And if that were not enough, . . . he had been condemned to the worst form of death: he had to endure being fastened to the cross with nails" (Hengel, 1971, 4–5). For people of the ancient world (i.e., Greeks, Romans, barbarians, and Jews), the cross was not just "any kind of death. . . . It was an utterly offensive affair, 'obscene' in the original sense of the word" (Hengel, 1971, 22). The shame and scandal of the cross seems to have put early Christians somewhat on the defensive: Justin Martyr describes the offense caused by the Christian message to the ancient world as "madness": "They say that our *madness* consists in the fact that we put a *crucified man* in the second place after the unchangeable and eternal God, the Creator of the world" (Hengel, 1971, 1).

Yet this Jesus, rejected and abandoned by his friends and feeling himself as rejected by God on the cross, is experienced by some as incarnating God. The experience of rejection, isolation, and abandonment is, as we have seen, the very essence of shame. If we could not understand Jesus as experiencing shame and suffering, the Gospel narrative of the Christ event would be all but meaningless. Dietrich Bonhoeffer, writing from prison shortly before his own execution, put it this way:

> God lets himself be pushed out of the world on to the cross. He is weak and powerless in the world, and that is precisely the way, the only way, in which he is with us and helps us. Matt. 8:17 makes it quite clear that Christ helps us, not by virtue of his omnipotence, but by virtue of his weakness and suffering. . . . [*O*]*nly the suffering God can help. . . . That is a reversal of what the religious man expects from God. Man is summoned to share God's sufferings at the hands of a godless world.* (Bonhoeffer, 1971, 360–361, emphasis added)

The Jesus of the Gospel narratives accomplishes great deeds of healing and power, he teaches and ministers from a profoundly powerful place in his center that is filled with God consciousness. But the Jesus of the Gospel narratives, when stripped of his Sunday school gloss, also suffered isolation, loneliness, anguish, and shame. His own triumphant struggle with these feelings, accomplished through constant prayer and brutal honesty, allowed their transformation in himself and gave him the ability to be a psychological instrument for the transformation of shame in others.

We contemporary people can take in Jesus' real lessons. We can struggle honestly and courageously with our own shame issues. In the words of Paul, this means coming to feel that "power is made perfect in weakness" (2 Cor. 12:9).

Conclusion

I have attempted in this article to demonstrate the ubiquity in human life of the shame experience and its centrality in the tension between the human condition of creatureliness and our awareness of godliness. The work of depth psychologists gives us a place to stand in understanding the roots of and the power and potential of shame in human life. This understanding gives us courage and hope as we seek God's grace in transforming healthy shame.

The biblical portrait of the Christ event—the Incarnation—constellates the shame archetype. Jesus' ministry with shamed and rejected individuals, and his own birth, passion, death, and resurrection, give us paradigmatic models of shame transformed.

Note

1. This table is reprinted with permission from Lynd, 1958, 208–209.

References

Bonhoeffer, D. (1955). *Letters and Papers from Prison*. London: SCM Press.

Bonhoeffer, D. (1971). *Letters and Papers from Prison*. London: SCM Press.

Bradshaw, J. (1988). *Healing the Shame That Binds You*. Deerfield Beach: Health Communications, Inc.

Capps, D. (2000). *Jesus: A Psychological Biography*. St. Louis: Chalice Press.

Crossan, J. D. (1995). *Jesus: A Revolutionary Biography*. San Francisco: Harper SanFrancisco.

Edelman, S. (1998). *Turning the Gorgon*. Woodstock: Spring Publications.

Episcopal Hymnal. (1982). Church Hymnal Corporation, New York.

Erikson, E. (1958). *Young Man Luther*. New York: W. W. Norton & Company.

Freud, S. (1917). *Mourning and Melancholia*. In *The Standard Edition of the Complete Psychological Works of Sigmund Freud*, vol. 14, J. Strachey, ed. and trans. London: Hogarth Press, 1966, 243–258.

Goffman, E. (1963). *Stigma: Notes on the Management of Spoiled Identity*. New York: Simon and Schuster.

Hawthorne, N. (1999). *The Scarlet Letter*. New York: Signet Classics.

Hengel, M. (1971). *Crucifixion in the Ancient World and the Folly of the Message of the Cross*. Philadelphia: Fortress Press.

Hick, J., & Goulder, M. (1983) *Why Believe in God?* London: SCM Press.

Hultberg, P. (1988). Shame: A Hidden Emotion. *Journal of Analytical Psychology*, *33*, 109–126.

Jacoby, M. (1996). *Shame and the Origins of Self Esteem: A Jungian Approach*. New York: Routledge Press.

Jung, C. G. (1950). Aion, *Collected Works*, R. F. C. Hull, ed. & trans. (Vol. 9). Princeton: Princeton University Press, ii.

Jung, C. G. (1952a). Answer to Job, *Collected Works*, R. F. C. Hull, ed. & trans. (Vol. 11). Princeton: Princeton University Press, 357–470.

Jung, C. G. (1952b). Synchronicity: An Acausal Principle, *Collected Works*, R. F. C. Hull, ed. & trans. (Vol. 8). Princeton: Princeton University Press, 421–519.

Jung, C. G. (1964). The Meaning of Psychology for Modern Man, *Collected Works*, R. F. C. Hull, ed. & trans. (Vol. 10). Princeton: Princeton University Press, 134–156.

Kennedy, E. (2001). *The Church and Human Sexuality: The Unhealed Wound*. New York: St. Martin's Griffin.

Lewis, H. (1971). *Shame and Guilt in Neurosis*. London and New York: International Universities Press.

Lewis, M. (1995). *Shame: The Exposed Self*. New York: The Free Press.

Lynd, H. (1958). *On Shame and the Search for Identity*. London: Routledge. (Reprinted 1999)

May, R. (1989). *The Art of Counseling* (Rev. ed.). Lake Worth: Gardner Press.

McClintock, K. (2001). *Sexual Shame: An Urgent Call for Healing*. Minneapolis: Augsburg Fortress Press.

Moltmann, J. (1993). *Crucified God*. Minneapolis: Fortress Press.

Nathanson, D. (1992). *Shame and Pride: Affect, Sex and the Birth of Self*. New York: W. W. Norton & Company.

Neyrey, J. (1981). *Honor and Shame in the Gospel of Matthew*. Louisville: John Knox Press.

Otto, R. (1958). *The Idea of the Holy*, J. Harvey, trans. New York: Oxford University Press. (Original work published 1923)

Pattison, S. (2000). *Shame: Theory, Therapy, Theology*. Cambridge: Cambridge University Press.

Patton, J. (1985). *Is Human Forgiveness Possible?* Nashville: Abingdon Press.

Perkins, P. (1995). The Gospel of Mark. In *New Interpreter's Bible Commentary* (Vol. 8). Nashville: Abingdon Press, 509.

Pilch, J., & Malina, B., eds. (1998). *Handbook of Biblical Social Values*. Peabody: Hendrickson Publishers.

Roland, A. (1996). Cultural Pluralism and Psychoanalysis. London: Routledge.

Rollins, W. (1999). *Soul and Psyche: The Bible in Psychological Perspective*. Minneapolis: Fortress Press.

Rollins, W. (2001, November 19). Lecture presented at the annual meeting of the Society of Biblical Literature, Denver.

Schneider, C. (1977). *Shame: Exposure and Privacy*. Boston: Beacon Press.

Scroggs, R. (1982, March). Emerging Trends in Biblical Thought. *Christian Century*, 99, 335–338.

Tillich, P. (1957). *Systematic Theology* (Vol. 2). Chicago: University of Chicago Press.

Tomkins, S. (1963). *The Negative Affects: Vol. 2. Affect, Imagery Consciousness*. New York: Springer.

Wimberly, E. (1999). *Moving from Shame to Self Worth*. Nashville: Abingdon Press.

Winnicott, D. W. (1986). Children Learning. In *Home Is Where We Start From*. New York: W. W. Norton & Company, 142–149.

Winnicott, D. W. (1988). *Human Nature*. Levittown: Brunner/Mazel.

Wurmser, L. (1997). *The Mask of Shame*. Northvale: Jason Aronson, Inc.

Yarbrough, C. D. (1999). Fragments of Our Lives. In *Preaching Through the Year of Mark: Sermons That Work* (Vol. 7), R. Alling & D. Schlafer, eds. New York: Morehouse Publishing, 28–31.

CHAPTER 15

BIBLICAL IMAGERY AND PSYCHOLOGICAL LIKENESS

David L. Miller

Cosmopolitan magazine, for its December 1958 issue, asked a number of well-known persons what would happen if Jesus were to return to earth. The respondents included Aldous Huxley, Pitrim Sorokin, Billy Graham, and Norman Vincent Peale. They also included C. G. Jung, then eighty-three years old, who responded with a brief reply in English. He wrote, very much unlike the others, that if this were to happen, because of the photographs and interviews from the media, Jesus "would see himself banalized beyond all endurance" (Jung, 1976a, 638). Jung's choice of words may seem odd, but it was in fact apt. Originally the term "banal" referred to a kind of feudal service whereby the tenants of a certain district were obliged to carry their grain to be ground at a certain mill and to be baked at a certain oven, a practice that was to the economic benefit of the lord of the manor, a sort of company store. Although the word "banal" now denotes "commonness," its history implies not variety and difference but monopoly.

This anecdote is, I believe, relevant to reflections in a work on psychology and the Bible. One might have conceived former tendencies in biblical interpretation to have been *banal* in both senses of the word—i.e., having become in our time common historiographically and theologically. But this may be the result of monopolistic perspective, even though, at first blush, it would appear that there has actually existed a hermeneutic binarism since the eighteenth century.

On the one hand, there seems to have been an assumption by some that the text of the Bible has doctrinal referents. That is, it is taken for granted in this perspective that biblical representation ultimately signifies tenets of belief, that the images and narratives of various pericopes have to do with ideas and thoughts to which a person in our own day may either give assent in faith or not. Faith, then, is imagined to be the work of the volitional ego. Mysteries of religion are located in the mind and the spirit of the human. This places the signifying function of the biblical text in the realm of what in philosophy is referred to as that of intelligibles.

On the other hand, different interpreters (or the same interpreters at different times or with different texts) seem to have assumed that the referent of the biblical text has to do with sensible rather than intelligible reality. It refers, these persons imagine, historically, and its message points to doings and experiences rather than to being and meaning. The stories and images of religion, in this view, have to do with the pietisms of everyday personal (i.e., egoic) life and morality. Their meaning belongs to the realm of the sensibles.

As biblical scholarship has swung back and forth between these (largely unconscious) hermeneutic perspectives, the effect on the religious imagination has been to split dogma and piety, mind and heart, spirit and flesh, ideal and real, thought and feeling, infinite and finite, supernatural and natural, transcendent and immanent. Yet these apparent oppositions do not in logical fact indicate real differences. Rather, philosophically understood, they are both representational and referential with regard to signification and they thereby carry an unwitting metaphysics of presence as a part of their perspectival baggage. Psychologically put, they locate religion as a function of ego, that is, ego's beliefs and doctrines, thoughts and ideas, or ego's experiences and history and behaviors (see Miller, 1981, xv–xxiv; 1986, 1–10). Furthermore, this monopolistic binarism (an ontotheology of ego) tends to locate the function of a religious text in the past (history, *Heilsgeschichte*, the sins of the fathers) or in the future (the kingdom of heaven, eschatology, tomorrow's moral imperative). What is missed is the psychological possibility that there may be an impact of biblical imagery in the here and now, a signifying that is different from, without being opposed to, historical or theological meanings, a textual intentionality and function that refers to a dimension of selfhood that is other than ego.

To put the matter another way, if assuming a theological and doctrinal significance to texts puts the interpreter in a deductive and rationalistic mode of thinking, and if assuming a historical and experiential significance implies an inductive and empirical strategy, there is yet a third possible way. The historian of religions, Henry Corbin, called this alternative way and its domain by the name *mundus imaginalis*, which was his translation into Latin of the Arabic *alam-al-mithal* (Corbin, 1970, 240; 1972, 1–19; 1979, 7–19). This "imaginal realm" functions similarly to the *metaxy* of Plato and of Plotinus, for both of whom the "middle realm" between mind's intelligibles (*nous*) and experience's sensibles (*aisthetikoi*) is the domain of soul (*psychē*) and carries the workings of imagination (*phantasia*). The realm of soul is logically situated between body and mind or spirit; it is the realm of imagination between rationality and empirical sense.

This "between realm" can be understood from everyday experience. If I attempt to communicate an idea to someone who does not understand, I might offer an illustration (i.e., giving image to an otherwise abstract idea). On the other hand, if I try to communicate an experience to someone who has never had such an experience, I might give a likeness or metaphor (i.e., giving image to an otherwise idiosyncratic empirical reality). Not only can the person sense the likeness of the idea or experience in the image, but he or she also and simultaneously is able to have a feel for the idea or, on the other hand, a cognition concerning the experience. Idea and experience come together in imagination's images. From Corbin's perspective, imagery functions in a modality other than that of reason and sensation. Yet it integrates these epistemic aspects that otherwise tend to split off from one another.

Think of the Bible in this imaginal manner (see Miller, 1980, 78–88). The biblical text is a treasure-house of images that are contextualized in a variety of genres (myth, history, parable, poetry, letter, prophecy, and apocalypse). These may be viewed not only as historical and/ or eschatological referents but also as profound psychological life-likenesses. For example, we are thrown into a world where things need naming; we have been excluded from paradisiacal bliss; we are confused by the world's towering babel; we are deluged and flooded; we are in bondage, yet from time to time we are able to walk dry through the sea's tempests and over its waves, even if it leads to more wilderness wandering; we are drawn to idols of gold and want a king like the others; we are exiled on an ash heap, yet we experience that we sometimes get guidance from our whirlwinds; we may even discover that something sacred is born from a virginal place; we have also been nailed, betrayed by our nearest friend, torn to pieces, and yet, miraculously, we manage to go on after three days or so; we find ourselves waiting for spirit to come; and we experience apocalypse now: "My God, my God! Why hast Thou forsaken me?" This is as articulate a psychology as one can find anywhere. The biblical images are "as-structures," as Heidegger called such, of the ideas (fantasies) and feel-ings of the psyche (Heidegger, 1962, 189). They body forth the uncon-scious complexes of a rich and multifaceted psyche.

Freud and Jung, who were known for drawing upon Greek mytho-logical images for their psychological tropings, both knew this psy-chological dimension of the Bible as well as the biblical dimension of the modern psyche. It is not surprising to find Jung saying that "we must read the Bible or we shall not understand psychology. Our psychology, whole lives, our language and images are built upon the Bible" (Jung, 1976b, 156). But Freud's concurring words may for some be unanticipated: "My deep engrossment in the Bible story (almost as soon as I had learnt the art of reading) had, as I recognized much later, an enduring effect on the direction of my interest" (Freud, 1959, 8).

If the psychological hermeneutic is more obvious after Freud and Jung, it is nonetheless neither new nor unique to depth psychology. The here-and-now life-likeness approach to biblical texts was, to give only one example, already conceptualized by Origen of Alexandria. In his third-century work, *On First Principles*, Origen was worrying the problem of a discrepancy between the twenty-sixth and twenty-seventh verses of the first chapter of Genesis. He wrote: "'And God said, Let us make man in our own image and likeness.' Then he [Moses] adds afterward, 'And God made man; in the image of God made he him. . . .' Now the fact that he said, 'He made him in the image of God,' and was silent about the likeness, points to nothing else but this, that man received the honor of God's image in the first creation, whereas the perfection of God's likeness was reserved for him." (Origen, 1966, 245). The implication for biblical study is that the text of the Bible reveals a world of images that are given by God but that the work of men and women in this life is to continue the creation of worlds of meaning by seeing likenesses to life among these images, as in the examples given two paragraphs above. The task is to turn image to likeness or to see likeness in biblical imagery and narrative.

This is, of course, an old strategy that is still very much the main-stay of poets, whether by way of metaphorical or metonymical con-sciousness. Three examples will make the point. The second part of Wallace Stevens's poem "The Owl in the Sarcophagus" describes the function of seeing the resemblance of life and image:

There came a day, there was a day—one day
A man walked living among the forms of thought
To see their lustre truly as it is

And in harmonious prodigy to be,
A while, . . .
. . . , a likeness of the earth,
That by resemblance twanged him through and through,

Releasing an abysmal melody,
A meeting, an emerging in the light,
A dazzle of remembrance and of sight.

(Stevens, 1975, 432–433)

Stevens's twang and dazzle is an amplification of a similar function reported in the tenth *Duino Elegy* by Rainer Maria Rilke:

And yet, they were waking a likeness within us, the endlessly dead,
look, they'd be pointing, perhaps, to the catkins, hanging
from empty hazels, or else they'd be meaning the rain
that falls on the dark earth in the early Spring.

And we, who have always thought
of happiness climbing, would feel
the emotion that almost startles
when happiness falls.

(Rilke, 1939, 85)

James Tate echoes analogical happiness in his poem "Entries," which is cited by both David Tracy (1981, 446) and Wendy Doniger (1998, 28–29) in books that argue in a manner similar to the present essay:

When I think no thing is *like* any other thing
I become speechless, cold, my body turns silver
and water runs off me. There I am
ten feet from myself, possessor of nothing,
uncomprehending of even the simplest particle of dust.
But when I say, You are *like*
a swamp animal during an eclipse,
I am happy, full of wisdom, loved by children
and old men alike. I am sorry if this confuses you.
During an eclipse the swamp animal
acts as though day were night,
drinking when he should be sleeping, etc.
This is why men stay up all night
writing to you.

(Tate, 1972, 90)

Goethe's sensibility, at the end of part two of *Faust*, explains the condition that makes possible Stevens's, Rilke's, and Tate's celebration of life-likenesses. He writes: "*Alles vergängliche / Ist nur ein Gleichnis*" (Everything that passes / is only a likeness) (Goethe, 1962, 502; my translation). This seeing of the likeness of "everything"—the transformation of everyday images into psychological life-likenesses, which is the stock and trade of poets—can include the poetics of biblical imagery.

To be sure, not everyone is convinced. Typical critiques of seeing depth-psychological meaning in the biblical images fall into three categories: attacks on essentialism, comparativism, and reductionism. I shall address each of these reticences in turn.

Essentialism/Difference

One typical criticism of a depth-psychological interpretation of biblical texts goes somewhat as follows: by assuming that the biblical imagery has archetypal psychological meaning, one implies a world of essences and essential forms of human meaning. The problem with such an assumption—or so goes the critique—is that it does not have adequate regard for the otherness of the divine or for the otherness of other persons. It elides not only the "infinite qualitative distinction" between the divine and human but also the fundamental differences of persons of various races, classes, and genders.

This criticism, however, is unsophisticated about the notion of "archetype." Ironically, it is a criticism concerning difference that itself fails to draw upon an important difference, a difference that is poignantly illustrated by an anecdote about C. G. Jung and Mircea Eliade.

In the context of their friendship at the Eranos Conferences in Ascona, Switzerland, Eliade, late in 1954, sent Jung a copy of his then-new book on yoga. Eliade speaks in that work about what he takes to be the archetypal significance of mandala images from south Asian yogic contexts and quotes Jung in support of his point about these being structurally archetypal. Eliade clearly thought that he was agreeing with what he took to be Jung's universal and essentialist point on the appearance of similar mandala imagery in his patients' spontaneous drawings. But much to Eliade's astonishment, instead of receiving a pleasant thank-you note Jung sent in reply a diatribe that indicated a profound difference between a philosophical (Platonic-Augustinian) use of the notion of "archetype" as an essential intellectual form (i.e., Eliade's notion) and a depth-psychological use of what many wrongly assume is the same notion (Jung, 1975a, 210–212). So crucial was the difference to Jung that it seems to have threatened the personal friendship between the two men. However, Eliade changed the citation to Jung in a subsequent edition of the work and wrote an apologetic clarification in the introduction of a still later book (Eliade, 1958, 219–227; 1959, vii–ix).

The difference in the two ideas concerning psychological images may be understood as the difference between material likenesses of something that appears among images that seem to be the same and formal likenesses of something that does not appear (unconsciously) among images that differ. In the *Enneads*, 1.2.2, Plotinus calls this distinction the difference between likenesses of like things, which the philosopher takes to be superficial, and likenesses of unlike things, that is, a likeness that does not appear and that is based upon difference (see Miller, 1986, 41–51). The former tends to function as a stereotype. Jung wanted to reserve the idea of archetype for the latter (even if many latter-day Jungians themselves seem to entertain the same confusion that Eliade did).

Martin Heidegger articulated the difference that Jung draws Eliade's attention to in a lecture on the "principle of identity" given in June 1957. The lecture became the book *Identity and Difference*. Heidegger argued that "the close relation [*die Zusammengehörigkeit*; the "belonging together"] of *identity* and *difference* . . . is that which gives us thought" (Heidegger, 1969, 21, 84). But Heidegger claims that identity and difference cannot come into an integrated relationship so long as one thinks of the identity of belonging together as a belonging *together* (*die ZUSAMMENgehörigkeit*), because this suggests, in Hegelian fashion, "the unity of a manifold, combined systematically, mediated by a unifying center of authoritative synthesis" (Heidegger, 1969, 9, 92). According to Heidegger's reasoning there is another way to think about the nature of identity and difference: namely, as *belonging together* (*die ZusammenGEHÖRIGKEIT*). In this way of thinking, the unity is determined by the belongingness of difference, rather than belongingness being determined by the unity. In the variety of unlikenesses in life one may begin to sense a vibrant resonance (*der in sich schwingende Bereich*) wherein things that one may not have thought belong *together* nonetheless *belong* together (Heidegger, 1969, 37, 102).

Jung, like Heidegger, was firmly post-Kantian concerning essence and difference, even if the former's language sideslipped from time to time. Jung saw clearly that the "self" is both the object and the subject

of the psychological work and that all psychological knowledge is
therefore hypothetical, having no claim to universal essentialist validity, being thereby confessional in its logical status and nature (see
Jung, 1971, 8–9; 1976a, 125–127; 1982, 181–183, 185). This implies
that "archetype" is by no means a metaphysical postulate but rather is
heuristic in function (Jung, 1969, 306). Jung's own strategy in psychological interpretation was to focus upon difference (see Hillman, 1988,
12–13). Individuation (growth and maturation in psychological insight)
was thought of as differentiation rather than as identification, the separation of the parts of a whole rather than an achievement of wholeness, the latter of which Jung thought impossible (Jung, 1971, 424, 448;
1985, 196–198). Individuation, Jung said provocatively, is becoming
that which one is not, and it is accompanied by the feeling of being a
stranger (Jung, 1972, 73, 174; 1975b, 31). So much is this the case that
it has led James Hillman, a postmodern archetypalist after Jung, not to
use the word "archetype" as a noun (as if it referred to some "thing" or
essence) but to use the adjective "archetypal," which Hillman says "is
a move one makes rather than a thing that is" (Hillman, 1983, 13).

A truly *depth*-psychological reading of biblical images, then, is a move
that is being made, and it is a move that, if properly understood, is
hardly vulnerable to an essentialist critique. This criticism is a misunderstanding; indeed, it is psychologically a projection. It could be
argued that an authentically depth-psychological hermeneutic precisely deessentializes the meaning of the text rather than locating
what someone might think of as an essential meaning or a psychological essence. Biblical images as life-likenesses are likenesses based on
fundamental difference rather than on sameness, what David Tracy
called "similarity-in-difference," recalling the words of Aristotle: "To
spot the similar in the dissimilar is the mark of poetic genius" (Tracy,
1981, 410). The life-likenesses are (un)grounded upon that which the
person is not, upon an otherness with which the psyche resonates even
while being different. As Wendy Doniger has put it: "Comparison is
our way of making sense of difference" (Doniger, 1998, 28).

Comparativism/Historicism

A second critique of a depth-psychological hermeneutic fears any
archetypal reading of meaning because of its putative ignoring of par-
ticularistic difference: namely, historical and temporal distinctiveness.
The criticism is that a psychological interpretation wittingly or unwittingly presupposes that meaning in texts is separate and separable

from a social, historical, and political context. The images of a narrative or a poem—so goes this assumption—signify similarly across temporal and spatial boundaries. A psychological reading leads inevitably to a comparativism in which everything is finally everything. It is likeness run amok, devoid of real everyday reality.

A first response to this charge must entail a reality check in the form of a few statements by Jung himself on the issue that is at stake, since it is Jung, rather than Freud, who is typically the target of this attack. To make the point as strongly as possible, I shall cite four of Jung's remarks:

> Primordial images and the nature of the archetype took a central place in my researches, and it became clear to me that without history there can be no psychology, and certainly no psychology of the unconscious. A psychology of consciousness can, to be sure, content itself with material taken from personal life, but as soon as we wish to explain a neurosis we require an anamnesis which reaches deeper than the knowledge of [personal ego] consciousness. (Jung, 1963, 205–206)

> It is . . . a grave mistake to think that it is enough to gain some understanding of the images and that knowledge here can make a halt. Insight into them must be converted into an ethical obligation. Not to do so is to fall prey to the power principle and this produces dangerous effects which are destructive not only to others but even to the knower. (Jung, 1963, 192–193)

> For me . . . irreality was the quintessence of horror, for I aimed, after all, at this world and this life. No matter how deeply absorbed or how blown about I was, I always knew that everything I was experiencing was ultimately directed at this real life of mine. (Jung, 1963, 189)

> Everything has its history, everything has "grown," and Christianity, which is supposed to have appeared suddenly as a sudden revelation from heaven, undoubtedly also has its history. . . . It is exactly as if we had built a cathedral over a pagan temple and no longer know that it is there unendingly. (Jung, 1970, 342)

These citations have at least the complicating effect of putting in the mouth of Jung the very words some critics use against him, which suggests that the supposed critique may well be itself a psychological projection that is ill-informed and lacking in serious scholarship, even if unintentionally so. There is, after all, a certain irony in critics of depth psychology's purported ahistoricism being themselves not altogether realistically contextualized. But the matter is as complex as it is ironic.

Jonathan Z. Smith has quoted Burton Mack approvingly concerning

the matter that Jung refers to above concerning the ahistorical nature
of certain self-espoused historicist hermeneutics of Christianity:

> The fundamental persuasion [of many scholars] is that Christianity
> appeared unexpectedly in human history, that it was (is) at core a brand
> new vision of human existence, and that, since this is so, only a startling
> moment could account for its emergence at the beginning. The code word
> serving as a sign for the novelty that appeared is the term unique. . . . It
> is this startling moment that seems to have mesmerized the discipline
> and determined the application of its critical methods. (Smith, 1990,
> 38–39)

The point, I take it, is that a so-called historical hermeneutic of
Christianity since the Enlightenment has given a reading of Christianity that is ahistorical (i.e., that denies Christianity's historical context). This suggests that the historical critique of depth-psychological
hermeneutics as being ahistorical has itself been involved in a reading
of Christianity that is archetypal and ahistorical, whereas Jung, for
one, wants archetypal readings to be grounded historically and to
have political and real-life effects.

The larger problem with this comparativist-historicist binarism is
that it may have been a false split from the beginning. Jonathan Z.
Smith has already been mentioned, and it has been his work for the
past twenty years that has aimed at correcting the simplistic dualism.
Smith is presuming the unwitting assumption that Nietzsche's Zarathustra (1966) calls "the myth of the Immaculate perception," that is,
the naively realistic assumption that historical readings bear a trans-
parency to some past real reality free of interpretative perspective.

Smith's point has been that differentiating historical work always
and already involves comparison, in spite of itself or its claims. In a lecture at Arizona State University in 1985, Smith gave examples of Saint
Paul, John of Plan del Carpini, and Jan von Ruysbroeck, as well as the
Israelites in the Bible, to show that "a theory of difference, when applied
to the proximate 'other,' is but another way of paraphrasing a theory
of 'self'" (Smith, 1992, 14). Smith called this "differential equations,"
and he noted that if there were "actual remoteness," authentic historical
otherness and some fundamental and separable difference, there would
be "mutual indifference." It is not a matter of whether comparativist
identifications take place in historiography but of whether such com-
parisons are made conscious or not. Psychological interpretations
become a convenient scapegoat for historians who may be unconsciously anxious about the subjective nature of their own purportedly
objective work. Think of the histories written about the Civil War!

Furthermore, as Smith says in an earlier work, "comparison itself requires the postulation of difference as the grounds of its being inter-esting (rather than tautological) and a methodological manipulation of difference, a playing across the 'gap' in the service of some useful end" (Smith, 1982, 35; cf. Smith, 1990, 38–39). Just as historical particularism implies comparison, so comparison implies difference and particularity. Smith says: "The process of comparison is a fundamental characteris-tic of human intelligence. Whether revealed in the logical grouping of classes, in poetic similes, in mimesis, or other like activities, comparison, the bringing together of two or more objects for the purpose of noting either similarity or dissimilarity, is the omnipresent substructure of human thought" (Smith, 1978, 240). This is, of course, the point about seeing psychological life-likenesses of biblical images, and to be sure, such a depth-psychological hermeneutic can be viewed as a very histor-ical and particular activity, even against those who imagine otherwise.

In his recent book, *The Savage in Judaism*, Howard Eilberg-Schwartz has made an argument that is adjacent to Smith's, one that reveals the naïveté of the historicist critique of a depth-psychological compara-tivism. Eilberg-Schwartz writes: "Determining what is 'the context' is itself always an interpretive act" (Eilberg-Schwartz, 1990, 95). That is, the distinction between a historical-contextualist and a psycholog-ical-comparativist paradigm breaks down in the end. Are Jewish reli-gion and history the context for Christian origins? Should the social and historical context be extended to Greco-Roman culture? Egyp-tian? And if these, should one not note the Persian and Indian contex-tualizations? And East Asian? Eilberg-Schwartz notes what must be apparent but is often not acknowledged. "Comparative analysis is sim-ply unavoidable. If an interpreter repudiates it, it comes in the back door" (Eilberg-Schwartz, 1990, 99). "History, like ethnography, always already presupposes comparative inquiry. . . . What this means is that there is no escaping the comparative enterprise. Even the most con-crete, contextualist study presupposes certain notions about societies, cultures, and persons formulated to explain human behavior and expe-rience in diverse contexts" (Eilberg-Schwartz, 1990, 99; cf. 1994, 173–178). It is not only "comparativists" who are comparativist, just as it is not only "historicists" who are grounded in real life.

Psychologism/Reductionism

A third typical critique remains, even if the other two were able to be met satisfactorily. It is the familiar charge of a humanization of things divine, of bringing the larger into the domain of the smaller, of the reductionism of psychologism.

To be sure, reductionism is a perduring risk. But one wonders if it is any more a risk in psychological than in historical and theological readings. It goes without saying that there are many humanistic ego-psychological readings that reduce. Indeed, Jung complained in his Tavistock Lectures that Freud's method of "free association" was reductive and offered his own "seeking the parallels" in larger arche-typal contexts (myth, folktale, religion, the arts) as a corrective in the direction of "amplification," seeing the smaller in terms of the larger, what Proclus calls *epistrophē*, a "leading back" of human things to their larger archetypal contexts (Jung, 1976a, 82–83).

Just here is the point. A given interpretation that proceeds by seeing psychological life-likenesses in biblical images may indeed itself be interpreted by some as reductive. But it may also be imagined other-wise. Rather than being a matter of psychologizing the Bible, it can be understood as the experience of "biblicizing" the psyche, of imagining human thoughts and feelings in terms of biblical images, divinizing the human rather than humanizing the divine. It is not that Jacob and his mother and father are in an Oedipal complex, but rather that a given sense of the familial mess can be seen as a Jacob complex.

This takes seriously Jung's saying that "we must read the Bible or we shall not understand psychology" (Jung, 1976b, 156). It is what Heinz Westman had in mind when he attempted with historical and psychological realism to acknowledge that his patients had biblical as well as Greco-Roman complexes, that the Bible is the "code" not only of Western literature (as Northrop Frye has noted) but also and equally tacitly that it is one of the codes of the Western psyche gener-ally (see Westman's books *The Springs of Creativity* [1961] and *The Structure of Biblical Myths* [1983]).

The hermeneutic goal is a psychology understood in biblical fig-ures, not a biblical text understood egoically. One speaks of *depth* psy-chology precisely because the aim is not to be reductive (not an ego-psychology or a humanistic psychology). In fact, one may be reductive by not taking realistic account of the profound aspects of selfhood occasioned by biblical insight. As Walter Wink once said: "We have analyzed the Bible; now we may wish to find ways to let it analyze us" (Wink, 1978, 141).

Note

Permission is granted from the following sources to reprint material quoted in this article: Alfred A. Knopf (New York) for Wallace Stevens, *Collected*

Poems (1975, pp. 432–433); Little, Brown (Boston) for James Tate, *Absences: New Poems* (1972, p. 90); and W. W. Norton (New York) for Rainer Maria Rilke, *Duino Elegies* (1939; translated by J. B. Leishman and S. Spender).

References

Corbin, H. (1970). *Creative Imagination in the Sufism of Ibn 'Arabî*, R. Manheim, trans. London: Routledge and Kegan Paul.

Corbin, H. (1972). Mundus Imaginalis, or the Imaginary and the Imaginal. *Spring*, 1–19.

Corbin, H. (1979). *Corps Spirituel et Terre Céleste*. Paris: Éditions Buchet/Chastel.

Doniger, W. (1998). *The Implied Spider*. New York: Columbia University Press.

Eilberg-Schwartz, H. (1990). *The Savage in Judaism*. Bloomington: University of Indiana Press.

Eilberg-Schwartz, H. (1994). Voyeurism, Anthropology and the Study of Judaism. *Journal of the American Academy of Religion, 62* (1), 173–178.

Eliade, M. (1958). *Yoga*, W. Trask, trans. New York: Pantheon.

Eliade, M. (1959). *Cosmos and History*. New York: Harper and Row.

Freud, S. (1959). *Standard Edition of the Complete Psychological Works* (Vol. 20), J. Strachey, trans. London: Hogarth.

Goethe, J. W. von. (1962). *Faust*, W. Kaufmann, trans. Garden City: Doubleday.

Heidegger, M. (1962). *Being and Time*, J. Macquarrie & E. Robinson, trans. London: SCM Press.

Heidegger, M. (1969). *Identity and Difference*, J. Stambaugh, trans. New York: Harper and Row.

Hillman, J. (1983). *Archetypal Psychology*. Dallas: Spring Publications.

Hillman, J. (1988). Jung's Daimonic Inheritance. *Sphinx, 1*, 9–19.

Jung, C. G. (1963). *Memories, Dreams, Reflections*, R. Winston & C. Winston, trans. New York: Pantheon.

Jung, C. G. (1969). *Collected Works*, R. F. C. Hull, trans. (Vol. 11). Princeton: Princeton University Press.

Jung, C. G. (1970). *Psychological Reflections*, R. F. C. Hull, trans., A. Jaffé, ed. Princeton: Princeton University Press.

Jung, C. G. (1971). *Collected Works*, H. G. Baynes & R. F. C. Hull, trans. (Vol. 6). Princeton: Princeton University Press.

Jung, C. G. (1972). *Collected Works*, R. F. C. Hull, trans. (Vol. 7). Princeton: Princeton University Press.

Jung, C. G. (1975a). *Letters*, R. F. C. Hull, trans. (Vol. 2). Princeton: Princeton University Press.

Jung, C. G. (1975b). Psychological Commentary on Kundalini. *Spring*, 1–32.

Jung, C. G. (1976a). *Collected Works*, R. F. C. Hull, trans. (Vol. 18). Princeton: Princeton University Press.

Jung, C. G. (1976b). *The Visions Seminar*, M. Foote, ed. Zurich: Spring.

Jung, C. G. (1982). *Collected Works*, R. F. C. Hull, trans. (Vol. 3). Princeton: Princeton University Press.

Jung, C. G. (1985). *Collected Works*, R. F. C. Hull, trans. (Vol. 16). Princeton: Princeton University Press.

Miller, D. L. (1980). Theology's Ego/Religion's Soul. *Spring*, 78–88.

Miller, D. L. (1981). *Christs: Meditations on Archetypal Images in Christian Theology*. New York: Seabury.

Miller, D. L. (1986). *Three Faces of God: Traces of the Trinity in Literature and Life*. Philadelphia: Fortress Press.

Nietzsche, F. (1966). *Thus Spoke Zarathustra*, W. Kaufmann, trans. New York: Viking Press.

Origen of Alexandria. (1966). *On First Principles*, G. W. Butterworth, trans. New York: Harper and Row.

Rilke, R. M. (1939). *Duino Elegies*, J. B. Leishman & S. Spender, trans. New York: W. W. Norton.

Smith, J. Z. (1978). *Map Is Not the Territory*. Leiden, The Netherlands: Brill.

Smith, J. Z. (1982). *Imagining Religion*. Chicago: University of Chicago Press.

Smith, J. Z. (1990). *Drudgery Divine*. Chicago: University of Chicago Press.

Smith, J. Z. (1992). *Differential Equations*. Tempe: Arizona State University Department of Religion.

Stevens, W. (1975). *Collected Poems*. New York: Alfred A. Knopf.

Tate, J. (1972). *Absences: New Poems*. Boston: Little, Brown.

Tracy, D. (1981). *The Analogical Imagination*. New York: Crossroads.

Westman, H. (1961). *Springs of Creativity*. New York: Atheneum.

Westman, H. (1983). *The Structure of Biblical Myths: The Ontogenesis of the Psyche*. Dallas: Spring Publications.

Wink, W. (1978). On Wrestling with God: Using Psychological Insights in Biblical Study. *Religion in Life*, 47, 136–147.

CHAPTER 16

Psyche, Soul, and Self in Historical and Contemporary Perspective

Wayne G. Rollins

Pity poor psychology. First it lost its soul, then its mind, then consciousness, and now it's having trouble with behavior.

—*New Encyclopedia Britannica*, 1989, 322

The general devaluation of the human soul is so great that neither the great religions nor the philosophies nor scientific rationalism have been willing to look at it twice. . . . very little attention is paid to the essence of man, which is his psyche.

—Jung, 1971, 93

You will never explore the furthest reaches of the soul, no matter how many roads you travel.

—Tertullian, *De Anima 2.6*, citing Heraclitus, 1950 [ca. 200 A.D.]

In an interview in 1955, Carl Jung told of his enjoyment in pointing out to medical students the view of the psyche found in the "old textbook for the Medical Corps in the Swiss army." It offered a description of the brain as a "dish of macaroni, and the steam from the macaroni was the psyche" (Jung, 1977, 262). Jung expressed his good-humored disdain for this mechanistic view of the psyche and countered it with his conviction of its immense importance and his commitment to its exploration. Jung states, "The reality of the soul [psyche] is the hypothesis with which I work and my main activity consists in collecting factual material and describing and explaining it" (Wehr, 1971, 153–154). For both Freud and Jung, the terms *psyche* and *soul* (they used the terms virtually interchangeably) denoted the totality of human psychic functions and constituted the heart of their lifelong research.

Although the understanding of psyche as "steam" has largely disappeared from the scene, one still finds a problem in the use, or lack of use, of the term among psychologists today. One reason may be that academic "psychology" finds difficulty in constructing an empirically verifiable model of the psyche. In any event, one looks in vain for references to psyche in introductory academic psychology texts, histories of psychology, and even texts on the psychology of religion.

An attendant irony is that despite this marginalizing of the term *psyche* we find the field of psychology continuing to manufacture *psyche*-rooted neologisms to describe new activities in the field, such as psychometrics, psychodynamics, psychosomatic, psychiatrist, psychotherapy, psychoanalysis, psychedelic, psychosocial, psychopathology, psychosexual, and psychohistory—but with no effort or apparent desire to define what the *"psych-"* element in these terms might mean.[1]

A comparable muddle exists with theologians and biblical scholars on the word *soul*. *Soul* appears hundreds of times as a translation term for the biblical words *nephesh* and *nishamah* in the Hebrew Bible and for the Greek word *psyche* in the New Testament (it occurs 105 times). Readers of the Bible seem to have no difficulty understanding the Hebrew Bible when it asks, "Why are you cast down, oh my soul [*nephesh*], and why are you disquieted within me?" (Ps. 42:5), or when the New Testament asks, "What does it profit a person if he gains the whole world and loses his soul [*psyche*]?" (Mark 8:36). But were biblical exegetes asked to define the terms, telling us precisely what *nishamah*, *nephesh*, or *psyche* refer to in the experience of being human, they would be hard-pressed.

The aim of this essay is to add some substance to our understanding of the terms *psyche*, *soul*, and *self*, with a review of the history of each of these terms, their changing meanings, and their use today. I contend that all three, in the end, refer to the same entity. All three denote the total system of conscious and unconscious life in the human personality. Certainly they are at home in different settings, with nuanced differences in connotation and denotation: *psyche* functions in the psychoanalytic and intellectual communities; *soul* in religious contexts and more recently in the culture at large; and *self* both in the culture at large and more recently among professional psychologists. But the phenomenon to which they point is the same.

Psyche in Historical and Contemporary Usage

Historians of psychology tell us that Aristotle's essay, *Peri Psyches* (*Concerning the Psyche*; Latin: *De Anima*), advanced the "first systematic psychology" in the West, laying "down the lines along which the relationship between various manifestations of soul and mind were conceived" for two millennia (Peters & Mace, 1967, 1, 4). Aristotle, in concert with Greek and Roman successors, collectively provided a detailed analysis of the nature and habits of the human psyche that was not improved upon until the eighteenth century. Aristotle defined *psyche* as the animating principle that catalyzes life in the body and is the source of all of the animating functions we associate with being human. He developed a catalogue of these functions—reason, will, desire, memory, sensation, perception, learning, motivation, emotion, socialization, personality, and imagination—and provided a "systematic psychology" that set the standard for 2,000 years. His successors in Greco-Roman philosophy and in patristic, medieval, and scholastic theology added little to Aristotle's observations, at best debating finer points. Aside from recurring philosophical and religious questions about the preexistence, immortality, and transmigration of the psyche, the term has functioned much as it does today, connoting the totality of the vital, animated self.

As Franz Delitzsch pointed out in his 1869 work, *A System of Biblical Psychology*, the word *psyche* was also a household item in early church philosophical and theological debate. Delitzsch opens his book with the statement that "biblical psychology is no science of yesterday. It is one of the oldest sciences of the church" (Delitzsch, 1869/1966, 3–5). Writing one year before Sigmund Freud's birth, twenty years before Carl Jung's, and twenty-three years before Wilhelm Wundt, the "founder of modern psychology," established his first psychological laboratory, Delitzsch provided a history of the dialogue that early church fathers engaged in with the writings of Aristotle, Plato, and the Stoics on the nature of the psyche (or Latin *anima*).

It is no small wonder, therefore, that the term psychology itself was born out of this dialogue. It is interesting to compare the appearance of the term "biology," in 1802, and the term "sociology," in 1840, with the appearance of the term "psychology," in 1530, three centuries earlier. "Psychology" was introduced to the academic world by none other than a biblical scholar, Philipp Melanchton, in a series of lectures beginning in 1530 that were later rendered as a Commentary on Aristotle's *Peri*

Psyches (1540). Melanchton had fostered the word "psychology" as a way to talk about the "spiritual" faculties of humans, as opposed to animals and angels.

It is this same term, *psyche*, that Wilhelm Wundt retained as the controlling concept of his "new psychology." Although Wundt issued a disclaimer, warning that he will use *psyche* in a strictly scientific sense, dismissing metaphysical connotations acquired in Western philosophical and religious tradition, he leaves no doubt that he uses it in its classic sense, namely, to refer to the totality of the psychic life (Hunt, 1993, 129).

Freud and Jung also turned to psyche to express the idea of the unified psychic self, freely employing the German *Seele* (*soul*) as a fitting translation (although, like Wundt, dismissing all metaphysical considerations). The precedent for using *Seele* as a synonym for *psyche* in academic psychological circles is found in the work of two German psychologists at the University of Göttingen, Johann Friedrich Herbart (1776–1841) and Rudolf Hermann Lotze (1817–1881). What Herbart and Lotze, Freud and Jung meant to denote by the terms *psyche* and *Seele* was the objective nature of the spiritual, mental, emotional, soulful self, not reducible to somatic and physical factors—the same self that Aristotle and his successors had described. In Freud and Jung's case, however, the concept of psyche is enlarged to include the newly highlighted realm of the unconscious.

In the early 1900s, the terms *psyche* and *soul* become problematic; an increasingly empirically oriented environment made it difficult to talk about realities that defy precise, scientific measurement. The result is a certain terminological uncertainty among psychologists, evident as early as 1910 in Sir William Hamilton's gerrymandering definition of psychology as "the science conversant about the phenomena or modifications, or states of the mind, or [of] conscious subject, soul or spirit, or self or ego" (Sanday, 1911, 137). The roots of this terminological uncertainty can be traced to the influence of the seventeenth-century mechanistic psychology of René Descartes and the rise of British empiricism, which led to a "banishment of the intangible" (Fuller, 1986, 76). Already in the 1600s, Thomas Hobbes had repudiated the term and concept of *soul* (*psyche*) as "pernicious Aristotelian nonsense," preferring instead to think of psychological phenomena as derivatives of the nervous system and brain (Hunt, 1993, 73). This drive to reduce "psychic" qualities to reflexes activated in the somatic system by environmental stimuli came to its fullest expression with the advent of behaviorism in the 1920s with J. B. Watson (1878–1958) and his celebrated successor B. F. Skinner (1904–1990). Watson and Skinner eliminated not only *psyche* and *soul* but added *instinct, consciousness, mind,* and *thinking* itself to the list of casualties, leading to the quip (when Skinnerism began to fade as the premier voice in the field), "Pity poor psychology, first it lost its soul, then its mind, then consciousness, and now it is having trouble with behavior" (*New Encyclopedia Britannica*, 1989, 322).

The result of this perspectival shift in academic psychology between the 1920s and 1960s (marked by various schools of thought and driven to no small degree by the professional desire among psychologists to achieve recognition for psychology as a bona fide scientific discipline) is the virtual disappearance of *psyche* from academic psychological discourse, a loss felt yet today. This shift was evident, as Bruno Bettelheim noted, in English translations of Freud that transmogrified Freud's humane language into mechanistic jargon: it rendered "soul" (*Seele*) as "mental," "structure of the soul" as "mental apparatus," "organization of the soul" as "mental organization," and in many instances completely eliminated Freud's references to soul (Bettelheim, 1982, 52–93).

This apparent ostracizing of the term *psyche* among academic psychologists did not go unchallenged. A "correction" set in with two developments in the 1960s and 1970s. The first was "third-force" or "humanistic" psychology, the second was a resurgent interest in Freud and Jung. Abraham Maslow advanced third-force or humanistic psychology to provide an alternative to the theories of human nature of the two dominant psychologies of the time, behaviorism and Freudian psychoanalysis. Psychologists who shared his objectives include Gordon Allport, Erich Fromm, Karen Horney, Carl Rogers, Viktor Frankl, Carl Jung, and Ira Progoff. Humanistic psychology confronted the dominant psychologies on four fronts. First, it challenged the reduction of human nature to the "material" and "efficient" causes of neurophysiology or environment, evident especially in behaviorism. Second, it contended that humans are driven ultimately not just by the need for Freudian *homeostasis*, or inner balance, but by "final causes" manifested in the "organism's inherent tendency toward . . . Self-transcendence." These "causes" impel humans beyond survival needs and physical needs to higher values, such as self-esteem and competence, and at the highest level, self-actualization, aesthetic pleasure, and understanding, where innate "potentialities, capacities, and talents" are actualized (Fuller, 1986, 155, 158–159). Third, humanistic psychology repudiated the "cellar view" of the unconscious proposed by Freud, preferring Jung's formulation that holds the unconscious to be not just a repository of the repressed but, more importantly, the source of an intuitive function that guides the organism toward self-actualization. Carl Rogers writes, "Our organisms as a whole have a wisdom and purpose which goes well beyond our conscious thought" (see Fuller, 1986, 88). Fourth, humanistic psychology treats the individual as subject as well as object. It takes seriously the "individual's subjective experience of the world" (Fuller, 1986, 88) as important data for constructing a model of the self, reclaiming the method of William James, who welcomed the "facts directly observable in ourselves" (James, 1971, 196).

As effective as humanistic psychology was in reclaiming a sense of psyche or soul, it did not construct a comprehensive model of the psyche. For the rudiments of such a model we must turn to the thought of Carl Gustav Jung. Jung uses the term *psyche* in its classical, historical sense to refer to the "totality of all psychic processes, conscious as well as unconscious," generally reserving *Seele* or *soul* to refer to the unconscious realm of the psyche, although sometimes using *psyche* and *Seele* interchangeably (Jacobi, 1968, 5). For Jung, the psyche is the matrix of all human culture. He sees it as the force "primarily responsible for all the historical changes wrought by the hand of man on the face of this planet" (1953–1978, vol. 10, 526), holding that all human artifacts, compositions, creations, and achievements are the product of the human psyche. As such it is "the womb of all the arts and sciences" (1953–1978, vol. 15, 33).

For this reason, Jung would maintain, the psyche deserves our keenest interest, despite the fact that "neither the great religions nor the philosophies nor scientific rationalism have been willing to look at it twice" (Jung, 1971, 93). He complains,

> In a period of human history when all available energy is spent in the investigation of nature, very little attention is paid to the essence of man, which is his psyche, although many researches are made into its conscious functions. . . . Man's greatest instrument, his psyche, is little thought of, if not actually mistrusted and despised. "It's only 'psychological'" too often means: it is nothing. (Jung, 1971, 93)

But Jung also acknowledges the impossibility of offering any final or complete description of the psyche:

> The phenomenology of the psyche is so colourful, so variegated in form and meaning, that we cannot possibly reflect all its riches in *one* mirror. Nor in our description of it can we ever embrace the whole, but must be content to shed light only on single parts of the total phenomenon. Since it is a characteristic of the psyche not only to be the source of all productivity but, more especially, to express itself in all the activities and achievements of the human mind, we can nowhere grasp the nature of the psyche *per se* but can meet it only in its various manifestations. (Jung, 1972, 85)

Even though it is "quite impossible to define the extension and the ultimate character of psychic existence," and even though the psyche is "an ineffable totality which can only be formulated symbolically," it is nevertheless real (Jung, 1953–1978b, 140). As an empirical reality it warrants close attention, not only because it is the progenitor of human culture but also because of its ineluctable role in the destiny of world affairs. Jung writes, "It seems to me far more reasonable to accord the psyche the same validity as the empirical world, and to admit that the former has just as much 'reality' as the latter" (1953–1978c, 375).

Soul in Historical and Contemporary Usage

The term *soul* has a similar history. It was introduced as an English translation for *psyche* in its Greek context, *anima* in its Latin context, and *Seele* in its German psychoanalytic context. Its past is more complex and problematic than that of *psyche* because of the tendency, especially in English-speaking religious circles, to use it exclusively as a reference to the disembodied self before or after death—a concept objectionable not only to Aristotle but to Freud, Lotze, and Herbart as well. The result is that for the first two-thirds of the twentieth century, *soul* was either absent from discourse among psychologists and theologians or distorted by translating Freud's *Seele* as *mind* or *mental*. Writing in 1967, James Hillman lamented the loss of the term *soul*: "As a term, . . . [the word *soul*] has all but vanished from contemporary psychology; it has an old-fashioned ring, bringing echoes of peasants on the Celtic fringes or reincarnating theosophists. Perhaps it is still kept alive as some vestigial organ by village vicars and by seminary discussion of patristic philosophy" (Hillman, 1967, 40–41). Although calls for the reclamation of *soul* appeared sporadically in the first two-thirds of the twentieth century, neither Hillman nor academic psychology nor theology could have anticipated the resurgence of the term in academic and popular circles in the 1980s and 1990s.

One example from academic discourse is William Barrett's *Death of the Soul: From Descartes to the Computer* (1986). Barrett derides the materialistic, mechanistic reductionism of the physical sciences that would "snuff out this little candle [of soul] as unnecessary and paradoxical." He "recall[s] with Kant . . . that it is the power of mind that creates the systems of mechanics that here seek to extinguish it." He urges a return to Descartes's dream, which he describes as "the universe as a single machine [that has] there, inside it, at its center, . . . that miraculous thing, his own consciousness, in the light of which he sees and meditates."

The book closes with an apt biblical metaphor: "What shall it profit a whole civilization, or culture, if it gains knowledge and power over the material world, but loses any adequate idea of the conscious mind, the human self, at the center of all that power?" (Barrett, 1986, 164, 166)

In a similar vein, Richard Swinburne, in his 1983–1984 Gifford Lectures later published as *The Evolution of the Soul* (1986), issues the charge that "scientists have tended to regard the life of conscious experience as peripheral, not central to understanding man." But, he argues, "we must not fall into the trap of believing that that which we cannot explain . . . does not exist. The conscious life evidently exists— that we have sensations and thoughts, feelings and hopes is the most evident thing that there is." For Swinburne, *soul* denotes the conscious, moral, conative, affective, experiencing, sensate self, dominated by "mental life." He "takes seriously the fact of human conscious experience, its continuity and it causal efficacy." He proceeds to trace the leap from the primordial soup of inanimate life that brings consciousness of mental life into being with its "sensations, thoughts, purposes, desires and beliefs." What relationship has conscious life to body? "Though dependent on physical processes," Swinburne states, "the soul (or mind) is not the body," which is an ordinary material object like the brain. But the body "is connected to a soul which is the essential part of a man, and which is the part which enjoys the mental life" (2–4). This "mental life" is characterized by two qualities that differentiate humans from other animals: "complex and logically ordered thought" and "awareness of moral goodness and obligation." Two additional differences are "free will" ("in the sense that their choices are not totally predetermined by their brain-states") and "structure of character" (Swinburne, 1986, 2–4).

One of the most compelling calls for the reclamation of *soul* is found in the ten essays edited by social scientists Richard K. Fenn and Donald Capps, *On Losing the Soul: Essays in the Social Psychology of Religion* (1995). The editors state that their purpose is "to expand the discourse of the social sciences about the self by reintroducing the word 'soul,' " noting that it has fallen out of use among sociologists and anthropologists (as well as psychologists). One of the contributors, Bernice Martin, offers an autobiographical response to the question "What is 'soul'?"

> "Soul," to my mother and the people with whom I grew up in that working class industrial town, was a word used unself-consciously to mean the ultimate core or essence of the individual's being. . . . People talked of the soul as if it were the irreducible, indestructible part of the person which, perhaps, continued to exist after death. . . . The word . . . suggests

to me the possibility of recognizing—hinting at—a level of discourse which accords some ultimate significance to the person beyond what can be said by the expert social scientific disciplines. The metaphysical and theological connotations of "soul" suggest a dimension of the integrity of persons, which is not fully captured by the vocabulary of "self" and "selfhood." The death of the soul is of greater moment than the death of the self. (Fenn & Capps, 1995, 70)

Another contributor, David Martin, characterizes soul as the "essential or animating element of any human being, and the spiritual quiddity, characterized ideally by reason and integrity and wholeness considered together" (Fenn & Capps, 1995, 39). Richard Fenn adds that it is also constituted of the mystery within a person that provides the capacity to act with freedom in the face of those longstanding social and cultural forces that some anthropologists, such as Victor Turner, see as absolutely determinative. How do we measure soul or gather data on it? Fenn contends that its presence, like a black hole, can only be inferred from its effects, since it cannot be seen directly (Fenn & Capps, 1995, 3). Or as Bernice Martin adds, "Few would have been able to define it; the meaning lay in the usage and the usage, as often as not, involved the telling of stories and the repetition of 'sayings'" (Fenn & Capps, 1995, 70).

As striking as the reclamation of *soul* is in academic quarters, its phenomenal renascence in popular culture in the 1980s and 1990s is all the more remarkable. Just the number of books with the word *soul* in its title is impressive: Alan W. Jones, *Soul-Making: The Desert Way of Spirituality* (1985); Gary Zukav, *The Seat of the Soul* (1989); Robert J. Drinan, *Stories from the American Soul* (1990); Larry Dossey, MD, *Recovering the Soul: A Scientific and Spiritual Search* (1990); Thomas Moore, *Care of the Soul* (1991) and *Soul Mates* (1994); Jack Canfield and Mark Victor Hanson, *Chicken Soup for the Soul* (1993), with a series of sequels; Marjorie Thompson, *Soul Feast* (1995); William J. Doherty, *Soul Searching: Why Psychotherapy Must Promote Moral Responsibility* (1995); Henry H. Mitchell and Nicholas Cooper-Lewter, *Soul Theology: The Heart of American Black Culture* (1996). One of the most comprehensive studies of "soul language" across world cultures is the anthology edited by Phil Cousineau, *Soul, An Archaeology: Readings from Socrates to Ray Charles* (1994), with 130 literary selections, including an Egyptian Gnostic myth of the soul's origin, a West African folktale, essays by psychologists, theologians, anthropologists, novelists, mystics, shamans, poets, and philosophers, and selections from sacred texts. Even popular science has broached the subject, evident in a jointly authored *Time* magazine feature article in 1995 entitled "In Search of the Mind: Glimpses of the Brain," which asks, "What, precisely, is the mind. . . where is it located? . . . Does it arise from purely physical processes. . . . Or is it something beyond the merely physical— something ethereal that might be close to the spiritual concept of the soul? (Lemonick, Nash, Park, and Willwerth, 1995, 49).

How is one to account for the resurgence of *soul* at the end of the twentieth century? From the perspective of the history of ideas, the shift can be seen as a popular manifestation of postmodern consciousness, with its negative suspicions of the positivistic and scientistic approach of behaviorism and radically empirical psychology. From a psychodynamic perspective, the answer may be found in the Freudian concept of the "return of the repressed." It is demonstrated in the return of a long-repressed cultural need for a term to speak of the complex but unified self that most people understand themselves to be, one that cannot simply be reduced to the somatic and physical factors that for so long had been enlisted by behaviorism and empirical psychology to justify the banishment of *psyche* and *soul* from the language. In terms of cultural history, Philip Cousineau confirms the existence of a universal linguistic need for a word to express the idea of soul when he lists the many terms that are "sacred words used by primal peoples the world over for the surge of life itself, linguistic cousins of what was called *sawol* in Old English, *sawal* by the Anglo-Saxons, *sala* by the Icelandic folk, and eventually, . . . what we now call *soul* (Cousineau, 1994, xx).

Self in Historical and Contemporary Usage

The term *self,* surprisingly, has had a history in psychological circles comparable to that of *psyche* and *soul*. It was often rejected by psychologists because it defied empirical description, but it was reinstated when the need arose for a word to express the concept of the whole person. Plato, Augustine, Descartes, Kant, and Hume had conceived of the self as that conscious inner agent that observes oneself having experiences. H. D. Lewis summarizes this idea of self as an "abiding subject distinct from all the particular items apprehended" (1990, 1125). Kant and Hume, however, resisted any attempt at a description of the self because of its unavailability to empirical observation. Self was a matter for philosophical speculation, not psychological study. British Associationist psychologists had "sloughed it off as no more than the connected chain of passing effects" (Hunt, 1993, 157).

Against this position, William James, in his 1890 *Principles of Psychology*, revived interest in the concept of self with a theory of its four dimensions: the material self, which includes body, family, and possession; the social self, consisting of interpersonal sentiments; the spiritual self, comprising the "inner" or subjective sense of being and the psychic faculties and dispositions; and the pure ego, which functioned as an inner principle of personal unity. James's most important contribution, however, was the distinction he drew between "self" as subject or knower, which he termed the "I," and "self" as object or known, the "me"; thus, he effectively reintroduced the "subjective self" into a conversation from which it had long been excluded (Hunt, 1993, 157).

James's theory was crowded out by the materialist views of behavioralism and the rational objectivism of early experimental psychology appearing in the early 1900s. One of his former students, Edward Titchener (1867–1927) of Cornell, was persuaded in time that "the concept of self should be left out of psychology because it would bring in the realm of meaning, that which . . . lay beyond the purview of psychology as a descriptive science." This point of view effectively excluded the concept of self from most academic psychological discourse for half a century (Mahoney, 1991, 216).

By the second half of the twentieth century, however, the term began to reappear under the sponsorship of clinical and developmental psychology, the arts, and the humanities. Alfred Adler spoke of the "creative self" as a key ingredient of his "individual psychology." The personality theories of Gordon Allport, Erik Erikson, and Erich Fromm began to speak of "self-concept," "self-attitudes," and "self-esteem." Jung spoke of "Self" as the supreme archetype to which the individual aspires. Rogers and Maslow introduced the notions of "self-actualization" and "self-realization," referring to a unified drive or tendency within the organism to grow and to realize its potentialities. Karen Horney wrote of "Self-analysis" and Heinz Kohut developed "Self Psychology."

By the last decade of the twentieth century, *self* had made its return within the guild of academic psychologists. In a chapter on "The Self in Process" in his 1991 volume *Human Change Processes: The Scientific Foundations of Psychotherapy*, Michael J. Mahoney writes,

> The cognitive, developmental, and emotional (r)evolution(s) have redirected mainstream experimental psychology back "inside" the organism; and the "modern synthesis" in psychology is, in part, an attempt to integrate and transcend inside/outside and mind/body dualisms. What cognitive and life scientists found when they looked inside the most "promising primates," however, was much more than they had antici-

pated. The recent and ongoing (re)discoveries of emotionality, unconscious processes, and personal meanings are cases in point. But perhaps
the single most important (re)discovery of twentieth century psychology has been that of the self, which has (again) become a cardinal concept after a moratorium that lasted over half a century. As Louis A. Sass
quipped, "The 'self,' once banished by mainstream psychology to the
cloudland of unobservable and irrelevant abstractions, seems to have
returned with a vengeance.". . . Whether it is a vengeful return or simply
the persistence of a centuries-old mystery, however, self studies are now
center stage in psychological laboratories and clinics around the planet.
(Mahoney, 1991, 211)

Academic psychology in the twenty-first century is beginning to
sense the loss of the *psyche* in psychology and the need for a model of
the self that will honor the reality of an entity that James had described
at the turn of the last century and that Aristotle and the biblical tradition had recognized long before.

On the basis of the foregoing, we suggest that there is sufficient justification for reinstating the triad of *psyche, soul,* and *self* as the historically most appropriate terms and culturally the most fitting terms to
refer to the total system of conscious and unconscious life in the human
personality. By way of a single definition that encompasses all three, I
offer the following:

The common semantic content of the terms *psyche, soul,* and *self*
includes reference to the totality of the conscious and unconscious
individual. This totality encompasses (1) the individual's powers
and functions: emotional, conative, affective, intuitive, imaginative,
perceptive, rational, sensate, moral, spiritual, and aesthetic; (2) the
individual's development, behavior, character, and acts, as these are
informed, shaped, and motivated by instincts, aspirations, innate
physical and psychodynamic proclivities and drives, as well as positive and negative external reinforcements; and (3) the individual's
personal capacities—self awareness, free will, aesthetic appreciation, moral judgment, seeking and creating of meaning, creativity,
and spiritual sensitivity—all of which can be bent to constructive
or destructive ends and, depending on the circumstances, be the
expression of healthy or pathological states.

If, as Jung said, this human psyche/soul/self is "primarily responsible for all the historical changes wrought by the hand of man on the
face of this planet" (1953–1978, vol. 10, 526), this means that every
human artifact—from the Eiffel Tower to nuclear weapons to Bach's

B Minor Mass to the Great Wall of China to Van Gogh's sunflowers to arthroscopic surgery to the great universities of the world to the Mars probe and to the concept of a free society—all are the products of a human being, sitting virtually naked, with no resource other than the virtually marginless repository of the human psyche. The psyche with its immense conscious and unconscious depths, the soul with its broad capacities for imagination and spirituality, and the self, capable of focused, centered action, constitute an immensely significant entity worth giving further thought to, both by psychologists and biblical scholars. It is time to restore the *psyche* to psychology and to come to a fuller understanding of what Scripture might mean when it suggests that the ultimate peril is not loss of life but loss of psyche/soul/self (Matt. 10:28; Mark 8:36).

Notes

This article is excerpted from W. Rollins (1999). *Soul and Psyche: The Bible in Psychological Perspective.* Minneapolis: Fortress. Reprinted with permission.

1. For example, Wulff's widely used *Psychology of Religion* (1991) lists no occurrences of the term *psyche* but includes ten references to *soul*.

References

Barrett, W. (1986). *Death of the Soul: From Descartes to the Computer.* New York, Doubleday.

Bettelheim, B. (1982, March 1). Reflections: Freud and the Soul. *New Yorker,* 52–93.

Canfield, J., & Hanson, M. V. (1993). *Chicken Soup for the Soul.* Daytona Beach: Health Communications, Inc.

Cousineau, P., ed. (1994). *Soul: An Archaeology: Readings from Socrates to Ray Charles.* San Francisco: HarperSanFrancisco.

Delitzsch, F. (1869/1966). *A System of Biblical Psychology,* A. E. Wallis, trans., Grand Rapids: Baker Book House. (Originally published as *System der biblischen Psychologie.* Leipzig, Germany: Dörffling & Franke, 1861; English translation, Edinburgh: T&T Clark, 1869)

Doherty, W. J. (1995). *Soul Searching: Why Psychotherapy Must Promote Moral Responsibility.* New York: Harper & Row.

Dossey, L. (1990). *Recovering the Soul: A Scientific and Spiritual Search.* New York: Bantam Books.

Drinan, R. S. J. (1990). *Stories from the American Soul.* Chicago: Loyola Press.

Fenn, R. K., & Capps, D., eds. (1995). *On Losing the Soul: Essays in the Social Psychology of Religion.* Albany: SUNY Press.

Fuller, R. C. (1986). *Americans and the Unconscious*. New York: Oxford.

Hillman, J. (1967). *Insearch: Psychology and Religion*. New York: Scribner's.

Hunt, M. (1993). *The Story of Psychology*. New York: Doubleday Anchor Books.

Jacobi, J. (1968). *The Psychology of C. G. Jung*. New Haven: Yale University Press

James, W. (1971). *A Pluralistic Universe*. New York: E. P. Dutton.

James, W. (1890). *Principles of Psychology*. New York: Henry Holt.

Jones, A. W. (1985). *Soul-Making: The Desert Way of Spirituality*. New York: Harper & Row.

Jung, C. G. (1953–1978a). *The Collected Works of C. G. Jung*, R. F. C. Hull, trans. (Vol. 10). Princeton: Princeton University Press.

Jung, C. G. (1953–1978b). *The Collected Works of C. G. Jung*, R. F. C. Hull, trans. (Vol. 11). Princeton: Princeton University Press.

Jung, C. G. (1953–1978c). *The Collected Works of C. G. Jung*, R. F. C. Hull, trans. (Vol. 13). Princeton: Princeton University Press.

Jung, C. G. (1953–1978d). *The Collected Works of C. G. Jung*, R. F. C. Hull, trans. (Vol. 15). Princeton: Princeton University Press.

Jung, C. G. (1971). *Man and His Symbols*. New York: Dell Publishing.

Jung, C. G. (1972). Psychology and Literature. *The Spirit in Man, Art, and Literature*. Princeton: Princeton University Press, 84–108. (Original work published 1930)

Jung, C. G. (1977). *C. G. Jung Speaking: Interviews and Encounters*. Princeton: Princeton University Press.

Lemonick, M. D., Nash, J. M., Park, A., & Willwerth, J. (1995). In Search of the Mind: Glimpses of the Brain. *Time, 146*(3), 44–52.

Lewis, H. D. (1990). Philosophy of Self. In *Dictionary of Pastoral Care and Counseling*, R. Hunter, ed. Nashville, Abingdon, 1125–1126.

Mahoney, M. J. (1991). *Human Change Processes: The Scientific Foundations of Psychotherapy*. New York: BasicBooks, HarperCollins.

Melanchton, P. (1540). *Commentarius de anima*. Paris: Witebergae.

Mitchell, H. H., & Cooper-Lewter, N. (1996). *Soul Theology: The Heart of American Black Culture*. Nashville: Abingdon Press.

Moore, T. (1991). *Care of the Soul*. New York: HarperCollins.

Moore, T. (1994). *Soul Mates*. New York: HarperCollins.

New Encyclopedia Britannica: Macropedia. 15th ed. (Vol. 26). (1988). Chicago: Encyclopedia Britannica, Inc., 322.

Peters, R. S., & Mace, C. A. (1967). Psychology. In *The Encyclopedia of Philosophy*. (Vol. 7), P. Edwards, ed. New York: Macmillan, 1–27.

Sanday, W. (1911). *Christology and Personality*. New York: Oxford University Press.

Swinburne, R. (1986). *The Evolution of the Soul*. Oxford: Clarendon.

Tertullian, Q. S. F. (1950). *De Anima, Tertullian, Apologetical Works and Minucius Felix Octavius*, R. Arbesmann, Sr. E. Daly, & E. A. Quain, trans. New York: Fathers of the Church, Inc.

Thompson, M. (1995). *Soul Feast: An Invitation to the Christian Spiritual Life*. Louisville: Westminster/John Knox Press.

Wehr, G. (1971). *Portrait of Jung: An Illustrated Biography*, W. A. Hargreaves, trans. New York: Herder & Herder.

Wulff, D. M. (1991). *Psychology of Religion: Classic and Contemporary Views*. New York: John Wiley and Sons.

Zukav, G. (1989). *The Seat of the Soul*. Seattle: S. & S. Kenmore.

CHAPTER 17

"Begotten, Not Created": The Gnostic Use of Language in Jungian Perspective

Schuyler Brown

Gnosis, broadly defined,[1] might be called *introverted religious knowledge*. If understood in this way, gnosis poses a continuing challenge to religious orthodoxy, whether Jewish, Christian, or Muslim.

Within the New Testament canon, Paul and the author of the Fourth Gospel, not to mention Jesus himself, exhibit a spiritual knowledge that commended them to later Gnostic writers. But Paul's letters and the Johannine corpus also show a concern for the threat that religious individualism can represent for any collective church structure.

The creative tension that we find in these New Testament writings was abandoned in later letters attributed to Paul, in which "what is falsely called knowledge" (1 Tim. 6:20), with its "myths and genealogies," was rejected in favor of "sound doctrine" (1 Tim. 1:4, 1:10, 4:7, 6:3; 2 Tim. 1:13, 4:3–4; Titus 1:9, 1:14, 2:1, 3:9).

This exclusion of the Gnostics from the church was more damaging to the Christian movement, from a psychological point of view, than any subsequent schism, whether between the Eastern and Western churches or between Catholics and Protestants. For this first Christian schism involved not simply different interpretations of revelation but differences over the nature of revelation itself.

In my opinion, the church and gnosis need each other. Without gnosis, Christianity ossifies into a dogmatic structure and "faith" comes to mean paying lip service to that structure. But once gnosis had been excluded from the church it simply disappeared from history, except as an underground phenomenon. The reappearance in our own day of Gnostic churches suggests that the collective and individual expressions of religious experience need to remain on speaking terms.

In declining to respond to "the Gnostic question" with a simple pro or con, I am following the lead of C. G. Jung, who affirmed the importance of gnosis for Christian renewal[2] but who also acknowledged the psychological value of the church as a protective container against the destructive inroads of the unconscious.[3]

My appreciation of the importance of gnosis did not come easily. Since I had been reared in the rationalism of mainline Christianity and schooled in the rationalism of the university, my initial reaction to Gnostic literature was one of bewilderment and disdain. I wondered how such material could ever have constituted a serious threat to the church.

In 1978, when I entered Jungian analysis, my attitude began to change, as I noticed the correspondence between my own strange dream world and the strange world of the Nag Hammadi texts. I came to realize that whatever has not yet been incorporated into consciousness must seem alien to the rational ego. But such alien intrusions, over which the ego has no control, may point to a way out of a diminished existence that has become insupportable.

The relationship between the image and the text in gnosis is the subject of this essay. I have come to believe that the significance of the rediscovery of ancient gnosis lies not so much in the bizarre ideas attacked by the heresiologists as in the use of the written word to express and evoke a visual image. Gnosis and orthodoxy represent two different ways of thinking, two different ways of reading, and two different ways of using language.

Gnosis and Orthodoxy: Fantasy Thinking versus Directed Thinking

C. G. Jung has distinguished between "directed," or logical, thinking and "fantasy," or "dream," thinking (1967, 18). Directed thinking is adapted to reality. It takes for granted the principle of contradiction, and it imitates the causal sequence of events taking place outside the mind. Fantasy thinking works spontaneously and is guided by unconscious motives. It sets free subjective tendencies. Rather than adapting itself to reality, fantasy thinking adapts external reality to its own inner world. Contradictions abound, as our own dreams testify every

night. In Freudian terms, fantasy thinking is primary process thinking and directed thinking is secondary process thinking.

Fantasy thinking, for Jung, is characteristic of antiquity: "to the
classical mind everything was still saturated with mythology" (1967,
20). Jung's characterization of mythic thinking describes many of the
texts that we now know from Nag Hammadi: "This creative urge
explains the bewildering confusion, the kaleidoscopic changes and syn-
cretistic regroupings, the continual renovation of myths in Greek culture" (1967, 20–21). The prevalence of this kind of thinking in Gnostic
literature explains why the church fathers regarded gnosis as a relapse
into paganism.

Directed thinking finds its ultimate achievement in modern science
and technology. Mythic projections upon the universe are withdrawn
in the interest of "devising formulas to harness the forces of nature"
(Jung, 1967, 20). Christian orthodoxy is linked to the thinking of
antiquity insofar as its subject matter is religious fantasy, but this fan-
tastic subject matter is treated dialectically, through directed thinking.
In this sense, orthodox scholasticism "is the mother of our scientific
method" (Jung, 1967, 20).

The Gnostic and the orthodox had the same Scripture, but they read
it differently. The directed thinking that is characteristic of doctrinal
orthodoxy leads to directed reading: the reader constructs a story
"behind" the text. A directed reading of the opening chapters of Genesis leads to the orderly sequence of "salvation history" that is familiar
to us from dogmatic theology: the creation of the world, the creation
of Adam and Eve,[4] the Fall, and the promise of redemption contained
in the *protoevangelium* (Gen. 3:15). In such an "objective" reading, a distinction must be made between the historical events (objective redemption) and the appropriation of this redemption by the individual (subjective redemption).

The Gnostic reading of Scripture is characterized by the infre-
quency of explicit Scriptural citations, which inhibits any distinction
between text and interpretation or between "then" and "now." Salvation history is indistinguishable from the psychic awakening of the
reader: the creation story is paradigmatic for anyone who receives
the revelatory gnosis.[5] In a Gnostic reading, the ceaseless crisscrossing
and interweaving of themes and characters preclude referentiality: the
feminine characters in particular—Barbelo, Sophia, the serpent, heavenly Eve, Epinoia—all seem to be expressions of the same force, rather
like Olympia, Antonia, and Giulietta in Offenbach's opera *Tales of Hoff-
mann*. The Gnostic creation stories do not show us a world distinct

from ourselves: objective reality is renounced for the sake of an imaginal noesis that can exist only in a twilight that rational clarity dispels.

Gnostic interpretation of Scripture gives free rein to the inner promptings of the imagination. The text serves as a catalyst for the release of natural symbols arising out of the unconscious, and the text becomes, in turn, the screen upon which these unconscious contents are projected. The inner is expressed in terms of the outer. By pointing away from itself to express an experience that is beyond rational discourse, the imagistic language of gnosis forestalls any idolatry of the word. Gnostic writing does not point to self-consistent and unchanging realities beyond the empirical world but rather uses religious images to interpret existence (LaFargue, 1985, 207).

A Difference in Root Metaphors: Speech versus Sexuality

The Gnostics and the orthodox seem to be guided by two different root metaphors, both of them derived from a common Scripture. In the Genesis story, creation comes about through God's word: "God said, . . . and it was so." The Prologue to the Fourth Gospel personifies this divine word: "The Word was with God, . . . and without him not one thing came into being" (John 1:1, 1:3). The masculine Logos replaces the feminine figure of Sophia, who, according to the Old Testament wisdom tradition, was beside God "like a master worker" (Prov. 8:30).

Sophia (personified Wisdom) becomes the protagonist of the Gnostic creation story. She is given the epithet *prouneikos* (Pasquier, 1988), which suggests impetuosity, wantonness, libido (in the inclusive sense used by Jung of any form of psychic energy [1967, 132–170]). As the connecting principle between the deity and creation, on the one hand Sophia is God's "delight" while on the other hand she is "delighting in the human race" (Prov. 8:30–31).

In the Johannine Prologue, where the feminine principle has been excluded, the sexual imagery is still present insofar as the incarnate word is the "Father's only Son" (John 1:14). In the Gnostic reading of Scripture, sexuality, not speech, is the root metaphor. The beginning of the cosmic process is not the divine word but an act of autoeroticism. Sophia conceives a thought from herself, through the invisible spirit's foreknowledge, and reveals an image from herself, but without her consort's approval (Apocryphon of John; Robinson, 1988, 119–123).[6]

Sexuality is also operative in the Gnostic interpretation of the Adam and Eve story. Death comes into being through the separation of Eve from Adam, and it will only be overcome through the reintegration of the masculine with the feminine, as symbolized by the sexual act (Gospel of Philip; Robinson, 1988, 150).

The Gnostic preference for fantasy thinking has consequences for the evaluation of the senses. In the orthodox conception, hearing is the most important sense, and it is through hearing that the word of faith is received (Rom. 10:8, 10:14, 10:17). For gnosis, however, seeing, tasting, and smelling are more highly valued. The Gnostic is the fragrance of the Father, and what comes through the ears is less effective, less direct, and less intimate than what comes through *pneuma*, which has the double meaning of "spirit" and "breath" (Gospel of Truth; Robinson, 1988, 47).

Psychological and Philosophical Critique of Religious Rationalism

Having grown up in a parsonage of the Swiss Reformed Church, Jung was keenly aware of the devastating psychological consequences of religious rationalism.[7] His concern was for those parts of the psyche that are not reached by rational discourse and that, in turn, rational discourse is unable to bring to expression.[8]

Jung was also thoroughly familiar with Kant's philosophical critique of metaphysics and metaphysically based theology. The language of directed thinking turns outward and is used for the purpose of communication (Jung, 1967, 18). For communication to take place effectively, language must be used as univocally as possible, so that misunderstanding can be avoided. Language is a social artifact, and for it to function in the public arena it must be strictly governed by social convention.

The truth of such rational discourse is measured by its correspondence with external reality, which it is presumed to mirror. Such discourse is an essential tool for *Homo faber* ("Man the maker") as he strives to control the world in accordance with his intentions. When, however, such discourse ventures into areas where no empirical verification is possible, its truth claims are suspect. In this conviction, Jung was at one with the tradition of negative theology, also called the *via negativa*, which believes that we can know only what God is *not*. This philosophical position has been confirmed by modern studies of language. No element can function as a sign without relating to another element that is not itself present. This means that every linguistic element is constituted by the trace of something absent. Nothing in language is ever simply there (Derrida, 1981, 26).

In other words, there can be no one-to-one correspondence between language and external reality. The common-sense position of philosophical realism is an illusion. Language does not mirror the outer world but interprets it, and no interpretation is uninfluenced by the interpreter. Objective reality finds expression in language as a creation of human consciousness.

If this is true even of discourse concerning the familiar world we think we know, its consequences for religious rationalism are devastating. The *deus absconditus* is revealed not through the powers of human reason but only through "metaphors transparent to transcendence" (Campbell, 1989, 28).

Language and the Poetic Imagination

Although for some religious traditions the ineffability of God excludes the use of Scripture, the Gnostics did not go this route. Yet, instead of using language to try to construct a rationally consistent theological system, the Gnostics related the word to the image through which the divine is revealed. In Thunder: Perfect Mind, Sophia proclaims, "I am . . . the word whose appearance is multiple" (Robinson, 1988, 298). The Gospel of Philip declares, "Truth did not come into the world naked, but it came in types and images."

"The world will not receive truth in any other way" (Robinson, 1988, 150). Using the paired opposites that are characteristic of mythic speech, Sophia declares, "I am the honored and the scorned one. I am the whore and the holy one. I am the wife and the virgin. I am the mother and the daughter" (Thunder: Perfect Mind; Robinson, 1988, 297).

The primacy of the image in Gnostic writing and the lack of concern for rational consistency suggest that we are dealing here with poetic discourse. This realization has been missed by many students of the Nag Hammadi texts, for they, like the ancient heresiologists, interpret gnosis as a doctrinal system.

Paul Kugler (1982) has related the poetic language of the soul to a psychology of the imagination. This approach applies beautifully to the Gnostic writings. Ever since Ferdinand de Saussure, it has been customary to distinguish the manifestation of linguistic competence in speech and writing (*parole*) from the supraindividual stock of linguistic elements and the rules for combining them. This linguistic system (*langue*) is what makes human communication possible, but it is not consciously known or reflected upon in the act of speaking or writing (Culler, 1976).

Through the unconscious assimilation of this linguistic system, which begins in earliest childhood, "man is separated from the material world (external objects of reference) and initiated into a shared archetypal system of meaning-relations—a system that collates meanings imaginally through a parity of phonetic values" (Kugler, 1982, 117). The unconscious web of linguistic associations, both semantic and phonetic, interacts with emotionally charged patterns of meaning that also lie outside consciousness and that are called complexes.[9] These inner connections between language and the psyche are particularly crucial for fantasy, in which the ordinary reference of language is abolished and phonetic associations seem to predominate.

Kugler is concerned with the relation between language and images in dreams, but the Nag Hammadi texts cannot be considered to be direct transcriptions of psychic material. The ancient Coptic manuscripts are translations, perhaps by Pachomian monks, of lost Greek originals. However, Kugler has shown that the invariant relationship among concepts, realized by an invariant phonetic pattern, transcends the differences among particular languages (1982, 51–52). That is to say, the same phonetic pattern is found in languages that have no relationship with one another. It is therefore possible that the correspondence between phonetic patterns, unified by acoustic archetypal images, and psychologically charged patterns of meaning may have been preserved in the transmission of these texts from Greek to Coptic and from Coptic to modern vernacular translations.

In rational discourse, the individual uses language; in poetic discourse, language uses the individual, who is said to be "inspired" by the Muse. What is thereby brought to expression is an underlying deep structure that imaginally connects disparate concepts. Conceptual language is not abolished but transcended.

For analytical psychology, rational discourse is not the highest form of symbol making. Behind and beneath the word there is always something more ultimate: the image, which is the expression of archetypal energy that is simply there. As Jung has written, "The protean mythologem and the shimmering symbol express the processes of the psyche far more trenchantly and, in the end, far more clearly than the clearest concept; for the symbol not only conveys a visualization of the process but—and this is perhaps just as important—it also brings a re-experiencing of it" (1968c, 162–163).

In the *descensus ad inferos* familiar to the mystics, human reasoning is of no avail, and the imaginative function of mythology replaces the use of rational discourse.

Gnostic Reflection on Language

The doctrinal interpretation (and discreditation) of gnosis ignores not only the central importance given to the image in the passages already cited but also some clearly deconstructionist statements about language, found particularly in the Gospel of Philip.

In an extraordinary anticipation of Derrida, we find this statement about the differential nature of language: "Light and darkness, life and death, right and left, are brothers of one another. They are inseparable" (Robinson, 1988, 142). From this point it follows that nothing can be understood in isolation: "Because of this neither are the good good, nor the evil evil, nor is life life, nor death death" (Robinson, 1988, 142).

The text goes on to draw the consequences for "God-talk": "Thus one who hears the word 'God' does not perceive what is correct, but perceives what is incorrect. So also with 'the father' and 'the son' and 'the holy spirit' and 'life' and 'light' and 'resurrection' and 'the church' and all the rest" (Robinson, 1988, 142). The literalistic interpretation of religious language leads to deception, which only the inner knowledge of the Gnostic can escape (Robinson, 1988, 142).

Of course, the Nag Hammadi texts include didactic as well as mythic material, and the Gnostic creation myth itself has been given a doctrinal interpretation. But these explicit statements from the Gospel of Philip give an indication of what kind of language game is being played.

To be sure, Nag Hammadi scholars can readily identify a welter of ideas and doctrines with parallels in other writings from late antiquity. But from a psychological point of view, the crucial thing is how such ideas and doctrines are being used.

A Gnostic Parable about Language?

There is an obscure passage in the Gospel of Philip that suggests the contrast between the rational and the archetypal dimensions of language that has been the central focus of this discussion. The text is stressing the difference between creating and begetting. A creator works openly, but begetting is done in private (Robinson, 1988, 157–158).

In the Gnostic creation myth it is the Demiurge and his archons who create Adam from the elements. But Adam has no real life in him. Only the highest being can confer upon him the divinity that will exalt him above the Demiurge and make him capable of receiving salvation (Rudolph, 1987, 94–95). The Demiurge who vainly boasts, "I am a jealous God" (Exod. 20:5) and "besides me there is no god" (Isa. 45:5) corresponds psychologically to the rational ego, which proclaims its self-sufficiency, unaware of its own roots in the unconscious.

The primary expression of ego consciousness is rational discourse. It "works openly." It is exoteric and relies for its intelligibility upon social convention. Begetting is an esoteric action, done "in private," away from ego consciousness. It is also instinctual, thus paralleling the archetypes, which, like biological instincts, "direct all fantasy into its appointed paths" (Jung, 1968b, 66).

If understood with reference to language, "begetting" can refer to the unconscious associations that are grouped around an archetypal image. The author challenges the orthodox view that the same creator God is responsible for both the creation of the world and the begetting of the Son: "he who creates cannot beget." That is to say, rational discourse and fantasy language come from different parts of the psyche. Gnostic texts are esoteric because their meaning depends not on the public conventions of rational discourse but on correspondences hidden in the deep structure of language, to which ego consciousness has no direct access.

According to the instruction of Father Zosima in *The Brothers Karamazov*, "Much on earth is hidden from us, but to make up for that we have been given a precious mystic sense of our living bond with the other world, with the higher heavenly world, and the roots of our thoughts and feelings are not here but in other worlds" (Dostoevsky, 1976, 299). For the Gnostic, the link between "things visible and invisible" is founded not on an act of creation but on a begetting from above (cf. John 3:3). The connection between the visible image and its invisible source is the result of an inner process, like the resemblance between a woman's child and the man who loves her (Gospel of Philip; Robinson, 1988, 156).

Consequently, the paradigm for the Gnostic use of language is to be sought not in the word's creative power but in the eternal process of generation through which the word came to be: "begotten, not created." The hidden correspondences between the two worlds are expressed not through rational discourse, the creation of ego consciousness, but through the power of fantasy language, which wells up from the deep structure that is eternally there.

Jung and the Gnostic Worldview

Jung's attraction to gnosis raises a question that calls for comment. Jung tells us that, for him, the irreality to which Nietzsche succumbed "was the quintessence of horror, for I aimed, after all, at *this* world and *this* life" (1961, 214). How, then, could Jung have anything but a negative reaction to Gnostic writings, which have nothing good to say about the material world, the body, and human sexuality and which understand the purpose of life to be escape from the world back to the divine *pleroma*?

I propose two responses to this question. First of all, our critique of the doctrinal interpretation of gnosis should make us cautious about taking such dark statements at face value. Of course, it is possible that the Gnostics shared the disparagement of the body and sexuality that was common in late antiquity. But far more importantly, the body, for the Gnostics, was a symbol of the ignorance of the spiritual world that gnosis strives to overcome. The cosmos, the body, and human sexuality all have powerful symbolic potential, and statements made about them in our texts may well represent the inner work of active imagination.

Second, the interest that Jung expressed in the Gnostics had to do not with their lifestyle but with the proximity of their writings to unconscious processes: "Most of [the Gnostics] were in reality theologians who, unlike the more orthodox ones, allowed themselves to be influenced in large part by inner experience. They are therefore, like the alchemists, a veritable mine of information concerning all those natural symbols arising out of the repercussions of the Christian message. (Jung, 1968a, 269)

In *Symbols of Transformation*, Jung wrote a commentary on the fantasies of a young woman who became psychotic because, in Jung's view, she had been unable to understand the significance of her own unconscious material and so was unable to draw the consequences for her personal life.[10] Unfortunately, the Nag Hammadi texts provide no biographical information about the authors, all of whom are anonymous.[11] We can therefore draw no inferences about how they interacted with the world in which they lived. Whether, from a modern psychological point of view, they were successfully individuated human beings we simply do not know.

Conclusion: Reading the Nag Hammadi Texts Today

The characters in the Gnostic creation myth bear a striking resemblance to the Jungian model of the psyche: the *pleroma* = the unconscious; the Demiurge = the ego; Sophia = the anima. For a Jungian, such correspondences confirm the psychological origin of these texts.

Nevertheless, this kind of interpretation runs the risk of becoming just one more variant of the doctrinal interpretation of gnosis criticized in this essay.

In keeping with the position that I have taken, I suggest that we read the Nag Hammadi texts as poetry, whatever their formal literary genre. Speaking for an ironic age, W. H. Auden declared, "Poetry makes nothing happen."[12] Nevertheless, no one who actually reads poetry believes this to be true. Poetry *has* the power to make something happen, and reading the Nag Hammadi texts can be a highly activating experience, if only the reader is able to defer the critical question: what does this *mean?*

Jung said, "Every interpretation is an hypothesis, an attempt to read an unknown text" (1977, 150). From this it would seem to follow that, before beginning the interpretive task, the reader must encounter the unknown text, in all its strangeness, on the experiential level. For Jung, the encounter with Gnostic literature is bound to be disorienting: "I read like mad, and worked with feverish interest through a mountain of mythological material, then through the Gnostic writers, and ended in total confusion. I found myself in a state of perplexity similar to the one I had experienced at the clinic when I tried to understand the meaning of psychotic states of mind" (Jung, 1961, 186).

The proximity of these texts to the unconscious stirs up unconscious contents in the reader, breaking the grip of the fixed structures of objectivity and referentiality.

The world of gnosis, now available to us as never before through the Nag Hammadi texts, is a world from which mythological thinking has not yet been banished in the interest of doctrinal and ethical uniformity. Such mythological understanding returns the Christian symbols to the psychic matrix from which they once came and removes the barrier between religion and experience. It is that barrier that Jung considered to be the greatest weakness of Western religion.

Notes

Reprinted by permission of Open Court Publishing Company, a division of Carus Publishing Company, Peru, IL, from *The Allure of Gnosticism*, ed. Robert A. Segal, copyright © 1995 by Schuyler Brown.

1. Since my interest in this chapter is in the broad definition of the Gnostic phenomenon, I shall use the Greek word *gnosis* (knowledge) rather than the English neologism "Gnosticism," which refers specifically to the developed Christian systems of the second and third centuries.

2. "Disparagement and vilification of Gnosticism are an anachronism. Its obviously psychological symbolism could serve many people today as a bridge to a more living appreciation of Christian tradition" (Jung, 1969, 292).

3. Jung refers to the church as "a mighty, far-spread, and venerable institution," and he illustrates its containing function with the example of the Swiss mystic and hermit, Brother Nicholas of Flue. He reported that Brother Klaus received a vision "so terrible that his own countenance was changed by it," but by means of an illustrated devotional booklet by a German mystic, Klaus was able to "elaborate" his visionary experience into the so-called "Trinity Vision," which he painted on the wall of his cell (Jung, 1968b, 8–9). Referring specifically to *gnosis*, Jung remarks, "Recognizing the danger of Gnostic irrealism, the Church, more practical in these matters, has always insisted on the concretism of the historical events" (1969, 287).

4. "These two sections of this 'primal history' [i.e., cosmogony and anthropogony] belong closely together and are only artificially separated by us" (Rudolph, 1987, 95).

5. "Adam or the first earthly man is for Gnosis the prototype of men in general; his destiny anticipates that of the mankind which is to follow. For this reason all these narratives have not only an illustrative but above all an existential significance. They are expressions of knowledge about the whence and whither of mankind" (Rudolph, 1987, 95).

6. The Gnostic texts cited in this essay are all to be found in Robinson (1988).

7. "[T]he distinguishing mark of the Christian epoch, its highest achievement, has become the congenital vice of our age: the supremacy of the word of the Logos, which stands for the central figure of our Christian faith" (Jung, 1970, 286).

8. "The spirit does not dwell in concepts. Words butter no parsnips" (Jung, 1961, 167).

9. Kugler builds upon the word-association experiments carried out by Jung (1973) at the Burgholzli Clinic.

10. "Had I treated Miss Miller I would have had to tell her some of the things of which I have written in this book, in order to build up her conscious mind to the point where it could have understood the contents of the collective unconscious" (Jung, 1967, 442).

11. What the heresiologists have to say about the lives of Gnostic teachers is naturally suspect.

12. Quoted in Culler (1981, 140).

References

Campbell, J. (1989). *This Business of the Gods: In Conversation with Fraser Boa.* Caledon East, Ontario, Canada: Windrose Films.

Culler, J. (1976). *Saussure.* Glasgow: Fontana

Culler, J. (1981). *The Pursuit of Signs.* Ithaca: Cornell University Press.

Derrida, J. (1981). *Positions,* A. Bass, trans. Chicago: University of Chicago Press.

Dostoevsky, F. (1976). *The Brothers Karamazov,* C. Garnet, trans. New York: Norton.

Jung, C. G. (1961). *Memories, Dreams, Reflections,* A. Jaffe, ed., R. Winston & C. Winston, trans. Glasgow: Fount.

Jung, C. G. (1967). Symbols of Transformation, *The Collected Works of C. G. Jung* (Vol. 5). Princeton: Princeton University Press. (Original work published 1911–1912)

Jung, C. G. (1968a). Aion, *Collected Works* (Vol. 9, pt. 2). Princeton: Princeton University Press. (Original work published 1951)

Jung, C. G. (1968b). The Archetypes and the Collective Unconscious, *The Collected Works of C. G. Jung* (Vol. 9, pt. 1). Princeton: Princeton University Press. (Original work published 1959)

Jung, C. G. (1968c). Paracelsus as a Spiritual Phenomenon, *The Collected Works of C. G. Jung* (Vol. 13). Princeton: Princeton University Press, 109–189. (Original work published 1942)

Jung, C. G. (1969). Transformation Symbolism in the Mass, *The Collected Works of C. G. Jung* (Vol. 11). Princeton: Princeton University Press, 201–296. (Original work published 1954)

Jung, C. G. (1970). Civilization in Transition, *The Collected Works of C. G. Jung* (Vol. 10). Princeton: Princeton University Press. (Original work published 1964)

Jung, C. G. (1973). Experimental Researches, *The Collected Works of C. G. Jung* (Vol. 2). Princeton: Princeton University Press.

Jung, C. G. (1977). The Practice of Psychotherapy, *The Collected Works of C. G. Jung* (Vol. 16). Princeton: Princeton University Press. (Original work published 1954)

Kugler, P. (1982). *The Alchemy of Discourse: An Archetypal Approach to Language.* Toronto, Canada: Associated University Presses.

LaFargue, M. (1985). *Language and Gnosis: The Opening Scenes of the Acts of Thomas.* Philadelphia: Fortress.

Pasquier, A. (1988). Prouneikos. A Colorful Expression to Designate Wisdom in Gnostic Texts. *Images of the Feminine,* K. L. King, ed. Philadelphia: Fortress, 47–66.

Robinson, J. M., ed. (1988). *The Nag Hammadi Library in English* (3rd ed.). San Francisco: Harper & Row.

Rudolph, K. (1987). *Gnosis,* R. M. Wilson, trans. San Francisco: Harper & Row.

GLOSSARY

Active imagination: A Jungian technique of exploring levels of meaning in a dream image by expressing that image in new forms, for example, poetry, art, dance, or clay. Jung had observed that "often the hands know how to solve a riddle with which the intellect has wrestled in vain" (Jung, 1953–1978, 8:86).

Amplification: A Jungian technique of dream interpretation that consists of introducing parallels to dream images from folklore, mythology, the history of religions, and personal history, toward the end of finding associations that will assist in the conscious clarification of the dream images.

Analytic psychology: The phrase Jung chose for his psychological approach in distinction from the term *psychoanalysis* used by Freud and *individual psychology* used by Adler.

Anima/animus: Latin for "soul," "person," "life," or "mind." Jung adopted these terms to refer to the unconscious archetypal depiction of the opposite gender. *Anima* refers to the image of the feminine in the masculine psyche; *animus* is the image of the masculine in the feminine psyche. Because these images are unconscious, they can be projected on members of the opposite sex, producing "love at first sight."

Archetype/archetypal image: Jungian psychology speaks of a pattern-making tendency of the collective psyche to portray mainstay human experiences, conditions, and life crises with a glossary of typical images that recur recognizably in slightly different garb in the literature and lore of cultures around the world, past and present. Although this patterning tendency is unconscious, and therefore cannot be directly observed, it can be seen at work in the "archetypal images" it produces in its "stories." These include transculturally recurrent figures such as the primordial garden, the divine child, the trickster, the golden age, the wise old man, the suffering servant, the patriarch, the virgin mother, the stages of history, and so on.

Behaviorism: A school of psychology, associated for decades with B. F. Skinner, that holds that the only proper subjects for psychological inquiry are the facts of human and animal behavior and animals and their conditioning. Behaviorism regarded the mind, the psyche, and the soul as inaccessible to psychological inquiry.

Biblical criticism: The art of the scholarly study of biblical texts that emerged in its modern form in the mid-nineteenth century. Until the 1960s, the enterprise involved the diachronic examination of Scripture from the standpoint of the historical, archaeological, literary, and theological critic. Since the 1960s, synchronic forms of biblical criticism have developed that include, among others, rhetorical, feminist, canonical, ideological, social scientific, and psychological criticism.

Canon: Within the field of biblical studies, the word *canon* refers to the collection of writings officially approved by a religious body. For Judaism the canon consists of the Hebrew Scriptures (Old Testament), and for Christianity the Old and New Testaments.

Cognitive dissonance: The discomfort that comes with the tension that can emerge out of a discrepancy between the realities of one's world and one's expectations, or between what we know and what we do. The condition can lead to paralysis of action, or it can serve as motivator to take steps to reduce the inconsistency.

Cognitive psychology: The fundamental assumption of cognitive psychology is that fears, complexes, and generally negative emotions can be traced to faulty ideas, distorted perceptions, and destructive attitudes or cognitions. The therapeutic goal of cognitive psychology is to change cognition and to examine the way in which the client construes reality.

Collective unconscious: In Jung's psychology the collective unconscious (or *objective unconscious*), in distinction from the personal unconscious, represents the deepest and broadest level of the unconscious, an inherited function common to the human race. It is the origin of the primordial archetypal images that are the common heritage of humankind.

Complex: Jung coined this term to refer to a psychologically significant entity on which an individual has focused a near-addictive amount of energy and feeling.

Cura animarum: A medieval ecclesiastical phrase meaning "the care or cure of souls" that has been used to define the mission of the church. It is also regarded in some therapeutic circles as the goal of psychology.

Defense mechanism: Also called *ego-defense mechanisms*, these are strategies, often unconscious and neurotic, for defending the self from unpleasant persons or situations. They include the strategies of displacement, denial, repression, suppression, compulsive behavior, transference, sublimation, projection, and reaction formation. In modern psychoanalytic theory they differ from the conscious "coping mechanisms" that a mature person employs to meet threatening circumstances (Hunter, 1990, 269 [E. M. Pattison]).

Demythologization: The term was introduced by New Testament scholar Rudolf Bultmann in the 1950s as a tactic for getting behind the literal meaning of biblical myths to their originating intent and existential relevance.

Displacement: A defense mechanism of redirecting one's defensive or belligerent feelings from the person who "deserves" them to a less threatening person who does not, like the man who barks at his wife at home rather than at the offending boss at work.

Dissociation: The psychological description of an unconscious defense mechanism of the splitting off from consciousness of certain uncomfortable, threatening, or disturbing realities in one's life, resulting in the possibility of memory loss, depression, or even multiple personality.

Exegesis: Derived from a Greek word that means "to lead out," it is used by scholars and literary critics to refer to the scholarly process of "leading out" the meaning of a text, focusing on the meaning of the words in their original historic context and within the framework of the world in which they were written. Exegesis is often described as the art of discerning "what the text said."

Feminist criticism: A school of biblical scholarship that studies Scripture with an eye to the role, valuation, and treatment of women. Three branches have developed: one that focuses on what is perceived as the incorrigibly androcentric and patriarchal character of the Bible; a second that focuses on those voices in the Bible that oppose human oppression, including the oppression of women; a third that seeks to bring to light the significant role of women in biblical culture, despite a perceived male-dominated tendency to dismiss it as unimportant.

Form criticism: A branch of biblical criticism originating in the 1920s aimed originally at studying the "forms" in which the oral traditions behind the Gospels were preserved and transmitted (for example, miracle stories, parables, sayings). In time, it was conceived more broadly as the study of the form or genre of biblical writings and their constituent parts, mindful of the different kinds of meanings and "truths" each conveys and the different functions each is designed to serve (for example, myth, legend, fable, law, psalm prophetic utterance, epistle, gospel, and apocalypse).

Hellenistic Judaism: The vast population of Jews living in the Mediterranean world between the second century B.C.E. and the second century A.D. who spoke Greek, produced the Greek translation of the Hebrew Bible, and developed a literature that incorporated Greek philosophical learning. A good example is Philo Judaeus of Alexandria.

Hermeneutics: Derived from a Greek root that means "interpretation," the term is used currently to refer to the study of the meaning transacted in the exchange between a text and a reader. It is often described as the art of determining "what the text says," with emphasis on the meaning(s) it can convey or catalyze for a present-day reader and on the meaning that the reader brings to the text.

Hermeneutics of suspicion: A phrase introduced by Paul Ricoeur that endorsed the need to read alerted to the ulterior motives, special interests, and ideologies that might be operative in the text being read.

Heuristic: Derived from the Greek root "to find," it refers to an idea or method that is employed toward the end of finding or teasing out further discoveries.

Humanistic psychology: A movement within psychology in the second half of the twentieth century that provided an option to psychoanalytic and behaviorist psychologies in its emphasis on human subjectivity, human potential, and strategies for self-improvement.

Ideological criticism: A branch of biblical studies that seeks to uncover ideologies (for example, racial, ethnic, class, social, political, gender-oriented) implicit in particular biblical authors, biblical texts, and biblical readers and interpretations.

Individuation: A Jungian term for the goal of the life process of becoming the "individual" one uniquely is, through a lifelong process of integrating the psychic components in one's life, and bringing the unconscious to fuller consciousness.

Logia: Greek for "sayings." A technical phrase in New Testament studies referring to the "sayings" of Jesus preserved in oral and literary tradition.

Myth: A foundational story within a culture that provides an interpretation of "how things are." Distinct from fables, which aim at providing moral examples, and legends, which enhance national figures of the past, the myth provides a "storied" introduction to a culture's understanding of physical, metaphysical, cultural, social, familial, personal, and cosmic realities and their meaning.

Neurosis/neurotic: A clinically imprecise term for emotional, behavioral, or cognitive disturbance that is distressing but not totally incapacitating for an individual. With respect to the cause of neurosis, Freud observed that behind a neurosis there is often concealed all the natural and necessary suffering the patient has been unwilling to bear. Karen Horney defined *neurotic anxiety* as a pathological, dysfunction-generating state in which anxiety is disproportionate to reality.

Pathogenic: Producing illness, disease, or dysfunction, physical or psychological.

Persona: A term popularized in Jungian psychology to refer to the face or "mask" one selects consciously or unconsciously as part of the task of adapting to and presenting oneself to the world. Jung commented, "one could say, with a little exaggeration, that the persona is that which in reality one is not, but which oneself as well as others think one is" (Jung, 1963, 397).

Personal unconscious: A Jungian phrase for that part of the unconscious that derives from personal experience of the individual, as opposed to a collective unconscious common to the species.

Post-traumatic stress disorder: "An anxiety disorder characterized by a pattern of symptoms attributable to the experience of a traumatic event. The symptoms of PTSD include (1) re-experiencing the traumatic event, (2) emotional numbing, and (3) any of a variety of autonomic, cognitive or behavioral symptoms" (Hunter, 1990, 931 [N. C. Brown]).

Projection: "A defense mechanism in which one unconsciously attributes one's own unacceptable feelings, desire, thoughts, and impulses to another person. This removes the responsibility for unacceptable qualities or feelings from oneself, thus protecting the ego. An example is a husband who is barely able to control his anger toward his spouse and subsequently becomes suspicious that *she* is angry" (Hunter, 1990, 960 [J. Estelle]).

Psyche: A term used in classical and biblical Greek to refer to the vital force, life, breath, true self, or soul; ultimately adopted in psychoanalytic tradition to refer to the totality of the psychic processes, conscious and unconscious, including affect, perception, cognition, conation, intuition, imagination, rationality, and spirituality, among others.

Psychodynamics: A term that means literally the "power of the psyche," referring to any "psychological theory or therapeutic method that explains and approaches psychological processes in terms of motives and drives" (Hunter, 1990, 989 [M. A. Woltersdorf]). It is also used currently to refer to the dynamic interactive psychic factors at work in human relations, whether in real time or as portrayed and expressed in art and literature.

Psychological biblical criticism: A branch of biblical studies that applies psychological and psychoanalytic insight to the study of the Bible, its origins, its content, its interpretation, and the history of its effects.

Psychologizing: The practice of explaining the essence or origin of events, persons, or entities (for example, art, religion, politics) in exclusively psychological terms.

Q: A code word in New Testament studies to refer to a collection of traditional sayings of Jesus that appear in the Gospels of Matthew and Luke but not in Mark or John. The collection includes the Lord's Prayer and the Sermon on the Mount, among many other "logia" or "sayings" of Jesus. The letter *Q* is an abbreviation of the German word *Quelle* for "source." It is believed that Matthew's sources include the Gospel of Mark, Q, and Matthew's own special material (or M). Luke's sources include the Gospel of Mark, Q, and Luke's own special material (or L).

Reader-response criticism: A branch of literary and biblical criticism that focuses on reading as an act of "construction" and on the role of the reader's values, responses, and attitudes in the process.

Redaction criticism: A branch of biblical studies that examines the effect of biblical authors on their texts, with respect to the principles of organization, selection of materials, interpretive cues, written and oral sources, vocabulary, and points of view they have enlisted or employed in creating and shaping their texts.

Repression: One of several defense mechanisms that consists of excluding unwanted memories, thoughts, or concerns from conscious awareness; living in denial.

Rhetorical criticism: A branch of literary and biblical criticism that focuses on the rhetorical or "persuasive" character, design, and function of a text or text unit within the original rhetorical context of its writing. Rhetoric has been defined as "that quality of discourse by which a speaker or writer seeks to accomplish his purposes." Accordingly rhetorical critics examine the rhetorical literary units, the rhetorical situation or problem, devices of style, and the writer's objective in context (Coggins & Houlden, 1990, 599–600 [J. I. H. McDonald]).

Self: Jungian psychology uses this term to refer to the archetype of the individuated person. This view of self, usually achieved in the second half of life, displaces the personal ego as the center of one's conscious life.

Self psychology: Psychologies that place the self at the center of personality and make the growth or actualization of the self the primary goal of life in general and of psychotherapy and counseling in particular (Hunter, 1990, 1137 [P. C. Vitz]). Representative "self psychologists" include Alfred Adler, Erich Fromm, Carl Rogers, Abraham Maslow, Rollo May, and Heinz Kohut. Kohut's psychology offers a positive perspective on narcissism (Wulff, 1991, 353).

Sitz im Leben: A phrase originating in German biblical scholarship to refer to the "life-setting" (lit., "seat in life") of a biblical text or event. Thus one might speak of the *Sitz im Leben* of John's Gospel, that is, the historical and cultural circumstances of the author of the Gospel and his community at the time the Gospel was being written.

Social scientific criticism: In its broadest sense, social scientific criticism "applies methods and theories to biblical texts in an attempt to reconstruct the social worlds behind these texts . . . while simultaneously illuminating the lives of the people living in these worlds" (Hayes, 1999, 2:478 [N. Steinberg]).

Superego: The part of the psyche in Freudian psychology that represents the introjection of societal, religious, and/or familial values, obligations, and obsessions that exercise unconscious inner authority in an individual's thoughts, values, and decisions.

Textual criticism: One of the earliest of biblical critical disciplines, dating to the sixteenth century. It began with the recognition that we do not have the original Hebrew or Greek "autograph" text of any biblical book but only centuries of handwritten copies. Furthermore, although the copies largely agree with one another, close inspection reveals that no copy agrees with any other copy in every detail. The task of textual criticism is to devise scholarly techniques for deciding which of the variant readings are corruptions and which are most likely the original.

Unconscious: "That part of the mind or psyche containing information that has never been conscious, or that was once conscious but is no longer" (Hunter, 1990, 1290 [H. Coward]). Jung defined the contents of the unconscious as including "everything of which I know, but of which I am not at the moment thinking, everything of which I was once conscious but have now forgotten; everything perceived by my senses, but not noted by my conscious mind; everything which, involuntarily and without paying attention to it, I feel, think, remember, want, and do; all the future things that are taking shape in me and will sometime come to consciousness" (Jung, 1963, 401).

References

Coggins, R. J., & Houlden, J. L. (1990). *A Dictionary of Biblical Interpretation.* Philadelphia: Trinity Press International.

Hayes, J. H., ed. (1999). *Dictionary of Biblical Interpretation.* Nashville: Abingdon.

Hunter, R., ed. (1990). *Dictionary of Pastoral Care and Counseling.* Nashville: Abingdon.

Jung, C. G. (1953–1978). *The Collected Works of C. G. Jung.* Princeton: Princeton University Press.

Jung, C. G. (1963). *Memories, Dreams, Reflections.* New York: Vintage Books.

Wulff, D. (1991). *Psychology of Religion: Classic and Contemporary Views.* New York: John Wiley.

INDEX

About the Contributors

PAUL N. ANDERSON is professor of biblical and Quaker studies and chair of the Department of Religious Studies at George Fox University, where he has served since 1989, other than a year as a visiting professor at Yale Divinity School (1998–1999). He is author of *The Christology of the Fourth Gospel: Its Unity and Disunity in the Light of John 6* (1996) and *Navigating the Living Waters of the Gospel of John: On Wading with Children and Swimming with Elephants* (2000). In addition, he has written many essays on biblical and Quaker themes and is editor of *Quaker Religious Thought*. He serves on the steering committee of the Psychology and Biblical Studies Section of the Society of Biblical Literature and teaches the New Testament Interpretation course in the PsyD program of George Fox University. His PhD in New Testament is from Glasgow University (1989), his MDiv is from the Earlham School of Religion (1981), and his BA in psychology and BA in Christian ministries are from Malone College (1978).

ANTHONY BASH serves as honorary fellow in theology and director of Studies in New Testament in the Department of Humanities on the faculty of the University of Hull, England. His fields of specialization include New Testament studies, biblical studies, and the use of social sciences in biblical studies. He has recently written one of the first articles to be published in the *Journal for the Study in the New Testament* on the application of psychological models to biblical interpretation, "The Interpretation of 2 Corinthians 10–13" (2001).

LYN M. BECHTEL received her PhD in biblical studies from Drew University prior to her appointment as visiting associate professor of Hebrew Bible at Drew Theological School and associate professor of Hebrew Bible at Moravian Theological Seminary. Her areas of specialization include the books of Genesis and Job, psychoanalytic theory and the Hebrew Bible, feminist interpretation of the Hebrew Bible, and the biblical experience of shame and shaming. Her publications include "Shame as a Sanction of Social Control in Biblical Israel: Judicial, Political, and Social Shaming" (*Journal of the Study of the Old Testament*, 1991) and "Genesis 2.4b–3.24: A Myth about Human Maturation" (*Journal for the Study of Old Testament*, 1995).

KAMILA BLESSING is an Episcopal priest of twenty years' standing and an "intentional interim" specializing in the health and healing of congregations. She has graduate training in family systems therapy, a PhD in information systems (studying the "people systems" in organizations and their communication) from the University of Pittsburgh, and a PhD in New Testament from Duke University. Her research in New Testament includes the applications of systems theories to Bible interpretation as well as the role of narrative in the maintenance of religious identity groups. Her publications include "Murray Bowen's Family Systems Theory as Bible Hermeneutic using the Family of the Prodigal, Luke 15:11–32" (*Journal of Psychology and Christianity*, 2000) and "The 'Confusion Technique' of Milton Erickson as Hermeneutic for Biblical Parables" (*Journal of Psychology and Christianity*, 2002).

SCHUYLER BROWN received his BA in classical languages from Harvard University in 1952, and as a member of the Jesuit order in the 1950s and 1960s, Brown received licentiates in philosophy (1957), theology (1964), and biblical studies (1969). He received his DrTheol from the University of Münster (Westphalia) in 1969. His academic appointments have included teaching positions at Woodstock College, General Theological Seminary in New York City, the University of London, and as professor of New Testament at the University of Toronto (St. Michael's College). He has served as a lecturer at the Jung Institute in Zurich and in the Training Program of the Ontario Association of Jungian Analysts. His wife, Margaret Eileen Meredith, is a graduate of the Jung Institute in Zurich and a practicing Jungian analyst in Toronto. Brown's publications include *The Origins of Christianity: A Historical Introduction to the New Testament* (1984; rev. ed., 1993) and *Text and Psyche: Experiencing Scripture Today* (1998, 2002).

MARTIN J. BUSS, professor of religion at Emory University, received a BD and a ThM from Princeton Theological Seminary in 1954 and 1955 and a PhD from Yale University in 1958. He has taught in the Department of Religion at Emory University from 1959 until the present, with a specialization in Hebrew Bible. He has examined this literature from a number of perspectives: anthropological, sociological, psychological, and philosophical. His first essay dealing with a psychological approach to the Hebrew Bible was "Self-Theory and Theology" (*Journal of Religion*, 1965).

DONALD CAPPS, psychologist of religion, is William Hart Felmeth Professor of Pastoral Theology at Princeton Theological Seminary. In 1989 he was awarded an honorary doctorate from the University of Uppsala, Sweden, in recognition of the importance of his publications. He served as president of the Society for the Scientific Study of Religion from 1990 to 1992. Among his many significant books are *Men, Religion, and Melancholia: James, Otto, Jung and Erikson and Freud* (1997); *The Freudians on Religion: A Reader* (2001); *Social Phobia: Alleviating Anxiety in an Age of Self-Promotion* (1999); and *Jesus: A Psychological Biography* (2000). He also authored *The Child's Song: The Religious Abuse of Children* (1995).

JAMES H. CHARLESWORTH is the George L. Collord Professor of New Testament Language and Literature as well as editor and director of the Princeton Theological Seminary Dead Sea Scrolls Project at Princeton University. He received his PhD from Duke University and has advanced degrees or study at Edinburgh, the École Biblique de Jerusalem, the Hebrew University, the University of Tübingen, and elsewhere. Charlesworth is editor of the *Old Testament Pseudepigrapha* and *The Dead Sea Scrolls* (the Princeton critical edition and translation). He has written or edited more than sixty-five books and completed the first in-depth study of serpent symbolism in antiquity and the Bible. He introduced the term "Jesus research" into the study of the historical Jesus.

HAL CHILDS is psychotherapist and clinical director at the California Counseling Institute, San Francisco. He holds the degrees of MDiv, MA, and PhD. He is closely affiliated with the work of the Guild for Psychological Studies in San Francisco. His field of specialization is New Testament interpretation and depth psychology, as is amply demonstrated in his trail-blazing doctoral dissertation, now published as *The Myth of the Historical Jesus and the Evolution of Consciousness* (2000).

DERECK DASCHKE received his MA and PhD in Divinity from the University of Chicago Divinity School and is presently assistant professor of philosophy and religion at Truman State University, Kirksville, Missouri. His fields of interest include religion and culture, psychology and religion, religion and health, new religious movements, and apocalypticism and millennialism. His publications include "Mourning the End of Time: Apocalypses as Texts of Cultural Loss" in *Millennialism from the Hebrew Bible to the Present*, edited by Leonard J. Greenspoon and Ronald A. Simpkins (2002) and "Desolate among Them: Loss, Fantasy, and Recovery in the Book of Ezekiel" (*American Imago*, 1999).

CHARLES T. DAVIS III studied at Emory University with Dr. Norman Perrin, graduating with BD and PhD degrees after special study at the University of Heidelberg. Although specializing in New Testament studies, he has also published articles and book reviews in the fields of American religion, computers and the humanities, philosophy, and Buddhist studies. He is the author of *Speaking of Jesus* and currently serves as professor of philosophy and religion at Appalachian State University in Boone, North Carolina, where he teaches biblical literature, Islam, and seminars on symbols and healing.

J. HAROLD ELLENS is a research scholar at the University of Michigan, Department of Near Eastern Studies. He is a retired Presbyterian theologian and ordained minister, a retired U.S. Army colonel, and a retired professor of philosophy, theology, and psychology. He has authored, coauthored, or edited 104 books and 165 professional journal articles. He served fifteen years as executive director of the Christian Association for Psychological Studies and as founding editor and editor in chief of the *Journal of Psychology and Christianity*. He holds a PhD from Wayne State University in the psychology of human communication, a PhD from the University of Michigan in biblical and Near Eastern studies, and master's degrees from Calvin Theological Seminary, Princeton Theological Seminary, and the University of Michigan. His publications include *God's Grace and Human Health* (1982) *Jesus as Son of Man, the Literary Character: A Progression of Images* (2003), *The Destructive Power of Religion, Violence in Judaism, Christianity, and Islam* (2004), and *Psychotheology: Key Issues* (1987) as well as chapters in *Moral Obligation and the Military*, *Baker Encyclopedia of Psychology*, and *Abingdon Dictionary of Pastoral Care*.

JAMES W. FOWLER is Professor of Theology and Human Development at Emory University in Atlanta and lecturer at Candler School of Theology. He was formerly on the faculty of Harvard University. He is currently the director of the Center for Faith Development and one of its primary research project directors. His prolific publications list includes such notable works as *Stages of Faith*; *Life-Maps*; *To See the Kingdom: The Theological Vision of H. Richard Niebuhr*; and *Becoming Adult, Becoming Christian, Adult Development and Christian Faith*. Professor Fowler is one of the great developmental theorists and researchers of the late twentieth and early twenty-first century.

DAVID G. GARBER JR., a PhD candidate at Emory University, is currently completing his dissertation, titled "Trauma, Memory, and Survival in Ezekiel 1–24." After receiving a BA in religious studies from Baylor University, he completed master of divinity and master of theology degrees from Princeton Theological Seminary. For the past two years, he has served as an adjunct professor at the McAfee School of Theology of Mercer University, Macon, Georgia, teaching courses in Hebrew Bible and biblical languages.

ITHAMAR GRUENWALD has served on the faculty of Tel Aviv University since 1967 in the Department of Jewish Philosophy and Program in Religious Studies. He has also been affiliated on a visiting basis as fellow with the Institute for Advanced Studies, Hebrew University; guest professor at the Revell Graduate School, Yeshiva University, New York; Martin Buber Guest Professor at the J. W. Goethe Universität, Frankfurt; and fellow at the Institute for Advanced Studies in Religion, University of Chicago. He has participated as chair and member of various committees of the Council for Higher Education in Israel. His publications include *Apocalyptic and Merkavah Mysticism* (1980), *From Apocalypticism to Gnosticism* (1988), and *Rituals and Ritual Theory in Ancient Israel* (2003).

DAVID JOBLING recently retired as professor of Hebrew Scriptures at St. Andrews College, Saskatoon, Canada, a post he had held since 1978. A native of England, he received his MA from Cambridge University and his PhD from Union Theological Seminary, New York City. He is the author of *The Sense of Biblical Narrative* (2 volumes) and of *1 Samuel* (Berit Olam series). As a member of the Bible and Culture Collective he coauthored *The Postmodern Bible* and coedited *The Postmodern Bible Reader*. He is a former general editor of the journal *Semeia* and a past president of the Canadian Society of Biblical Studies.

D. ANDREW KILLE received his PhD from the Graduate Theological Union in Berkeley in psychological biblical criticism. He is the author of *Psychological Biblical Criticism: Genesis 3 as a Test Case* (2001). As a former pastor, he teaches psychology and spirituality in the San Francisco Bay Area and is principal consultant for Revdak Consulting. He has served as co-chair of the Psychology and Biblical Studies Section of the Society of Biblical Literature and on the steering committee of the Person, Culture, and Religion Group of the American Academy of Religion.

ANDRÉ LACOCQUE is emeritus professor of Hebrew Scriptures at the Chicago Theological Seminary and emeritus director of its doctoral Center for Jewish–Christian Studies. He received his PhD and ThD from the University of Strasburg and honorary degrees from the University of Chicago and the University of Brussels. He is a long-standing member of the American Academy of Religion and the Chicago Society of Biblical Research, and he served as president of the Middle West Region of the Society of Biblical Literature (1973–1975). His publications include *Jonah, a Psycho-Religious Approach to the Prophet* (with Pierre-E. Lacocque, 1990) and *Thinking Biblically* (with Paul Ricoeur, 1998), which has been translated into Spanish, French, Portuguese, Italian, Polish, Hungarian, and Rumanian, with additional translations in progress in Greek and Korean. In 2001, colleagues published a Festschrift in his honor: *The Honeycomb of the Word: Interpreting the Primary Testament with André LaCocque*, edited by W. Dow Edgerton.

BERNHARD LANG received the degree of DTheol from the University of Tübingen and the DHabil from the University of Freiburg. He serves on the Faculty of Arts and Humanities at the University of Paderborn, Germany. He also holds the position of honorary professor of religious studies at the University of St. Andrews, U.K. His fields of specialization include biblical studies, the cultural history of the biblical world, history of Christian spirituality, and the anthropology and theory of religion. His major publications include *Drewermann, interprète la Bible* (1994); *Heaven: A History* (2nd ed., 2001, with many translations); *Sacred Games: A History of Christian Worship* (1997); and *The Hebrew God: Portrait of an Ancient Deity* (2002).

JILL L. McNISH received her JD from Rutgers University, and MDiv and a PhD in psychology and religion from Union Theological Seminary, New York City. Her field of specialization is the interface between psychology, theology, and spirituality. She is currently working in the Blanton-Peale Institute Pastoral Studies Program, New York City, and is engaged in interim ministry with the Episcopal Diocese of Newark. She is author of *Transforming Shame: A Pastoral Response* (2004) and "Uses of Theories of Depth Psychology in Ordained Ministry and the Institutional Church"(*Journal of Pastoral Care*, 2002).

PETRI MERENLAHTI received his PhD from the University of Helsinki and is currently working as research fellow in its Department of Biblical Studies. His field of specialization is narrative criticism of the New Testament and Gospels, with special interest in the Gospel of Mark. He has been a regular participant in the national programs of the Psychology and Biblical Studies Section of the Society of Biblical Literature. His publications include *Poetics for the Gospels? Rethinking Narrative Criticism* (2002).

DAN MERKUR received his PhD from the University of Stockholm and is currently in private practice as a psychoanalytic psychotherapist. He is affiliated with the Department for the Study of Religion, University of Toronto, and enrolled as a candidate at the Toronto Institute for Contemporary Psychoanalysis. His field of specialization is comparative religions. His publications include " 'And He Trusted in Yahweh': The Transformation of Abram in Gen 12–13 and 15" (*Journal of Psychology of Religion*, 1995–1996) and *Mystical Moments and Unitive Thinking* (1999).

DAVID L. MILLER holds a BD degree from Bethany Theological Seminary (1960) and a PhD from Drew University (1963). Until 1999 he was the Watson-Ledden Professor of Religion at Syracuse University (New York), and until 2003 he served as a core faculty person at Pacifica Graduate Institute in Santa Barbara. He specializes in the fields of religion and literature, and psychology and mythology, and is the author of four books—*Christs: Archetypal Images in Christian Theology* (1981); *Three Faces of God* (1987); *Hells and Holy Ghosts: A Theopoetics of Christian Belief* (1989); and *Gods and Games: Toward a Theology of Play* (1970)—as well as the editor of the book *Jung and the Interpretation of the Bible* (1995).

JOHN MILLER holds a ThD from the University of Basel and is professor emeritus of religious studies at Conrad Grebel College, University of Waterloo, Ontario. He was cofounder and co-chair of the Historical Jesus Section in the Society of Biblical Literature. He also served as director of Psychiatric Rehabilitation Services at Chicago State Hospital. His writings include *The Origins of the Bible: Rethinking Canon History* (1994); *Biblical Faith and Fathering* (1989); and *Jesus at Thirty: A Psychological and Historical Portrait* (1997).

DIETER MITTERNACHT holds the MDiv, MTheol, MPhil, and DTheol degrees and is currently researcher and lecturer at Lund University in Sweden. He also serves as visiting lecturer at the Swedish Agricultural University and as fellow of the Swedish Council of Research with the research project Social Cognition and Strategies of Persuasion in Pauline Letters. His fields of specialization include Pauline studies, texts and communication (rhetoric and epistolography in antiquity), early Christian identity, and sociopsychological approaches to exegesis. He is also a specialist on the ancient synagogue, participating as a fellow of the research project The Ancient Synagogue: Birthplace for Two World Religions. His publications include "By Works of The Law No One Shall Be Justified" (1988) and *Forum für Sprachlose: Eine kommunikationspsychologische und epistolär-rhetorische Untersuchung des Galaterbriefs* (1999). He has coedited *The Synagogue of Ancient Ostia and the Jews of Rome: Interdisciplinary Studies* (2001).

WILLIAM MORROW received his PhD from the University of Toronto; currently he is associate professor of Hebrew and Hebrew Scriptures at Queen's Theological College and the Department of Religious Studies, Queen's University, Kingston, Ontario. He is the author of *Scribing the Center: Organization and Redaction in Deuteronomy 14:1–17:1* (1995) and various articles related to the composition of biblical law. His publications in the area of psychological biblical criticism include "Toxic Religion and the Daughters of Job" (*Studies in Religion*, 1998).

ROBERT H. NEUWOEHNER earned his doctorate through the University of Denver and Iliff School of Theology joint PhD program in religious and theological studies, where he concentrated his research on the feminine symbolism in the Gospel of John. He has presented papers at national and regional meetings of the American Academy of Religion and the Society of Biblical Literature, and he recently published a psychosymbolic interpretation of John 20:14–18 in the Jungian journal *Psychological Perspectives*. Drawing on thirty years of work with Jungian theory, he has begun developing and offering seminars and workshops to provide "education for the second half of life."

MICHAEL WILLETT NEWHEART is associate professor of New Testament language and literature at Howard University School of Divinity, where he has taught since 1991. He holds a PhD from Southern Baptist Theological Seminary and is the author of *Wisdom Christology in the Fourth Gospel* (1992) and *Word and Soul: A Psychological, Literary, and Cultural Reading of the Fourth Gospel* (2001) as well as numerous articles on the psychological and literary interpretation of the New Testament.

ILONA N. RASHKOW is professor of Judaic studies, women's studies, and comparative literature at the State University of New York, Stony Brook. She has also been the visiting chair in Judaic studies at the University of Alabama. Among her publications are *Upon the Dark Places: Sexism and Anti-Semitism in English Renaissance Bible Translation* (1990); *The Phallacy of Genesis* (1993); and *Taboo or Not Taboo: Human Sexuality and the Hebrew Bible* (2000). Her areas of interest include psychoanalytic literary theory as applied to the Hebrew Bible and, more generally, as applied to Judaic studies, religious studies, feminist literary criticism, and women's studies.

WAYNE G. ROLLINS is professor emeritus of biblical studies at Assumption College, Worcester, Massachusetts, and adjunct professor of Scripture at Hartford Seminary, Hartford, Connecticut. He has also taught at Princeton University and Wellesley College and served as visiting professor at Mount Holyoke College, Yale College, College of the Holy Cross, and Colgate Rochester Divinity School. His writings include *The Gospels: Portraits of Christ* (1964); *Jung and the Bible* (1983); *Soul and Psyche: The Bible in Psychological Perspective* (1999); and numerous articles on psychology and biblical studies. He received his BD from Yale Divinity School and his PhD in New Testament studies from Yale University. He served as president of the New England section of the American Academy of Religion (1984–1985) and is the founder and past chair (1990–2000) of the Society of Biblical Literature Section on Psychology and Biblical Studies.

JOHN SCHMITT is associate professor in the Department of Theology at Marquette University. His special interests lie in the field of monastic and interfaith studies. His publications include, as coauthor,

The Prophets II, volume 7 of *The Storyteller's Companion to the Bible* (1995); "Samaria in the Books of the Eighth Century Prophets" in *The Pitcher Is Broken: Memorial Essays for Goesta W. Ahlstroem*, edited by Steven W. Holloway and Lowell K. Handy (1996); and "The City as Woman in Isaiah 1–39" in *Writing and Reading the Scroll of Isaiah: Studies in an Interpretive Tradition* (1997).

KARI SYREENI received his doctor of theology from the University of Helsinki, Finland, and is professor of New Testament studies at the University of Uppsala, Sweden. His special research interests include the Gospels, New Testament hermeneutics, psychological exegesis, and the Bible and modern literature. His publications include *The Making of the Sermon on the Mount: A Procedural Analysis on Matthew's Redactional Activity. Part I: Methodology and Compositional Analysis* (1987); "Separation and Identity: Aspects of the Symbolic World of Matt. 6:1–18" (*New Testament Studies*, 1994); Metaphorical Appropriation: (Post-) Modern Biblical Hermeneutic and the Theory of Metaphor" (*Literature and Theology*, 1995); and a forthcoming work, *In Memory of Jesus: Grief Work in the Gospels*.

RALPH L. UNDERWOOD, BD, MTh, MA, PhD, is emeritus professor of pastoral care at Austin Presbyterian Theological Seminary, Austin, Texas. He has been a member of the faculty there since 1978. He retired at the end of 2001. Before teaching at Austin Seminary he was director of the Wholistic Health Center in Woodridge, Illinois. His terminal degree is from the University of Chicago Divinity School in religion and psychological studies. A United Methodist minister, he was ordained in 1961. In addition to his article cited in the note of his chapter, his relevant publications are *Pastoral Care and the Means of Grace* (1993) and "Scripture: The Substance of Pastoral Care" (*Quarterly Review*, 1991).

ANDRIES G. VAN AARDE, DD, PhD, is on the faculty of theology and professor of New Testament at the University of Pretoria, South Africa. He is a member of the Context Group and the Jesus Seminar and co-chair of the Matthew Seminar of the International Society of New Testament Studies. His publications include *Fatherless in Galilee: Jesus as Child of God* (2001); "Jesus as Fatherless Child" in *The Social Setting of Jesus and the Gospels*, edited by W. Stegemann, B. J. Malina, and G. Theissen (2002); "Jesus and Perseus in Graeco-Roman Literature" (*Acta Patristica et Byzantina*, 2000); and "Jesus' Father: The Quest for the Historical Joseph" (*HTS Theological Studies*, 1998).

WALTER WINK is professor of biblical interpretation at Auburn Theological Seminary in New York City. Previously he was a parish minister and taught at Union Theological Seminary in New York City. In 1989 and 1990, he was a peace fellow at the United States Institute of Peace. His most recent book is *The Human Being: The Enigma of the Son of the Man* (2001). He is author of *The Powers*; and a trilogy, *Naming the Powers: The Language of Power in the New Testament* (1984), *Unmasking the Powers: The Invisible Forces That Determine Human Existence* (1986), and *Engaging the Powers: Discernment and Resistance in a World of Domination* (1992). *Engaging the Powers* received three Religious Book of the Year awards for 1993, from Pax Christi, the Academy of Parish Clergy, and the Midwestern Independent Publishers Association. His other works include *Jesus and Nonviolence* (2003); *The Powers That Be* (1998); and *When the Powers Fall: Reconciliation in the Healing of Nations* (1998). He has published more than 250 journal articles.

About the Series Editor and Advisers

J. HAROLD ELLENS is a Research Scholar at the University of Michigan, Department of Near Eastern Studies. He is a retired Presbyterian theologian and ordained minister, a retired U.S. Army Colonel, and a retired Professor of Philosophy, Theology and Psychology. He has authored, coauthored, and/or edited 104 books and 165 professional journal articles. He served fifteen years as Executive Director of the Christian Association for Psychological Studies, and as Founding Editor and Editor-in-Chief of the *Journal of Psychology and Christianity*. He holds a PhD from Wayne State University in the Psychology of Human Communication, a PhD from the University of Michigan in Biblical and Near Eastern Studies, and master's degrees from Calvin Theological Seminary, Princeton Theological Seminary, and the University of Michigan. He was born in Michigan, grew up in a Dutch-German immigrant community, and determined at age seven to enter the Christian Ministry as a means to help his people with the great amount of suffering he perceived all around him. His life's work has focused on the interface of psychology and religion.

ARCHBISHOP DESMOND TUTU is best known for his contribution to the cause of racial justice in South Africa, a contribution for which he was recognized with the Nobel Peace Prize in 1984. Archbishop Tutu has been an ordained priest since 1960. Among his many accomplishments are being named the first black General Secretary of the South African Council of Churches and serving as Archbishop of Cape Town. Once a high school teacher in South Africa, he has also taught theology in college and holds honorary degrees from universities including Harvard, Oxford, Columbia, and Kent State. He has been awarded the Order for Meritorious Service presented by President Nelson Mandela, the Archbishop of Canterbury's Award for outstanding service to the Anglican community, the Family of Man Gold Medal Award, and the Martin Luther King Jr. Non-Violent Peace Award. The publications Archbishop Tutu authored, coauthored, or made contributions to include *No Future Without Forgiveness* (2000), *Crying in the Wilderness* (1986), and *Rainbow People of God: The Making of a Peaceful Revolution* (1996).

LEROY H. ADEN is Professor Emeritus of Pastoral Theology at the Lutheran Theological Seminary in Philadelphia, Pennsylvania. He taught full-time at the seminary from 1967 to 1994 and part-time from 1994 to 2001. He served as Visiting Lecturer at Princeton Theological Seminary, Princeton, New Jersey, on a regular basis. In 2002 he co-authored *Preaching God's Compassion: Comforting Those Who Suffer* with Robert G. Hughes. Previously, he edited four books in a Psychology and Christianity series with J. Harold Ellens and David G. Benner. He served on the Board of Directors of the Christian Association for Psychological Studies for six years.

DONALD CAPPS, Psychologist of Religion, is William Hart Felmeth Professor of Pastoral Theology at Princeton Theological Seminary. In 1989 he was awarded an honorary doctorate from the University of Uppsala, Sweden, in recognition of the importance of his publications. He served as president of the Society for the Scientific Study of Religion from 1990 to 1992. Among his many significant books are *Men, Religion and Melancholia: James, Otto, Jung and Erikson and Freud*; and *The Freudians on Religion: A Reader*; and *Social Phobia: Alleviating Anxiety in an Age of Self-Promotion*; and *Jesus: A Psychological Biography*. He also authored *The Child's Song: The Religious Abuse of Children*.

ZENON LOTUFO JR. is a Presbyterian minister (Independent Presbyterian Church of Brazil), a philosopher, and a psychotherapist, specialized in Transactional Analysis. He has lectured both to undergraduate and graduate courses in universities in São Paulo, Brazil. He coordinates the course of specialization in Pastoral Psychology of the Christian Psychologists and Psychiatrists Association. He is the author of the books *Relações Humanas* [Human Relations]; *Disfunções no Comportamento Organizacional* [Dysfunctions in Organizational Behavior]; and coauthor of *O Potencial Humano* [Human Potential]. He has also authored numerous journal articles.

DIRK ODENDAAL is South African; he was born in what is now called the Province of the Eastern Cape. He spent much of his youth in the Transkei in the town of Umtata, where his parents were teachers at a seminary. He trained as a minister at the Stellenbosch Seminary for the Dutch Reformed Church and was ordained in 1983 in the Dutch Reformed Church in Southern Africa. He transferred to East London in 1988 to minister to members of the Uniting Reformed Church in Southern Africa in one of the huge suburbs for Xhosa speaking people. He received his doctorate (DLitt) in 1992 at the University of Port Elizabeth in Semitic Languages. At present, he is enrolled in a master's course in Counseling Psychology at Rhodes University.

WAYNE G. ROLLINS is Adjunct Professor of Scripture at the Hartford Seminary and Professor Emeritus of Theology at Assumption College, Worcester, Massachusetts, where he served as Director of the Ecumenical Institute and Graduate Program of Religious Studies. He has also taught on the faculties of Princeton University and Wellesley College, with visiting lectureships at Yale College, The College of the Holy Cross, Mt. Holyoke, and Colgate–Rochester Divinity School. An ordained minister in the United Church of Christ, he received the BD, MA, and PhD degrees from Yale University, with post-graduate study at Cambridge University (U.K.), Harvard University, and the Graduate Theological Union in Berkeley, California. His writings include numerous articles and three books: *The Gospels: Portraits of Christ; Jung and the Bible*; and, most recently, *Soul and Psyche: The Bible in Psychological Perspective*. He is the founding chair of the Psychology and Biblical Studies Section of the Society of Biblical Literature, an international organization of biblical scholars.